LOREN MILLER is a judge of the Los Angeles Municipal Court. His father, John Bird Miller, was born a slave, only two years after the Dred Scott case; all of the great decisions affecting Negroes during and after the Civil War were delivered by the Supreme Court during the lifetime of father and son. Born in Pender, Nebraska, in 1903, Loren Miller was educated in the public schools of Kansas and Nebraska. He attended the University of Kansas and Howard University, and received his LL.B. from Washburn Law School in Topeka, Kansas. As a practicing lawyer in Los Angeles for 25 years, Miller appeared before the United States Supreme Court on numerous occasions, particularly in cases involving claims on discrimination in housing. A vice president of the NAACP, he was formerly publisher of the *California Eagle*, a Los Angeles Negro newspaper.

THE PETITIONERS

PANTHEON BOOKS

A Division of Random House / New York

The Petitioners

THE STORY OF THE SUPREME COURT

OF THE UNITED STATES AND

THE NEGRO *by Loren Miller*

To my wife, Juanita, for her unflagging faith;

to my father, John Bird Miller, born a slave,

whose love of liberty inspired me to become a lawyer,

and to my mother, Nora Herbaugh Miller, whose love of

my father led her across the color line and to my birth,

I dedicate this book.

Preface

There is a grave risk in attempting a history of the Supreme Court's decisions on a specific issue, particularly on such an explosive and controversial one as its pronouncements on the constitutional rights of the Negro, as slave, freeman, and citizen. The Court does not, indeed cannot, deal with any issue in isolation. All constitutional decisions are imbedded in the social context of their times, and the very act of isolating one issue invites distortion, perhaps makes a certain distortion inevitable. That is a calculated risk that must be run.

Supreme Court language is not always clear. Lawyers and judges are forever engaged in debate as to what the Court, or any court for that matter, meant to decide by the use of certain words or phrases. Language itself undergoes changes in shades of meaning, and in retrospect a meaning may be attributed to a declaration or decision that was not intended by the phrase maker. I have tried to eliminate that danger by seeking out the continuity that runs through the decisions.

It may seem that there is little to be gained from an examination of what the Supreme Court decided in cases involving slavery. We are accustomed to thinking of the abolition of slavery as marking a sharp and complete break with the past. The truth is that the long shadow of slavery still falls over the Negro and determines many present-day attitudes toward him. That is especially true in the case of legal and constitutional attitudes. Under our common-law system, judges look to precedents in adjudicating cases. A matter once decided becomes a precedent in its field, and judges display an understandable reluctance about disturbing rules that have become hallowed by prior decisions. Even where there has been constitutional or statutory change, courts constantly seek for continuity in the law and hark back to old cases to trace that continuity.

The Supreme Court that was called upon to interpret the Thirteenth, Fourteenth, and Fifteenth Amendments, with their revolutionary changes in constitutional law, was composed of judges steeped in pre-Civil War precedents. It is not at all surprising that the old familiar precedents conditioned their viewpoints. For the most part, the Supreme Court justices of the Reconstruction period and succeeding years were conservative; the dominant Reconstruction congressmen who framed the Civil War amendments were radicals. The judges sifted the radicalism of Congress through their own conservatism and their regard for precedent and arrived at decisions, sometimes at variance with what the framers intended. In their proper turn, those decisions became precedents for later decisions. Traced to their ultimate source, some of the Supreme Court's twentieth-century civil rights decisions are rooted in pre-Civil War adjudications.

I have not cited or discussed all Supreme Court decisions involving the Negro. Some of them treated matters of minor concern; others are simply restatements of what was decided in the great landmark cases. In other instances, I have had to consider and discuss cases in which the Negro was not directly involved, because they announced rules that so profoundly affected the Negro that to leave them out would distort history.

The sometimes extensive treatment of dissenting opinions occurs because the dissents often serve to illuminate the prevailing opinion. In other instances, the dissents are valuable because they point out a course that was open to the Court. If the Court had adopted the dissenting point of view, it would have profoundly altered the course of history. Other dissents are valuable because they have sometimes boldly and sometimes subtly become the majority point of view.

As will be apparent, I have felt it necessary to devote some time to historical narrative in order to put Supreme Court decisions in proper perspective. That is particularly true of the period from the making of the Constitution to the Dred Scott case in 1856 and that of the amending of the Constitution from 1865 to 1870.

Of course, I have tried to be objective, but my own viewpoint should not be overlooked. Quite frankly, I spent 25 years as an embattled advocate of complete equality before the law and in the process became steeped in Professor John W. Burgess's belief that "civil liberty is national in its origin, content and sanction" and that "There is no doubt that those who framed the Thirteenth and Fourteenth Amendments intended to occupy the whole ground and thought they had done so." He points out that the "opposition charged that these amendments would nationalize the whole sphere of civil liberty; the majority accepted that view . . ." and the legislation of Congress "proceeds upon that view." My acceptance of that view should be borne in mind by the reader.

A WORD OF GRATITUDE

My wife, Juanita, and my sons, Loren and Edward, sacrificed more than I can recount to the writing of this book. I can only repay them in this poor coin of public tribute for what they know of my neglect of them in my preoccupation with writing and research.

Other persons gave assistance that entitles them to special mention. Lawyers—particularly Stanley R. Malone, Jr., Nathaniel Colley, Jack Tenner, and my son Loren—read the manuscript, or parts of it, and ferreted out weak spots for my consideration and correction. Kathryn P. Carr, librarian, stretched rules and regulations to find needed texts and treatises. My secretary, Mary Thompson, assisted by Rosalie Freeman, was invaluable in her meticulous preparation of the manuscript and in keeping me reasonably close to deadlines. I thank them all.

Of course, mistakes and shortcomings are of my own making, and for them I accept full responsibility.

LOREN MILLER

Contents

Preface   **vii**

PART THREE   Through a glass, darkly

PART FOUR   The welcome table

Contents

Contents

PART ONE

What has been, has been

Not heaven itself upon the past has power;

But what has been, has been. . . . ❋ Alexander Pope,
Imitations of Horace

◄ 1 ► *The Least Noise*

*They that govern the most
make the least noise.*

JOHN SELDEN

All dressed up in his best Sunday suit, Bird Gee, my granduncle, walked into a Kansas restaurant on October 10, 1875, "for the purpose of partaking of a meal at the table of a certain inn under the management and control of Murray Stanley," as his intent was described in the quaint language of the law. Family lore has it that Uncle Bird, who had escaped from slavery as a youngster, was a contentious man as far as his rights were concerned; his detractors said he was a natural born troublemaker and agitator. It may well have been that he went to Mr. Stanley's restaurant to test his rights under the Civil Rights Act of 1875, passed by Congress and signed by President Ulysses S. Grant only a few short months before. If so, he achieved his purpose. Mr. Stanley's waiters told him in no uncertain terms that Mr. Stanley did not serve Negroes. Bird Gee made what was then called a beeline to U. S. District Attorney George R. Peck and poured out his grievance.

The federal Civil Rights Act of 1875 provided in part that "All persons within the jurisdiction of the United States shall be entitled to the full and equal accommodations, advantages, facilities, and privileges of inns, theaters . . . and other places . . . of public accommodation" and prescribed fines and imprisonment for violators. In due legal season, Mr. Stanley's conduct was laid before a federal grand jury, which returned an indictment on April 14, 1876, charging him with the criminal offense of refusing the "privileges of an inn to a person of color." It seemed as if Bird Gee had triumphed.

However, Mr. Stanley's lawyers went to federal circuit court and argued vehemently that Congress had no authority under either the Thirteenth or the Fourteenth Amendments to enact a public accommodations law and asked that the indictment be dismissed. District Attorney Peck was properly shocked at such sentiments, as lawyers always profess to be when their opponents express a view contrary to the posture they have assumed as an advocate of a cause. He decried the constitutional heresy that Congress lacked authority to protect the rights of the new freedmen and insisted with equal vigor that Mr. Stanley must be punished for his wrongdoing.

Caught in the crossfire of these arguments, the circuit judges couldn't make up their minds and certified the question to the Supreme Court of the United States for its consideration and determination. Bird Gee had fired the first gun in what would be a long constitutional war and end in a momentous Supreme Court decision construing the meaning of the clauses of the Fourteenth Amendment that provide that "No State shall . . . deny to any person within its jurisdiction the equal protection of the laws" and define the authority of Congress to legislate under the amendment.

The Supreme Court was in no hurry to settle the issue. It dallied along until October 15, 1883, when four similar cases were before it, and then held by an eight-to-one vote in what are known as the *Civil Rights Cases* that Congress had no constitutional authority to prohibit Murray Stanley from drawing the color line at his inn.[1] My Uncle Bird was given to strong language but unfortunately, or fortunately, neither legend nor history has preserved the purple prose with which he is said to have appraised the decision. Other Negroes and their friends across the nation held mass meetings at which they denounced the Court for its "betrayal" and charged it with "selling out to the Rebels." A determined minority of Americans cheered the Court wildly, but most Americans either didn't care or approved what the Court had done. Bird Gee left for Indian Territory with word that he was going to spend the rest of his life among the "heathens" where there was no racial discrimination. He did.

On December 14, 1964, long after Murray Stanley and Bird Gee had been gathered to whatever reward awaits civil rights litigants, the Supreme Court held that Congress *did* have constitutional authority to prohibit racial discrimination by innkeepers and upheld the Civil Rights Act of 1964, which also provides in part that Negroes are entitled to the full and equal facilities of places of public accommodation! There had not been a single change in the Fourteenth Amendment or in any other clause of the Constitution bearing on the subject in the 81-year span between 1883 and 1964. Neither proponents nor opponents of the law claimed that there had been any change. Much else had changed, however, between 1875, when Congress wrote public accommodations legislation that was found *unconstitutional,* and 1964, when it wrote almost identical legislation that was found *constitutional.* It is one of the accidents of history that the year 1883 lies almost halfway between the time when the Supreme Court was constituted in 1789 and the year 1965. The Court had begun to function 94 years before 1883; it had functioned 81 years after that time by 1964.

Much also happened in the 94 years of Supreme Court history between 1789 and 1883 as far as Negroes were concerned. In the beginning, the vast majority of them were slaves, with no constitutional rights or privileges, with no rights of any kind which a white man was bound to respect according to a distinguished Chief Justice.

By 1883 they were free men, they were citizens, they were entitled to vote without discrimination on account of their race or color, and the Supreme Court itself had said that they had all the constitutional rights and privileges possessed by white men. That change in status stemmed from the addition of the Thirteenth, Fourteenth, and Fifteenth Amendments to the Constitution, each of which provided that Congress should have power to enforce it through appropriate legislation. The amendments were equalitarian in purpose and outlook, and congressional legislation passed soon after their adoption was cast in that same mold. But the Supreme Court, either called upon to interpret, or seizing opportunities to interpret, the amendments and consequent congressional legislation put its own meaning on the amendments and the authority they vested in Congress.

It soon became apparent that Congress and the Court differed widely as to what the amended Constitution meant in respect of the civil rights of Negroes and the extent of congressional authority to protect those rights under the Civil War amendments. Bird Gee's case is a nearly perfect example of the disagreement, with Congress claiming the authority to enact public accommodations statutes and the Court denying and nullifying its authority to do so. There was nothing novel in the breach of opinion; Congress and the Court had been at loggerheads over similar issues prior to the Civil War. Congress enacted the Missouri Compromise Act prohibiting slavery in large portions of the Louisiana Purchase. Thirty years later, the Court nullified that legislation.

This is a full chronicle of what the Supreme Court has said and done in respect of the rights of Negroes, slave and free, between 1789 and 1965, including the constitutional mystery of how and why the Court decided that the 1875 Civil Rights Act was unconstitutional and the matching Civil Rights Act of 1964 was constitutional, when there had been no change in constitutional language between the two dates.

In some respects it is a new story because it has never been gathered together in one narrative before. In other respects it is an oft-told tale because each issue it presents has been reviewed and debated many times before.

As told here, it has been a straight-flowing chronicle, with each subject—the rights of slaves, the rights of Negroes to sit on juries, to vote, to use public accommodations, to attend public schools, and to claim many other rights and privileges—neatly packaged and told separately, as if the Court heard cases involving them and decided them in that manner. That is only a storytelling device. No such thing happened.

The Court heard and decided cases as they came to it. On some occasions it decided a variety of cases, or one case, presenting a multitude of issues. The questions it decided have been disentangled and told separately to expedite presentation and heighten understanding. The issues have been simplified and extracted from legal language that may obscure as well as illuminate.

There is nothing remarkable in the fact that the decision in *Civil Rights Cases* of 1883 loosed a tirade of invective against the Supreme Court. The Court has been the center of violent controversy since its earliest days. Shrill as they are, today's outcries against the Court's decision on civil rights, prayers in public school, legislative reapportionment, and the rights of unpopular minorities are muted in comparison to the criticisms of the past. Chief Justice John Marshall's decision in 1803 that the Court had power to declare a congressional statute unconstitutional was greeted by Thomas Jefferson with the charge that such power made "the Judiciary a despotic branch." [2]

Horace Greeley's *New York Tribune* said that the Dred Scott decision was "entitled to just so much moral weight as would be the judgment of a majority of those congregated in any Washington barroom" and the *Boston Chronicle* agreed that a "majority of the court are great scoundrels." [3] During the Civil War, the Court was branded a "nest of traitors" and a refuge for treason.[4] There is hardly even a remote possibility that recurrent demands for the impeachment of Chief Justice Earl Warren will ever be dignified by official action, but Justice Samuel Chase was put on trial before Congress in 1805 because of his judicial conduct in advising a grand jury.

The list of the Court's past critics is an imposing one and includes such great historical figures as Jefferson, Andrew Jackson, Abraham Lincoln, and the two Roosevelts, Theodore and Franklin D. Means of curbing its power have ranged from proposals to reduce its membership to three to increasing that membership to fifteen, and from recall of decisions by popular vote to stripping it of all power to hear appeals.

The most persistent criticism of the Court has been the charge that it has usurped power that properly belongs to other branches of the federal government or to the states, a reflection of the fact that it has become the final repository of power in our governmental system. In every organized society such power must rest somewhere, whether in the chief of a tribal system, the absolute monarch of the Middle Ages, the dictators of the past or present, or the legislature in parliamentary government. When all else fails, the supreme organ must settle the issues that confront the society, and the more controversial the issue, the more certain that lesser state organs will default and defer to the final expositor of governmental power. By the same token, the greater will be the outcry against whatever settlement is effected.

The single most controversial issue, and one that runs like a red thread through American history and has required governmental settlement is the relationship of Negroes to the American body politic. The attempt to formulate a Constitution almost foundered on the question of slavery and the foreign slave trade. Slavery kept the nation in turmoil for the first 73 years of its existence and finally led

to a bloody Civil War. The Civil War amendments glossed over the
wounds but, despite early appearances and vain hopes, did not
effect a resolution of the question of race relations. It hasn't been
settled yet.

As the Supreme Court's power grew, it was inevitable that it
would be called upon to say the final word and resolve the racial
conflict. It was just as inevitable that, whatever it said and whenever it pronounced a judgment, the Court would be involved in
heated controversy. The Court's decisions on the foreign slave trade,
interstate commerce in slaves, fugitive slave laws, the Dred Scott
case, interpretation of the Civil War amendments and modern civil
rights have touched off tirades against the judiciary. The recurrent
theme has been the charge of usurpation of power belonging to
other branches of government and to the states, just as in other
criticism of the Court. For reasons that will appear as the story
unravels, and beginning prior to the Civil War, the Court took the
rights of Negroes under its wing.

The result was that the Negro became the ward of the Supreme
Court for more than a hundred years.

As befits a dependent, the Negro has had to solicit the interces-
sion of his guardian when he has sought to exercise rights and privileges enjoyed by grown-up citizens as a matter of course. It is such
a commonplace that Americans see nothing remarkable in the fact
that Negroes have had to secure Supreme Court decrees in order to
do what white Americans may do without question, such as buy or
rent homes, vote in primary elections, ride on Pullman cars, attend
state-owned graduate and professional schools, read daily newspapers in city libraries, loll around in public parks, gain admission
to primary and secondary schools, eat in bus stations, or swim in
the ocean. The list could be extended.

The ultimate in Supreme Court guardianship was reached in
1955, when the Court decided that public schools must be open to
all pupils without racial restrictions, then fathered a scheme under
which federal district courts were ordered to exercise supervisory
powers over local school boards to see to it that schools were "desegregated" and Negro pupils admitted "with all deliberate speed." [5]
What the decision amounted to was that southern Negro youngsters have had to apply for school admission with a Court decree in
one hand and their credentials in the other.

Every decision holding that the Negro is entitled to exercise some ordinary right or privilege without restraint because of race has been hailed as proof that the Supreme Court has been faithful to its trust as the guardian of civil rights or has been denounced on the ground that it has exceeded those powers. The Court's function as a special overseer in the case of the Negro's day-to-day exercise of citizenship rights and privileges goes unquestioned. Yet the Founding Fathers, to whom we ascribe almost infinite wisdom and foresight, wrote no such provision into the Constitution and never even discussed, or came close to discussing, the matter.

Congressional framers of the Civil War amendments—the Great Charter of Civil Rights—were so hostile to a supreme tribunal that had rendered the Dred Scott decision and so certain of their own competency that they tacked on to the Thirteenth, Fourteenth, and Fifteenth Amendments the telling phrase, "Congress shall have power to enforce this article by appropriate legislation."

Immediately after the Civil War, Congress demonstrated what it meant by "appropriate legislation" by enacting a series of laws that ran the gamut from protecting the Negro's right to contract and purchase, lease, hold, inherit, and convey real property to guaranteeing him the vote, full and equal accommodations in inns, public conveyances on land and water, theaters and other places of public accommodation and amusement. It prescribed heavy penalties for persons who interfered with the Negro's exercise of almost every conceivable civil right.

If left untouched, and enforced, those statutes would have eliminated the necessity, indeed, the very possibility, of most of the Supreme Court's highly praised (and roundly condemned) civil rights decisions. They were neither left untouched nor enforced because they ran afoul of the Supreme Court's notions of what the Constitution permitted the legislative and executive branches of the federal government to do by way of protection of civil rights and its own appraisal of its supremacy as an interpreter of the Constitution.

The Court's dominant notion was that it, and not Congress, was the final arbiter of what the Constitution, as amended, meant and of how far the fundamental law took civil rights from the province of the states and placed them under protection of the national government. There was nothing novel in the doctrine it expounded; it was a modified exposition of a judicial point of view developed in a series of cases, capped by the Dred Scott decision, involving the rights of Negroes, free and slave, handed down prior to the Civil

War.[6] The importance of the Dred Scott case lay in the fact that the Court held that the Constitution itself contained implicit distinctions between Negroes and white residents of the nation, as far as the exercise of constitutional rights was concerned. White persons, it declared in essence, were born with certain rights; Negroes had rights only at the sufferance of the white man.

The Constitution, the Court said in the Dred Scott case, was made *by* and *for* white men; they were the People who had ordained it in order to secure the Blessings of Liberty for themselves and their posterity. On the other hand, said Chief Justice Taney, "neither that class of persons who had been imported as slaves nor their descendants, whether they became free or not, were a part of the People." Therefore, he reasoned, Negroes were not protected by federal constitutional guarantees. In the case of slaves, an obvious reason was offered: they were a species of property resigned by the Constitution to the entire control of the states in which slavery existed and in which they resided. Free Negroes were said to lack constitutional protection because the Court said they were not, and could not become, national citizens and "therefore can claim none of the rights and privileges which the Constitution provides for and secures to citizens of the United States."

The Chief Justice drew a rigid distinction between national citizenship and state citizenship. He said that it was true that all free persons might be citizens of the several states and, as such, must look to the states in which they were citizens for protection of whatever rights those states chose to accord them. Under no circumstances could the federal government intervene to compel the states to respect their civil rights, because such rights were solely matters of concern to the states, where they had reposed prior to the Constitution. The federal government, he said, was a government of limited powers, having only such powers as were delegated by states.

This duality of citizenship had little or no practical consequence for white Americans, since the states stood ready to safeguard their fundamental rights; their rights as national citizens were secure under the Constitution. It was enormously oppressive as far as Negroes were concerned, because some of the states were bitterly hostile to the exercise of civil rights by free Negroes and, under Taney's dictum, Negroes were not and could not become national citizens. In each instance, the states were declared to be vested with power to deal with their Negro residents, fairly or unfairly, as they chose, so long as they observed constitutional restrictions protecting the property rights of slaveholders and did not invest free Negroes with rights arising out of national citizenship. "The unhappy black race," said Taney, "were separated from the white by indelible marks," and it followed that the Constitution recognized and formalized the differences between the races.

In effect, the Court attributed to the Constitution a complete scheme defining the special relationship of Negroes, free and slave, to the federal government, to the states, and to the body politic, and asserted for itself the exclusive power to define the nature, character, and extent of those relationships through its own interpretation of the Constitution. Congressional legislation in conflict with that interpretation was declared void. A Negro, feeling himself aggrieved, had no place to turn for relief except to the Court. For better or worse, the Supreme Court had made the Negro its unwilling ward.

Opponents of slavery protested violently against the double standard created by the ruling in the Dred Scott case and raged at what they called judicial usurpation of power that properly belonged to Congress. When antislavery congressmen took control of Congress after secession and victory in the Civil War, they attempted to break the Supreme Court's claim of monopoly as far as delineation of the Negro's rights was concerned. By the Thirteenth Amendment abolishing slavery they effectively reversed the Court's decisions as to the disabilities imposed on slaves. By the express provision of the Fourteenth Amendment that all persons born or naturalized in the United States were citizens of the United States *and* of the states of their residence, they sought to undermine the Dred Scott holding that Negroes were denied parity with white persons under the federal constitution because of lack of national citizenship.

Their obvious intent was to abolish that duality of citizenship of which Taney had made so much. They bolstered the case by the Fourteenth Amendment provision forbidding the states to abridge the privileges or immunities of citizens of the United States or to deny to any person due process of law or equal protection of the laws. They clothed the Negro with the right to vote on a parity with other Americans by the Fifteenth Amendment. Finally, they placed, or thought they placed, civil rights under the dominion and control of the federal government and gave Congress the power to legislate for the enforcement of the equalitarian amendments they had added to the Constitution. And, as has been remarked, Congress did legislate.

The Supreme Court began the work of undoing congressional intent and action by blandly reasserting for itself the power it had claimed in the Dred Scott case to determine and define the relationship of Negroes to the federal government, to the states, and to the body politic. It found nothing in the War amendments that circumscribed that power, and it was as certain as it was before their enactment that its interpretation of the Constitution in respect of the rights and privileges of Negroes was binding on the legislative and executive branches of the federal government.

Thus self-armed, the Court narrowed the scope of the Fourteenth and Fifteenth Amendments; as the first step, it restored the old Dred Scott concept of two classes of citizenship—national and state—and then held that the privileges and immunities clause of the Fourteenth Amendment protected only national citizenship rights; it declared that civil rights were still under the exclusive control of the states, just as they had been prior to the Civil War; it riddled congressional legislation by invalidating many civil rights laws on narrow technical grounds and by holding that others were not warranted under the particular amendment they were designed to implement.[7]

The states were completely restored to the civil rights saddle by an 1883 decision holding that Congress had no power to interdict racial discrimination by individuals and that such power resided in the states, where it had reposed prior to the Civil War.[8] By 1896 the Court had edged close enough to the Dred Scott dictum that "the unhappy black race were separated from the white by indelible marks" to approve the doctrine that the states could constitutionally classify citizens of the United States on the basis of race and deny Negroes the use of public and public-utility facilities through such classification, as long as separate and equal facilities were provided. It scoffed at equalitarian laws: "Legislation," it said, "is powerless to eradicate racial instincts or to abolish distinctions based upon physical differences."[9]

In jubilant retrospect, a southern lawyer could say: "What gave satisfaction to the South and strength to bear the affliction in which they found themselves was the determination of the Court to maintain the *true character of government,* and to hold . . . that the existence of the states with powers of domestic and local government including the *regulation of civil rights* . . . was essential to the perfect working of our complex form of government." [10] Since the vast majority of Negroes lived in southern states, Supreme Court approval of state "regulation of civil rights" resigned most of them to the dominion of believers in white supremacy, who formalized and implemented that doctrine through Jim Crow laws and evasive restrictions on the franchise. In its proper turn, the Court, by the application of its own logic in upholding the separate-but-equal doctrine was constrained to sanction racial distinctions drawn by the states in their regulation of civil rights. History had come full circle: wittingly or unwittingly, the Court had returned to the Dred Scott dictum that the Constitution recognized and formalized "differences" between the races.

But the power of the states to regulate civil rights was not untrammeled. The states could not sanction slavery nor could they impose racial restrictions on the right to vote. Moreover, they could not, through legislative, executive, or judicial action, deny due process of law or equal protection of their laws on the basis of race.

The only way to test conformity of state action to these constitutional safeguards was through the long, slow, and tedious process of litigation on which the Supreme Court could say the last word. Thus, whenever a Negro has complained that state action, or individual action sanctioned by the state, has deprived him of some right or privilege guaranteed by the Constitution, or that some separate facility was, in fact, unequal, he has had to appeal to the Supreme Court for an interpretation of the particular constitutional provision alleged to govern the situation. The short of the matter is that the guardian-and-ward relationship between the Supreme Court and the Negro, originating before the Civil War, has persisted into our own times. The forced reliance of the Negro on Supreme Court action for vindication of ordinary rights and privileges of citizenship has bred the popular belief that the judicial branch of government is the proper forum for the redress of all racial grievances.

The congressional will to act as a reflex to popular sentiment atrophied during judicial pre-emption of action in the area of race relations for three quarters of a century. The 1957 Civil Rights Bill was the first federal legislation in the field for more than 80 years.

The efforts of Congress to enforce the Fourteenth and Fifteenth Amendments by "appropriate legislation" are still bitterly assailed as unconstitutional and as an invasion of states' rights whenever such legislation strikes down racial inequalities.

The scholarly Senator Richard Russell of Georgia railed at senatorial approval of the 1964 Civil Rights Bill as "mob rule" and as a "lynching." Arizona's Senator Barry Goldwater in hot pursuit of the 1964 Republican presidential nomination gave his sober opinion that Congress lacked power under the Fourteenth Amendment to enact equalitarian statutes giving Negroes access to places of public accommodation affected by interstate commerce or to interdict employer or union racial discrimination against a Negro workman. Both senators saw congressional action as an invasion of states' rights, thus underscoring the irony that those who insist loudest that the Civil War was fought on the issue of states' rights also insist with equal vehemence that the victors did not accomplish their purpose and that the states are still supreme as far as civil rights of Negroes are concerned. Their view rests largely on judicial construction of the Civil War Amendments during a 60-year span from 1873 to the middle 1930's.

The Supreme Court's response to the Negro's plea for the redress of his grievances has been uneven since it took his rights under its wing after the Civil War and rebuffed early congressional attempts to raise him to the status of a first-class citizen. For almost half a century, the Court spurned the Negro's claim that the Constitution was color blind or evaded his request for equalitarian treatment by torturing language out of its plain meaning, but the pendulum swung in the other direction beginning in the mid-1930's as the Court began a return to the original meaning and intent of the Civil War amendments.

As the Court progressed in that return, it overturned or ignored its own strangling precedents and even assumed an amazing leadership in the area of civil rights. By the sheer weight of its own example, it inspired something of a similar zeal on the part of the executive branch of government and ultimately helped create a climate of public opinion in which Congress was induced to act by passing the Civil Rights Acts of 1957, 1960, 1964, and 1965. The Court's equalitarian decisions beginning in the mid 1930's gave increasing freedom and opportunities to civil rights organizations to press it as well as the executive and legislative branches of government for ever widening reforms. As it made the Negro more and more a free man, it diminished the need for its guardianship over him and made him more and more a master in his own house.

This story, then, is an inquiry into the checkered relationship of the Supreme Court and the Negro—of its beginnings, of its growth; of its good and of its evil; of the manner in which its decisions have affected the lives of Negroes and the well-being of the nation; of its present and, inevitably, a forecast of the future. It begins with the background and the making and meaning of the Constitution the Supreme Court has construed.

How firm a foundation, ye saints of the Lord,
Is laid for your faith in His excellent word!

OLD HYMN

Thomas Jefferson's original draft of the Declaration of Independence arraigned the King of England on the ground that "he has waged cruel war against human nature itself, violating its most sacred rights of life and liberty in the persons of distant peoples who never offended him; captivating and carrying them into slavery in another hemisphere or to incur miserable death in their transportation thither . . . Determined to keep open a market where *men* should be bought and sold, he has prostituted his negative by suppressing every legislative attempt to prohibit or restrain this execrable commerce . . . he is now exciting those very people to rise in arms among us, and to purchase that liberty of which he has deprived them, by murdering the people on whom he has obtruded them; thus paying off former crimes committed against the *liberties* of one people with crimes which he urges them to commit against the *lives* of another." [1]

The argument was a neat and telling one. Jefferson was at once making the King a scapegoat for the slave trade, which he detested, and absolving the colonists of blame for the institution of slavery that troubled his conscience and the consciences of many of his colleagues, although he and many of them were slaveholders. The charge that the King was stirring up a slave insurrection was calculated to arouse fear and incite resentment against Britain and thus further the cause of independence. But Jefferson was more than a mere propagandist.

The natural rights theory which found its expression in the dogma that "all men are created equal [and] are endowed by their Creator with certain unalienable Rights, that among these are Life, Liberty and the pursuit of Happiness" required intellectual opposition to slavery by men who took its precepts seriously. Jefferson was such a man. He had searched his own conscience and was reluctant to rationalize slavery on the facile ground that Negroes were inferior, a conclusion that, he said, "would degrade a whole race of men from the rank in the scale of beings which their Creator may perhaps have given them." [2] In 1774, he had prodded fellow Virginians with the assertion that "the abolition of domestic slavery is the great object of desire in these colonies where it was unhappily introduced in their infant state. But previous to the enfranchisement of the slaves we have, it is necessary to exclude all further importations from Africa." [3] Jefferson had distinguished company among the men who subscribed to the Declaration, but his strictures against the King for maintaining the slave trade did not find their way into that great document.

John Adams, his discerning collaborator, remarked later that he was delighted with Jefferson's "flight of oratory . . . especially that concerning slavery; which, though I knew his Southern Brethren would never suffer to pass in Congress, I would certainly never oppose." [4] Adams's skepticism was based on the shrewd judgment that men of affairs seldom let their sentiments outrun their investments. He was right. The signers of the Declaration were content to stand on the resounding proposition that all men are created equal and let it go at that.

As the war progressed, the King's generals issued proclamations from time to time offering freedom to slaves who would join them, but they made no real effort to stir up the servile insurrection inveighed against by Jefferson. The Redcoats carried away and impounded literally thousands of slaves and enlisted a few in their armies. Continental policy varied from state to state. Free Negroes bore arms in most northern states and in some southern states. Under one policy, masters hired out their slaves as menials and in other instances sent bondsmen to serve in their stead when there was a call for men. Alexander Hamilton, Henry Laurens, and a few others proposed wholesale enlistment of Negroes, but Washington was cautious and other Southerners bitterly opposed such schemes.

The scanty records of the time indicate that some 4,000 Negroes served in the Continental Army, but their contribution was not decisive enough to disrupt the slave system. When peace came, His Britannic Majesty agreed to return "all negros and other property" taken from the colonists. The promise of freedom to Negroes who had borne arms was indifferently fulfilled; many were returned to slavery, and a Tennessee court later decided that title to land awarded a Negro slave as a bounty for his services as a soldier passed through him and lodged in his master because a slave could not own real property! [5] Luther Martin summed it all up: "When our liberties were at stake, we warmly felt for the rights of men. The danger being thought to be past . . . we are daily growing more insensible to those rights." [6]

War's end found slavery on the way toward extinction in the northern states and on the decline in the upper South. It was not too difficult under the Articles of Confederation to secure the passage of the Ordinance of 1787 prohibiting slavery in the Northwest Territory, which had been ceded to the national government by the states. A harbinger of things to come was southern insistence on a clause in the Ordinance which provided for the "return to service or labor" of any person who had escaped to that region, a euphemism that meant fugitive slaves must be returned to their masters.

When the Founding Fathers finally gathered in Philadelphia in 1787 to write a constitution for the new United States of America, they knew that one of their thorniest problems would be that of the manner in which the document dealt with slavery and the slave trade. Sectional feeling had firmed up and nobody believed that the new nation would, or could, interfere with slavery where it existed, but there were those who hoped that it would, at a minimum, prohibit the slave trade. The eggheads at the convention were primed to write a prohibitory slave trade clause into the Constitution, but as is usual in political gatherings, they ran into heavy opposition from the practical men who were there to represent the sentiments of their constitutents.

The format of the Constitution required the convention to deal with the question of apportionment of members for the House of Representatives before it reached the issue of the foreign slave trade. The first Census of 1790 showed that there were 1,900,976 whites and 27,112 free Negroes in the northern states, as against 1,271,488 whites and 32,354 free Negroes in the southern states. There were, however, only 40,364 slaves in the North and 657,533 in the South. The disparity, but not the exact figures, was known to the men who attended the convention. The fat was in the fire: should slaves be passed over as property or counted as men in apportioning representation? The answer, such as it was, is found in Article I, Section 2, of the Constitution which provides that in the apportionment for membership in the House, population should be "determined by adding to the whole number of free persons . . . excluding Indians not taxed, *three fifths* of all other persons." "All other persons" was a synonym for Negro slaves.

The debate over counting of slaves in apportionment opened up the whole controversy over slavery. Jefferson was absent in France and did not participate in the convention, but doughty little James Madison, who shared at least a portion of Jefferson's sentiments, was there to take careful notes and to do what he could to draft a document that would prohibit the foreign slave trade. Luther Martin, George Mason, and a few others restated as their own the views expressed on the trade in Jefferson's original draft of the Declaration, but most Southerners were adamant: the Constitution would never be ratified by their states if it prohibited importation of slaves. Even the most insistent Southerners were careful to say that they were not to be understood as being apologists for the slave trade but, they argued, slavery was a local problem of the several states and, as Charles Pinckney of South Carolina put it, "If the southern states are left alone, they will probably of themselves stop importation." [7] Abraham Baldwin of Georgia and other Southerners echoed that sentiment, thus setting a verbal style that obtains even today when there is national discussion of racial problems.

After the eighteenth-century equivalent of a modern senatorial filibuster had raged for some time, the Constitution makers drafted another neat compromise. What they wrote in Article I, Section 9, was that "the Migration or Importation of such Persons as any of the States now existing shall think proper to admit, shall not be prohibited by the Congress prior to the Year one thousand eight hundred and eight; but a tax or duty may be imposed on such Importation, not exceeding ten dollars for each Person. . . ." What they meant was that Congress could not prohibit the foreign slave trade for twenty years—until 1808—but could levy a head tax up to ten dollars on each slave who was imported.

There were other problems. The new constitution provided that Congress "could lay and collect taxes." Suppose that a Congress dominated by antislavery sentiment should lay on "all persons" who happened to be slaves a head tax so steep that it amounted to confiscation? That fear was set at rest by the fourth clause of Article I, Section 9, providing that "No Capitation, or other direct, Tax shall be laid, unless in Proportion to the Census or Enumeration herein before directed to be taken." That is, Congress couldn't tax slavery out of existence by a head tax.

At the time the convention was meeting, the air was full of talk about an English decision by Lord Mansfield holding that under the common law, a slave gained permanent freedom when he set foot on free soil. The decision had been rendered in 1771 and was believed to be a correct exposition of the law. It was apparent that all northern states were going to abolish slavery in the very near future. The Northwest Territory was already free soil by the Ordinance of 1787. What would be the status of a slave who escaped to the free states? If freedom attached to slaves under those circumstances, slavery was in jeopardy. An easy answer was at hand. The Founding Fathers simply rewrote the last clause of the Ordinance and provided in Article IV, Section 2, that "No person held to service or Labour in one State, under the Laws thereof, escaping into another, shall, in Consequence of any Law or Regulation therein, be discharged from such Service or Labour, but shall be delivered up on Claim of the Party to whom such Service or Labour may be due." A less squeamish convention might simply have adopted a provision to the effect that an escaped slave should be returned to his master wherever found.

There was one final matter. By its own terms, the Constitution could be amended at any time. There was the possibility, if not the probability, that the carefully contrived compromises prohibiting interdiction of the foreign slave trade until 1808 and restraining Congress from levying a confiscatory head tax on slaves might be amended out of the Constitution before the critical date. That possibility was eliminated in Article V by the proviso that "no amendment which may be made prior to the Year One thousand eight hundred and eight shall in any Manner affect the first and fourth

Clauses in the Ninth Section of the first Article." Slavery and the slave trade were safe until 1808, at least.

When their labor was done, the Founding Fathers had managed to write a Constitution without mentioning the words *slave* or *slavery*, but they knew, and the nation knew, that the document they had produced was designed to protect slavery where it existed. There were both idealistic and practical reasons for the verbal sleight of hand in the refusal to mention slavery. Many, perhaps most, of the men who wrote the Constitution believed (hoped may be a better word) that slavery was a dying institution; they did not want to give it recognition in the fundamental law of the land in such a manner as to stay its demise. More than that, the new nation had fought a revolutionary war on the ostensible ground of vindicating the proposition that all men are created equal, and the Founding Fathers were understandably uneasy about stultifying themselves in their own eyes and in the eyes of the world by a bald recognition of slavery in a constitution written to embody the political principles for which the people had fought. On the practical side was the fact that slavery did exist, that it was deeply rooted in the southern states, that it was believed to be essential to the southern economy, and that in any event the South was determined to hang on to it, and had made it plain that unless slavery was recognized and protected, that section would not join the new union.

The tacit toleration of slavery raised a difficult question for those who professed the belief that all *men* are created equal: was the slave a man or was he property? The practical answer was that he was both, but that answer settled nothing. It only raised new problems for men engaged in writing a constitution in which the slave's status had to be defined.

If the slave was mere property, he had no rights; he could be bought and sold with no more compunction than could a horse or a mule. If he was a man, he was entitled to the Rights of Man: the rights to "Life, Liberty and the pursuit of Happiness." There was no idealistic solution to that problem in a nation which, on one hand, condoned slavery and, on the other, based its fundamental law on the recognition of the dignity of the individual. The paradox could be glossed over by verbiage that might conceal or soften conflict (the Irrepressible Conflict, as it came to be called) until slavery died its hoped-for natural death. The Constitution makers, under Madison's prodding, agreed that it would be "wrong to admit,

in the constitution, that there could be property in man" [8] and decided to write a document that avoided overt recognition of slaves
as property. They were successful to the extent that they not only
avoided use of the terms *slave* or *slavery* but masked their references to the subject so skilfully that even today the layman cannot
identify the compromise clauses without the guidance of lawyers or
historians. Wherever slaves are referred to in the Constitution, they
are described as "persons," but language can obscure as well as
illuminate, and the felicitous word did not settle the issue of
whether a slave was to be dealt with as a man or property in the
eyes of the law. It merely befuddled the question and deferred it
for later generations of disputatious lawyers and judges.

Skill in masking constitutional recognition and protection of slavery did not eliminate the certainty that such recognition and protection were pregnant with the promise of difficulties for the new
nation. The single most important principle that suffused the Constitution and promised stability for the political institutions created
by it was the dignity of the individual and the inviolability of his
rights and privileges as protected by that instrument. In theory,
that principle demanded that every man be treated as, and function as, an individual, as a *person* in constitutional language. By
that reckoning, no such person had group identity in the eyes of the
law; he had no rights or privileges dependent upon his status as a
member of an ethnic, religious, economic, or political group. Similarly, no person was disadvantaged because of membership in any
such group. He stood not as Jew or Gentile, Catholic or Protestant,
rich or poor, before the law of the land. He was a *person*. As a
person he could claim the rights, privileges, and protections, implicit or expressed in the original Constitution and explicit in the
Bill of Rights. Plainly, the Constitution vindicated the principle for
white Americans. But recognition and protection of slavery inflicted a mortal wound on that principle as far as the overwhelming
majority of Negroes was concerned. For the word *slave* was to all
practical intents and purposes synonymous with the appellation
Negro.

The Constitution imposed implicit disabilities on the slave. And
the slave was a Negro, stripped of his individual dignity and denied
constitutional protection simply because of his status as a member
of an ethnic group. He stood, not as a person, but as a slave before
the law of the land. He existed beyond the pale of the protections

of the original Constitution and the guarantees of the Bill of Rights. He was a stranger in a strange land. Nor did the freeborn or emancipated Negro entirely escape the disabilities laid on his slave kinsman. For his very freedom was suspect; it was not his by right of ancient inheritance but a boon conferred on him or his ancestors by some individual who had been born as a person. The Constitution could be construed as saying that these freeborn blacks, or those upon whom freedom was conferred, were indeed *persons*, but the document contained no safeguards against their degradation.

There was no national citizenship except as a derivative of state citizenship, and the states were left constitutionally free to impose disabilities because of race; they could, and most of them did at the time the Constitution was adopted, bar Negroes from the ballot box, the jury, the privilege of bearing witness against white persons, the public schools, and almost every conceivable right or privilege. The Constitution was silent on the question of whether or not the implicit or expressed protections of the original document and the explicit guarantees of the Bill of Rights accrued to free Negroes. That issue was dependent on whether or not they held national citizenship derived from their state citizenship.

From the very first, free Negroes and their Abolitionist allies clamored that they were indeed persons in the constitutional sense and, hence, national citizens and sought to bolster their case by quoting the language of the Constitution, which even spoke of slaves as persons. But no matter what the theory, the practice was that the national government laid racial disabilities on them, and in the fullness of time, the Supreme Court decided the issue against them. In retrospect, it is easy to see that the Negro's long struggle for what he calls first-class citizenship has been, and is, nothing more or less than an effort to gain status as an individual, as a *person*, because it is only as a person that he can claim the rights, privileges, and protections enjoyed by white Americans who are born as persons.

The astute Founding Fathers were well aware of the contradictions implicit in recognition of slavery in the Constitution side by side with the guarantees of individual rights. That they glossed over these contradictions does not convict them of hypocrisy. The belief in the inferiority of Negroes was widespread and deeply rooted. Even Jefferson vacillated, giving it support and sanction more often than not. The Founding Fathers could not be sure that

Negroes were capable of exercising the rights of, or shouldering the responsibilities of, citizenship. Time would tell. Time, it was also hoped, would bring the demise of slavery and acquit Negroes of its disabilities, and there was also vague hope that as slaves became free men, they would become persons in reality as well as in constitutional fiction. But slavery did not die, and the perceptive Jefferson ultimately cried out that it was the Rock on which the Union would break. That lay in the future in 1787.

There were fitful denunciations of the slavery compromises when the Constitution was submitted to the people, but objections never assumed serious proportions. The proud young nation embarked on its voyage with a Constitution that (1) ordered the counting of three fifths of all slaves in the apportionment of congressmen, (2) forbade congressional interference with the foreign slave trade until 1808, (3) prohibited Congress from taxing slavery out of existence, and (4) provided that a slave who escaped to a free state should be returned to his master. Cutting deeper than these obvious accommodations to political realities was the fact that the Constitution implicitly recognized the existence of slavery in the several states and the correlative right of slave states to its exclusive control and regulation within their borders.

Important questions were left unanswered. The Constitution specified that a slave escaping to a free state should be "delivered up on Claim of the Party" by whom he was held in slavery, but it did not specify the duty, or lack of it, of the asylum state in the case where a fugitive was demanded. Similarly, the Constitution gave Congress the power to regulate foreign and interstate commerce, but it was silent on the question of whether or not the states could control interstate commerce in slaves, although such commerce was extensive at the time the Constitution was framed and adopted. Article IV, Section 2, provided that, "The Citizens of each State shall be entitled to all Privileges and Immunities of Citizens in the several States," but there was no definition of citizenship in the Constitution and no specific language to indicate whether free Negroes were, or were not, citizens vested with these priceless privileges and immunities in the states of their residence. Obviously, slaves were not citizens of a free republic, but if free Negroes had that status in one state, did they have national citizenship? Could they exercise their state citizenship rights in another state? Or could the slave states exclude free Negroes altogether? The Constitution did not say. Nor did the Constitution vest Congress with specific power to enact fugitive slave legislation, control the flow of slave property in interstate commerce, determine the citizenship status of free Negroes, or define their rights in slave states. It could have been predicted that a weak central government would leave such matters to state comity, while a strong, or stronger, central government would insist on its own solutions.

There was an unanswered question of another hue. Congress was given power to "make all needful Rules and Regulations respecting" the territory belonging to the United States, but that provision was not as complete as it seemed. The issue would arise as to whether it applied only to territory then owned by the United States or to territory that the nation might acquire in the future. Indeed, there was no constitutional warrant for acquiring new territory. When new territory was acquired, despite constitutional silence, by the Louisiana Purchase and the Mexican War, the question arose as to the extent of congressional control over slavery in that new territory. Slaveholders soon asserted a right to take their slaves into new territory, with the argument that slaves were property and that the Constitution protected the right of every citizen to hold property in federal territories and empowered them to invoke constitutional protection against impairment of property rights. Opponents of slavery answered that congressional protection or recognition of slavery in such territories amounted to establishment of slavery where it did not exist, and they argued that neither Congress nor any other agency of the federal government had any such power. New territory meant new states; another ambiguity was added. Could the citizens of a new territory organize for statehood and apply for admission to the Union as a slave state, and would the admission of a new state as a slave state amount to federal establishment of slavery?

The Constitution did not resign resolution of these unanswered questions to the Supreme Court in so many words. Nor did it specifically take them away from Congress. What the Constitution did do was to provide that it should be the Supreme Law of the Land and binding on all state judges, that the judicial power of the United States should be vested in a Supreme Court and such inferior courts as Congress might establish, and that the judicial power should extend to all cases arising under the Constitution, laws, and treaties of the United States. The exact meaning of that provision became a matter of debate, but regardless of what it meant when the Framers wrote it, the Court gradually expanded it to mean that the judiciary was clothed with exclusive power to interpret the Constitution and, ultimately, to invalidate congressional enactments found to be in conflict with its notions of the meaning of the Constitution.

Early in the history of the nation, Congress enacted the Judiciary Act of 1789 giving the Supreme Court power to affirm or reverse state judicial decisions declaring invalid "a treaty or statute of, or an authority exercised under the United States," or which might sustain the validity of state laws which are "repugnant to the constitution, treaties or laws of the United States." Plainly, men who were contemporaries of the Founding Fathers were satisfied that the Constitution contemplated a measure of judicial review of legislation. In 1803, Chief Justice John Marshall took a bold step in an obscure case, *Marbury v. Madison,* in which he purported to declare that a federal law in conflict with the Constitution was void.[9]

He seized on the occasion to write: "It is, emphatically, the province and the duty of the judicial department, to say what the law is. Those who apply the rule to particular cases, must of necessity expound and interpret that rule. If two laws conflict with each other, the courts must decide on the operation of each. So, if a law be in opposition to the constitution; if both the law and the constitution apply to a particular case, so that the court must either decide the case conformably to the law, disregarding the constitution; or conformably to the constitution, disregarding the law; the court must determine which of these conflicting rules governs the case: this is of the very essence of judicial duty. If, then, the courts are to regard the constitution, and the constitution is superior to any ordinary act of the legislature, the constitution, and not such ordinary act, must govern the case to which they both apply." This was a sweeping claim; it made the Court the final repository of national power, and it aroused violent opposition, particularly from Jeffersonians who insisted that each department of government could, and should, determine for itself the meaning of the Constitution. John Marshall's doctrine of judicial supremacy was destined to have enormous consequences in the area of American race relations and on the issue of slavery.

Judicial supremacy was not established overnight, and in the meanwhile, Congress placed its own interpretation on portions of constitutional language and found its own answers to some of the open questions.

Whether slavery was debated in Congress or in the courts, the slaveholding states adopted as their central theme the proposition that the Constitution left the whole matter to the states. That constant harping on the rights of states in respect to slavery nourished the growth of the states' rights doctrine which, of course, had other roots as well. In its final form, the states' rights doctrine asserted that the states had entire control over slavery within their own borders; that interstate commerce in slaves was beyond the control of Congress; that free Negroes held no national citizenship and, hence, were not beneficiaries of the privileges-and-immunities clause; that slaveholders had a right to take their property into all federal territories, and that residents of territories applying for statehood had a right to secure admission of new states as slave states.

In short, this doctrine resolved every constitutional ambiguity in favor of slavery and the slave states. Having justified those positions on a claim of paramountcy of states' rights, proponents of slavery then took the inconsistent position that Congress, and not the states, was supreme as far as the return of fugitive slaves was concerned, and that Congress alone could legislate on that issue. They wanted national fugitive slave laws because they didn't trust the northern states to return their slaves. Conversely, opponents of slavery deprecated the right of the states as to slavery, except for the admission that the states did have a right to exercise control over slavery within their own borders. They tended to argue for federal supremacy in every other instance except in the case of fugitive slaves, where they, too, became inconsistent and asserted that the return of fugitives was a matter of state comity over which Congress could exercise no control. It suited their purpose to insist on states' rights in that instance, because they wanted to hamper return of fugitives. Consistency is never a virtue in political controversy.

The initial battles to settle the unanswered constitutional questions were fought in Congress, because the Supreme Court had not completely established its supremacy and was reluctant to tackle what it regarded as a political question, and because both sides were content to let the matter rest there. The number of free and slave states was put on a parity and kept there for many years, thus guaranteeing an equal division in the Senate and near-equality in the House. Neither side could impose its will on the other. The early skirmishes took the form of trying to upset congressional equilibrium and were settled by the kind of compromises that are inevitable in a democratic system. As compromises wore thinner and thinner and as judicial power grew, the struggle to shape national policy as respects slavery shifted more and more to a struggle to determine the content, and import, of Supreme Court decisions and then to induce the Court to take jurisdiction of the whole controversy. The Court was ultimately induced to assert power to settle all issues involving slavery, and in the process of doing so, it took the lives and liberties of all Negroes, free and slave, under its judicial wing. It also helped precipitate the Civil War. That war disrupted, but did not destroy, the Court's assumption of power. The path toward judicial power was a long and twisting one through uncharted constitutional territory.

⚜ 3 ⚜ *An Agreement with Hell*

*The compact which exists between
North and South is a covenant with
death and an agreement with hell.*

Motto, GARRISON's *Liberator*

If an American citizen should go to the Los Angeles suburb of Alta-
dena next Independence Day, desecrate a copy of the Constitution
and brand it as subversive of liberty and decency, he would undoubtedly be hailed before the House Committee on Un-American
Activities or the Senate Internal Securities Committee, or both, in-
terrogated as to his beliefs and associations, past and present, and
upon failure to answer, he would certainly be cited for contempt of
Congress unless he took quick refuge in the Fifth Amendment.
Nothing of the kind happened to William Lloyd Garrison who
went to Framingham, near Boston, on July 4, 1854, burned a copy
of the Constitution, denounced it as a covenant with death and an
agreement with hell and urged his hearers to cry amen!

There were no such congressional committees in Garrison's day,
and there was so much controversy over the Constitution and slavery that extravagance was expected. There were voices all over the
land, even in the Senate, calling for secession and disunion. Also,
what Garrison said on that Independence Day of 1854 was anticli-
max. Of the Constitution he had cried out in 1832: "A sacred compact, forsooth! We pronounce it the most bloody and heaven-
daring arrangement ever made by men for the continuance and
protection of a system of the most atrocious villainy ever exhibited
upon earth." Since 1843, his newspaper, *The Liberator*, had borne
the slogan, "The compact which now exists between the North and

South is a covenant with death and an agreement with hell—involving both parties in atrocious criminality . . ."

Garrison had not always taken such a dim view of the Constitution. When he began publication of *The Liberator* in 1831, he had regarded the document as the surest haven of free men and had urged Negroes to put their faith in the Constitution: "Thanks be to God that we have such a Constitution. Without it, the liberties of every man—white as well as black would be in jeopardy. There it stands, firm as the Rock of Gibraltar, a high refuge from oppression." That early estimate had been made at a time when Garrison had his eyes glued on the guarantees of personal liberty in the Constitution and the Bill of Rights, and when he was beguiled by the belief, or hope, that those guarantees inured to every *person* of whom it spoke. He reasoned that adherence to such a Constitution and to laws enacted under it and interpreted in its spirit would preserve and enhance the liberties of every man, white and black. His disillusionment grew not only out of an increasing awareness that the Constitution protected slavery in the states in which it existed and that the legislative, executive, and judicial branches of the federal government were compelled to further that protection but also to a rising conviction that all doubts as to constitutional meaning were being resolved in favor of the slave power by congressmen, the chief executive, and especially the Courts.

Chief Justice John Marshall, the guiding spirit in the Supreme Court from 1800 to 1835, and Justice Joseph Story, his ablest supporter, who went to the Court in 1811, were conservatives with a strong bias in favor of property rights. Their recognition of constitutional tolerance of slavery carried with it a correlative belief that the property rights of slaveholders were paramount in a judicial determination of questions affecting slavery. The distinction, whatever it is worth, of having been the first Negro to put his case before the Supreme Court belongs to a slave called simply "London" and described in court reports as Negro London.[1] Virginia law provided that a slave, brought into the state and kept there for a year or more, gained freedom unless his master, within 60 days after bringing him in, filed a declaration to the effect that the master intended to become a citizen of the state. London was taken to Virginia by the father of his owner and kept there for eleven months, without any declaration having been filed. Ultimately, the owner came to the state and within 60 days after his arrival filed the proper declaration, but only after London had been in the state more than a year. Chief Justice Marshall added to Negro London's distinction by writing the opinion in his case in 1806, holding that the law was satisfied when the real owner filed the declaration within the 60 days of his arrival, regardless of the fact that the slave had been in the state more than a year. Negro London returned to obscurity and slavery—the ordinary slave didn't even have a surname in those days.

Negro Ben was before the Court in 1810 claiming freedom on the ground that he was being held in slavery in violation of a Maryland statute which required any person bringing a slave into that state to prove to the "satisfaction of the naval officer or collector of taxes that such slave had resided three years in the United States" prior to having been brought into the state.[2] Everybody agreed that no such proof had been offered when Ben was taken to Maryland, but the Chief Justice bypassed the law by holding that proof of such three-year residence was sufficient if it was offered at the trial of the suit for freedom. Negress Sally made a bid for freedom in 1816 on the ground that she had been taken to Maryland in violation of another law that prohibited importation of slaves, but Marshall frowned on her claim: her sojourn had been only temporary, he said.[3] Ben and Sally joined London in a return to the anonymity of slavery.

The law of slavery, perforce, developed in the slaveholding states, which meant that it was favorable to slavery as an institution of private property. Marshall's tactic, or more accurately, the tactic of the Court over which he presided, was to put the stamp of approval on state laws and state court decisions respecting slavery. Under the common law, which prevailed in the United States, a child followed the condition of its father as to freedom. The opposite rule that the child followed the condition of the mother—*partus sequitur ventrem*—obtained under the civil law of continental Europe. The slave states chose to follow the civil law, and the presence of 246,565 persons classed as mulatto slaves—that is, children of white fathers and Negro mothers—by the Census of 1850 bears statistical witness to the wisdom of their choice. The effect of the choice didn't stop there; it gave rise to the quaint conceit that one drop of African blood made a person a Negro and, hence, presumptively liable to the burdens of slavery, and that there was something morally reprehensible about sexual relations between Negro males and white females. There is no data on how many thousands of words have been uttered on the sanctity of white womanhood and the mongrelization of the races, with little more original justification than the fact that the offspring of a Negro man and a white woman would have been free persons under the law of slavery.

The question of whether a child followed the condition of the mother reached the Supreme Court in 1827. Chief Justice Marshall made short shrift of the matter: "The second point is, we believe, well settled. The issue is, we believe, universally considered as following the mother. . . ." [4] The Court buttressed the point in 1834, in a case where a slave woman had been given freedom at the end of a particular period. During that period and while she was still a slave, some children were born to her and the Court agreed that children born prior to her attainment of freedom were slaves: "Therefore, children of a slave mother born during the term . . . are slaves and must be held as such. . . ." [5] Slaves who sought freedom by trying to trace their descent from a white maternal ancestor were handicapped by rulings, again pronounced by the Chief Justice, that they could not sustain such proof by offering evidence of her reputation as a white woman. This was the ordinary, and often the only, manner in which matters of pedigree could be proved.

These restrictive decisions occasioned personal hardships and aroused humanitarian resentment, but the Court under Chief Justice Marshall did not hand down any decisions involving major constitutional questions on the issue of domestic slavery. It aroused far more controversy by its decisions on the foreign slave trade. After Congress legislated on the slave trade, the Court was presented with a series of cases involving forfeiture of ships engaged in the trade and the disposition of slaves taken from such ships. The most important of them was decided in 1825.

The Antelope, as the case is called, involved a slave ship of that name. [6] The *Columbia,* a privateer sailing under a Venezuelan commission, called in 1819 at Baltimore, where it took on an American crew of some 30 or 40 men. Fully equipped, it set sail, changed its name to the *Arraganta,* hoisted a foreign flag, and made its way to the African coast, where it preyed on Spanish and Portuguese slave ships. After having stolen a full complement of slaves, it captured the *Antelope,* which was also loaded with contraband slaves. The two ships sailed together to the Brazilian coast, where the *Arraganta* was wrecked. All slaves were transferred to the *Antelope,* which was finally captured while it was skulking around the American coast trying to unload its cargo. When it was towed to Savannah, four sets of claimants demanded the slaves. The captain claimed them on the obscure ground that he had taken them as contraband of war; the Spanish and Portuguese based their respective claims on the assertion that the slaves had been stolen from their vessels, and the United States government based a claim on the theory that the slaves had been transported in an American ship contrary to its laws and asserted that, therefore, the slaves were entitled to freedom under international law.

The case was important because it involved the reach and scope of American and international law as to the slave trade. Marshall took the occasion to write what he evidently regarded as a definitive opinion on the issues. Slavery, he said, is "contrary to the laws of nature . . . every man has a right to the fruits of his own labor." But, he noted, "whatever might be the answer of the moralist" on the issues before the Court, "a jurist must search for a legal answer." He had no doubt that "these negroes were property," and he took notice of the Spanish argument that the "slave trade originated in motives of humanity and was intended to avoid the greater evils growing out of the barbarous state of the African continent." The nub of the matter, as Marshall saw it, was whether or not slavery was contrary to the law of nations in the absence of treaties or of specific prohibitions of particular countries. "Among the most enlightened nations of antiquity," he ruminated, "the victor might enslave the vanquished. This, which was the usage of all could not be pronounced repugnant to the law of nations, which is certainly to be tried by general usage. That which received the assent of all must be the law of all." He agreed that the harsh law of war entitling the victor to enslave the vanquished was no longer in general vogue, but, he said, "Africa has not yet adopted these principles." Since international law was "decidedly in favor of the [slave] trade," in the absence of specific agreements to the contrary and since neither Spain nor Portugal had forbidden it, "a jurist could not say that a practice thus supported was illegal and that those engaged in it might be punished either personally or through deprivation of property." He devised a mathematical formula by which the slaves were divided between Spanish and Portuguese claimants and the American government.

Marshall's decision, which drew the approval of all of his colleagues, was a narrow one, undergirded by an insistence on the primacy of property rights. His appeal to the character of slavery as a by-product of war was misplaced. As government counsel pointed out, "Slaves are no longer acquired merely by capture in war or by trade; but free persons are seized and carried off by traders and agents." The terrible inhumanity of the slave trade was a matter of common knowledge, and everybody knew that African slaves were being bootlegged into the United States in sizable numbers. Critics charged that the Court had flubbed an opportunity to strike a blow at the illicit business, but anger was somewhat allayed by a simultaneous decision in a case styled *The Plattsburg*, in which the Court held that an American ship was subject to condemnation where it was outfitted for the slave trade although a portion of its business was legal.[7]

The foreign slave trade—like today's narcotic traffic—had few defenders albeit a substantial number of participants. Cases involving the trade often presented the Court with difficult technical questions concerning property rights in seized vessels and the quantum of proof necessary to convict owners and officers of engaging in the trade. Abolitionist attacks on the Court waxed and waned depending on the particular decision, but the common complaint was that it had far more concern with property rights than human rights. There were outbursts of rage, as when Justice Story wrote an opinion for a unanimous Court in 1827 dismissing on technical grounds an indictment against John Gooding, a notorious Baltimore slave trader, who was defended by Roger Taney, a rising young Baltimore lawyer.[8] A great hue and cry went up, charging the Court with not only going out of its way to shield the slave trade but also with granting practical immunity to rich and powerful slave traders. The thread of consistency that ran through the Court's decisions in respect to the slave trade was its narrow construction of the laws it was called upon to interpret. It stuck closely to textual terms and avoided dealing with the moral issues, thus enraging opponents of slavery.

Meanwhile, the real battle over slavery was being fought in Congress. The Founding Fathers had left little apparent room for federal legislation. By express constitutional provisions, Congress could levy a limited head tax on slaves imported prior to 1808 and could prohibit the importation of slaves after that date. There was

practically complete agreement that it could legislate for the return
of escaped slaves as it did in 1793, and that it could prohibit American citizens and American shipping from engaging in the foreign
slave trade even prior to 1808. It could not liberate a single slave in
a single state or even ameliorate the condition of his servitude. At a
glance, it would appear that Congress pretty well stuck to its constitutional last. It closed the slave trade to American citizens in
1794 and to American shipping in 1800; it prohibited the slave
trade as soon as possible; it passed two fugitive slave laws, one in
1793 and another in 1850, and it amended these basic laws from
time to time. Despite this seeming legislative moderation, Congress
was in turmoil over slavery from its first session until the Civil War.
It became a forum for debate between opponents and proponents
of slavery, principally because both sides believed that Congress,
and not the Supreme Court, was the proper agency of government
to answer the questions on the slavery issue left open by the Constitution.

A particular source of friction was the deluge of petitions that
descended on Congress from the very beginning. Congress was importuned from time to time to abolish slavery, to prohibit American
citizens from engaging in the slave trade, to close American shipping to the slave trade, to abolish slavery and the slave trade in the
District of Columbia, to prohibit interstate commerce in slaves, to
interdict slavery in the territories, to repeal fugitive slave laws, to
inquire into the re-enslavement of freed Negroes, and to do a dozen
and one other things that would restrict and hamper slavery and
limit its growth. Finally, it sought to solve, but only aggravated, the
petition problem with its famous gag rule of 1837, laying all antislavery petitions on the table without consideration.

One of the prime sources of trouble for Congress was a matter
that the Constitution makers thought was settled. The Constitution
provided that "New States may be admitted by Congress into this
Union" and that "Congress shall have power to dispose of and
make all needful Rules and Regulations respecting the Territory or
her Property belonging to the United States. . . ." Congress rati-
d the Ordinance of 1787 prohibiting slavery in the Northwest
rritory at its first session, thereby assuring the nation that all
st.tes carved out of that territory would be free. It was tacitly assumed that states formed out of the territory lying south of the
Ohio River and belonging to southern states would permit slavery.

Kentucky was admitted in 1792 and Tennessee in 1796, both as slave states. When Mississippi Territory, comprising the present states of Alabama and Mississippi, was organized in 1798, a congressional motion to prohibit slavery could muster only twelve votes in the House. The debate on the motion marked the first time Congress had faced the issue as to its competency to control slavery in federal territories. Its constitutional power to do so was not challenged.

The Louisiana Purchase threw the issue out of joint. Under French law, slavery was permissible in the entire area lying between the Mississippi River and the Rocky Mountains and stretching from Canada to the Gulf of Mexico. A great portion of the Purchase lay north of the line 36° 30′ north latitude, the tacit dividing line between free and slave states. Congress had kept the number of free and slave states in balance since the War of 1812, and when Missouri applied for admission in 1818, the balance required that it be admitted as a slave state. Missouri made such an application, only to run into a storm of opposition growing out of a congressional amendent to the admission bill which declared all of its inhabitants free who were born after admission and provided for gradual emancipation of those then held in slavery. Discussion of the amendment touched off a towering congressional debate on constitutional issues.

The essence of the antislavery position was that the Constitution lodged in Congress the right to impose whatever terms it chose for admission to the Union; the Southerners argued that Congress had no such power by constitutional warrant. The case for the North was well put by Congressman John W. Tyler of New York: "First. Has Congress power to require of Missouri a constitutional prohibition against the further introduction of slavery as a condition of her admission into the Union? Second. If the power exists, is it wise to exercise it?" [9] He answered both questions in the affirmative: "After the formation of a Territory the Congress may admit the state into the Union in pursuance of a power delegated by the same section of the Constitution, in the following words: 'New States may be admitted by the Congress into the Union.' This grant of power is evidently alternative; its exercise is committed to the sound discretion of Congress. . . . But if Congress has the power to altogether refuse to admit new States, much more has it the power of prescribing such conditions of admission as may be judged reasonable." As to expediency: "If we reject the amendment and suffer this evil, now easily eradicated, to strike its roots so deep in the soil that it can never be removed, shall we not furnish some apology for doubting our sincerity when we deplore its existence— shall we not expose ourselves to censure?"

Congressman Alexander Smyth of Virginia had an answer for his colleague: "The right to own slaves being acknowledged and se- cured by the Constitution, can you prescribe what the Constitution guarantees? Can you touch a right reserved to the States or the people? You cannot. If you possessed the power to legislate con- cerning slavery, the adoption of the proposition on your table, which goes to emancipate all children of slaves hereafter born in Missouri, would be a direct violation of the Constitution which pro- vides that 'no person shall be deprived of property without due process of law; nor shall private property be taken for public use without just compensation.' . . . It has been said that the Consti- tution vests in Congress a power to make all needful regulations respecting the territory of the United States; and this power, it is supposed, authorizes us to exclude slavery from the territories of the United States and also to demand from any of those territories about to become States a stipulation for the exclusion of slaves. The clause obviously relates to the territory belonging to the United States as property only. . . . A power to dispose of and make all needful regulations respecting the property of the United States is very different from a power to legislate over the persons and prop- erty of the people." [10] Congressman Robert Reid of Georgia met the argument as to expediency: "Slaves, divided among many masters, will enjoy greater privileges and comforts. . . . Danger from in- surrection will diminish. Confidence will grow between the master and his servant." [11]

Neither Tyler nor Smyth suggested that the issue was a judicial one, lying within the jurisdiction or competency of the Supreme Court.

The matter was finally settled by the famous Missouri Compro- mise Act of 1820, under which Missouri was admitted as a slave state, with the proviso that slavery was forever prohibited in all other portions of the Louisiana Purchase lying north of the line of 36° 30' north latitude. In accordance with the act, Missouri adopted a constitution and presented it to Congress for ratification. Trouble stirred again. The state constitution contained a clause obligating the legislature to pass laws against the entry of free Negroes. Northern representatives and senators objected on the ground that such a provision violated Article IV, Section 2, of the Constitution, that "the Citizens of each State shall be entitled to all Privileges and Immunities of Citizens in the several States." Another unanswered constitutional question was demanding an answer: Were free Negroes citizens of their states and, as such, entitled to the privileges and immunities safeguarded by the Constitution, which included the right to move freely from state to state? Congress did not solve that question. It temporized by a measure allowing the admission of Missouri, provided that its legislature should pass an act declaring that it would never exclude any citizen of another state from the privileges and immunities to which he was entitled under the Constitution of the United States. It dared not try to define privileges and immunities possessed by free Negroes.

The uneasy peace established by the Missouri Compromise lasted a quarter of a century. It was disrupted when Texas came barging into the Union in 1845, trailing the Mexican War in its wake and leading to the annexation of new territories neither open nor closed to slavery by American law. Under Mexican law, slavery was prohibited in the area belonging to it. Before the war was ended, Congressman David Wilmot of Pennsylvania proposed that "neither slavery or involuntary servitude" should exist in any part of territory procured from Mexico. The South was aroused anew. On February 19, 1847, Senator John C. Calhoun of South Carolina introduced a series of resolutions in the Senate and, by way of preface, cited statistics showing that the balance of power was shifting in favor of free states and asserted that unless all territory about to be acquired from Mexico, including that north of the antislavery line, was left open to slavery, "the Government would be overwhelmingly in the hands of the non-slaveholding States."

The Calhoun resolutions were based on the premise that no agency of the federal government, legislative, executive, or judicial, could interfere with slavery in the territories or attach any conditions to the admission of new states. In the fierce blaze of debate that followed, both the Wilmot Proviso and the Calhoun resolutions were defeated, with both sides reiterating and refining the arguments that had raged over the Missouri Compromise. Something new was added. A portent of the future came when several senators proposed that the entire matter be referred to the federal judiciary for settlement.

California knocked on the Union door in 1850, without having gone through a territorial apprenticeship. Senator Henry Clay of Kentucky seized the occasion as an appropriate time for a settlement of the most aggravated slavery questions that were plaguing the nation; he introduced what came to be called the Compromise of 1850. He proposed: the admission of California as a free state; the strengthening of the fugitive slave law; prohibition of the slave trade—not slavery—in the District of Columbia; that since "slavery does not by law, and is not likely to be introduced into any of the territory acquired by the United States from Mexico, it is inexpedient for Congress to provide by law either for its introduction into or its exclusion from any part of the said territory . . ." and that "Congress has no power to prohibit or obstruct the trade in slaves between the slaveholding states." Ultimately, and after extensive debate, rehashing previous arguments on the Missouri Compromise and the Wilmot Proviso, California was admitted as a free state, the slave trade was prohibited in the District of Columbia, the fugitive slave law was tightened up, and New Mexico and Utah were organized as territories without restrictions as to slavery. The nation was assured that the Compromise of 1850 had settled the slavery question forever. Forever lasted four years.

The slavery controversy broke out in new and renewed fury in 1854, when Congress was called upon to legislate on the organization of the Kansas and Nebraska Territories. Senator Stephen Douglas of Illinois proposed that the residents of those territories, both of which were free soil by virtue of the Missouri Compromise, should decide for themselves whether the new states should be free or slave. His proposal, which had cropped up on prior occasions, had the advantage of apparent fairness: What could be more democratic than letting the people of the new states decide for themselves? Appearances belied reality. Douglas was proposing the repeal of the Missouri Compromise, in effect if not in words, although he denied the charge and claimed that the compromise had been repealed by the Compromise of 1850. Moreover, he was placing the stamp of congressional approval on the southern doctrine, urged with increasing vigor, that slaves were mere property and that slave owners had the right to take that property into all territories of the

United States. Even more insidious from the antislavery point of view, he was stripping away the last pretense that slaves were "persons" within the purview of the Constitution and was stultifying the doctrine that slavery existed, and could only exist, by force of local law and never by reason of federal establishment or protection.

The Douglas proposal triumphed, with the explanation that it was "the true intent and meaning of this act not to legislate slavery into any Territory or State, nor to exclude it therefrom; but to leave the people thereof perfectly free to form and regulate their domestic institutions in their own way, subject only to the Constitution of the United States." The committee which had brought in the bill had remarked "that it is a disputed point whether slavery is prohibited in the Nebraska country by valid enactment" and whether the "8th section of the act preparatory to the admission of Missouri is null and void"—another of the increasing series of hints that the entire matter could be, and should be, settled by the Supreme Court.

Marshall and Story, the dominant figures on the Court until 1835, were not only conservatives but believers in a strong, or at least strengthened, central government. A review of nonslavery cases that came before the Court under Marshall shows that it very consciously and consistently upheld the right of Congress and the federal government as against the claims or objections of the states. In the language of the day, Marshall favored a broad construction of the Constitution. "The government of the United States," he said in a famous case involving banking, "though limited in its powers, is supreme." [12] And to attempts to limit and constrict the powers of the central government on broad issues, he abjured his brethren that "we must never forget that it is a constitution we are expounding." [13] In the landmark case of *Gibbons v. Ogden*,[14] for example, the Court upheld the power of Congress to control commerce between the states by giving a sweeping meaning to the term *regulate* and by holding that congressional action in the field precluded state attempts at regulation. The effect of the decision was to break up a virtual monopoly in shipping protected by New York law.

South Carolina and Virginia had intruded on congressional control of interstate commerce by laws directed against the entrance of free Negro seamen and by providing for their detention and custody until the vessels in which they had arrived should leave port. Acting under the theory enunciated in *Gibbons v. Ogden*, Justice

William Johnson, sitting as a circuit judge, held flatly that South
Carolina's statute was unconstitutional: the power to regulate commerce, he said, was vested in Congress.[15] South Carolina ignored
his decision.

Presented with the same problem in reference to the similar Virginia law, Marshall, also sitting as a circuit judge, sidestepped the
issue.[16] He was frank about his reasons for doing so and wrote Justice Story: "Our brother Johnson, I perceive, has hung himself on a
democratic snag in a hedge composed entirely of thorny States-
Rights in South Carolina. You have, it is said, some laws in Massachusetts, not very unlike in principles that to which our brother has
declared unconstitutional. We have its twin brother in Virginia; a
case has been brought before me in which I might have considered
its constitutionality, had I chosen to do so; but it was not absolutely
necessary and as I am not fond of butting against a wall in sport, I
escaped on construction of the act."

Meanwhile, Marshall was carefully nurturing and expounding
his theory, announced in *Marbury v. Madison* in 1803, that the Supreme Court's interpretation of the Constitution was binding on
the executive and legislative branches of government as well as on
the courts. That announcement had met bitter opposition. Jefferson
disputed it: "But the opinion which gives to the Judges the right to
decide what laws are constitutional, and what not, not only for
themselves in their own sphere of action, but for the Legislative
and Executive also in their spheres, would make the Judiciary a
despotic branch." Jefferson's triumph put the brakes on the open
exercise of judicial supremacy as Marshall conceived it, but the
struggle continued and it was one of the central issues that led to
the election of Andrew Jackson, a vigorous opponent of the Marshall doctrine of judicial supremacy. If accepted, the Marshall doctrine had enormous consequences: it meant that the Court, and not
Congress or the executive, was vested with the ultimate power to
decide what the Constitution commanded or interdicted and, more,
that if Congress did make constitutional judgments and enacted
laws on the basis of those judgments, the Court could strike them
down.

The Supreme Court could not, however, invalidate either state or
congressional legislation by reason of any supervisory power but
only by construction of statutes in cases coming before it for adjudication. Marshall's refusal to rule on the constitutionality of the

Virginia exclusion laws was, therefore, significant inasmuch as it was a deliberate refusal, for policy reasons, to exercise a power he claimed for the Court. The real issue for him was whether it was politic to act at that time. And what was politic today might not be so tomorrow or the next year.

Jackson was at the height of his power when Marshall died in 1835, and it was a foregone conclusion that he would choose a Chief Justice who agreed with him that each of the coordinate branches of government could determine for itself the constitutionality of its own acts and actions. Such an appointment would curb the Marshall claim that the judiciary was supreme. The choice fell on Roger Brooke Taney, a slaveholder who had freed all but two of his slaves,[17] and who had distinguished himself by his opposition to Chief Justice Marshall's claims of judicial supremacy.

⊰ 4 ⊱ *A Long Way from Home*

Sometimes I feel
Like a motherless child
A long way from home.

NEGRO SPIRITUAL

Roger Taney was popularly believed to have been the guiding legal genius behind Andrew Jackson's veto of the congressional act rechartering the Bank of the United States. In a message which disparaged the power of the Supreme Court, the President proclaimed, "If the opinion of the Supreme Court covers the whole ground of this act, it ought not to control the coordinate authorities of this Government. The Congress, the Executive and the Court must each for itself be guided by its own opinion of the Constitution. . . . The authority of the Supreme Court must not, therefore, be permitted to control the Congress or the Executive. . . ." [1] The rebuke was aimed at the contention that the Court was the supreme arbiter of constitutional interpretation and that what it held was binding on other branches of government.

Taney was one of that group of Democrats who had flocked to Washington to help effectuate Jackson's triumph over reaction in general and over John Marshall's federalist Supeme Court in particular. Conservative senators had ganged up to block his confirmation as Secretary of the Treasury and as an associate justice of the Supreme Court earlier in Jackson's term but were powerless to prevent Taney's confirmation as Chief Justice, an event that signalized the Jacksonian victory in all branches of the government. By 1836, five of the seven Supreme Court Justices were Jackson's appointees and, by 1837, six of the nine had been named by him. The Supreme

Court, it seemed, had been reduced to its proper place as one of three coordinate branches of government, supreme in its own sphere, as Congress and the Executive were in theirs.

The most sensational case involving slavery to reach the Taney Court in its early years was the *Amistad* decision in 1841.[2] A French ship of that name took on a cargo of Negro slaves who had been captured in Africa and landed in Cuba. After the ship sailed from Havana, the slaves revolted, killed the captain, and ordered the mate to sail for Africa. Instead, he piloted the ship toward New York, and it was seized off Long Island. The revolt captured popular imagination, and John Quincy Adams, former President, came out of virtual retirement to represent the slaves in the Supreme Court, where they asserted their freedom against Spanish claimants. Justice Story wrote an opinion for the Court, holding that the slaves had been kidnapped in violation of international law and ordering them set free. Only Justice Baldwin dissented. There was great rejoicing on the part of antislavery people, who hailed the decision as a practical reversal of Marshall's ruling in the *Antelope* case.

A month earlier and almost obscured by the excitement over the *Amistad* revolt, the Court had decided a case of different import, and of far greater importance on the issue of domestic slavery. Mississippi's 1822 constitution expressly prohibited the "introduction of slaves in this state as merchandise or for sale" after May 1, 1833. After the critical date, Robert Slaughter, a Louisiana slave trader, took some slaves to Mississippi and sold them to John W. Brown, whose note for payment was guaranteed by Moses Groves and others. Brown defaulted in his payments and Slaughter filed suit, choosing the federal court as a forum, since he was a citizen of one state and Groves of another. Groves pitched his defense on the claim that the sale was void because it was prohibited by the Mississippi constitution.

Groves v. Slaughter,[3] as the case was styled, raised the grave question of interstate commerce in slaves. Antislavery people were bombarding Congress with petitions demanding that it prohibit such traffic under the constitutional provision giving Congress the power to "regulate commerce . . . among the several states." Their lawyers pointed to the decision in *Gibbons v. Ogden*,[4] in which the Court had held that Congress had exclusive power to regulate interstate commerce. Since, they argued, slaves were regarded as articles of commerce, it followed that Congress could regulate the interstate slave trade in the same manner that it could regulate commerce in other property. Proponents of slavery vigorously denied that Congress had any power over the interstate slave traffic; they contended that slaves were property of a peculiar kind and that the right to buy and sell them in interstate commerce was, as they phrased it, higher and deeper than the Constitution.

The logical next question was whether or not a state which tolerated slavery within its own borders could prohibit the importation and sale of slaves as merchandise, as the Mississippi constitution put it. And again, proslavery adherents answered the question in the negative, basing their contention on the ground that such action would deprive slaveholders of a valuable property right. A slave state, they said, could no more prohibit its citizens from buying or selling slaves in interstate commerce than it could deprive them of the right to buy, or sell, any other commodity from, or to, citizens of other states. What proponents of slavery were insisting on was an answer to the question left open by the Constitution on the issue of interstate traffic in slaves, and, of course, the answer they proposed was entirely favorable to slavery.

No matter what he may have thought of the merits of the constitutional issue raised by his opponents, Groves was intent on escaping liability on the note he had signed, and he fought fire with fire by clothing his own argument in the bright raiment of states' rights. As a sovereign state, he said, Mississippi had the right to control its own affairs, even to the extent of prohibiting importation of slaves if it chose to do so. He bolstered his case by citing a Mississippi court decision which apparently agreed with his claim. The economic issue was important, for despite the plain prohibitions of the Mississippi constitution, there had been a wholesale importation of slaves into the state by speculators, and it was said that if Groves prevailed and escaped payment, creditors stood to lose more than two million dollars. The importance of the case can be gauged from the fact that Henry Clay and Daniel Webster appeared for Slaughter in the Supreme Court and that the opinions of the various justices occupy 70 pages in the Court reports. The arguments of Groves's lawyer occupy another 86 pages in the appendix.

Justice Robert Thompson who wrote what is regarded as the opinion of the Court reduced the case to a narrow compass in order to avoid the larger constitutional issues. "The question arising un-

der the constitution of Mississippi," he wrote, "is whether this prohibition, *per se*, interdicts the introduction of slaves as merchandise
. . . or is directory only to the legislature, and requiring their action
in order to bring it into full operation." He came to the conclusion
that the prohibition was directory only and that, since the legislature had not acted as directed, there was no restraint on bringing slaves into the state for sale as merchandise. "This view of the
case," he reminded his brethren, "makes it unnecessary to inquire
whether this article is repugnant to the Constitution of the United
States; and, indeed, such inquiry is not properly in the case, as the
decision has been placed entirely upon the construction of the constitution of Mississippi." Since a majority of the Court agreed with
Thompson's construction, the case should have come to an end at
that point. It is a cardinal article of Supreme Court faith that no
more is ever decided in a case than is necessary for its disposition as
between litigants. But the other justices would not let the matter
rest; the Court was heading toward a constitutional stand on slavery issues.

Justice John McLean opened up the discussion of what he called
the "momentous and delicate question" of these constitutional issues. He began with the amazing statement that "Although the
question I am to consider *is not necessary* to a decision of the case
. . . I deem it fit and proper to express my opinion upon it." He
cited *Gibbons v. Ogden* and reminded the Court that the case "decided that the power to regulate commerce is exclusively vested in
Congress and that no part of it can be exercised by a state." But
that was not the end of the matter, he said, because "The Constitution treats slaves as persons. But if slaves are considered in some
states as merchandise, that cannot divest them of the leading and
controlling quality of persons, by which they are designated in the
Constitution." Since slaves were persons and not property in the
constitutional sense, McLean concluded that states had the power
to exclude such unwanted persons, even though they could not regulate interstate commerce: "The right to exercise this power, by a
state, is higher and deeper than the Constitution. The evil involves
the prosperity and may endanger the existence of a state. Its power
to guard against, or to remedy the evil, rests upon a law of self
preservation."

Chief Justice Taney was as candid as McLean: "I concur that the
[constitutional] point is not involved in the case before us. But as

my brother McLean has stated his opinion upon it, I am not will-ing, by remaining silent, to leave any doubt as to mine." He had no doubt that, as far as interstate traffic in slaves was concerned, "the action of the several states cannot be controlled by Congress; either by virtue of its power to regulate commerce, or by virtue of any power conferred by the Constitution of the United States."

Justices Story, Wayne, Thompson, and McKinley agreed that the "provision of the Constitution of the United States which gives the regulation of commerce to Congress, did not interfere with the provisions of the constitution of the state of Mississippi which re-lates to the introduction of slaves as merchandise or for sale." Jus-tice Henry Baldwin went even further; he was certain that federal laws forbidding states to "entirely prohibit the importation of slaves" would be "anti-national, subversive of the harmony which should exist between the states as well as inconsistent with the most sacred principles of the Constitution. . . ." Almost as an after-thought, Justices Story and McKinley agreed with Moses Groves that the provisions of the Mississippi constitution were operative and that he ought not be held liable on the note. But they were in the minority, and Groves had to pay.

The Court had taken a long step toward asserting its supremacy in constitutional questions respecting slavery. The flat statements of the justices that Congress could not legislate on the interstate slave traffic between slave states were stern warnings that they were pre-pared to invalidate congressional enactments on the subject. Ap-parently, as far as slavery was concerned, the Jacksonians were ready to jettison their doctrine that the authority of the "Court must not be permitted to control Congress or the Executive. . . ." It was apparent, too, that there was a strong sentiment on the Court favoring the proposition that a slave state could not prohibit the importation of slaves. Baldwin, who was its foremost exponent, said that had "the contract in question been *invalid* by the Consti-tution of Mississippi, it would have been *valid* by the Constitution of the United States," because "wherever slavery exists, by the laws of a state, slaves are property in every constitutional sense, and for every purpose. . . ."

A year later, the Court took another stride toward establishing its supremacy in the slavery controversy by invalidating a Pennsyl-vania law enacted to govern the return of fugitive slaves. The law had been passed after consultation and agreement with Maryland, the chief source of Pennsylvania fugitives, to effectuate the constitutional provision that persons "held to Service or Labour" in one state and escaping to another "shall be delivered up on the Claim of the Party to whom such Service or Labour may be due." The Pennsylvania law provided that a person claiming a fugitive must secure a warrant for the escaped slave's arrest, and then take the fugitive before a magistrate and secure an order for his removal to the state from which he had fled. Removal of a person from Pennsylvania without following the required steps and securing the order itself was denounced as kidnapping.

Margaret Morgan, a Maryland slave, escaped to Pennsylvania with her child in 1832. Another child was born in Pennsylvania after her escape. In 1837, Edward Prigg, a slave catcher, arrived in Pennsylvania with affidavits proving that she was the escaped slave of Margaret Ashmore and secured a warrant for Margaret Morgan's arrest, but when he took her before a magistrate, that official refused to sign a removal order. Prigg then spirited Margaret Morgan and her two children out of the state and was indicted and charged with kidnapping because the magistrate had not ordered the removal. Maryland cooperated by returning him for trial. The jury found that Margaret Morgan was born a slave, that she had escaped from Maryland, and that she and her two children were slaves since the children followed the condition of the mother. Upon that finding, the trial court held Prigg guilty of kidnapping for failure to secure the magistrate's removal order. The Pennsylvania Supreme Court affirmed the conviction in such a perfunctory manner that Justice McLean was later led to remark that he supposed the "case had been made up to bring the question" to the Supreme Court.

When the case—*Prigg v. Commonwealth*[5]—got to the Supreme Court, Pennsylvania justified the conviction on the ground that return of fugitives was a matter of state comity and that state law must be followed to the letter. It pointed out that the Constitution did not give Congress express power to legislate on the matter, and it asserted that the federal Fugitive Slave Law of 1793 was invalid as an invasion of states' rights. "The obligation" to return fugitives "is on the states, and for the states," Pennsylvania's attorney general told the Court: "The states' power is left perfectly free and untrammeled." Prigg's lawyers were properly shocked at this enunciation of states' rights and countered with the argument that the Fugitive

Slave Law had been enacted in 1793 when constitutional meanings were fresh in the minds of congressmen. They found it perfectly in order that Congress had passed a statute setting up procedures for the reclaiming of fugitives. Congress, they said, was supreme in the field, and neither Pennsylvania nor any other state could enact laws on the subject.

Justice Story, chosen to write the opinion for the Court, began by reassuring the nation that there was no animosity between the contestants: "The cause has been conducted in the Court below and has been brought here by the cooperation and sanction both of the state of Maryland and the state of Pennsylvania, in the most courteous and friendly spirit." The owner of a slave, he said, must "have the right to seize and repossess the slave, which the local laws of his own state confer upon him as property." He rejected the contention that the rendition of fugitive slaves was a matter of comity between the states and held that state laws were not binding on slave owners or their agents, who were perfectly free to secure their own property as long as they did not breach the peace and complied with federal law. It was well known, Story wrote, that many constitutional "provisions were matters of compromise of opposing forces and opinions." The article respecting the return of fugitives was such a compromise, and its plain purpose was to "secure to citizens of the slaveholding states the complete right and title of ownership in their slaves." He refuted the claim that Congress lacked power to legislate on the subject, despite the absence of an express grant of such power in the Constitution, because, he said, "where an end is required, means are given, and where duty is enjoined, ability to perform it is contemplated to exist on the part of the functionaries to whom it is entrusted."

Pennsylvania's assertion that its laws must be complied with in any event was rebutted on the ground that Congress, having the power to act, had legislated on the subject and thus pre-empted the field: "It would seem, upon just principles of construction, that the legislation of Congress, if constitutional, must supersede all state legislation upon the same subject. . . ." In the course of the argument, Pennsylvania had made much of the fact that the Fugitive Slave Law required state magistrates to assist in the return of fugitives and had attacked that requirement as being in derogation of state sovereignty. Story agreed that "it might well be deemed an unconstitutional exercise of the power of interpretation to insist that the states are bound to provide means to carry into effect the duties of the national government." State magistrates, he said, "may, if they choose, exercise that authority, unless prohibited by state legislation."

The Court was unanimous in upholding the validity of the Fugitive Slave Law, but that unanimity did not extend to all aspects of the case. The most troublesome point was that involving the duties of the states in respect of fugitives. Chief Justice Taney was dissatisfied with Story's opinion that Congress had exclusive power to legislate on the subject: "I think the states are not prohibited; and that, on the contrary, it is enjoined upon them as a duty to protect and support the owner when he is endeavoring to obtain possession of his property found within their respective territories. . . . I dissent therefrom . . . from that part of the opinion of the Court which denies the obligation and the right of state authorities to protect the master. . . ."

Justice Baldwin, adhering to his die-hard view that slaves were property under any and all circumstances, concurred in the judgment but "dissented from the principles laid down by the Court as grounds for their opinion." Justice McLean was "brought to the conclusion that, although, as a general principle, Congress cannot impose duties on state officers, yet in the case of fugitives from labor and justice, they have the power to do so." But the right was a barren one, he said, for "The power may be resisted by a state and there is no means of coercing it." He also thought that there was a place for state legislation not inconsistent with congressional enactments, and he, alone, would have affirmed Prigg's conviction on the ground that the Pennsylvania law requiring the claimant to take the fugitive before a magistrate and secure an order for removal was a valid exercise of state police power aimed to prevent "the forcible abduction of persons of color."

The Prigg decision drew angry protests from opponents of slavery, who knew full well that state control over rendition of fugitive slaves, such as that attempted by Pennsylvania, played into their hands. They looked forward to legislation by northern states which would impose severe restrictions on slave claimants and would extend the right of trial by jury to, and the utilization of habeas corpus by, fugitives. Under the circumstances, they were quite willing to switch sides and cover their purposes with the mantle of the states' rights doctrine.

The South moved to consolidate its victory by the Fugitive Slave Law of 1850, which proposed to remedy what were regarded as the defects of the earlier congressional legislation. It provided for federally appointed commissioners to exercise the powers granted judges in the 1793 act. These commissioners were given concurrent jurisdiction with United States judges to give certificates to claimants and order the removal of fugitives. United States marshals and deputies were required to execute writs under the act on penalty of $1,000 fine, and if a slave escaped from the marshal, "with or without his assent," that official became liable for the value of the slave. A certificate of removal was required on the affidavit of a claimant, and the fugitive was prohibited from giving evidence in his own behalf. Commissioners were to be paid ten dollars for each fugitive ordered returned but only five dollars when the claim was refused! On an affidavit by the claimant that he feared a rescue, the marshal was required to take the fugitive directly to the demanding state. A claimant of a slave might make an affidavit in his own state describing the fugitive, and when authenticated, that record was conclusive proof that the fugitive was a slave. Persons who aided or abetted in the rescue of a fugitive were liable to heavy fines and imprisonment.

Free states retaliated with "personal liberty" laws. These laws generally prohibited the use of state jails for detention of fugitives, provided state assistance of counsel for fugitives, secured jury trials and the writ of habeas corpus for fugitives, required proof of identity of the fugitive by at least two witnesses, forbade state judges from assisting in the return of fugitives, and levied heavy fines on persons seizing a free Negro and claiming him as a slave.

Conflict was inevitable.

Sherman M. Booth, editor of an abolitionist newspaper, was arrested in 1854 on a warrant issued by a federal commissioner in Wisconsin for participating in the rescue of an escaped slave near Racine. He applied for habeas corpus to the state courts on the ground that the Fugitive Slave Law of 1850 was unconstitutional, because (1) Congress had no power to legislate on the subject; (2) the law required the return of a person without a trial by jury; and (3) the act vested in commissioners judicial powers that properly belonged to the courts. The Wisconsin Supreme Court set Booth free, with one judge holding that all grounds of the petition were valid, another agreeing that the law as written was unconstitutional, and the third dissenting and holding that the law was valid. The United States attorney promptly appealed. While that appeal was pending, Booth was formally indicted by a United States grand jury for assisting in the escape of the fugitive. He was convicted in federal court and again applied for habeas corpus to the state courts. The Wisconsin Supreme Court again ordered his release on the ground that the Fugitive Slave Law of 1850 was invalid because Congress had no power to enact such legislation and because the act did not provide a jury trial for the *person* involved. The holding flew straight in the fact of the decision in the Prigg case and, of course, the United States district attorney had no choice but to appeal. The two appeals were decided together.

Chief Justice Taney wrote an opinion for a unanimous court in 1858 reversing both cases and ordering Booth jailed.[6] Booth again sought his release from the custody of the United States marshal on a writ of habeas corpus, but the Wisconsin courts rejected that plea. State officers obstructed federal officials at every turn. On occasions, fugitives were taken from the custody of the United States marshals. Estimates had it that there were 15,000 to 30,000 escaped slaves living openly in the North, with the masters unable to seize and return merchandise worth more than a million dollars.

As resistance spread, attacks on the Supreme Court mounted from both sides, and the Court sought to extricate itself by extreme care in its pronouncements lest it inadvertently weaken the fabric of its developing case law on slavery. The extent of its caution is well illustrated in the so-called *Passenger Cases*,[7] which were decided in 1849. New York and Massachusetts had passed laws imposing taxes on alien passengers arriving at their ports. The statutes did not concern, or even mention, slavery; they were attacked on the ground that they were violating the clause giving Congress the power to regulate commerce with foreign nations. The real issue was almost ignored in the Supreme Court while the justices wrangled over the slavery issue that lurked beneath the surface. The quarrel was so intense that the official court reporter wrote resignedly that, "Inasmuch as there was no opinion of the court, as a court, the reporter refers the readers to the opinions of the judges for an explanation of the statutes and the points in which they conflicted with the constitution and laws of the United States." A reading of the various opinions reveals that the Court held the statutes invalid by a five-to-four vote.

Justice Wayne, writing for the majority, was sure that "The fear expressed, that if the States have not the discretion to determine who may come and live in them, the United States may introduce into the Southern States emancipated negroes from the West Indies and elsewhere, has no foundation. . . . It will be found, too, should this matter of introducing free negroes into the Southern States ever become the subject of judicial inquiry, that they have a safeguard against it in the Constitution. . . ."

Chief Justice Taney, speaking for the minority, was not reassured by Wayne's words: "I cannot believe that it was ever intended to vest in Congress, by the general words in relation to the regulation of commerce, this overwhelming power over the states. For if the treaty stipulation before referred to can receive the construction given to it in the argument . . . then the emancipated slaves of the West Indies have at this hour the absolute right to reside, hire houses and traffic and trade throughout the Southern States in spite of laws to the contrary, inevitably producing the most serious discontent, and, ultimately, leading to the most painful consequences."

The case dragged on for pages, with all justices agreeing that the states had the right to exclude Negroes, but with a majority of five holding that invalidation of the New York and Massachusetts passenger laws would not prevent the states from ordering that exclusion, while a minority of four argued to the very limit of judicial restraint that "it would be difficult to imagine the mischiefs" if the states could not enact such legislation because "if it should suit the commercial speculations of British subjects to land within the territory of any of the States cargoes of negroes from Jamaica, Hayti or Africa," it would be virtually impossible to "designate any legitimate power in the States to prevent invasion of their domestic security."

The controversy over slavery was becoming all-pervasive. Congress found it increasingly difficult to organize new territories and admit new states. There were bitter disputes which brought threats of secession and disunion and predictions of an irrepressible conflict between "opposing and enduring forces."

There simply *had* to be a final solution.

Out of desperate hope, politicians began to express their belief that the solution could lie in a definitive judicial determination of the entire slave question: Let the Supreme Court decide! The idea was attractive to men seeking a way out of the impasse into which

the slavery controversy had landed the nation. Surely, the argument ran, final power to settle even the most vexing question must
reside somewhere under the constitutional system. John Marshall
had asserted it for the Supreme Court, but the Jeffersonians and
later the Jacksonians had contested and weakened that claim with
their insistence that each department—judicial, executive, and legislative—was supreme within its own sphere. But the Marshall doctrine of judicial supremacy, although quiescent and in eclipse, had
never died. De Tocqueville had noted it and remarked that the
power to declare a law unconstitutional was "the only one peculiar
to the American magistrate." That power, he remarked, gave "rise
to immense political influence," because, as he pointed out, "few
laws can escape the searching analysis of judicial power for any
length of time." [8]

Congress had its share of members who were weary of the endless controversy over slavery and who were quite willing to rid
themselves of the political liabilities entailed in taking stands on the
issue. The proposal that the Supreme Court step in and settle the
slavery issue in the territories was bruited about in the Senate in
connection with a bill framing territorial governments for New
Mexico and California. In a debate that began on July 18, 1848,
Senator John M. Clayton of New Jersey, chairman of the committee in charge of the bill, proposed that territorial governments of
the two areas be deprived of the right to legislate on slavery and
that the right to introduce or prohibit slavery be determined by an
examination of the Constitution "as the same should be expounded
by the judges, with a right of appeal to the Supreme Court." He
said that "this bill resolves the whole question between the North
and the South into a constitutional and judicial question. . . . If
the Constitution settles the question either way, let those who rail
at the decision vent their indignation on their ancestors who
adopted it." [9]

Senator Thomas Corwin of Ohio twitted the Jacksonian Democrats for what he called their newly found willingness to defer to
the Supreme Court: "I recollect very well when we did not stop to
inquire how the Supreme Court had decided or ordained. I had
decided with John Marshall at its head . . . that Congress had
power to establish a bank as you had; but with what infinite scorn
did Democratic gentlemen . . . Jackson Democrats as they chose
to be called . . . curl their lips when they referred to that decision

of the Supreme Court. Then the cry was 'We are judges for ourselves; we make no law unless we have the power to enact it.' Now, however, the doctrine is that there is only one tribunal competent to put the matter at rest forever." [10]

Senator Reverdy Johnson of Maryland, one of the most distinguished constitutional lawyers of his time, thought that "While statesmen, politicians, were found differing on a subject, the Supreme Court was unanimous . . . the members of the Supreme Court are not politicians. They were born in a different atmosphere and they address themselves to different hearers. Politicians are always differing and disputing—one taking this side of a question, and another taking an opposite view, all equally honest. How desirable in a case of such importance as this, to call in a third party, rather than that we should be driven to despair, above all to bloodshed." As the debate went on, Johnson summed up his views: "The South has asked us only to keep off legislative action on the subject. They asked only that the question be submitted to the Supreme Court to be decided upon in conformity with the Constitution." [11]

In his annual message at the opening of the December, 1848, session of Congress, President James K. Polk suggested that "If Congress, instead of observing the course of non-interference leaving the adoption of their own domestic institutions to the people who may inhabit such territories; or if, instead of extending the Missouri Compromise line to the Pacific, shall prefer to submit the legal and constitutional questions which may arise to the decision of judicial tribunals . . . an adjustment may be affected in this mode. If the whole subject be referred to the judiciary, all parts of the Union should cheerfully acquiesce in the final decision of the tribunal created by the Constitution for the settlement of all questions which may arise under the Constitution, treaties, and laws of the United States." [12]

Although neither the debaters nor President Polk suggested that the Supreme Court be invited to pass on the validity of the Missouri Compromise Act, it is hard to escape the conclusion that if the Court did have the power to pass on the constitutionality of slaveholding in new territories, it had the right to examine past enactments to see whether or not they squared with the Constitution. That very contention had been pressed in argument in a Missouri court in a case styled *Dred Scott, man of color, v. Emerson.*[13]

Senator Sydney Breese of Illinois suggested the format of a suit to test the constitutionality of congressional enactments: "If the senator from New Jersey will allow me, I will ask him if the question of servitude could not be brought before the Supreme Court of the United States, very readily, by an action, by the slave, of assault and battery and false imprisonment? Such a suit would bring up the question fairly, and without the intervention of a jury. The person claimed as a slave brings his action . . . the master pleads to the action that true it is that he holds plaintiff in his custody as he has a right to do, for he is a slave . . . the plaintiff demurs and the question of law arising therefrom is decided by the court, and, if the decision be against the slave, the Supreme Court has jurisdiction . . . because a decision has been pronounced against a right claimed under the Constitution." [14]

When the Senate committee headed by Stephen A. Douglas of Illinois reported on the proposal to organize the Kansas-Nebraska Territory in 1853, it remarked pointedly that "it is a disputed point whether slavery is prohibited in the Nebraska country by valid enactment. The decision of this question involves the constitutional power of Congress to pass laws prescribing and regulating the domestic institutions of the various territories of the Union. In the opinion of these eminent statesmen who hold that congress is invested with no rightful authority to legislate upon the subject of slavery in the territories, the 8th section of the act preparatory to the admission of Missouri is null and void; while the prevailing sentiment in large portions of the Union sustains the doctrine that the Constitution of the United States secures to every citizen an inalienable right to move into any of the territories with his property, of whatever kind and description to hold and enjoy the same under the sanction of law." [15] The committee disclaimed any intention to rule on the validity of the Missouri Compromise Act or to impair it in any manner, but its words were an open invitation to the Supreme Court to step in and settle the matter.

Antislavery lawyers sitting in the Senate, such as Salmon P. Chase of Ohio and Charles Sumner of Massachusetts, stood on the proposition that no judicial interpretation whatever was needed to demonstrate the antislavery character of the Constitution. As Chase put it in the course of debate on the repeal of the Missouri Compromise: "And now, sir, let me ask the attention of the Senate to the Constitution itself. That charter of our government was not formed upon pro-slavery principles, but upon anti-slavery principles. It nowhere recognizes any right of property in man. It nowhere confers upon the Government which it creates any power to establish or continue slavery." [16]

The Constitution, Chase argued, "denies absolutely to Congress the power of legislating for the establishment or maintenance of slavery." He turned to the familiar proposition that the Constitution does not speak of slaves as property: "Upon this state of things the Constitution acts. It recognizes all men as persons. It confers no power, but on the contrary, expressly denies to the Government of its creation all power to establish or continue slavery. Congress has no more power under the Constitution to make a slave than to make a king; no more power to establish slavery than to establish the Inquisition." Charles Sumner echoed Chase's argument in the same debate: "The Constitution regards slaves always as 'persons' and never as property. When it is said, therefore, that every citizen may enter the national domain with his property, it does not follow by any rule of logic or law that he may carry his slaves." [17]

It is noteworthy that neither Chase nor Sumner invited the Supreme Court to settle the slavery issue. Their premise was that the Constitution had settled the issue with finality and that its tolerance of slavery was limited to the states in which slavery existed at the time of its adoption as a matter of state law. The Constitution, they contended, circumscribed both Congress and the Supreme Court to the extent that neither could take any action which would protect slavery in the territories, for the very invocation of such protection would in effect establish slavery where it did not exist by positive law: the Supreme Court, like Congress, "had no more power to make a slave than to make a king."

And if the Supreme Court did venture to assert constitutional protection of slavery in the territories, some antislavery congressmen were prepared to disregard its fiat as far as legislation was concerned. Sumner said as much in 1852 in a debate on the fugitive slave law; referring to the Prigg case, he argued that Story's opinion "cannot arrest our duty as legislators." [18] He quoted the veto message on the bank controversy and continued: "With these authoritative words of Andrew Jackson, I dismiss the topic . . . the decisions of the Supreme Court cannot stand in our way." Plainly, those for whom Chase and Sumner spoke were not in agreement with President Polk's dictum that "all parts of the Union should cheerfully acquiesce" in a Supreme Court settlement of the slavery issue.

But Chase and Sumner did not speak for all opponents of slavery.

There was a moderate wing of the antislavery movement emergent in the new Republican party which was willing to submit the controversy to the Court for settlement. Abraham Lincoln of Illinois spoke for that group at Galena, Illinois, on August 1, 1856, when, in discussing the Missouri Compromise, he told an audience: "I grant you that an unconstitutional act is not law; but I do not ask you, and will not take, your construction of the Constitution. The Supreme Court of the United States is the tribunal to decide such a question, and we will submit to its decision; and if you do, there will be an end to the matter." [19]

Although embittered partisans later charged that the Supreme Court hatched a plot in the Dred Scott case and arrogated to itself the power to decide the entire slavery controversy, that accusation is wide of the mark. The Court bumbled its way into the controversy. Both sides were suspicious of the Court. Abolitionists described it as the "very citadel of slavery," [20] but Senator George Badger of North Carolina demurred to the proposal to submit the slave controversy to the Court, saying that he had a "respect for the Supreme Court, but was not willing to leave the decision of the question to a court, so large a portion of which were opposed to slavery." [21] These charges and countercharges are eloquent of the fact that the justices were divided. Some were in favor of a sweeping judicial pronouncement on slavery, others were resistant, and still others were doubtful of the advisability of trying to settle the issues.

That the Court was jockeyed into a position where it was willing to undertake decision of the question was due to many factors. The argument that the peace and harmony of the nation depended upon it must have struck a responsive chord among some justices. Presidential iteration of the claim that the whole nation would acquiesce in whatever decision it might make carried weight. Lawyers know that every court likes to broaden its own jurisdiction, and the growth of the doctrine of judicial supremacy carried with it a bid for the Court to entertain suits that enhanced its importance and prestige. As the Court's power grew, there was an increasing tendency to refer controversies to the Court for final solution, and the mere mortals who peopled it must have enjoyed their prerogatives. Also, the Court's exercise of power had dulled the Jacksonian concept that the Supreme Court could not impress its will on the coordinate branches of government. The opportunity to "settle the peace and harmony of the country . . . by judicial decision," as one justice was to phrase the matter at a later date, was thrust on the Court in its consideration of a case presented to it by the moderates seeking to forestall the spread of slavery. The Court embraced that opportunity only after long vacillation and as a result of the interplay of forces set in motion by political rivalries.

On April 6, 1846, an obscure Missouri Negro, born plain Sam, who had picked up the more euphonious name of Dred Scott, began fumbling his way through a series of lawsuits designed to secure freedom for himself, his wife, and his two daughters. Born a slave in Missouri, Scott was purchased for $500 in 1832 by Dr. John Emerson, a graduate of the University of Pennsylvania. Emerson, an army surgeon, held Scott in slavery in St. Louis until 1834. Transferred to Rock Island, Illinois, in that year, Emerson took his slave with him. As luck would have it, another army officer, Major Laurence Taliaferro, was stationed at the same post with his female slave, Harriett. Scott's former wife had been sold away from him, and he was ready for another fling at matrimony. The two slaves struck up an affair, and when their masters were transferred to Fort Snelling in what is now Minnesota, Dred and Harriet were married. One child, Lizzie, was born to them in their new home. Illinois was free both by state law and by virtue of congressional enactment of the Ordinance of 1787, prohibiting slavery in the Northwest Territory. Fort Snelling lay in a part of the Louisiana Purchase above the line of 36° north latitude in which slavery had been prohibited by the Missouri Compromise Act of 1820.

Dr. Emerson returned to St. Louis in 1838 with his slave couple and their one child. Another child, Eliza, was born after the return to Missouri. When Emerson died in 1843, his wife became executrix of his will. As executrix she was entitled to possession of the slaves, but her right to sell them was somewhat doubtful. Scott, who had made some money hiring himself out with Mrs. Emerson's consent, tried to buy his freedom and that of his family, but she refused his offer. His savings of some $300 were adequate to hire a lawyer, who not only filed suit in the Missouri state court for freedom for Scott and his family but also laid claim to damages accruing to Scott for the time he had been held in slavery since his return to St. Louis. There was every prospect of success, because the Missouri Supreme Court had previously held that residence in free territory conferred freedom on a slave. The case was filed on April 6, 1846, and finally tried on June 30, 1847, but much to Dred's, and his lawyer's, dismay, the jury ruled in favor of Mrs. Emerson.

Scott filed a motion for a new trial and for some obscure reason filed another suit in the state court on July 2, 1847, claiming his freedom. When he got the new trial, he dismissed the second suit and the original action was retried on January 12, 1850. Scott triumphed. Mrs. Emerson appealed, and in 1853 the Missouri Supreme Court overruled former decisions and held that the "voluntary removal of a slave by his master to a State Territory, or Country in which slavery is prohibited does not entitle the slave to sue for his freedom in this State." [22] The case was sent back to the trial court for a new trial, but the ruling practically erased any chance Scott had of winning his case in the state courts.

Meanwhile, luck of a sort had intervened again. In 1850, Mrs. Emerson married the well-known Massachusetts antislavery congressman, Calvin G. Chaffee, who did not fancy being cast in the role of a slaveholder even through the attenuated fact that the slaves belonged to his wife. Under Missouri law, a married woman could not serve as executrix of her deceased husband's will, and Mrs. Emerson-Chaffee's duties were assumed by her brother, Dr. John F. A. Sanford, a citizen of New York. The Chaffees were rid of all ostensible connections with slavery, and any further proceedings that Scott might take would have to name Sanford as his legal opponent. Scott had all but lost out completely in the Missouri courts, but now he had a chance to resort to the federal courts because Sanford was a citizen of New York and the federal courts had jurisdiction to hear suits between citizens of different states—that is, he had a chance to get into federal court if he could show that he was a "citizen" of Missouri. He had nothing to lose by making the claim.

When United States Circuit Judge Robert Wells opened federal court in St. Louis, Scott's lawyers showed up, on November 2, 1853, and filed a suit under the style of *Dred Scott v. John F. A. Sanford*.[23] They alleged, and lawyers for both sides later agreed, that Scott had been "sold" to Sanford, but that was only a legal fiction, probably stipulated to in order to expedite the lawsuit. Scott, of course, alleged that he was a citizen of Missouri and that Sanford was a citizen of New York. The case excited little attention in St. Louis and less interest in the nation, and on May 4, 1854, a federal circuit court jury decided in favor of Sanford. Scott and his family remained slaves. He appealed, or at least his lawyers appealed, to the U. S. Supreme Court.

The long and tortuous story of what happened to Dred Scott and his case in the Supreme Court requires telling in great detail because Dred Scott's case grew so much bigger than Dred Scott that his personal fortunes were forgotten in the midst of a furious and nation-shaking debate over great constitutional issues. If Scott, who couldn't read or write, was like most litigants, he never understood the complex legal and constitutional questions that shaped the outcome of his case. What he could understand was that on March 6, 1857—exactly ten years and eleven months after he had filed his first suit seeking freedom—word came from Washington that he, Harriett, Lizzie, and Eliza were still slaves in the eyes of the law

✦ 5 ✦ *The Summer Is Ended*

*The harvest is past, the summer
is ended, and we are not saved*

JEREMIAH 8:20

No person was less affected by the outcome of the Dred Scott case in the Supreme Court than Dred Scott. Three months later, he was given the formal freedom that had been his and his family's, to all practical intents and purposes, prior to the filing of his case in the federal courts. He had simply received top billing in a great and dramatic contest between opposing and enduring forces, to borrow a phrase. For the Dred Scott case in the federal courts was a contrived lawsuit in which little was what it seemed. The complaint was filed as a prosaic action for damages for battery and false imprisonment, but the real purpose of those who originally filed it was to test the question of whether Scott and his family were free persons or slaves. Those who later kept it alive fathered it and furthered it to test great constitutional principles. It oscillated between comedy and tragedy from beginning to end.

There was a touch of slapstick in the circumstances that an indolent clerk misspelled the name of Scott's legal opponent and changed it from Sanford to Sandford, and there was cruel irony in the fact that "Sandford" was not the slave-beating villain of the piece, as was alleged and as is commonly supposed; he never struck Scott in his life. He was a foil who lent his name, not to keep Scott, whom he never owned in slavery, but to help in the test of constitutional principles. In fact, there is every evidence that Dr. Sanford wanted to lose his own lawsuit!

There was high comedy of another sort in the spectacle of the nine justices of the United States Supreme Court writing a small volume of 240 pages in a marathon debate on how to settle "the peace and harmony of the country . . . by judicial decision," some of them tittering like a bunch of schoolboys and tattling judicial secrets on the progress and outcome of the case to friends and political associates, oblivious to the fact that a house divided against itself on the great issue before them could not stand. There was tragicomedy of a powerful sort in Chief Justice Roger B. Taney, Jacksonian Democrat, writing an opinion composed in varying parts of suspect law, garbled history, and shoddy sociology to demonstrate that the believers in the theory of the Natural Rights of Man who subscribed to the Declaration of Independence and who had framed the Constitution had permanently frozen into that document the dogma that a Negro "had no rights which a white man was bound to respect."

There was even a little rescue scene when Senator Reverdy Johnson of Maryland, bosom friend and dinner companion of the Chief Justice—he who had said that "members of the Supreme Court are not politicians" and that the Court should be called in to settle the slavery issue "rather than that we should be driven to despair, above all to bloodshed"—volunteered his services at Supreme Court argument in order to be sure that the justices had the full benefit of the proslavery position. There was the final futility of Congress appropriating $6500 to print and distribute the opinion in order to let the nation know that the slavery issue had been settled!

The decision foreshadowed tragedy a-plenty and for all: tragedy for Roger B. Taney, proslave in sentiment but able lawyer and competent Chief Justice, whose name would be forever linked with what men remember as the infamy of the Dred Scott case; tragedy for the arrogant and unseeing men who cajoled and goaded a majority of the Court into a decision that would hasten the destruction of many of their fortunes, their homes, and their lands; tragedy tinged with inevitability for the stubborn antislavery men, because it made clear that their prophecy of Irrepressible Conflict was terribly and irrevocably true; tragedy for ponderous James Buchanan, whose vision was so limited that he could believe that the nation would "cheerfully submit" to a judicial decision opening all federal territory to slavery and putting free Negroes outside the pale of national citizenship; tragedy above all for the nation, because the decision was confirmation of the fact that the time had passed when the slavery issue could be settled otherwise than by force of arms.

The script for the Dred Scott case had been written, or spoken, by Senator Sydney Breese of Illinois when he asked the Senate if "the question of servitude [in the territories] could not be brought before the Supreme Court of the United States very readily, by an action, by the slave, of assault and battery and false imprisonment . . . ?" Scott sued Sanford, admittedly a citizen of New York, for damages on a fictitious claim of assault and battery, charging that Sanford had "severely beaten" him, his wife, and two children, and on the ground that he and his family had been falsely imprisoned by being held in slavery. In law, a master could neither assault nor falsely imprison his slaves, and the very filing of the suit meant that Scott claimed freedom for himself and his family. The suit was filed in the federal court and, since the Constitution permitted the filing of such a suit only if the plantiff was a citizen, Scott was, in effect, claiming national citizenship and citizenship of Missouri, a status he could have had only if he was a free man.

Apparently, Sanford's lawyers had also been reading Senator Breese's script, because they filed what lawyers call a plea in abatement, a document saying that no matter what had happened to him or his family, Scott could not sue in federal court. That court, they intoned, "ought not to have or take further cognizance of the action aforesaid, because said causes of action . . . accrued to the said Dred Scott out of the jurisdiction of said court and exclusively within the jurisdiction of the courts of Missouri; for that, to wit, the said plantiff Dred Scott is not a citizen of the state of Missouri . . . because he is a negro of African descent, his ancestors were of pure African blood and were brought into this country and sold as negro slaves. . . ."[1] What they were saying was that Scott, *as a descendant of slaves,* regardless of whether he was slave or free, could not be a citizen of a state in a constitutional sense and, hence, could not file suit in the federal courts. As Breese had suggested, Scott's lawyers promptly demurred; that is, they admitted for purposes of the lawsuit the truth of the plea that he was a descendant of slaves but asserted that such a fact did not bar him from citizenship.

Judge Wells, who presided over the case, agreed with Scott's lawyers that the plea in abatement was ineffective to dispose of the case, ruling that Scott's descent from slaves did not, in and of itself, prevent him from being a citizen of Missouri and holding that a Negro claiming to be free was entitled to sue in federal court on his claim for damages when the person disputing that claim was a citizen of another state. Technically, the judge sustained the demurrer to the plea in abatement. When that was done, Sanford had the choice of appealing to the Supreme Court or of filing an answer and trying the case on the merits of Scott's claim that he and his family had been beaten and falsely imprisoned. He could not do both. He chose to file an answer. Lawyers for both sides collaborated in drawing up a statement—not altogether faithful to the facts—reviewing Scott's initial slavery, his residence in Rock Island and Fort Snelling, his marriage, the birth of the two children, his return to Missouri, and the history of his case in the Missouri courts.

The judge read the statement to the jury, and then advised it that it must find against Scott and in favor of Sanford on the ground that, although Scott had the right to sue as a Negro, he could not prevail because his status as a slave or free man depended on the law of Missouri and that, since the highest court of that state had decreed that he was a slave, he must be determined to be a slave in a proceeding in a federal court sitting in Missouri. The jurors heeded the judge's admonition and Scott lost his case. As later events were to prove, Sanford had no intention—assuming he had the power—of holding Scott in slavery, but Scott's lawyers weren't ready to drop the case. They wanted a ruling from a higher court.

The impoverished and illiterate Scott had no hand in getting his case before the U. S. Supreme Court. That task fell to his lawyers, who were determined to get a final ruling on the legal questions they had raised. They persuaded Gamaliel Bailey, editor of the Washington newspaper *New Era,* to post the necessary bond for costs and looked around for a lawyer who would argue the case without a fee. They approached Montgomery Blair, slaveholder and former mayor of St. Louis, who would become postmaster general in Lincoln's cabinet and whose father had been a close friend and confidante of Andrew Jackson. He consented after some urging by his father and Bailey. Sanford was represented by a lawyer who had appeared for him in other litigation, Senator Henry Sheffie Geyer of Missouri, a Supreme Court advocate of some distinction.

The stage was set for one of the most famous cases in Supreme Court history and for a decision that would profoundly affect the lives of all Americans, white and black, born and unborn.

The question confronting the Supreme Court was the apparently simple one of whether or not Scott was a citizen of Missouri and of the United States within the meaning of the Constitution and, thus, had the right to sue for damages in a federal court. In its proper turn, the question of his citizenship drew into dispute the issue of whether he was a slave or a free man. If he was a slave, the case was at an end; if he wasn't a citizen, he couldn't sue. If he was free, there remained the question of whether, as a descendant of slaves, he was a citizen of Missouri, the issue involved in the plea in abatement. Of course, it didn't seem to make a bit of difference to Scott whether he couldn't sue in the federal court because he was a slave, or whether that right was denied him because he was a descendant of slaves. In either event, he was going to lose his case. But that neat technical point made a great deal of difference to Scott's lawyers, who were looking beyond his case and had their eyes fixed on more than the question of whether or not he was going to win an award of damages.

They were trying to establish two very important propositions: (1) that slavery not only could not exist in the territories above the antislavery line of 36° 30′ north latitude but that the taking of a slave north of that line changed his status to that of a free man, and (2) that a free Negro was a citizen of the state wherein he resided and of the United States. Their triumph would strike a double blow at slavery. It would demolish the contention of slaveholders that the Constitution vested them with the right to take their slave property into all federal territories, and it would bolster the claim that free Negroes, as national citizens, were clothed with all of the rights inhering in such citizenship. Scott's lawyers were not leaving him in the lurch by pressing these issues; if those questions were decided in his favor, he could maintain his lawsuit and at the same time establish a very important legal principle.

The proposition that a descendant of slaves was not, by virtue of that fact alone, debarred from citizenship had been decided in Scott's favor when his demurrer to the plea in abatement was sustained, and his lawyers were determined to hang on to that legal advantage. They argued vigorously in their briefs that Sanford's failure to appeal from the ruling on the demurrer had put that

question in repose and that the only issue before the Supreme
Court was whether their client gained freedom and consequent capacity to sue by his residence, first in Rock Island, Illinois, and,
later, in Fort Snelling, Minnesota Territory.

Their insistent argument presented the Court with a tricky procedural question that had importance beyond its technical aspects.
Admittedly, Sanford's failure to appeal from the ruling on the demurrer to the plea in abatement made it extremely difficult for the
Court to review the correctness of that decision. But the Supreme
Court's failure to disturb the circuit court's holding that Scott, as a
descendant of slaves, had standing to sue in federal court would
leave room for future contention that the Court had set a precedent
for full citizenship claims by free Negroes. If the whole matter was
settled, as the circuit court had decided, on the ground that the
decision of the Missouri courts was controlling, the Supreme Court
would be taxed with evasion and with failure to discharge its duty.
The case was getting sticky.

The Supreme Court heard the case argued twice, first on February 11, 1856, and again on December 15, 1856. The dates are significant because the presidential election of 1856 intervened between the two arguments. After a conference on April 7, 1856, the
Court decided to dispose of Scott's lawsuit, now called *Dred Scott
v. Sandford,*[2] without a ruling on the constitutional questions.

Justice Samuel Nelson was apparently commissioned to write the
opinion of the Court after that first conference, and although what
he wrote never became the official opinion, Justice Nelson stuck to
it and ultimately inserted it in the Supreme Court reports as if it
were.[3] In that opinion, he used the term *we*, the language used to
indicate the opinion of the majority, and proceeded as if he were
speaking for the majority of the court, as indeed he must have been
at the time he was writing.

In the opinion he proposed for the Court, Nelson turned to the
vexing procedural question raised by Sanford's failure to appeal
from the ruling on the plea in abatement but remarked: "In the
view we have taken of this case, it will not be necessary therefore to
pass on it and we shall proceed at once to an examination of the
case on its merits." He described the question of whether Scott was
a slave at the time the suit was filed in federal court as a "question
exclusively of Missouri law, and which, when determined by that
State, it is the duty of the Federal Courts to follow. . . ." He noted

the argument that the Missouri Compromise Act was unconstitutional but went on to say that "we are satisfied . . . that even conceding, for the purpose of the argument, that this provision is valid . . . it can have no operation or effect" to compel Missouri courts to recognize its efficacy in that state. Nelson stubbornly refused to be drawn into the larger constitutional issues: they were beyond the boundaries of the case, he said, and when such questions as "the right of a master with his slave of transit through a free state on business or commercial pursuits or in the discharge of a federal duty . . . arises, we shall be prepared to decide it." He rejected the argument that the federal courts could substitute their judgment for that of the Missouri judges and held with finality: "Our conclusion is that the judgment of the court below should be affirmed."

The proposed disposition of the case was narrow; it would have left Scott and his family in apparent slavery but would have precipitated a minimum of public controversy, because it glossed over the underlying and explosive constitutional issues. But the case was not permitted to die with a whimper instead of a bang, because it had become a pawn in a struggle for political power as it dragged its way through the courts. Those who had chosen it as a test case were, in modern parlance, moderates. They were not abolitionists, sworn to an immediate destruction of slavery, but Free Soilers, men who were determined to arrest the spread of slavery and restrict it to existing slaves states. Their long-term view was that, thus arrested and restricted, slavery would collapse and die of its own weight. They were convinced that the Supreme Court would rule with them on the issues in the Scott case and strengthen their position.

Lincoln had admitted in 1856 that "an unconstitutional act is not law" and had said that "The Supreme Court of the United States is the tribunal to decide such a question, and we will submit to its decision; and if you do there will be an end to the matter." [4] The "we" to whom he referred and for whom he spoke were the Free Soilers; the "you" to whom he directed his remarks were the proslavery people. As practical politicians, Lincoln and the Free Soilers were not unaware of the fact that the success of their program would curb the power of the slaveholders, and they were certainly not averse to that result. Their political star was ascendant; their vehicle was the new Republican party, founded in 1854.

Ranged on the other side were moderates of another hue, men who espoused the southern cause of slavery but who were profoundly alarmed by the increasing clamor for secession and who were determined to preserve the Union. Their wish was father to their thought that the nation would "cheerfully submit" to, or at least acquiesce in, a Supreme Court determination that Congress could not exclude slavery from federal territories and that the Constitution did not sanction citizenship for free Negroes. Their hope was that such a decision would allay southern fears and cut the ground from beneath the disunionists.

After the Court had agreed to the disposition of the Scott case without settlement of the constitutional issue, wheels began to turn. One of the men with a weather eye on the Republican presidential nomination of 1856 was Justice John McLean of the U. S. Supreme Court. His ambitions were a matter of common knowledge. Immediately after the Court conference of April 7, 1856, his colleague Justice Benjamin Curtis wrote his uncle that "Judge McLean hopes, I think, to be a candidate for the office. He would be a good president but I am not willing to have a judge in that most trying position of being a candidate for this great office." [5] McLean was more than a politician with a yen for the presidency; he was an opponent of slavery who had dissented on phases of the Prigg and Slaughter cases and who had made it plain that he was prepared to help arrest the spread of slavery. Justice Curtis was in general agreement with McLean. He had been appointed to the Court in 1851 and was already preparing to retire. In the letter to his uncle, he complained that the Court was getting ready to "evade" the constitutional issues in the Scott case. There were other leaks to the same effect. Horace Greeley's *New York Tribune* reported that Justice McLean was readying a strong dissent and would score the Court for its failure to shoulder its constitutional responsibilities. [6]

Word got out that McLean would take the view that Sanford lost his right to question the correctness of the circuit court ruling (sustaining the demurrer to the plea in abatement) by reason of his failure to appeal from the decision that Scott, as a descendant of slaves, had access to the federal courts. Rumor had it that he would assert that the Court must consider the case on its merits, that is, on the question of whether Scott had become free by reason of his residence in Illinois and in Minnesota Territory, and that he would argue vigorously that Scott was free because of his sojourn in territory where slavery was prohibited by the Northwest Ordinance and by the Missouri Compromise Act. He would insist that the Court was not bound by the determination of the Missouri courts that Scott lost his right to assert his freedom by his return to Missouri, but that the Court was free to substitute its own correct opinion— the correct opinion being that Scott and his family were free. He would make it plain that, as a free man, Scott was a citizen who had access to the federal courts to press his suit. By a happy coincidence, McLean's views would parallel those almost certain to be espoused by the Republican party when it held its convention in June. Rumor also had it that Justice Curtis would support McLean in most respects. Other wheels began to turn. Justice McLean's dissent was not issued in the midst of the 1856 presidential campaign, because on May 7, 1856, Chief Justice Taney and a majority of the Court ordered the case reargued—after the fall election. McLean didn't get the Republican nomination either. That plum went to the popular John C. Fremont, who was defeated by the Pennsylvania Democrat James Buchanan.

Justice McLean's widely publicized plan to dissent from the majority ruling had thrown the spotlight on the Scott case, and by the time of reargument in December, pressure mounted to dissuade the Court from its determination to "evade" the constitutional issues. Senator Reverdy Johnson translated his belief that the slavery question was one for judicial decision into action and volunteered his services to assist in presentation of the case. Alexander Stephens, who would become vice-president of the Confederacy, wrote his brother, "I have been urging all the influence I could bring to bear upon the Supreme Court to get them to postpone no longer the case on the Missouri restriction." [7] He predicted success. Montgomery Blair, Scott's lawyer, decided that he needed help and tried to secure the services of the proslavery moderate Senator George Badger of North Carolina. Turned down in that quarter, he enlisted the association of George Ticknor Curtis, who happened to be Justice Curtis's brother. The arguments were long and brilliant, but how much they influenced the Court is another matter. Apparently, they had little effect on Justices McLean and Curtis, whose dissents had been accurately predicted the previous spring when the Court planned to by-pass the constitutional questions.

There were other factors at play. The Democratic victory in the 1856 election was used as an argument that the results showed the people were tired of the slavery controversy and were ready for a final judicial settlement. The Free Soilers, original protagonists of the case, lost the initiative to proslavery adherents who now "waylaid the judges . . . generally emphasizing the opportunity which lay before the Court to fulfill a public and patriotic duty by forever quieting a discussion injurious to the country's welfare. Declare all such restrictions as the Missouri Compromise unconstitutional, it was urged, and the North will acquiesce and the Union will be preserved." [8]

President-elect Buchanan injected himself into the deliberations, and by February 19, 1856, Justice John Catron was writing him a letter: "Will you drop Grier a line saying how necessary it is—and how good the opportunity is, to settle the agitation by an affirmative action of the Superior Court . . . ?" [9] Four days later, Justice Robert Grier wrote to the incoming President: "Your letter came to hand this morning. I have taken the liberty to show it in confidence to our mutual friends Judge Wayne and the Chief Justice. We fully appreciate and concur in your views as to the desirableness at this time of having an expression of the opinion of the Court on this troublesome question. With their concurrence, I will give you in confidence the history of the case before us, with the probable result." [10]

When President Buchanan asked the nation in his inaugural address to cheerfully submit to the decision, he knew what the Court was going to say. The rest of the nation had to wait two days, until March 6, 1857, for Chief Justice Taney to announce the Court's opinion that he had been commissioned to write on February 14. There were, the Chief Justice said, two important questions for consideration: (1) Did the circuit court have jurisdiction to consider the case? (2) If it had jurisdiction, was the judgment which it had given erroneous? He did not say so in so many words, but the second question raised three correlative issues: (a) Were the federal courts bound by the ruling of the Missouri courts that Scott was a slave? (b) If the federal courts were not bound by the Missouri ruling, did Scott gain freedom by being taken, first to Illinois, and later to Minnesota Territory? (c) Did Scott lose the opportunity to assert his freedom by voluntarily returning to Missouri with his master?

The Chief Justice began with an examination of national citizenship. "The question before us," Taney elaborated, "is: whether the class of persons [Negroes] described in the plea in abatement compose a portion of this people and are constituent members of the sovereignty? We think they are not, and that they are not included, and were not intended to be included, under the word 'citizen' in the Constitution and therefore can claim none of the rights and privileges which that instrument provides for and secures to citizens of the United States." The question of national citizenship, Taney insisted, was to be determined solely by the sentiments and intentions of the Framers of the Constitution: "No one, we presume, supposes that any change in public feelings or opinion, in relation to this unfortunate race, in . . . Europe or in this country, should induce the Court to give a more liberal construction in their favor than they were intended to bear when the [Constitution] was adopted." Free Negroes, he said, were "not even in the minds of the framers of the Constitution when they were conferring special rights and privileges upon citizens of a State in every other part of the Union."

History, Chief Justice Taney said, bore out his contention that the Framers did not intend to include free Negroes under the protection of the Constitution: "In the opinion of the court the legislation and history of the times and the language used in the Declaration of Independence, show that neither the class of persons who had been imported as slaves, nor their descendants, whether they became free or not, were then acknowledged as a part of the people, nor intended to be included in the general words used in that memorable instrument. . . . It is difficult at this day to realize the state of public opinion in relation to that unfortunate race which prevailed in the civilized and enlightened portions of the world . . . when the Constitution of the United States was framed and adopted. . . . They had, for more than a century before, been regarded as beings of an inferior order and altogether unfit to associate with the white race, either in social or political relations; and so far inferior that they had no rights which the white man was bound to respect. . . ." He drew a distinction between state and national citizenship.

Chief Justice Taney's distinction between state and national citizenship had few, almost no, practical consequences for white Americans. National citizenship at that time was a derivative of state citizenship; a person was a citizen of his state and, as a consequence, of the nation. The rights of that citizen were secure if he was a white man; the state would safeguard his priceless privileges and immunities in his own state; the national government would preserve his constitutionally protected rights and those established in the Bill of Rights and, more, would stand sentinel for his privileges and immunities in the other states. National and state citizenship rights were two sides of the same coin for the white person. As one person, he possessed both.

Taney's doctrine of duality of citizenship was simply a device to bolster and support the slave power. In fact, its burden fell on the Negro alone. In application, it meant that Negroes were resigned to the entire control of the states, an end for which proponents of slavery had always clamored. He had withdrawn all federal protection of Negroes, stripping them of all constitutional rights and privileges, including, by fair implication, even the right to live under a republican form of government. They had neither civil nor political rights, except such as might be granted by a magnanimous state government within its own borders. A state that bestowed full citizenship on a Negro could not protect him outside its jurisdiction nor call upon the federal government for aid under the privileges-and-immunities clause. Worst of all, there was no way that a Negro could attain national citizenship.

Turning to the fact that free Negroes undoubtedly enjoyed some rights as citizens of particular states, the Chief Justice took pains to restrict the exercise of those rights to the states of their residence: "It does not by any means follow because he has all the rights and privileges of a citizen of a State, that he must be a citizen of the United States. . . . Those rights which he would acquire would be restricted to the State which gave them. . . ." He argued that "No state can introduce a new member into the political community of the United States." And since the citizenship rights of a free Negro were restricted to the state that granted them, it followed that "the provision in the Constitution giving privileges and immunities in other states does not apply to them."

If there were historical reasons for denying national citizenship to free Negroes, Taney urged, there were also practical reasons: "For if they were so received, and entitled to privileges and immunities of citizens, it would exempt them from operation of special laws and from the police regulations considered to be necessary for their own safety. It would give to persons of the negro race who were recognized as citizens in any one State of the Union the right to enter every other State whenever they pleased, singly or in companies, without pass or passport; and, without obstruction, to sojourn there as long as they pleased at every hour of the day or night without molestation, unless they committed some violation of law for which a white man would be punished; and it would give them full liberty of speech in public and private upon all subjects upon which its own citizens might speak; to hold public meetings upon political affairs, and to keep and carry arms wherever they went. And all of this would be done in the face of the subject race of the same color, both free and slaves, and inevitably producing discontent and insubordination among them and endangering the peace and safety of the State."

At least five other justices agreed with their chief that Dred Scott wasn't a national citizen and couldn't be such a citizen because he was a descendant of slaves and, hence, had no right to sue in the federal courts. If they were correct, the case was at an end: the circuit court lacked jurisdiction to entertain the suit and should have dismissed it. But Chief Justice Taney was not ready to stop. As Justice Curtis put it in his dissent: "Having first decided that they were bound to consider the sufficiency of the plea to the jurisdiction of the Circuit Court, and having decided that this plea showed that the Circuit Court had no jurisdiction, and consequently that this is a case to which the judicial power of the United States does not extend, they have gone on to examine the merits of the case as they appeared on the trial . . . and so have reached the question of the power of Congress to pass on the Act of 1820. On so grave a subject as this, I feel obliged to say that, in my opinion, such an exertion of judicial power transcends the limits of authority of this court. . . ." Justice Curtis was right. The Court has always insisted that it has no general lawmaking power and that it cannot decide more in a particular suit than is necessary for the disposition of the case before it. Even the Chief Justice was troubled by this limitation. He met it by arguing that, since error appeared in the circuit court's decision on the merits of the case, "there can be no doubt as to the jurisdiction of this court to revise the judgment of a circuit court and to reverse it for any error apparent on the record. . . ." He was determined to reach the issue of the constitutionality of the Missouri Compromise Act. And he did.

The Constitution provides that "Congress shall have power to dispose of and make all needful rules and regulations respecting the territory or other property belonging to the United States." But the Chief Justice contended that the provision applied only to territory belonging to the United States at the time of the adoption of the Constitution. Under that interpretation, Congress could make whatever rules it chose for Illinois, which was part of the Northwest Territory ceded to the federal government by the original thirteen states. The Ordinance of 1787, adopted under the Articles of Confederation, prohibited slavery in that territory, and Congress adopted the ordinance after the formation of the Union. Taney agreed that Congress, therefore, was within constitutional bounds in forbidding slavery in Illinois. But Minnesota Territory, in which Fort Snelling was located, was another matter. It was a portion of the Louisiana Purchase not owned by the United States when the Constitution was adopted.

When the United States acquires territory, the Chief Justice argued, "the Government and the citizen both enter it under the authority of the Constitution." Under the Constitution, he said, slaves were not only property like any other property but were in fact a class of property particularly favored by the Constitution and placed under its protection: "The rights of property are united with the rights of person, and are placed on the same ground by the Fifth Amendment to the Constitution . . . which provides that no person shall be deprived of life, liberty, or property without due process of law. And an Act of Congress which deprives a citizen of the United States of his liberty or property merely because he came himself or brought his property into a particular Territory of the United States . . . could hardly be dignified with the name of due process of law." He was ready for the cutting thrust: "Upon these considerations it is the opinion of the Court that the Act of Congress [the Missouri Compromise Act] which prohibits a citizen from holding property of this kind in the Territory of the United States north of the line mentioned is not warranted by the Constitution, and it is therefore void; and that neither Dred Scott himself, nor any of his family, were made free by being carried into this territory, even if they had been carried there by the owner with the intention of becoming a permanent resident." In sum, the Missouri Compromise Act was unconstitutional. Congress had no power to prohibit slavery in any federal territory, except in the Northwest Territory, and a slaveholder was free to take his slaves into any other federal territory and hold them in slavery.

In his zeal to reach the question of the Missouri Compromise Act and invalidate it, the Chief Justice had skipped over the fact that Dred Scott's first place of residence on free soil was in Rock Island, Illinois. Illinois was doubly free, first by virtue of the admittedly valid Ordinance of 1787 and, secondly, by state law. Chief Justice Taney settled that aspect of the case by holding that Scott's return to Missouri had given the courts of that state exclusive jurisdiction to determine the issue of his slavery or freedom and that the federal courts were bound by the state court rulings. If he was correct, he should have decided that question before ruling on the matter of Scott's residence in Minnesota Territory. Again, the case would have been at an end. The Missouri courts had ruled that Scott was a slave and since, as Taney said, the ruling of the Missouri court was binding on the federal court sitting in that state, it followed that the circuit court was right in adhering to the Missouri ruling.

The conclusion is inescapable that the Chief Justice was determined to let nothing stand in the way of his determination to invalidate the Missouri Compromise Act. He pronounced the final word: "Upon the whole, therefore, it is the judgment of the court that it appears by the whole record before us that the plaintiff in error (Scott) is not a citizen in the sense in which that word is used in the Constitution; and that the Circuit Court of the United States, for that reason, had no jurisdiction in the case and could give no judgment in it. Its judgment for the defendant must, consequently, be reversed and a mandate issued directing the suit to be dismissed for want of jurisdiction."

Dred Scott was right back where he started—in slavery. It made no difference to him that he was a slave by virtue of a Supreme Court decision holding that he was not, and could not become, a national citizen and that the Missouri Compromise Act was invalid, whereas, prior to the appeal, he had been held to be a slave because he had returned to Missouri with his master after residence in territory made free by terms of the Ordinance of 1787 and the Missouri Compromise Act. But it did make a difference, a tremendous constitutional difference, to the nation.

Six other justices agreed with their chief that Scott had made no case. Their reasoning varied, and all of them wrote opinions clarifying their stands. Justice James Wayne was blunt: "The case involves private rights of value and constitutional principles of the highest importance, about which there had become such a difference of opinion that the peace and harmony of the country required the settlement of them by judicial decision." Justice Robert Grier wrote a few lines to say that he agreed with Chief Justice Taney "that the plantiff cannot sue as a citizen of Missouri in the courts of the United States." Justice Nelson began by saying that he agreed with the Chief Justice but then inserted the text of his original opinion, obviously written before Taney's opinion, which did not deal with the larger constitutional issues. Justice Peter V. Daniel not only denied the right of any state to elevate persons of African descent to citizenship "by any direct or indirect proceeding" but went further and advanced the argument that both the Ordinance of 1787 and the Missouri Compromise Act were beyond the competency of Congress. Justice John A. Campbell, who would soon resign and cast his lot with the Confederacy, seemed to indicate complete agreement with the Chief Justice, although he later denied that he had. Justice Catron, who had sentenced men to hang in territorial courts under laws passed by Congress, thought it was "now too late" to question the congressional right to make rules for federal territories but asserted the Missouri Compromise was invalid because it breached the treaty by which France had ceded Louisiana to the United States.

Justice McLean wrote the kind of a dissent he had planned the previous spring, laying heavy emphasis on the fact that the purport of the decision was to establish slavery in the federal territories. He insisted that the federal government had no such power and that, while the Constitution tolerated slavery where it existed at the time of the formation of the union, it went no further. Taking his colleagues to task for venturing to consider the question of the Missouri Compromise Act, he charged that "a majority of the court have said that a slave may be taken by his master into a Territory of the United States, the same as a horse, or any other kind of property. It is true this was said by the Court, as also many other things which are of no authority. Nothing that has been said by them which has not a direct bearing on the jurisdiction of the court against which they decided can be considered as an authority. I shall certainly not regard it as such. The question of jurisdiction, being before the Court, was decided authoritatively but nothing beyond that question. A slave is not a mere chattel. He bears the impress of his Maker and is amenable to the laws of God and man and he is destined to an endless existence."

Justice Curtis centered his fire on the Chief Justice's history, and he had no trouble in showing that free Negroes were citizens and voters of at least five states at the time of the adoption of the Constitution. He quoted a North Carolina case, particularly telling because it came from a slave state, in which the supreme court of that state rejected the proposition that free Negroes were less than citizens and laid emphasis on the commonly held doctrine that there was no intermediate class between citizens and slaves. "It has often been asserted," he pointed out, "that the Constitution was made exclusively by and for the white race. It has already been shown that in five of the original thirteen States, colored persons then possessed the elective franchise and were among those by whom the Constitution was ordained and established. If so, it is not true in point of fact that the Constitution was made exclusively *by* the white race. And that it was made exclusively *for* the white race is, in my opinion, not only an assumption not warranted by anything in the Constitution but contradicted by its open declaration that it was ordained and established by the people of the United States for themselves and their posterity. And, as free colored persons were then citizens in at least five states, and so, in every sense, part of the people of the United States, they were among those for whom and whose posterity the Constitution was ordained and established." He dissented from that "part of the opinion of the majority of this court in which it is held that a person of African descent cannot be a citizen of the United States" and from "what I deem their assumption of authority to examine the constitutionality of the act of Congress commonly called the Missouri Compromise Act."

When the justices of the Supreme Court concluded their mighty war of words over Dred Scott and his case, it was readily apparent that they had decided, with only two dissents, that he was not a national citizen and could not sue in the federal court; that because the Missouri Compromise Act was unconstitutional, he had not become free by having been taken to Fort Snelling, and that since he had voluntarily returned to Missouri, his claim to freedom because of his residence in Illinois was solely a matter for the Missouri courts. But the Court had done more, much more. Dred Scott was not a Negro island, entire unto himself.

The Court had construed the Constitution in such a manner as to create a class of beings, those of African descent, who were ineli-

gible to national citizenship. Free beings of that intermediate class
—neither national citizens nor slaves—could claim no protection
from the federal government. Although Taney's assertion that a
Negro had no rights which a white man was bound to respect was
made as the historical assessment of a belief prevailing at the time
of the adoption of the Constitution, it was, nonetheless, a definition
of an existent condition, because the Chief Justice said, and the
majority agreed, that the full measure of the Negro's rights was that
intended by the Framers as of the time the Constitution was
adopted. Slaves were not constitutional persons, despite constitutional language; they were, in the emphatic terms of Justice Daniel,
"property, in the strictest sense of that term." The holding that the
Missouri Compromise Act was unconstitutional was more than a
passing invalidation of a congressional enactment; it purported to
strip Congress of all power to control slavery in the territories and
to vest supervision of the matter in the courts.

Some of the more important aspects of the constitutional rights
of slaveholders were outlined. They could take their *property* into
federal territories at will; they could invoke the due-process-of-law
clause of the Fifth Amendment to shield their right to buy and sell
and hold that property; they could, if they chose, return the property to the states from which they had come without fear that the
slave could claim freedom through territorial residence; they were
secure against congressional interference with this complex of
rights.

The short of the matter was that the Court had made Negroes,
free and slave, its wards by attributing to the Constitution a complete scheme defining and regulating their relationships with the
federal government, the states, and the body politic, and by arrogating to itself the exclusive power to assess the nature, character,
and extent of those relationships. The conditions of the guardianship were onerous indeed. Lincoln, reviewing the case, commented
that "all the powers of the earth" seemed to be combining against
the Negro, and "now they have him, as it were, bolted in with a
lock of a hundred keys, which can never be unlocked without the
concurrence of a hundred men, and they scattered to a hundred
different and distant places." The unwilling wards were helpless,
and virtually hopeless. They had no rights secured by the Constitution.

Congress could do nothing beyond enacting legislation expediting their return to slavery if they escaped; free states could not elevate free Negroes to the status of national citizenship, and if they conferred state citizenship, it was counterfeit beyond the boundaries of the particular state; slave states held Negroes free and slave at their mercy, and Negroes were most numerous where the states were most merciless; white men were liable to heavy penalties if they aided an escaping slave in the North, and to heavier penalties if they spoke out against slavery in the South. The very Court that claimed the guardianship, and defined its terms and conditions, professed an entire lack of power to mitigate its burdens, or to countenance congressional or executive interference, because, it said, the rigid scheme which oppressed its wards was imbedded in the fundamental law of the land and, as Taney said tartly, "If any of the provisions are deemed unjust, there is a mode prescribed in the instrument itself by which it may be amended."

A roar of rage and disapproval greeted the decision. Antislavery lawyers led the attack with the charge that a majority of the Court had carefully stage-managed the case in order to reach and invalidate the Missouri Compromise Act. They argued persuasively that the majority's initial ruling that the circuit court had no jurisdiction to entertain the suit because of Scott's lack of national citizenship put a legal end to the case and whatever was said thereafter was mere *obiter dictum*, judicial talk without binding effect. Most lawyers still agree with that estimate.

Taney's history was bombarded as heavily, and as effectively, as his legal conclusions. Justice Curtis's long and discursive opinion had riddled the Chief Justice's conclusions as to the intentions of the framers. As Lincoln remarked, the "Dred Scott decision was, in part, based on assumed facts which were not really true." As the opinion circulated and the North understood the ramifications of the majority opinion, the attacks grew in intensity and bitterness. Boston Negroes held a meeting to remonstrate against it and were told by Governor John Andrews of Massachusetts that the decision was wrong "because of its injustices to the colored race." [11] The legislatures of Ohio, Vermont, and Maine passed resolutions assailing the decision and saying that it was not the law of the land. The Northern Methodist Conference, meeting in 1857, said that the decision "has overwhelmed us with surprise and affords additional assurance that the decisive battle of freedom is yet to be fought." [12]

It would be almost a hundred years before another Supreme

Court decision, the School cases of 1954, would stir a similar outburst.

Argument gave way to invective. Senator William F. Seward of New York told the Senate and the listening North that the decision was the result of a conspiracy between Buchanan and a Taney-led majority of the Court.[13] the *Boston Atlas* shrieked that "the names of the judges will go down in history with Arnold, the traitor." [14] And the *Boston Chronicle* agreed that "a majority of the court are great scoundrels." [15] Greeley's *New York Tribune* put it that the majority opinion was "entitled to just so much moral weight as would be the judgment of a majority of those congregated in any Washington bar room." [16]

In the midst of the raging storm, Dred Scott, *né* Sam, lay down and died of galloping consumption on September 17, 1858. But the controversy he had stirred up in his decade-long battle for his freedom was not interred with his bones.

An uncertain sound

For if the trumpet give an uncertain sound,

who shall prepare himself to the battle? . . . ❋

I CORINTHIANS 14:8

PART TWO
An uncertain sound

◄§ 6 §► *Let My People Go!*

*Go down Moses,
'Way down in Egypt land,
Tell old Pharaoh
To let my people go!*

NEGRO SPIRITUAL

On September 22, 1862, four years and five days after Dred Scott's
death, Abraham Lincoln warned residents of the states still in rebellion that unless they laid down their arms by January 1, 1863, he
would exercise his war powers and free their slaves. When the
Emancipation Proclamation was issued as promised, or threatened,
it left slavery untouched in the border states and in those areas of
the Confederacy under control of Union arms, but everybody knew
that the end had come for the South's peculiar institution. Less than
two years later, the Thirteenth Amendment, ratified on December
18, 1865, did what Dred Scott's case had failed to do: it settled the
slavery issue. "Neither slavery nor involuntary servitude," it provided, "except as punishment for crime whereof the party shall
have been duly convicted shall exist in the United States, or any
place under their jurisdiction."

Mindful of the long controversy over the scope and reach of its
power in reference to slavery, Congress was determined to leave
nothing to chance or judicial interpretation as to its primacy under
the freedom amendment. Its determination was expressed in phras-
ing that was direct and used for the first time in a constitutional
amendment: "Congress," the framers said in so many words, "shall
have power to enforce this article by appropriate legislation." That
clause drew dissent; it would, opponents cried, produce "a centrali-

zation of power and a consolidated Government . . . it overturns and sets at naught all local laws."[1] Moreover, the dissenters argued in words that sound as if they were uttered only yesterday in current civil rights controversies, the provision would "invade the states," strike down the "cornerstone of the Republic," and cripple the "right of the States to domestic government."[2] The language remained intact and seemed to clear the way for congressional supremacy beyond the possibility of judicial invalidation of any legislation enacted within the broad scope of the amendment.

There seemed to be little immediate prospect of Supreme Court intervention with congressional action on the slavery issue. The Court, in the words of one of its chroniclers, was in eclipse.[3] For one thing, the opinion was widespread that it harbored enemies of the Union cause. Many blamed its Dred Scott decision for the bloody civil war. At late as 1863, five members of the Dred Scott majority, including Chief Justice Taney, were sitting on the Court. In 1865, three of that majority and Nathan Clifford, a Buchanan appointee, still wore its judicial robes.

Taney died in 1864 but not before he had measured arms with Lincoln. He ordered the release of John Merryman, who had been imprisoned by the military after the President suspended the writ of habeas corpus in Maryland in 1861. Lincoln ignored the order which had been issued by the Chief Justice sitting in the Baltimore Circuit Court. Taney struck back by filing his opinion in *ex parte Merryman*[4] and sending a copy under seal to the White House. The chief executive was unmoved by the opinion that he could not suspend the writ, and his attorney general backed him up. Merryman stayed in jail, while Taney lamented that "I have exercised all the power which the constitution and laws confer upon me, but that power has been resisted by a force too strong for me to overcome."

Another attempt at judicial interference with executive conduct of the war came in 1863 on a challenge to a blockade order issued by Lincoln on April 27, 1861. Certain ships sailing into southern ports were seized by the Navy, and their owners brought suit for their return in the so-called *Prize Cases*[5] on the claim that the President had no power to issue the blockade order. The case was decided on March 10, 1863, in the critical days of the war, and Lincoln was upheld by a narrow five-to-four majority. Three Lincoln

appointees and two members of the old Dred Scott court constituted the majority, while Taney, Nelson, Catron and Clifford, all
holdovers, dissented. The case and the close decision created a stir
of anger, but the practical effect was to bolster the power of the
executive in the war crisis. Lincoln, the Father Abraham of popular song, was in the ascendant as the great Father Figure of the nation, and when an attempt was made in 1864 to secure the release
of Clement Vallandigham, southern-sympathizing Ohio politician
who had been jailed by a military tribunal, the Supreme Court declined to take jurisdiction on technical grounds.[6] That same year,
in a case designed to test the validity of paper currency issued to
finance the war effort, the Court again found technical grounds for
refusal to act, but it said nine years later in less perilous times that
its decision was erroneous.[7]

Cases concerning conduct of the Civil War and the extent of
presidential war powers did not directly involve Negroes. They are
important here only insofar as they shed light on Supreme Court
attitudes and illuminate congressional motives in proposing and
wording constitutional amendments and in enacting legislation to
implement those amendments. The ratifying southern states were
greatly concerned about congressional implementation of the Thirteenth Amendment.

A Mississippi legislator feared that the section giving Congress
legislative power contained "something which may be destructive
to the welfare of the South." [8] South Carolina resolved that "any
attempt by Congress towards legislation upon the political status of
former slaves, or their civil relations, would be altered by the proposed amendment. . . ." [9] The basis for these fears lay in the fact
that there was a substantial body of opinion, lay and legal, to the
effect that, if Negroes were granted unqualified freedom, in distinction to mere release from bondage, they would be vested at once
with all the constitutional rights and privileges enjoyed by white
men, a theory that rested on a belief that certain natural rights
inhered in free men. The bedrock on which Taney had based his
Dred Scott opinion was that the constitution itself differentiated
between Negroes as slaves and descendants of slaves and free
white men who composed the body politic. Southerners who had
become reconciled to the abolition of slavery, and many Northerners, did not want to disturb the distinction that had been drawn

between Negroes and whites in the exercise of their rights, and they feared that Congress would seize upon the Negro's status as a free man to invest him with full civil rights. Their fears were justified.

Congress began its work with the original Civil Rights Act, that of April 9, 1866. The very first section of that ten-section enactment struck at Taney's elaborate citizenship argument by providing that all persons born in the United States and not subject to any foreign power (excluding Indians, of course) were citizens of the United States. Such citizens, Congress provided, "shall have the same right in every state and territory" to contract, sue and be sued, inherit, sell and lease property, give evidence, and "have full and equal benefits of all laws and proceedings for the security of person and property as is enjoyed by white persons and shall be subject to like punishment, pains and penalties and to none other, any law, statute, ordinance, regulation or custom to the contrary notwithstanding." Persons acting under "color of law . . . or custom" who deprived any other person of such rights "on account of such persons having been held in a condition of involuntary servitude" were declared guilty of a misdemeanor. Moreover, federal courts were given exclusive jurisdiction of "all causes, civil or criminal, affecting persons who are denied or cannot enforce in [state] courts or judicial tribunals . . . the rights secured to them" by the act. Congress, claiming to exercise the power conferred on it by the Thirteenth Amendment, was acting to enforce that article by "appropriate legislation" and in the process was arrogating to itself many of the rights claimed by the states. The constitutional propriety of the legislation depended on the extent to which civil rights had been placed under federal control by the amendment.

The first Supreme Court test of civil rights legislation enacted under the Thirteenth Amendment came, curiously enough, in 1872, after the passage of the Fourteenth Amendment, in the case of *Blyew v. United States.*[10] Blyew was indicted and convicted for the murder of a Negro woman, and the case was removed to federal court because all witnesses were Negroes, and Kentucky law did not permit Negroes to testify against a white man. Blyew attacked his conviction on the ground that the dead woman was not a "person" entitled to the benefits of the 1866 Act, since she was not in existence and none of her rights could possibly be affected. Justices Bradley and Swayne would have none of that facile argument and asserted in dissent that "the entire class of persons under disability is affected by prosecutions for wrongs done to one of their number, in which they are not permitted to testify in State Courts."

Justice Bradley went out of his way to justify the constitutionality of the 1866 Civil Rights Act, although the majority had not spoken on that subject. "I have no doubt," he said, "of the power of Congress to pass the laws now under consideration. Slavery, when it existed, extended its influence in every direction, depressing, disfranchising the slave in every possible way. . . . The power to enforce the [Thirteenth] Amendment by appropriate legislation must be a power to do away with the incidents and consequences of slavery, and to instate the freedmen in full enjoyment of that civil liberty and equality which the abolition of slavery meant." Nobody contradicted that exposition of natural rights, but the majority freed Blyew by holding that "the person murdered [was not] . . . affected by the cause. Manifestly, the Act refers to persons in existence." The Court majority's restrictive view of the legislation had been forecast in other cases in which Negroes were not involved and in which the Civil Rights Act was not drawn into controversy.

Augustus Garland had been admitted to practice in the Supreme Court in 1860, but when Arkansas seceded, he cast his lot with his native state and served in the Confederate Congress, where he was still sitting in the spring of 1865. President Andrew Johnson granted him a full pardon in July of that year, and in 1867 he applied for readmission to the Supreme Court. He ran into trouble because Congress had passed an act requiring all lawyers appearing before federal courts to take an oath saying that they had never "sought, accepted, or attempted to exercise the functions of any office whatsoever under any authority or pretended authority in hostility to the United States." The Supreme Court had amended its rule to require that same oath. Garland was apparently disqualified, but he pressed his application, and by a five-to-four vote in *ex parte Garland*,[11] the Court held the congressional act invalid and said that its own rule had been adopted "inadvisedly."

Justice Stephen Field, a Lincoln Democratic appointee, speaking for the majority, held that the law imposed punishment for an act which was not a crime when committed. Therefore, he reasoned, it violated constitutional interdictions against bills of attainder and *ex post facto* laws. Justice Miller was caustic, and right, in dissent on the proposition that restrictions on the privilege of practicing law fell under neither bills of attainder nor prohibitions against *ex post facto* legislation. The majority opinion, he said, was based on "those elastic rules of construction which cramp the powers of the Federal Government when they are to be exercised in certain directions and enlarges them when they are to be exercised in others. No more striking example of this could be given than the cases before us, in . . . which the Constitution of the United States is held to confer no power on Congress to prevent traitors from practicing in her courts. . . ."

Congressmen saw great significance in the fact that four members of the old Dred Scott court had joined with a Democratic appointee to invalidate an act of Congress. Congressman Thaddeus Stevens growled that "although not in terms as infamous as the Dred Scott decision, [it] is yet far more dangerous in its operation upon the lives and liberties of the loyal men of this country." [12] Robert Bingham, his colleague, who would become the father of the Fourteenth Amendment, said that if the "Court usurps power to decide political questions," the "insulted and defied" people would soon "demonstrate that the servant is not above his lord, by procuring a further Constitutional amendment . . . which will defy judicial usurpation, by annihilating the usurpers, in the abolition of the tribunal itself." [13]

Lawyer Garland not only got himself readmitted to the Supreme Court but soon turned up as an attorney for the state in the case of *Mississippi v. Johnson*,[14] in which that state sought to enjoin the President from enforcing Reconstruction legislation. The Court declined to take jurisdiction on the ground that the issue was a political one, but Garland and his associates made two other attempts in *Georgia v. Stanton*[15] and *Mississippi v. Stanton*,[16] the variant being that injunction was sought against the Secretary of War instead of the President. Again they were rebuffed on the grounds that the "bill and prayers for relief call for the judgment of the court upon political questions." The states' lawyers then asked permission to amend their bill by eliminating political issues and pitching their case on alleged interference with private property rights of the states. Three members of the old Dred Scott court and Field voted to permit the amendment to the pleadings, but Grier, the other Dred Scott judge, was absent, although he was said to favor amendment. The equal division forestalled the attempt to amend the pleadings, and Charles Warren, official historian of the Court, later observed that "owing to the absence of Judge Grier . . . the question whether the Court could interfere with the Reconstruction legislation in order to protect the public property of a State remained undecided; and Congress was left with a free hand." [17]

That Congress intended to keep its free hand in Reconstruction was proved when William McCardle, a Mississippi editor, was jailed for violation of one of the first Reconstruction acts. Existent law gave him access to federal courts, and when the case got to the Supreme Court docket as *ex parte McCardle*,[18] his lawyer, Jeremiah Black, who had been Buchanan's attorney general, moved to advance the case on the court calendar. A by-now familiar division cropped up, with Justices Grier, Nelson, and Clifford, joined by Field and Davis, in favor of advancement, and Chief Justice Chase, and Justices Swayne and Miller in opposition.

Newspaper reports had it that the ultimate decision would reflect that same division against the validity of the Reconstruction act. The case was argued on January 31 and February 1, 1868, on the issue as to whether the Court had jurisdiction. It held it did have on February 17 and set the case for final argument in early March. Congress took no chances. On March 27, it passed a law over Johnson's veto stripping the Court of jurisdiction to decide the case. The justices bowed to congressional will, with the order that "we are not at liberty to inquire into the motives of the legislature . . . without jurisdiction the court cannot proceed at all in any cause. . . ." Congress had won the battle against judicial interference with its notions of Reconstruction.

There were some congressmen and many lawyers who did not believe that the Thirteenth Amendment vested Congress with the right to enact the Civil Rights Act of 1866. Their skepticism did not spring from doubts as to the natural rights of man sought to be vindicated, but rather from the belief that under the constitutional system, the states, and not the federal government, were supreme in the area of civil rights. Some of these congressional doubters wanted to leave those state rights undisturbed, but the majority was convinced that federal intervention was necessary to raise the Negro to full citizenship status and protect him from punitive action by the southern states. In their view, the remedy lay in another constitutional amendment that would shift the power to protect and guarantee civil rights from the states to the federal government.

There were other congressmen who believed that the Civil

Rights Act of 1866 was constitutional but who feared that the act would be repealed by a subsequent congress; they proposed to abort that possibility by grafting the essence of the Civil Rights Act onto the Constitution. The work of framing the proposed amendment began while the Civil Rights Act was still under consideration, and in June, 1866, two months after passage of the act, the Fourteenth Amendment was submitted to the states.

Congressman Bingham, who deserves more credit than any other single individual for the format of the Fourteenth Amendment, was an abolitionist from the Western Reserve who subscribed wholeheartedly to the social compact doctrine of liberty, equality, and protection which was the stock-in-trade argument of all abolitionists. The creed stemmed from the Declaration of Independence: governments were instituted among men to guarantee unalienable rights. Free men, they argued, owed allegiance to government and, in its proper turn, government owed free men the duty of protecting them in the exercise of their natural rights: those privileges and immunities spoken of in the original Constitution and those rights enumerated in the first eight amendments. The essence of the problem confronting Bingham and his supporters was that under the original Constitution, privileges and immunities were attributes of state citizenship with the correlative duty of state protection, while the guarantees of the Bill of Rights were operative only against the federal government. In the course of his vigorous constitutional opposition to passage of the Civil Rights Act, Bingham proposed a constitutional amendment on January 12, 1866, which provided that "Congress shall have power to make all laws necessary and proper to secure to all persons in every State within the Union equal protection in their rights of life, liberty and property." [19] He ran into trouble on three fronts.

States' rights advocates obviously wanted no part of an amendment that would make the federal government supreme in the area of civil rights. Moderates were not ready to back a law that would entirely destroy federalism, even if they did desire federal supervision of civil rights. Some of Bingham's own followers pointed out that the amendment would do nothing beyond giving Congress the power to pass civil rights legislation which might be repealed by later congressional enactments; they wanted an amendment that would guarantee civil rights in and of itself *and* give Congress the power to implement the guarantees. After numerous refinements, the final draft of Section 1 of the amendment was hammered out. It was deceptively simple:

> *All persons born or naturalized in the United States and sub-. ject to the jurisdiction thereof, are citizens of the United States. and of the state wherein they reside. No State shall make or enforce any law which shall abridge the privileges or immunities of citizens of the United States; nor shall any state deprive any person of life, liberty, or property without due process of law; nor deny to any person within its jurisdiction the equal. protection of the laws.*

The opening citizenship sentence on which, as we shall see, so much was made to depend in later Supreme Court decisions, was an afterthought added at the last minute on the Senate floor. Section 1 fulfilled the demands of the abolitionists turned Republicans —the so-called Radicals—that the amendment contain positive guarantees of civil rights. It is cast in the negative although its mandate is affirmative because, as Bingham explained, it was drawn to conform to constitutional style. Section 5 also conformed to a new style: "Congress shall have power, by appropriate legislation, to enforce this article."

We tend to think of the Fourteenth Amendment in terms of its first section, but Congress spent a great deal of time debating the other four sections. Section 2 was an oblique attempt to coerce enfranchisement of the freedmen by providing that any state which denied the ballot to any of its citizens except for crime or rebellion should have its representation in Congress "reduced in proportion which the number of such male citizens shall bear to the whole number of male citizens twenty-one years of age in such State." The provision was believed to have been superseded by the Fifteenth Amendment with its wholesale prohibition of all racial restrictions on voting, and when it became apparent that the states were able to evade the command of the voting amendment, the time had passed when Congress was willing to act. The provision has never been enforced.

Section 3 of the amendment disqualified from holding federal office all persons who had aided the rebellion, but it provided that Congress could remove the disability by a two-thirds vote. Section 4 validated the public debt incurred in the Civil War, forbade federal or state assumptions of debts incurred by the seceding states in

prosecution of the war, and interdicted "any claim for loss or emancipation of any slave." Section 5 gave Congress the power to enact
appropriate legislation.

The phrase *privileges and immunities* has virtually dropped out
of popular and legal usage, primarily because the Supreme Court
found that, as used in the Fourteenth Amendment, it did not place
civil rights under federal protection as Congress obviously intended. It had great significance to the framers of the amendment.
The Founding Fathers had also deemed it important; they had provided in Article IV, Section 1, of the original Constitution that "The
citizens of each State shall be entitled to all privileges and immunities in the several States."

The phrase had never been defined with exactitude, but lawyers
and laymen alike put great store in *Corfield v. Coryell,* a decision
by Supreme Court Justice Bushrod Washington, nephew of the im-
mortal George, in which he defined privileges and immunities of
citizenship as those rights "which are, in their nature fundamental;
which belong of right to the citizens of all free governments." Some
of these rights, he said, are ". . . protection by the government; the
enjoyment of life and liberty, with the right to acquire and possess
property of every kind; and to pursue and obtain happiness and
safety. . . . The right of any citizen of one state to pass through or
reside in any other state, for purposes of agriculture, professional
pursuits or otherwise; to claim the benefit of the writ of habeas
corpus; to institute and maintain actions of any kind in the courts of
the state; to take, hold, and dispose of property either real or personal. . . ."

That the Fourteenth Amendment provision forbidding any state
to "make or enforce any law which shall abridge the privileges or
immunities" of citizens of the United States had great significance
to those who enacted it is plain from congressional debate on the
subject. Congressman Andrew J. Rogers, an all-out opponent of the
amendment, pointed out that "all the rights we have under the laws
of the country are embraced under the definition of privileges and
immunities." He was certain that if the clause "ever becomes a part
of the fundamental law of the land, it will prevent any state from
refusing to allow anything to anybody embraced under the term
privileges and immunities. . . . It will result in a revolution worse
than that through which we have just passed." [20] Nobody disputed
him.

Bingham adverted to the matter in debate a short time after Rogers had spoken. The clause, he said, would supply "the power in the people, the whole people of the United States, by the express authority of the Constitution, to do that by congressional enactment which hitherto they have not had the power to do, and have never even attempted to do; that is, protect by national law the privileges and immunities of all the citizens of the Republic and the inborn rights of every person within its jurisdiction whenever the same shall be abridged or denied. . . ." [21] When the bill got to the Senate, Senator Jacob Howard agreed with Bingham: "The great objective of the first section of the amendment is, therefore, to restrain the power of the states and compel them at all times to respect these great fundamental guarantees. . . . Here is a direct affirmative delegation to Congress to carry out all the principles of all of these guarantees, a power not found in the [original] Constitution." [22]

The phrase *due process of law* is a hallowed one in Anglo-American jurisprudence, harking back to the Magna Carta concept of "the law of the land." It had found its way into constitutional language in the Fifth Amendment, and Taney had invoked it in the Dred Scott case to protect the rights of slaveholders. Restricted in original meaning to procedural safeguards, it had begun to mean much more by the time of the Civil War and had been extended to cover all arbitrary discrimination against the individual and to comprehend protection of personal and property rights against governmental invasion. Thus, when the amendment provided "nor shall any state deprive any person of life, liberty or property without due process of law," the plain and intended meaning was that the states must conform laws and procedure to a pattern that would give every man "his day in court, and the benefit of the general law." [23]

The last clause of the trinity of rights enumerated in the first section of the amendment was that no state shall "deny to any person within its jurisdiction the equal protection of the laws." There had been no direct mention of equal protection in the original Constitution or in the Bill of Rights, and the states were perfectly free to visit all manner of inequalities on their own residents. As pointed out, northern and southern states alike had denied free Negroes the right to attend schools, hold public office, sit on juries, or exercise other privileges. Continuing that practice, the southern states sought to reduce Negroes to peonage by the Black Codes enacted after passage of the Thirteenth Amendment. Moreover, as congressional committees complained, these states made no effort to protect Negroes against wholesale murders, beatings, and other forms of violence. True enough, the Civil Rights Act of 1866 had been aimed at these evils, but the framers of the amendment wanted to give corrective measures constitutional sanction. The obvious congressional purpose in the equal-protection clause was to strike down invidious state laws on the one hand and to compel state protection of the lives and liberties of all persons on the other. Its thrust was to condemn unequal state laws or unequal enforcement of state law and to require the states to provide or afford equal protection to all persons at all times.

If language has any meaning, the equal-protection clause means that laws unequal on their face or laws that were unequally administered are automatically void. The grant of congressional power to enforce the provisions of the amendment meant that Congress could supply the protection which the states could not or would not afford—it could correct state action of commission or omission by supplying positive protection. There remained the question of what "laws" the amendment spoke when it required "equal protection of laws."

The answer is plain when the three clauses of the first section are read together as they were linked together: it meant equal protection of all laws respecting the rights of life, liberty, and property outlined in the due-process clause and the laws protecting privileges and immunities as tacitly defined in the privileges-and-immunities clause. These were the natural rights of free men, those rights "which are in their nature fundamental; which belong of right to the citizens of all free governments," in the language of Justice Washington. They were the unalienable rights white men had enjoyed as free men, guaranteed and safe-guarded by the free government instituted in the United States by the Constitution. Negroes, now free men, were to enjoy these rights also; the Constitution as amended would be as a sword and a shield to protect them.

The Fourteenth Amendment was ratified on July 28, 1868. Seven months later, amid cries that the Republican party was seeking to perpetuate itself in power, Congress submitted the Fifteenth Amendment to the states: "The right of citizens to vote shall not be denied or abridged by the United States or by any State on account of race, color, or previous condition of servitude." And, of course: "The Congress shall have power to enforce this article by appropriate legislation." Ratification was proclaimed on March 30, 1870.

A Mississippi fieldhand, born of a slave mother and father three years *after* Dred Scott filed his first suit for freedom in the Missouri courts, was now a free man, a citizen of the United States and of the State of Mississippi, entitled to all the privileges and immunities of a white man, guaranteed due process of law, protected against state denial of equal protection of the laws, and protected against discrimination in the priceless privilege of voting in state and federal elections. Moreover, Congress had the power to protect those rights by appropriate legislation.

Congressional understanding of what the Thirteenth, Fourteenth, and Fifteenth Amendments meant can be gathered from what Congress did to implement their meanings and what congressmen said in debate on laws they proposed for that implementation. Within five years after ratification of the Fifteenth Amendment, Congress took three giant steps under its power to enforce the amendments by "appropriate legislation": In 1870 it passed the Enforcement Act updating and re-enacting the sweeping Civil Rights Act of 1866; in 1871 it passed and amended the so-called Klan Act, and it capped its work with the 1875 "Act To Protect All Citizens in Their Civil and Legal Rights." Significantly, each of these acts proscribed discrimination by individuals as well as discriminatory conduct by state officials.

In debate on the passage of the 1875 Act, Charles Sumner could say "that hereafter in all of our legislation, there shall be no such word as 'black' or 'white' but that one shall speak only of citizens." [24] And Senator O. P. Morton of Indiana was certain that "The remedy for the violation of the Fourteenth and Fifteenth Amendments was expressly not left to the courts. The remedy was legislative, because in each case the amendment itself provided that it shall be enforced by legislation on the part of Congress." [25]

The spirit in which Congress approached the task of enacting appropriate legislation had been outlined by Thaddeus Stevens in debate on the Fourteenth Amendment: "The first section," he said, "prohibits the States from abridging the privileges and immunities of citizens of the United States, or unlawfully depriving them of life, liberty, or property, or of denying to any person within their jurisdiction the 'equal' protection of the laws. I can hardly believe that any person can be found who will not admit that every one of these provisions is just. They are all asserted in some form or other, in our Declaration or organic law. But the Constitution limits only the action of Congress, and is not a limitation on the states. This amendment supplies that defect, and allows Congress to correct the unjust legislation of the States, so far that the law which operates upon one man shall operate *equally* upon all." [26]

The equalitarian command of the Civil Rights Act of 1866, re-enacted in the Enforcement Act of 1870, was expressed in the phrase that all persons, without regard to race, color, or previous condition of servitude, should have the *same* right as white persons to exercise the ordinary rights of citizenship in regard to contracts or land tenure. It prescribed punishment for any person who, under "any law, statute, ordinance, regulation or custom," subjected any inhabitant of any state or territory to any different punishment on account of race or color than that prescribed for punishment of "white persons" and lodged jurisdiction in federal courts to punish such offense. The act also implemented the right to vote without distinction as to race or color and made it a felony for two or more persons to conspire together to violate the act "or to injure, oppress, threaten, or intimidate any citizen with intent to hinder his free exercise of any right or privilege granted by the Constitution." Those who subjected any inhabitant to deprivation of the right to sue, enforce contracts, give evidence, or to enjoy "the full and equal benefit" of all laws because of the race or color of the person deprived of such rights were declared guilty of a felony.

The sweeping and rhetorical language of the statute echoed abolitionist sentiment and was plain, and painful, to opponents who protested vainly that the rights of the states were being crushed beneath a Republican juggernaut.

After three years of intermittent debate, Congress enacted the Civil Rights Act of 1875, with a preamble which stated that Congress deemed it essential to just government that "we recognize the equality of all men before the law, and hold that it is the duty of government in all its dealings with the people to mete out equal and exact justice to all, of whatever nativity, race, color, or persuasion, religious or political" and that it is "the appropriate object of legislation to enact great fundamental principles into law."

The act provided that "All persons within the jurisdiction of the United States shall be entitled to the full and equal enjoyment of the accommodations, advantages, facilities, and privileges of inns, public conveyances on land or water, theaters, and other places of public amusement; subject only to the conditions and limitations established by law, and applicable alike to citizens of every race and color, regardless of any previous condition of servitude." The aggrieved person could sue in federal court and recover $500. The violator was also guilty of a misdemeanor cognizable in the federal courts. As originally proposed by Senator Sumner, the act also covered churches, but his senatorical colleagues evidently thought that such a prohibition laid too great a strain on institutions committed to the brotherhood of man and struck out that provision. The Senate also included a ban on segregated public schools and cemeteries, but the House dropped those two clauses from the bill.

Debates on the bills probed beliefs as to the scope and reach of congressional power. Bingham, insisting that he had written the first section of the Fourteenth Amendment except the citizenship sentence "letter for letter and syllable for syllable," argued that the amendment incorporated the first eight amendments of the Bill of Rights and that Congress had unlimited power to protect constitutional rights against both official and private action, even to the extent of displacing state authority altogether, without awaiting infringements of constitutional rights.[27] James A. Garfield, who would become President, was a little more constrained; he thought the provision that "the States shall not 'deny equal protection of the laws' implies that they shall afford equal protection."[28] Senator George Edmunds of Vermont, a distinguished constitutional lawyer, was certain that the equal-protection clause was affirmative in nature and "grants an absolute right" which traced back beyond Magna Carta.[29] Senator Frederick Frelinghuysen of New Jersey argued that the equal-protection clause, combined with the privileges-and-immunities grant, extended to all discrimination because of race "in favor of perfect equality before the law."[30] There was more in the same vein, all directed to the proposition that the Fourteenth Amendment was equalitarian in thrust and import.

The consensus that emerged from the debates on "appropriate" legislation was that the equal-protection clause did more than condemn official or state action, and that at the very least it vested Congress with power to set aside unequal state legislation and with power, when needed, to afford protection to all persons in their enjoyment of constitutional rights when the states failed either through neglect to enact needed laws or by refusal or impotence to enforce them. Congress, it was agreed, was the primary organ for implementation of the guarantees of due process, equal protection, and privileges and immunities. There was no doubt in the minds of the majority of congressmen that the equal-protection clause meant perfect and absolute equality before the law and condemned every discrimination flowing from unequal laws, inadequate law, or mal-administration of the law, by courts or executives, and discrimination in places of public accommodation. Consistent with these views, and inherent in them, was the proposition that whenever racial segregation provoked inequality, it, too, fell under the constitutional ban.[31]

Congressional solicitude for its own power to enforce the amendments reflected the deep distrust of the judiciary in general and the Supreme Court in particular. The Supreme Court decisions in the Garland case, its assumption of jurisdiction in the McCardle appeal, and its attitudes in some other instances loosed a tirade of invective in which the Court was denounced as a refuge for traitors and usurpers basing opinions on politics and not on law. Bills were introduced to curtail and in some instances abolish its jurisdiction on appeals and diminish its numbers. On one occasion, Bingham suggested that the number of justices be reduced to three.[32]

Fear that Negroes would be unable or unwilling to carry their own cases to court led to passage of legislation imposing criminal penalties, so that the government would be able to protect the equality Congress demanded despite fear, ignorance, or indifference on the part of Negroes. This does not mean that Congress intended to bypass all judicial action in protection of civil rights; what it did intend was that in the construction of the system of law it had enacted, discretion in the determination of civil rights was reduced to a minimum or rendered nonexistent. The courts, it was believed, would be compelled to lend their process to enforcement without regard to their notions of policy.

The long sickness had come to end; now the majestic rhetoric of the Declaration of Independence had full meaning: "*All* men are created equal [and] are endowed by their Creator with certain unalienable Rights, that among these are Life, *Liberty* and the pursuit of Happiness." The "Government . . . instituted among men" in the United States of America was committed to "secure these rights" and to safeguard them against the aggressions of individuals, of the states, and of their agents and servants. By constitutional fiat and statutory direction, the national writ would run to guarantee privileges and immunities, due process, and equal protection of the laws for every man, white and black. In spirit, "in all of our legislation," there was "no such word as black or white . . . only . . . citizens."

Every caveat taken by Chief Justice Taney in Dred Scott's case had been met: Negroes were citizens of the United States *and* of the states in which they resided; they were part of the body politic; they enjoyed privileges and immunities conferred by the Constitution; they had the *same* rights as white men, and white men were bound to respect those rights under the pains and penalties of punishment—the "indelible marks" that once separated the white from the "unhappy black race" had been erased. There was neither color nor caste; there were only Americans.

These great, new guarantees were written into the Constitution, binding on the states, binding on unseeing men blinded by the prejudices evoked by 250 years of slavery, binding on legislators and administrators and judges. And whenever the need arose to implement these rights, Congress had power to enact appropriate legislation—the very important power to immunize these newly established rights against judicial impairment.

Or so it was written.

⊰ 7 ⊱ *Less Than True*

Although these words are false, none shall prevail
To prove them in translation less than true. . . .

ELINOR WYLIE, *Angels and Earthly Creatures*

That the equalitarian flame that had burned so brightly in the Reconstruction Congresses flickered feebly in the Supreme Court of the United States, as proponents of civil rights feared and charged, was made abundantly plain in the initial court test of the first section of the Fourteenth Amendment. The test came in 1873 in a case called the *Slaughter House Cases*,[1] and by one of those perversities of history that lead to endless "iffy" speculations, it did not involve the rights of Negroes guaranteed under the carefully contrived privileges-and-immunities, due-process, and equal-protection-of-the-laws clauses of the amendment. It revolved around the privilege of white butchers to ply their trade in a New Orleans slaughter house. The confusion was compounded by the fact that the law was assailed as the corrupt product of a carpetbag legislature, and when the case finally got to the Supreme Court, one of the attorney-defenders of the amendment was John A. Campbell, who had sat with, and agreed with, Chief Justice Taney in Dred Scott's case and had left the Court to cast his lot with the Confederacy, while ranged on the other side was Matthew H. Carpenter, who had voted for the amendment as a senator![2] The law, like politics, sometimes makes strange bedfellows.

In 1869, the Louisiana legislature passed a law regulating slaughter houses in Orleans, Jefferson, and St. Bernard parishes. In effect, the statute gave a certain corporation a monopoly on the maintenance of slaughter houses, ordered the closing of all other such places, required the slaughter of all animals at the specified houses, and directed the favored corporation to permit the use of its facilities by all butchers. It was justified as a health measure. The opposition set up a howl of favoritism, legislative corruption, and monopoly, and appealed to the state courts for relief. The state tribunal could find nothing wrong.

The issue got to the U. S. Supreme Court because opponents of the legislation added the charge that the law, in effect, curtailed the right of a butcher to make a living and, they said, the right to make a living was a property right, one of those precious privileges and immunities guaranteed to citizens of the United States by the new Fourteenth Amendment. Of course, the chances are that the legislature hadn't given the amendment a thought—it had been ratified in 1868, and the law had been passed barely a year later. Moreover, discussion and debate on the amendment had centered around the issue of Negro rights and the provincial-minded state legislators had probably never considered it in connection with slaughter houses. It was certainly true that prior to the amendment, the law was within the competency of the states. But the fact remained that the Fourteenth Amendment was cast in general terms and that it did say: "All persons born or naturalized in the United States and subject to the jurisdiction thereof are citizens of the United States and of the State wherein they reside. No State shall make or enforce any law which shall abridge the privileges or immunities of citizens of the United States."

The first sentence was not included in the draft of the amendment sent by the House to the Senate but was tacked on at the last minute by senators to remove all doubts about Negro citizenship and to dissipate the old Dred Scott dictum that Negroes could not achieve national citizenship. The practical effect was to create a unitary citizenship: a native-born or naturalized person was at once a citizen of the United States *and* of the state of his residence.

Congressional proponents of the Fourteenth Amendment were clear enough on the scope and reach of the privileges-and-immunities clause. Senator Jacob Howard of Michigan, a member of the committee that framed the amendment, told his colleagues: "I look upon the first section [of the amendment] as very important. It will, if adopted by the States, forever disable everyone of them from passing laws trenching on those fundamental rights which pertain to citizens of the United States and to all persons who may happen to be within their jurisdiction. It establishes equality before the law, and it gives to the humblest, the poorest, the most despised of the race the same rights and the same protection before the law as it gives the most powerful, the most wealthy, or the most haughty. . . ." [3]

The Supreme Court, sharply divided five-to-four and speaking through Justice Samuel F. Miller, astounded the nation by holding that there were still two categories of citizens—national and state— and that the privileges-and-immunities clause did not protect rights flowing from state citizenship but only those arising out of national citizenship. National citizenship rights were very narrowly limited; state citizenship rights were broadly defined to include all civil rights, and it was said that it was "not the purpose of the Fourteenth Amendment . . . to transfer the security and protection of . . . civil rights . . . from the states to the federal government. . . ." Forty years later, a constitutional lawyer remarked dispassionately, "Thus the Supreme Court of the United States began its series of adjudications under the Fourteenth Amendment by substantially repudiating it." [4]

The Court's action can be evaluated and understood only in the context of the times and in light of the attitudes of the judges who rendered the decision. Two primary factors were at play. First, there was judicial reluctance to upset a policy decision of a state legislature which had enacted a law that could not have been challenged in federal courts prior to the enactment of the Fourteenth Amendment. That reluctance was tempered, of course, by the sobering knowledge that failure to explain and rationalize the decision and square it with the amendment would be unthinkable. The Supreme Court judges who had to undertake what seemed to them that delicate task were lawyers who by long training were steeped in the doctrine that civil rights were matters of state concern; they were loathe to abandon that view for the new and revolutionary concept forced on the states by Congress, which had nationalized civil rights and placed them under congressional control.

Strengthening the judges' hands was the fact that the Court had notions and traditions of its own, institutionalized in its decisions and persuasive as precedents, that ran contrary to the nationalizing command of the Fourteenth Amendment. The case invited assertion of judicial supremacy under all the circumstances, because strong and self-willed judges who successfully assert the power to determine the constitutionality of legislation are prone to confuse that power with the power to assess the *wisdom* of legislative action, a temptation that is especially great where there has been a sharp break with tradition, as was the case with the Fourteenth Amendment. Justice Miller, we are told by a friendly biographer, was convicued from a study of Reconstruction that Congress was "the least reliable branch of government." [5]

In the second place, there was a rising tide of belief that centralization of federal power had gone too far and that it was time to call a halt. A southern lawyer, reviewing the case in a southern law journal five years later, observed, "The truth is that when this amendment first came before the Supreme Court for construction, the minds of patriotic men were filled with alarm at the centralizing tendency of the government. The President of the United States was holding a half dozen states under the heel of military despotism; the Congress of the United States was indicating its disposition, strongly and more strongly at each successive session, to encroach upon the reserved rights of the states. . . . No one can deny that the disposition of the majority of the court to put some construction upon this amendment which would curb the progress of Federal power was a most patriotic one. But was it wise? Can it ever be wise for the court to force a meaning upon the language of the Constitution to avert a fancied or threatened danger?" [6]

Whether wise or not, the majority had its way. After all, judges are only men, all too often insulated against the harsh realities that move those who must make political decisions. By 1873, the high tide of moral fervor that had gripped the nation at the close of the Civil War was ebbing away, as such tides generally recede after great crusades. The country was ready for what another generation after another conflict would call a return to normalcy.

Justice Miller's prevailing opinion for the majority reflected these ambivalences, and these contradictory factors and attitudes. "No questions," he said, "so far reaching in their consequences, so profoundly interesting to the people of this country and so important in their bearing upon the relations of the United States and of the several States to each other, and to the citizens of the States and of the United States, have been before this Court during the official life of any of its present members." The "one pervading purpose" of the Civil War Amendments, he said, was "the freedom of the slave race, the security and firm establishment of that freedom, and the protection of the newly made freeman from the oppression of those who had formerly exercised unlimited dominion over him." He did not wish to be understood as saying that none but the Negro "can share in this protection. . . . But what we do say . . . is that in any fair and just construction of any section or phrase of these amendments, it is necessary to look to the purpose which we have said was the pervading spirit of them all, the evil which they were designed to remedy. . . ."

This strong and emotional recital must have excited Justice Miller's listeners into the belief that he was about to announce complete agreement with what Thaddeus Stevens or Robert Bingham had said on the floor of Congress in debate on the Fourteenth Amendment. Not so. He turned to the first sentence of the amendment: "All persons born or naturalized in the United States and subject to the jurisdiction thereof are citizens of the United States and of the state wherein they reside." There was no question in his mind but "That its main purpose was to establish the citizenship of the negro. . . ." He then considered the second sentence which reads, "No state shall make or enforce any law which shall abridge the privileges or immunities of citizens of the United States." That sentence, he said, "is more important. . . ." Its importance for him lay in his assertion that "the distinction between citizenship of the United States and the citizenship of a State is clearly recognized and established. . . . It is quite clear, then, that there is a citizenship of the United States, and a citizenship of a State, which are distinct from each other. . . ." The clarity was a judicial fiction.

What Justice Miller had done to support his position was to resort to the semantic device of tearing the second sentence from its context with the first sentence. Having done that, he pointed out that the first sentence made natural-born or naturalized persons citizens of the United States and of the states of their residence. He stopped there as if that were the end of the citizenship matter. Then he picked up the second sentence, as if a new subject matter had been introduced, and pointed out that the second sentence forbade infringement of the privileges and immunities of citizens of the United States. He had given his position the semblance of logic, but when the two sentences are read together as they are joined in the amendment, it is apparent that the meaning is that a person is a citizen of the United States *and* of the state of his residence and that the states are forbidden to impinge on *the citizen's* privileges and immunities. But logic does not undo history or reverse Supreme Court decisions; Justice Miller had restored to the amended Constitution the duality of citizenship Chief Justice Taney had found to exist in the original Constitution.

Apparently stung by critics who pointed out that there were very few rights inhering in national citizenship as such, Justice Miller enumerated a "few of them." He included the rights: to go to the seat of government, access to seaports, to petition for redress of grievances from the federal government, to freedom on the high seas and to use navigable streams. A Reconstruction Congress concerned with the rights of Negroes would hardly have got itself all worked up over these abstractions.

In the course of the argument, lawyers had pressed the contention that Congress had intended to place civil rights under the control of the federal government. Justice Miller had a question: "Was it the purpose of the 14th Amendment," he asked, "by the simple declaration that no State should make or enforce any law which shall abridge the privileges or immunities of citizens of the United States, to transfer the security and protection of all the civil rights which we have mentioned, from the states to the Federal government? And where it is declared that Congress shall have power to enforce that article, was it intended to bring within the power of Congress the entire domain of civil rights heretofore belonging to the States?" Reconstruction congressmen had replied in the affirmative, but Justice Miller returned a different answer: "We are convinced that no such results were intended by the Congress which proposed these Amendments nor by the legislatures of the States which ratified them."

When the decision was announced, Senator George Boutwell, who had sat on the committee that framed the amendment, said positively that the "Court had erred in holding that there were two classes of rights, National and State." Senator George F. Edmunds, another framer of the amendment and a noted constitutional lawyer, pointed out that every word in the amendment had undergone close scrutiny and said that the Court "differed [from Congress] in respect both to the intention of the framers and the construction of language used by them." Senator Timothy Howe, who had also voted for the amendment, was blunt: "The American people would say as they had about the Dred Scott case that it was not the law and could not be law."

The Court minority of four disagreed vehemently. Justice Stephen Field was contemptuous of the strained dual-citizenship argument. "A citizen of a State," he said, "is now only a citizen of the United States residing in that State. The fundamental rights, privileges and immunities which belong to him as a free man and a free citizen now belong to him as a citizen of the United States and are not dependent upon his citizenship of any State. . . ." He reviewed congressional passage of the Civil Rights Act of 1866 and its reenactment after the ratification of the Fourteenth Amendment as a demonstration of the intention of Congress to vest absolute equality in all citizens without regard to race or color. And just as the Reconstruction congressmen had done on so many occasions, he referred to Justice Bushrod Washington's decision in *Corfield v. Coryell*[7] as a shorthand definition of privileges and immunities guaranteed by that clause in the Fourteenth Amendment. They included, he said, "protection by the government; the enjoyment of life and liberty, with the right to acquire and possess property of every kind, and to pursue happiness and safety. . . ." He pointed out that Senator Lyman Trumbull of Illinois had enumerated these as "the very rights belonging to a citizen of the United States." In language reminiscent of debate on the floor of Congress, he insisted that "The privileges and immunities of the United States, every one of them, is secured against abridgement in any form by any state. The fourteenth amendment places them under guardianship of National authority." He could not resist adding that if the amendment meant no more than the majority said it did, "it was a vain and idle enactment, which accomplished nothing, and most unnecessarily excited Congress and the people on its passage." That the quip was an overstatement only proves that Supreme Court judges occasionally get all shook up.

Justice Noah H. Swayne joined the fray with the acid observation that "This Court has no authority to interpolate a limitation that is neither express nor implied. Our duty is to execute the law, not to make it. . . . It is objected that the power conferred is novel and large. The answer is that the novelty was known and the measure deliberately adopted. . . . The construction adopted . . . is . . . much too narrow. It defeats . . . the intent of those by whom the instrument was framed and of those by whom it was adopted. To that extent it turns . . . what was meant for bread into a stone." To the expressed fears that a broad construction of the amendment would lead to "enactments by Congress interfering with the internal affairs of the States," Justice Joseph P. Bradley answered that "The great question is: what is the true construction of the Amendment? When we find that we shall find means of giving it effect. . . . The national will and national interest are of far greater importance."

But the deed was done. The Supreme Court had breathed life into the defunct Dred Scott dogma that there were two categories of citizenship rights, national and state, with civil rights under state control. That duality boded ill for the Negro, just as it had in Dred Scott's day and for the same reason: many states were hostile, some bitterly so, to his claim of absolute equality with white citizens.

There were important differences between the judgments pronounced in the Dred Scott and Slaughter House cases. Admittedly, the federal Constitution of 1873, unlike that of 1858, commanded equality as far as national citizenship rights were concerned and forbade denial of due process and equal protection of the laws by the states as far as state citizenship rights were involved. In the course of discussion, Justice Miller had said in the *Slaughter House Cases* that "We doubt very much that any action of a State not directed against Negroes as a class, on account of their race will ever be held to come" within the purview of the equal-protection clause. How would the Court define due process and equal protection of the laws? Would its definitions of those clauses be as restrictive and as subversive of the congressional will as its views of the privileges-and-immunities phrase? The answers were not long in coming.

Congress had provided criminal sanctions in the Enforcement Act of 1870. One section made it a crime if "two or more persons shall band or conspire together . . . to injure, oppress, threaten or intimidate any citizen with intent to prevent or hinder his free exercise and enjoyment of any right or privilege granted or secured to him by the Constitution of laws of the United States. . . ."

A riotous group of one hundred white persons broke up a political meeting of Louisiana Negroes, and two of them were convicted of violating the quoted section of the Enforcement Act after a grand jury indictment. The major questions certified to the Supreme Court in the case, *United States v. Cruikshank*,[8] in 1875, were what "rights and privileges" are granted and secured by the Constitution, and the subordinate one of whether the indictment properly charged the offense. The first of the rights claimed to have been violated by the conspirators was the "lawful right to peaceably assemble together with each other and with other citizens of the United States for a peaceful and lawful purpose."

There was a vagrant hope in some quarters that the Court would hold that the privileges-and-immunities clause protected Negroes against discrimination in the exercise of civil rights despite what had been said in the *Slaughter House Cases,* but Chief Justice Waite chilled that hope in the very beginning by repeating that "The same person may be at the same time" a citizen of the United States and of a state, "but his citizenship under one of these governments will be different from those he has under the other." The federal government "can neither grant nor secure rights or privileges not placed . . . under its jurisdiction." Duality of citizenship was as much a fact for Negroes as it was for New Orleans butchers; their civil rights were also under the domain and control of the states. The fact was that Negroes, free and slave, had been denied the right of peaceable assembly in Louisiana prior to the passage of the Thirteenth and Fourteenth Amendments and that these enactments had granted and secured the right. But the Court ignored history: "The right of the people," it said, "peaceably to assemble for lawful purposes existed long before the adoption of the Constitution of the United States. It was not, therefore, a right granted by the Constitution." [9]

Other counts in the indictments charged that the conspirators had banded together to prevent the Negro victims from "bearing arms for a lawful purpose," sought to deprive them of "life and liberty without due process of law," and striven to prevent them from voting in Louisiana elections. The Court made short shrift of these contentions. The right to bear arms, it said, was only protected against federal infringement. Chief Justice Waite agreed that the "Fourteenth Amendment prohibits any State from depriving any person of life or property without due process of law; but this adds nothing to the rights of one citizen against another. It simply furnishes an additional guaranty against any encroachment by the states upon the fundamental rights which belong to every citizen as a member of society." The right to vote, the Court added, is not an attribute of national citizenship, "but exemption from discrimination in the exercise of that right on account of race" is. And since it could find no charge that the conduct of the conspirators was undertaken with an intent to prevent the victims from voting on account of their race, it held the indictment was defective in that respect.

The government had advanced the claim that Negroes had been denied equal protection of the laws in that the state had failed in its duty to protect them against mob violence and their right to assemble. The Court disagreed. The mob action was that of individuals, it said. "The Fourteenth Amendment," it insisted, "prohibits a State from denying to any person within its jurisdiction the equal protection of its laws; but this provision does not . . . add anything to the rights which one citizen has under the Constitution against another. The equality of rights of citizens is a principle of republicanism. Every republican government is in duty bound to protect all its citizens in the enjoyment of this principle, if within its power. That duty was originally assumed by the States, and it still remains there. The only obligation resting on the United States is to see that the States do not deny the right."

The Cruikshank decision was rendered at a time when the Ku Klux Klan was sowing to the wind of violence and would soon reap the whirlwind of complete destruction of Negro rights in the entire South, as any observer could see. The southern states were unwilling, or unable, to stay the holocaust, and Congress had acted, drawing its power from the enabling clauses of the Fourteenth and Fifteenth Amendments. In the case of the Fourteenth Amendment, Congress had been especially careful to tailor and fashion a source of constitutional power that would enable its laws to escape a judicial veto of the kind exercised in the Dred Scott case. Although most of the framers of the amendment claimed, and opponents admitted, much more, friend and foe alike agreed that at a very minimum, Congress had power to enact curative legislation under the equal-protection clause where the states failed to safeguard the rights of the freedmen. As the theorists of the time had it, a free man owed allegiance to the state, and the state in turn owed the free man protection.

The Enforcement Act and its proposed application in the Cruikshank case posed the almost classic instance for which the Fourteenth Amendment and enabling legislation were devised: the states had defaulted in their duty to protect the rights of their citizens, and the federal government was supplying the defect. Yet the Supreme Court decided that the congressional fiat was counterfeit! Its pious assertion that the states had the duty to protect the rights of their citizens was a sterile exercise in constitutional double-speak; the states would not protect the civil rights of Negroes; the Court would not permit Congress to do so. The claim that the burden of protecting "civil rights was originally assumed by the States; and it still remains there" was, to put it gently, less than true, as a cursory glance at congressional debates will show. Ominously, the three remaining justices, who had dissented so vigorously in the *Slaughter House Cases*, held their peace.

In any event, the Court had spoken on the due-process and equal-protection clauses. It had not completely emasculated them, as it had done in the case of the privileges-and-immunities clause, but it had severely limited their application and had given them much less scope than their congressional framers had contemplated.

The Court decided another case, *United States v. Reese*,[10] at the same term that it decided the Cruikshank case, and in the same narrow spirit. The voting aspects of the case deserve attention in another place, but here it is sufficient to observe that an election official was indicted for refusal to receive and count the vote of a Negro, William Garner, in a state election. The indictment was laid, as the lawyers say, under the third and fourth sections of the Enforcement Act. The first two sections of the act, entitled "An Act To Enforce the Right of Citizens of the United States To Vote in the Several States of the Union and for Other Purposes," denounced conduct calculated to deprive persons of the right to vote "on account of race or color." The third and fourth sections, under which the indictments were drawn, forbade refusal to receive and count votes for the reason "as aforesaid."

The Court, speaking again through Chief Justice Waite, reversed the conviction on the ground that the act was defective because it did not repeat the magic words "on account of race and color" in the third and fourth sections, and held that the words "as aforesaid" would not suffice. The holding led the official court reporter to note that "Congress has not yet provided by 'appropriate legislation' for the punishment of the said offense."

Justice Ward Hunt was aghast at what he regarded an example of judicial pettifoggery and said so in a vigorous dissent. "What," he asked, "do the words 'as aforesaid' mean? They mean for the causes and pretenses or upon the gounds in the 1st and 2d sections mentioned; that is, on account of the race or color of the person so prevented . . . by this application of the words 'as aforesaid' they become pertinent and pointed. Unless so construed, they are wholly and absolutely without meaning. No other meaning can possibly be given to them." What he meant was that no other meaning should be given to them. But it was.

The government sought to repair the damage done in the Cruikshank case by a carefully drawn indictment under provisions of the Enforcement Act of 1871 that were almost identical with those at issue in the Cruikshank case. The indictments under Section 2 of the act were obviously meticulously prepared in order to eliminate all technical objections, and the Court was presented with the single question of whether or not the section was constitutional. Its answer in *United States v. Harris*,[11] decided in 1883, was a resounding no. The facts were that an armed mob had taken some Negroes from the custody of a Tennessee sheriff, killed one of them, and beaten others. The government argued that the Negroes had been denied equal protection of the laws within the meaning of the Fourteenth Amendment through the failure of the state to protect them. Congress, it said, had the right and the duty to enact protective legislation under the equal-protection clause of the amendment, because that clause saddled the states with an affirmative duty to shield their citizens in the exercise of their citizenship rights, and where they failed to do so, the federal government could, and should, act.

Justice William B. Wood, as spokesman for the Court, rejected the government's argument. "The legislation under consideration," he said, "finds no warrant for its enactment in the 14th Amendment. The language of the Amendment does not leave this subject in doubt. When the State has been guilty of no violation of its provisions; when it has not made or enforced any law abridging the privileges or immunities of citizens of the United States; when no one of its departments has deprived any person of life, liberty or property without due process of law, nor denied to any person within its jurisdiction equal protection of the law; when, on the contrary, the laws of the State, as enacted by its legislative and construed by its judicial and administered by its executive departments, recognize and protect the rights of all persons, the Amendment imposes no duty and confers no power upon Congress. . . ."

The decision was an expansion of the ruling in the Cruikshank case, with the addition that the Court now recognized that discriminatory judicial and executive action, as well as legislative action, by the states might under some circumstances result in the denial of equal protection of the laws. But the all-important ingredient was the Court's insistence that the equal-protection-of-the-laws clause of the Fourteenth Amendment was limited to a "guaranty of protection against the acts of State Government itself." That clause, it was saying, interdicted sins of commission by the states but had no efficacy when a state's sins of omission tolerated violation of the Negro's right by individual citizens. That view was merely implicit in the Cruikshank case, but now it had been squarely decided that a federal law punishing individuals for engaging in mob violence to prevent Negroes from exercising their citizenship rights was invalid. Much had happened between 1875 and 1883.

The bitterly disputed Hayes-Tilden election had been held in the interim, and the compromise of 1876 had been effected. Federal troops had been withdrawn from the South, and the Redeemer governments were establishing white supremacy in the old Confederacy. The busy, bustling North was hard at work building railroads, spawning corporations, winning the West, creating great fortunes, welcoming hordes of immigrants from Europe to do the necessary labor—and quite willing to resign the Negro to the tender mercies of the South. Many former abolitionists had come to the conclusion, later expressed by Charles Francis Adams, that he had been "fundamentally wrong" in supposing that constitutional amendments would be effective to place former slaves "on an equality, political, legal, and moral, with those of the more advanced race." Segregation, he said "has . . . received the final stamp of scientific approval." [12] Frederick Douglass, the great Negro leader, surveyed the scene in 1880 and announced mournfully that "The citizenship granted in the Fourteenth Amendment is practically a mockery, and the right to vote, provided for in the Fifteenth Amendment, is literally stamped out in the face of government." [13] These facts of life were known to the judges who sat on the Supreme Court.

Judges do not arrive at decisions by taking Gallup polls or conducting popularity contests. They apply the law as they understand it.

The great business and industrial need of the latter half of the nineteenth century was for legal devices that would expedite growth and development of corporations and free them of crippling state restrictions. Successive appointments of successful corporate lawyers to the Court after the Civil War created a climate of judicial opinion in which the problems of growing business found a sympathetic audience.[14] Slowly, subtly, but surely, the Fourteenth Amendment was transformed into a charter to protect economic interests, chiefly of corporations. In 1960, Robert J. Harris made a study of 554 cases involving the equal-protection clause of the amendment and found that 76.9 per cent of them involved legislation affecting economic interests, while 14.2 per cent involved claims of racial discrimination! [15] Figures involving the due-process clause are even more disparate, as that clause came to be a refuge for corporate privilege and has had almost no utility in discrimination cases. It is no exaggeration to say that the Court lost sight of the real purpose of the amendment between 1883 and the early 1930's, with a few notable exceptions.

There is no direct conflict between use of the Fourteenth Amendment to protect economic interests and its utilization for its "all-pervading purpose" of protecting the rights of Negroes. But the Compromise of 1876 attendant on the Hayes-Tilden election was more than a bargain between the Democrats and the Republicans, by which the political rule of the South was resigned to Democratic control with a Republican warrant to pursue nationalizing economic policies. It was a moral commitment loosely, yet effectively, binding on the entire country, designed to lay the ghost of civil strife that had rent the nation. It signalized the restoration of the Union on terms acceptable to the South. The tremendously powerful judicial arm of the national government, the Supreme Court of the United States, had a vital role to play in making the compromise effective. On the one hand, it had to give free play to the nationalizing economic forces, and on the other, it had to carry into effect the bargain as it related to state control of civil rights—within the contours of the Fourteenth Amendment as interpreted by the Court.

This unspoken formula called for an expansive interpretation of the amendment in the area of economic interests and a restrictive interpretation in the sphere of civil rights. That is exactly what the Court did, and we need not cry corruption or charge cynicism to explain its actions. We need only see it in its proper historical perspective as a court of men, predominantly successful corporation lawyers, conservative in outlook, predisposed to the businessman's point of view, tragically mistaken but patriotic within their lights, and convinced that the destiny of the nation lay in giving free rein to the doctrine of laissez-faire economics. It was as easy for these men to tolerate the evils of the burgeoning Jim Crow system as it was for the Founding Fathers to accommodate themselves to the evils of human slavery. And for the same reason: both had blinded their eyes with visions of other goals.

Within a fifteen-year span, from 1868 to 1883, the Supreme Court struck down as unconstitutional four general congressional acts of importance to Negroes in the Garland, Reese, Harris, and Civil Rights cases (the latter not yet considered), a remarkable record in light of the fact that it had exercised that claimed right only once prior to the Civil War. It had also gutted the privileges-and-immunities clause and restricted the due-process and equal-protection-of-the-laws provisions of the Fourteenth Amendment. This wholesale undoing of the congressional will reflected both a deep hostility to the national legislative view of Reconstruction and an obvious determination to re-establish judicial supremacy, so badly damaged by congressional and popular reaction to the Dred Scott case and the Court's dilatory conduct during and after the Civil War.[16] That the Court re-established its supremacy at the expense of the Negro need occasion no surprise; the strong traditionally use the weak as stepping stones to power. There was remarkable unity in the Court itself, with few dissents on constitutional grounds in the Fourteenth Amendment cases during this period.

There was one dissent in *United States v. Harris,* and that without an opinion.[17] The dissenter was John Marshall Harlan, Kentucky-born former slaveholder, one time Union army officer, and initial enemy of the Thirteenth Amendment; Republican office seeker, who had been defeated for governor of his state and had then served the Hayes-Tilden Commission; an activist who understood slavery, the ramifications of the slave power, and the forces at play in Reconstruction; a man who had recanted his early racism and had accepted the necessity of absolute equality for the new Negro citizen. For the next three decades his would be a lonely voice crying his dissent in the wilderness of judicial revision against Supreme Court repudiation of the letter and spirit of the Fourteenth Amendment. Time would come full circle some three decades after his death, almost three quarters of a century after ratification of the Fourteenth Amendment, and the Court would begin a return journey to the principles he discerned so clearly and so early. By one of the accidents of history, one of the judges sitting on the Court on that return journey would be his grandson, John Marshall Harlan III, only lukewarm in attachment to his grandfather's great commitments. And as the Court retraced its steps, it would forbear to pay its full respects to the original John Marshall Harlan's prescience and judicial integrity. But no man could foresee that in 1883.

Justice Harlan's first written dissent on a civil rights issue came in the *Civil Rights Cases*, in which the Court made a final shambles of Reconstruction legislation. The details are revealing of the temper of the times; they deserve more than passing mention, but the case itself was preceded by a series of rulings on the right of Negroes to serve on juries and to be tried by juries from which Negroes had not been excluded.

⊰{ 8 }⊱ *Hinder the Wind*

You can't hinder the wind from blowing.
Who could live without hope?

CARL SANDBURG, *The People, Yes*

Every American accused of serious crime is entitled to be tried by a jury of his peers, and if he is denied that right, he can be granted a new trial by a reviewing court.[1] The slave was nobody's peer; he had no right to sit on a jury, but even he had a right to trial by jury when he was accused of crime, although in some states only slaveholders could sit in judgment on him.[2] Free Negroes fared little better prior to the Civil War. Most states barred them from jury service and, when accused of crime, they had to be content with all-white juries.

Section 4 of the 1875 Civil Rights Act provided that no otherwise qualified citizen "shall be disqualified for service as a grand or petit juror" in any state or federal court because of "race, color, or previous condition of servitude" and levied a fine of up to $5000 on any "officer or other persons charged with duty in the selection or summoning of jurors [who] excludes or fails to summon any citizen" for jury duty because of race. That is still the law.[3]

The obvious purpose of the section was to require integration of Negroes into the grand and trial jury systems of the states and in federal courts. As Justice William Strong put it in the original jury cases reaching the Supreme Court, exclusion of Negroes was "practically a brand upon them, affixed by law; an assertion of their inferiority, and a stimulant to that race prejudice which was an impediment to securing to individuals of the race that equal justice which the law aims to give them." [4] As is the case with other federal penal laws, prosecutions could be instituted under the 1875 Act by United States district attorneys.

The fact that criminal prosecutions could be initiated did not prevent a person from resorting to self-help if he was aggrieved at being indicted or tried by a jury from which Negroes had been wrongfully excluded. The command of the equal-protection-of-law clause of the Fourteenth Amendment seemed to cover the situation. When the purpose of the amendment was borne in mind, it was apparent that the state was sinning against that clause by discriminating against some of its citizens in respect of jury duty. The defendant concerned about exclusion of Negroes from jury service had the added problem of the manner in which he could protest his right.

The Civil Rights Act of 1866, re-enacted after passage of the Fourteenth Amendment, offered one way. It provided for removal to federal courts of "causes commenced in any State Court . . . against any person who is denied or cannot enforce in the judicial tribunals of the state . . . any right secured to him by any law providing for equal civil rights of citizens of the United States." Thus, the aggrieved person, confronted with a state law barring Negroes from jury service, could well say that one of the equal civil rights "secured to him" by law was that of indictment and trial by juries from which Negroes had not been arbitrarily excluded and ask to have his case removed to a federal court where there was no discrimination. Or he might be more direct about the whole matter and simply demand that the state court throw out the indictment returned by a grand jury from which Negroes were excluded, or ask the judge to summon a new panel when he was confronted with a trial jury where racial exclusion had been practiced.

Almost everybody agreed that these self-help remedies were available to a Negro defendant. Lawyers and judges were deeply committed to the proposition that a defendant—any defendant— had a right to be judged by a jury of his peers. As Justice Strong phrased the matter, "The very idea of a jury is a body of men composed of the peers or equals of the persons whose rights it is selected to determine; that is, of his neighbors, fellows, associations and persons having the same legal status in society as that which he holds. . . ." That concept had grown up in a society in which there was no disadvantaged group marked off by color or caste and where the defendant's objection was to the individual juror or jurors and not to such jurors as members of a hostile ethnic group or caste. The reality of southern life was that there were two separate and more or less hostile groups from which jurors could be drawn. Very few white Southerners regarded any Negro as a peer or as a person having their status in society. There were as few Negroes who did not know that their white neighbors harbored racial antipathies and hostility toward them. Thus, an objection to an all-white jury rested on racial, not individual, grounds. It seemed self-evident that a Negro could object to an all-white jury selected in violation of the 1875 Civil Rights Act. But what about a white defendant? Could he exercise that same right?

Not many white Americans, particularly Southerners, really wanted Negroes sitting on grand juries which indicted them or trial juries which tried them. But lawyers who defend persons accused of crime can't afford to be squeamish about utilizing ethical devices that will assist their clients. An error is an error, and where a legal mistake is made, a lawyer must be alert to pounce on it. Where the law prohibits racial discrimination in the selection of juries—as did the fourth section of the 1875 Civil Rights Act—and where such discrimination occurred, a lawyer for a white defendant would have been amply justified in seizing on that fact to register an objection on behalf of his client, if that objection were available to him. The question of his standing to object boiled down to whether a grand or trial jury, selected in violation of the act, was a properly constituted jury or whether the violation of law in its selection made all its acts void. If all of its acts were void, a white person had as much right to complain as a Negro.

There was little likelihood that a white southern defendant would challenge arbitrary exclusion of Negroes from juries in the formative years of constitutional law on the subject. The initial obstacles were the deep-seated belief of lawyers and judges that the individual defendant was solely concerned with the issue of whether or not a particular jury before which he appeared was composed of *his* peers and the belief of white defendants that Negroes were not their peers.

The second difficulty, bound up with the first, was that the Supreme Court does not decide abstract questions of law; it only considers actual cases and controversies brought before it. The temper of the times was such that it would have been extremely difficult to find a white defendant who was willing to fly in the face of public sentiment and challenge Negro exclusion from juries, even if it promised an apparent personal advantage. Success in establishing the legal proposition that juries selected in violation of the 1875 Act could not return valid indictments or render valid judgments would have undermined and destroyed the all-white jury as a southern institution. Most white Southerners believed that preservation of that system outweighed a personal advantage that might accrue from a successful challenge to it; public opinion restrained those who did not. There was a certain perverse merit in that view.

The all-white grand jury, selected in violation of federal law but accepted as a valid jury, in the absence of a challenge, could refuse to indict a white person charged with aggression against a Negro, and that was the end of the matter. Or an all-white trial jury, similarly selected and accepted, could acquit the white person of a crime against a Negro, and that, too, was the end of the matter. The white defendant would not complain in either instance; the Negro could not. Juries also pass on civil matters, and the illegally selected all-white jury could, and more often than not did, favor the white person in a contest between Negro and white litigants.

The policy of the federal government was also of critical importance. Under the 1875 Civil Rights Act, it had power to prosecute jury officials who arbitrarily excluded Negroes from jury service, and vigorous exercise of that power would have gone a long way toward compelling integration of Negroes into southern jury systems. Unfortunately, the act was passed on the eve of the compromise in the Hayes-Tilden election of 1876, after which the federal government did next to nothing by way of enforcement of civil rights laws. The Negro was pretty much left to shift for himself in the Supreme Court jury cases, with only one prosecution case reaching the tribunal.

It was in this atmosphere that the law in respect of jury exclusion was developed. Negroes challenged the all-white jury; whites did not, whether they had such a right or not. The courts soon agreed that Negroes, *as Negroes*, were entitled to juries selected without discrimination. In the absence of challenge to their validity, all-white juries continued to function in the cases of white defendants. Thus, an incipient separate-but-equal rule was intruded into the jury systems of southern states. The fact that white persons did not attack the jury selection practices of southern states did not settle the issue of whether or not arbitrary exclusion of Negroes from grand or trial jury panels in violation of the 1875 Act made the actions of such juries void in every particular. What it did mean was that the issue would have to be raised by Negroes. But lawyers for Negroes also subscribed to the common belief of their profession that the individual defendant was only concerned with the question of whether or not the particular jury considering *his* case was a jury of his peers. Generally, that was the way the question was posed to the Supreme Court. The broader and much more important issue of the validity, or invalidity, of all functioning of illegally selected grand or trial juries could not readily be raised by a Negro, but it cropped up in a tangential manner in the case where removal to federal courts was sought by a Negro defendant who charged jury discrimination.

The Supreme Court began consideration of the jury question in 1879, in the case of *Strauder v. West Virginia.*[5] That state's laws restricted both grand and trial jury service to white male persons. A West Virginia Negro, indicted for murder by a grand jury drawn in conformity with state law, asked for removal of his case to federal court and, out of an abundance of caution, as the lawyers say, also asked the judge to set aside his indictment by the all-white jury. The judge refused his request, and the Negro was tried and convicted by an all-white trial jury.

Justice Strong, speaking for a seven-to-two majority of the Court, readily agreed that the Negro's right to a jury, not restricted to white persons, "if not created, is protected, by the [Civil War] Amendments and the legislation of Congress under them." It followed that the defendant was correct in asking removal of his case to the federal court, and removal should have been granted before trial.

The justice treated the equal protection clause of the Fourteenth Amendment as creating a right in the Negro defendant, *as a Negro,* and took the occasion to explain the majority view. "At the time of the incorporation of the Amendments," he said, "it required little knowledge of human nature to anticipate that those who had been regarded as an inferior and subject race would . . . be looked upon with jealousy and dislike" by the formerly dominant whites. Therefore, the Fourteenth Amendment was "adopted to assure the colored race the enjoyment of all civil rights that under the law are enjoyed by white persons. . . ." Congress, he said, had power under the amendment to assure Negroes of a trial by a jury of their peers, "their neighbors, fellows, associates, persons having the same legal status," that is, by juries from which Negroes were not arbitrarily excluded.

Justice Strong did not count it significant that the amendment spoke in general terms or that its language was cast in the negative. He stressed the fact that the amendment prohibited denial of due process and equal protection of the laws. "What is this," he asked in a flight of oratory, "but declaring that the law in the states shall be the same for the black as for the white; that all persons, whether colored or white, shall stand equal before the laws of the states and, in regard to the colored race, for whose protection the Amendment was primarily designed, that no discrimination shall be made against them by law because of their color? The words of the Amendment, it is true, are prohibitory, but they contain a necessary implication of a positive immunity, or right, most valuable to the colored race—the right to exemption from unfriendly legislation against them distinctively as colored—exemption from legal discriminations, implying inferiority in civil society, lessening the security of their enjoyment of rights others enjoy, and discriminations which are steps toward reducing them to a subject race."

Negroes found great comfort in those resounding words. They still do. Their lawyers like to quote them whenever possible, but that does not alter the fact that all that the Court decided in respect of jury service was that Congress had power to enact the fourth section of the Civil Rights Act and the removal statute; that a Negro, as a Negro, could successfully attack a state statute restricting jury service to white persons, and that, upon his objection, his trial could be removed to a federal court. It did not declare that all acts of such a jury were void. The illegally selected jury could continue to function in the absence of a challenge to the court's jurisdiction.

Two other cases were decided the same day as the Strauder case. One of them, *Virginia v. Rives,*[6] also concerned the right of removal of a case to the federal courts. Two Negroes on trial for their lives were indicted and tried by all-white juries from which all Negroes had been excluded by the machinations of the jury commissioner. The defendants demanded that Negroes be summoned for the trial jury, but that demand was refused. Virginia law, unlike West Virginia statutes, did not restrict jury service to Negroes, and the jury commissioner had, in fact, discriminated against prospective and qualified Negro jurors in defiance of state law. Nevertheless, a federal judge, Alexander Rives, ordered the case removed to his court after convictions of the men, and Virginia sued to bring the case back to its own courts. By his removal order, Judge Rives had held in effect that the actions of grand or trial juries, selected in violation of the 1875 Civil Rights Act, could be declared void by a federal court on complaint of the affected Negro defendant at any stage of a trial, and that the federal court could enforce its order by removing the defendant from the jurisdiction of the state court.

The Supreme Court reversed Judge Rives and decided in favor of Virginia, holding that there was no right of removal to a federal court when a trial had actually been held or begun in a state court where a state statute did not bar Negroes from jury service. Justice Strong, again speaking for a seven-to-two majority, pointed out that there could be no claim that the "Constitution or laws of Virginia denied" Negroes the right to jury service. Under those circumstances, he said, a Negro defendant would have to present his objections to a jury to the Virginia courts and prove the discrimination of the jury commissioner or other state officials. If the trial judge refused relief, he would have to take an appeal in the state appellate court. In the event the highest court in the state denied his claim, then, and only then, could the matter be presented to the federal courts on a writ of error to the U. S. Supreme Court. In practice, the Supreme Court's reversal of Judge Rives meant that a state officer, in violation of the Civil Rights Act, could select all-white grand and trial jury panels that could indict and convict Negroes, with no remedy short of expensive appeals through the state courts and, ultimately, to the Supreme Court. That is precisely what did happen. Few Negroes were able to shoulder the burden of such complicated appeals.

The right to appeal from the state judge's decision to the Supreme Court was important and was affirmed over Virginia's vigorous objections. The notion that the Fourteenth Amendment only prohibited discriminatory action by the state and that Congress was powerless to interdict discrimination by individuals was gaining ever wider currency at the time. Virginia seized on that concept to argue that action by a state official in violation of state law was merely an individual dereliction and not state action. Therefore, Virginia's lawyers said, congressional statutes forbidding discrimination in selection of juries and providing for removal of cases to federal courts were valid only when state law excluded Negroes from jury service. If the jury commissioner had barred Negroes from jury service in violation of its laws, only Virginia could punish him or undo his wrongs, the lawyers argued. They were saying there was no state action. Justice Strong was unmoved by that contention. "A state may act through different agencies," he answered, "either by its legislative, its executive or its judicial authorities; and the prohibitions of the [Fourteenth] Amendment extend to all actions by the state." The action of a jury commissioner in excluding Negroes from juries was *state action*. Even if he acted in defiance of state law, his conduct fell under the ban of the equal-protection clause.

Like the Strauder case, the Rives case contains some glowing language about Negro rights, but the effect of the decision was to restrict the applicability of the removal statute to the case where a state statute barred Negroes from jury service. In all other cases, the Negro defendant would have to pursue the long and expensive course of trying to prove racial discrimination in jury selection in the very court that had countenanced it in the first place, of then appealing the almost certain adverse decision to a hostile state appellate court, where chances of success were not great, with a final appeal to the U. S. Supreme Court.

The Court made it plain that the burden of *proving* racial discrimination would lie on the Negro defendant in each case. There was an added restriction. The defendants in the Rives case had demanded that one third of the jury be composed of Negroes, a quota that corresponded to the proportion of Negroes to the general population. Justice Strong rejected this formula. "A mixed jury in a particular case is not essential to the equal protection of the laws," he said. He went on to explain that all the Negro defendant could ask under the Constitution and the 1875 Act were jury *panels* from which Negroes had not been excluded. A jury panel is simply the pool of jurors from which jurors are drawn to hear a particular case.

In sum, the decisions meant that (1) the Court regarded the 1875 law as giving a Negro defendant, as a Negro, a right to indictment and trial by juries chosen from *panels* on which Negroes had not been excluded because of race; (2) the Negro defendant must pursue his remedies in state courts in the absence of an exclusionary statute but with a final resort to the Supreme Court; (3) the Negro defendant must assume the burden of proving racial discrimination where there was an absence of Negroes from jury panels; and (4) the action of a state official in arbitrarily excluding Negroes from jury panels was state action.

The other case decided in 1879 was *ex parte Virginia*.[7] In that case, a Virginia judge who refused to summon Negroes for jury service was indicted for violating the 1875 Act. He sought release on the ground that Congress had no constitutional authority to control the actions of a state judicial officer and that the act was unconstitutional as applied to him. The claim of unconstitutionality revolved around the by now familiar argument that Congress had power only to prohibit discriminatory *state action*. He raised the contention repeated in the Rives case that, since he acted in defiance of Virginia's nondiscriminatory jury law, his action was not state action but a piece of individual wrongdoing. Justice Strong, the consistent spokesman for the Court in the series of cases, rebuffed the judge on both claims.

He began with a restatement of the purposes of the Civil War Amendments. The "one great purpose of these amendments," he reminded the judge, "was to raise the colored race from that condition of inferiority and servitude . . . into perfect equality of civil rights with all other persons within the jurisdiction of the States. . . . They were intended to be, what they really are, limitations of power of the States and enlargement of the powers of Congress. . . ."

Justice Strong went on to point out that the amendments gave Congress the power to enforce them by appropriate legislation: "It is not said that the *judicial power* of the general government shall extend to protecting the rights and immunities guaranteed. . . . It is the power of Congress which has been enlarged. Congress is authorized to *enforce* the prohibitions by appropriate legislation." That, of course, was what the framers had said in debate over and over again. He brushed aside the argument that Congress was invading the prerogatives of the states.

"Nor does it make any difference," he maintained, "that such legislation is restrictive of what the State might have done before the constitutional amendment." It was, he said, such changes that Congress was "empowered to enforce against State action, however put forth, whether that action be executive, legislative or judicial. Such enforcement is no invasion of State sovereignty. No law can be invalid which the people of the United States have, by the Constitution of the United States empowered Congress to enact." Again, he was voicing the sentiment uttered many times in the Reconstruction Congresses which had proposed the Fourteenth Amendment and enacted the various civil rights acts that protection of civil rights had been placed under the federal government.

Justice Strong betrayed impatience with the circuitous argument that a state officer who discriminated in violation of a state law could not be called to book by Congress on the thin claim that his defiance of state law divested him of his status as an officer of the state and made his action only an individual wrong. "We do not perceive how holding an office under a State, and claiming to act for the State, can relieve the holder from obligation to obey the Constitution of the United States or take away the power of Congress to punish his disobedience," he said sharply.

The decision was a very important one because it opened the way for federal prosecution of jury officials who violated the Civil Rights Act in selection of juries.

Justice Field disagreed with the Supreme Court majority and said so in dissents in which he was joined by Nathan Clifford, the final Buchanan holdover. The states, he thought, had the right to determine who should serve on juries. They also excluded women and also men over 65, both covered as persons by the equal-protection clause of the Fourteenth Amendment. If the states could exclude women and overage men, why could they not also exclude Negroes from service as jurors? It was Field's stress on this simplistic concept that led Justice Strong to stress the root purpose of the amendment as that of protecting the rights of Negroes.

Justice Field had another general argument: "The equality of protection secured," he argued, "extends only to civil rights as distinguished from those which are political, or arise from the form of government and its mode of administration." He regarded jury service as an unprotected political right. Finally, he challenged the constitutionality of the fourth section of the 1875 Civil Rights Act, because under the original Constitution, "The States required no aid from any external authority to manage their domestic affairs." The Fourteenth Amendment had not changed that central constitutional doctrine, he argued.

Justice Field was particularly outraged by the majority opinions in the two Virginia cases, which he saw as interference in the judicial affairs of the state. "Nothing," in his judgment, "could have a greater tendency to destroy the independence of the States; reduce them to a humiliating and degrading dependence upon the central government . . . than the doctrine . . . that Congress can exercise coercive authority over the judicial officers of the States."

It seemed plain to Justice Field that there was no state action involved where state law did not exclude Negroes from jury service. The state, he insisted, did not act where an officer did something in defiance of state law: "If an executive or judicial officer exercises power with which he is not invested by law, and does unauthorized acts, the State is not responsible. . . ." The essence of that argument was that if a jury commissioner or judge barred Negroes from juries where state law did not require it, the litigant must look to the state for relief. A judge, he said, "is responsible only to the State whose officer he is and whose law he is bound to enforce." Justice Field would have left Negroes to the entire mercy of the states in the whole realm of jury service. But, he said, they would not be without protection if that were done, for "Equality in their civil rights was in other ways secured to persons of the colored race, and the ballot being assured to them, an effectual weapon against unjust legislation was placed in their hands." He was a poor prophet.

Undeterred by Justice Field's dissents, the Court persisted in its jury trial philosophy in the case of *Neal v. Delaware,*[8] which reached it one year later, in 1880. Delaware's 1831 constitution restricted the right to vote to white male citizens, and its laws made only *voters* eligible for jury service. A Negro defendant asked to have his case removed to federal court on the ground that state law, in effect, excluded Negroes from jury service. When that motion was denied, he asked the state trial judge to quash the grand jury and trial jury panels, on the ground "That from the grand jury that found [the indictment] and from the . . . jury that was summoned to try" him, "citizens of the African race, qualified in all respects to serve as jurors, were excluded from the panels because of their race and color." In its review of the case, the Delaware appellate court virtually admitted that Negroes had been excluded because "the great body of black men residing in this State are utterly unqualified by want of intelligence, experience or moral integrity to sit on juries."

Justice Harlan assumed what was to become a familiar role as a protagonist of Negro rights by writing the opinion of the Court.

Following the precedent of the Rives case, he held that the removal request was correctly denied, because "Adoption of the Fifteenth Amendment had the effect, in law, to remove from the State Constitution, or render inoperative, that provision which restricts the right of suffrage to the white race. Thenceforward the statute [respecting jury service] was itself enlarged . . . so as to embrace all . . . who were qualified to vote." Therefore, Negroes were qualified for jury service by state law, and their exclusion was the wrongful act of state officials charged with selection of jury service. He said that the defendant's remedy lay in the motions to quash the indictment and the trial jury panel and, upon denial, an ultimate appeal to the Supreme Court. He reasoned that Delaware courts had erred in denying the motions to set aside the indictment and conviction, in light of the virtual admission that Negroes had in fact been excluded from the grand and trial jury panels. The case was sent back for indictment and trial by properly constituted juries from which Negroes had not been excluded.

The tired argument that there was no state action because the jury officials had acted in defiance of state law was summarily disposed of: "The action of those officers in the premises is to be deemed the acts of the State." Justice Harlan cemented the point with a quotation from *ex parte Virginia:* "Whoever, by virtue of public position under a State government, deprives another of property life, or liberty without due process of law, or denies or takes away the equal protection of the laws, violates the constitutional inhibition; and as he acts in the name of and for the State, and is clothed with the State's authority, his act is that of the State. This must be, or the constitutional prohibition has no meaning." Justice Field duly noted his dissent.

In its final resolution, *Neal v. Delaware* added nothing new to Supreme Court law respecting jury service. In an oblique way, it left the white jury *system* intact. Under the facts in the case, the Court could have seized the occasion to say that the trial court lost all jurisdiction in the case by acquiescing in indictment and trial by all-white juries selected in violation of the 1875 Act and that removal to federal court was justified. Such a ruling would have struck at the all-white jury systems.

Three years later, in 1883, the Court reiterated those views in *Bush v. Kentucky* and underscored the proposition that there is "no legal right in the accused to a jury composed in part of his race. All

that he could rightfully demand was a jury from which his race was
not excluded because of their color." [9]

The Court never made it plain how it had arrived at the doctrine
that the right of the Negro defendant was limited to that of grand
and trial jury panels "from which his race was not excluded because
of their color." Apparently, it was a judicial bow in the direction of
the 1875 Civil Rights Act, with its interdiction of racial exclusion
in the selection and summoning of juries, and an acknowledgment
of the requirements of due process and equal protection as voted in
the Fourteenth Amendment. In either case, the right was so limited
in application that it was almost sterile. It neither assured the Negro defendant of indictment or trial by a jury which included Negroes nor implemented the purpose of integrating Negroes in state
jury systems.

In practice, the decision led to tokenism on jury panels at best.
The rulings had absolutely no effect in requiring integration of Negroes into the jury systems of the states. The states could, and did,
devise all-white grand and trial jury systems. They were entirely
safe in doing so, because such juries, selected and summoned in
evasion, or violation, of the 1875 Act, were perfectly competent to
perform all jury functions insofar as they concerned white persons
—or Negroes, except the singular Negro defendant who might
complain and who had the resources to appeal. After the overthrow
of Reconstruction governments in the South, Negroes rapidly disappeared from the jury systems in that region.

There was a large flaw in the Supreme Court reasoning, as Justice Field pointed out with some malice in his dissent in *ex parte
Virginia:* "The position that in cases where the rights of colored
persons are concerned, justice will not be done unless they have a
mixed jury is founded upon the notion that in such cases white
persons will not be fair and honest jurors." He said he did not sub-
scribe to that position. But, he said, "If this position be correct there
ought not be any white persons on the jury. . . ." Nobody ever
tried to answer his observation, which reduced the whole issue to
an absurdity but which did lay a finger on the weakness of the
proposition that the Civil Rights Act meant that only a Negro could
complain of jury exclusion because, as a defendant in a particular
case, he was entitled to a jury of his peers, his "neighbors, fellows,
associates, persons having the same legal status."

The ruling that the complaining defendant must prove the willful exclusion of Negroes from jury service was onerous and restrictive. The poor and handicapped defendant had to match his prowess against that of the relatively all-powerful state, committed, by the very fact of exclusion, to depriving him of his rights. He had to conform to difficult procedural requirements in order to have his case heard on appeal, and he had to run the gamut of hostile courts from the trial tribunal to the state's highest appellate court. If he persisted and finally lodged his case in the Supreme Court, he learned all too often that his case must fail there because he had not conformed to state procedure or because his proof was held insufficient.[10]

In numerous cases, such a defendant was told by state supreme courts or by the U. S. Supreme Court that his proof that Negroes had never been permitted to serve on grand or trial juries or were persistently absent from them was no "proof" of willful or purposeful exclusion.[11] He had to pinpoint the discrimination which he claimed in his own case, although the discrimination was a matter of common knowledge in his community and in his state—indeed, in the nation at large. There was no sound reason for thrusting the burden of proof on the Negro defendant. The Civil Rights Act of 1875 had forbidden racial discrimination in state jury systems in order to implement the equal protection required by the Fourteenth Amendment. The states should have been required to show affirmative compliance with the highest law of the land where dereliction was charged, especially where there had been long continued absence of Negroes from juries.

A final effort to induce the Supreme Court to broaden its rule in the jury exclusion cases was made in 1895 in *Andrews v. Swartz*.[12] At his trial, a New Jersey Negro defendant charged deliberate exclusion of Negroes from the grand and trial juries that indicted and convicted him and made offers to prove his claims. His contention was overruled, his offers of proof rejected, and he was convicted and sentenced to death. A peculiar New Jersey law made an appeal from a death sentence an "act of grace" on the part of the state, and he was refused the right to appeal. He then went to the federal courts and sought a writ of habeas corpus, repeating in great detail his allegations of deliberate exclusion of Negroes from grand and trial juries in his county and again offering to prove his charges. He argued with a great show of reason that the trial court's erroneous refusal to grant his motion to quash the juries deprived that court of jurisdiction to try his case.

In effect, he was making the claim that a jury from which Negroes had been willfully excluded was a sham jury and that its actions were nullities as a denial of due process of law. The Supreme Court was being offered an opportunity to retrace its steps and, by nullifying the actions of an arbitrarily selected all-white jury, give meaning and content to the Civil Rights Act as an instrument for integrating Negroes into state jury systems. Justice Harlan, speaking for a unanimous Court, was unmoved by the contention. The defendant, he said, should have presented his case to the highest state court willing to hear it and then have gone to the Supreme Court on a writ of error. "Even if it be assumed that the state court improperly denied to the accused the right to show by proof that" Negroes were "arbitrarily excluded from the panel of the grand or petit jurors solely because of their race," the state court would not lose jurisdiction, he said. Habeas corpus would not lie; the accused remained in his death cell.

Southern states continued their implacable resistance to Negro service on grand or trial juries. Every evasive practice that ingenuity could devise was instituted. A favorite was that of disfranchising Negroes by onerous requirements and then of confining jury service to voters. In *Williams v. Mississippi*,[13] a state constitutional convention "swept the circle of expedients" to bar Negroes from the ballot and limited jury service to voters, but the Court held that it could not intervene.

Although *ex parte Virginia* cleared the way for prosecutions of state officials who excluded Negroes from juries for racial reasons, no such case came to the Supreme Court after 1879 for the simple reason that United States attorneys general and federal district attorneys did not prosecute offenders. The policy still obtains. In case after case, Negro defendants have proved against great odds that there has been wholesale and willful exclusion of Negroes from juries, but the executive arm of the government has been content to leave the jury issue to the individual. Significantly, the cessation of prosecutions began hard on the heels of the Compromise of 1876, in which control of political affairs was resigned into the hands of southern states.

The Supreme Court's role in the jury cases was a checkered one.

Within the narrow limits it pricked out in the early cases, it held fast to its originally announced doctrine. Its decisions had the effect of wiping out state statutes excluding Negroes from jury service. In individual cases it did upset indictments and convictions. Wherever a Negro defendant could meet its rigid rules and prove exclusion of Negroes from his grand or trial jury, it reversed his conviction and ordered reindictment or retrial. In obvious cases, it cut through tricky state procedural rules and regulations and ordered hearings on the merits of a Negro's claim that there had been discrimination in selection or summoning of juries.[14]

The Court held squarely that a state official who acts in apparent defiance of state law to discriminate acts in the name of and for the state and that his action is "state action" within the meaning of the Fourteenth Amendment, a ruling that has had great importance in other areas of the law. It upheld the right of the federal government to prosecute state officials who discriminated against Negroes in jury service. Its language in the jury cases hewed close to the line laid out in the Congresses that proposed the Fourteenth Amendment and enacted the various Civil Rights Acts. It did less to revise the congressional intent in this phase of the law than in any other issue that arose out of the Civil War Amendments.

On the other side of the ledger, the Court proceeded as if the due-process and equal-protection-of-law clauses of the Fourteenth Amendment and the 1875 Civil Rights Act cast no affirmative duty on the states to integrate Negroes into their entire jury systems. The states were left perfectly free to continue all-white jury systems, and those all-white juries, selected in obvious violation of the 1875 Act, were accorded full status as valid juries. As valid juries, they could, and did, discriminate in favor of white persons in indictment and trials in criminal and civil cases, to the obvious disadvantage of Negroes who were the victims of white aggression or who were defendants in civil litigation. The Court circumscribed the right of Negro defendants to object to arbitrary exclusion of Negroes from grand or trial juries.

It is true that the Court's opportunity to broaden its rule was limited by the fact that whites did not initially object to Negro exclusion, but it could have reached the problem by holding in *Neal v. Delaware, Virginia v. Rives,* and *Andrews v. Swartz* that a state court which tolerated an arbitrarily selected all-white jury was thereby deprived of jurisdiction to proceed with trials. If that concept had been introduced into the law, it would have served as precedent to encourage white defendants to assert that violation of the 1875 Act made indictments or convictions void in their cases, even where no racial conflict was present. Sooner or later, a desperate white defendant facing long imprisonment or execution would have to take that step.

It may seem at first blush that exclusion of Negroes from the jury systems of the southern states was a relatively minor matter. It was not. Disfranchisement of Negroes assured the election of white judges, sheriffs, jury commissioners, and prosecutors. The all-white jury system encouraged aggressions by white persons against Negroes because, in the context of southern life, the aggressive white had practical immunity from indictment or conviction.[15] Mob violence flourished, because juries would neither indict nor convict lynchers.[16] Brutal law enforcement officials could maim and even kill Negroes without fear of prosecution.[17] In civil litigation, the all-white jury effectively guaranteed success for the white exploiter in every phase of Negro-white relationships. Protection of civil rights, increasingly put under state regulation and control by Supreme Court decisions, was impossible where white juries were called upon to determine a right claimed by a Negro in defiance of local customs and traditions. The Negro had no place to turn. The fiat of the white man became law. The proud boast that "ours is a government of laws and not of men" was reversed as far as Negroes were concerned.

Although the Court must have believed that its reversals of verdicts in individual cases where racial exclusion in selection of juries was proved would prod the states into abandoning all-white jury systems, the burden it laid on the Negro defendant to prove the discrimination he asserted encouraged foot-dragging by southern jury commissioners and courts. It was only when the Court liberalized its rules of proof a half-century later that Negroes found some relief from the discrimination that had grown and flourished because of the Court's failure to take a broad view in its early rulings.

Throughout the jury cases the Supreme Court majority had held firmly to the proposition that the acts of state officials in excluding Negroes from juries even in violation of state law was *state action*, despite consistent dissents by Justices Field and Clifford. That very insistence was a significant omen: it signalized growth of the concept that the Fourteenth Amendment did not empower Congress to proscribe racial discrimination by individuals.

The first two sections of the 1875 Civil Rights Act did interdict individual discrimination by keepers of places of public accommodation, and there was a rising wind of opinion that the two sections were unconstitutional. That wind was assuming hurricane proportions, even as the Court was deciding the jury cases.

A new constitutional crisis was at hand.

◄ 9 ► *No Hiding Place*

Went to the rock to hide my face,
The rock cried out: no hiding place—
There's no hiding place down here.

NEGRO SPIRITUAL

The Civil Rights Act of 1875 was Charles Sumner's last testament to the American people. He introduced the original bill in 1872 and died in 1874, after two years of unrelenting effort to get it out of committee. As Whig, abolitionist, and Republican, Sumner had served for many years as the conscience of the Senate and was the most uncompromising political advocate of the Negro's complete equality before the law in his native Massachusetts and in the nation.[1] The original bill prohibited discrimination by all places of public accommodation, by churches and cemeteries, and interdicted segregation in public schools. The Senate deleted the church provision and Vice-President Henry Wilson's vote broke a Senate tie to approve the measure and send it to the House, where the school and cemetery clauses were dropped.

As finally approved by Congress and signed by President Grant, Sections 1 and 2 of the act were what are now called public accommodations laws. Anticipating by almost ninety years substantially identical provisions in the Civil Rights Act of 1964, the first two sections prohibited denial of "full and equal enjoyment of the accommodations, advantages, facilities and privileges of inns, public conveyances . . . theaters and other places of public amusement." Offenders were liable in damages of not less than $500 or to fines and imprisonment.

The three years of running debate on the measure and the fact that it was passed after the Supreme Court's emasculation of the privileges-and-immunities clause of the Fourteenth Amendment underscore the understanding of Congress that the due-process and equal-protection clauses gave it power to legislate to protect fundamental constitutional rights and enforce equality where the states failed to do so. Further, it reflected a strong and lingering belief that the Thirteenth Amendment also conferred similar power on Congress, a power exercised to some extent in the original Civil Rights Act of 1866. Above all, it demonstrated the congressional understanding that civil rights had been placed under protection of the federal government. Congressional debates centered on the policy and wisdom of such legislation, with little doubt as to constitutionality. Congress gave a broad construction to the clauses giving it power to enforce both amendments by "appropriate legislation." Its passage of the act showed its determination that the legislation was appropriate.

There was no immediate Supreme Court test of the act, and by the time the question reached the nation's highest tribunal in 1883 in the *Civil Rights Cases*,[2] the strong tide of equalitarianism that had led to its passage was ebbing away. The bargain of 1876 awarding the presidency to Rutherford Hayes had been cemented; the Court was well embarked on its course of restrictive interpretation of the Fourteenth Amendment and a critical textual review of Reconstruction legislation.

Bird Gee's original case had been joined by four others, one from San Francisco in which a Negro had been denied a seat in the dress circle at a theater; another from New York involving admission of a Negro to the Grand Opera house; one from Missouri respecting denial of hotel facilities to Negroes; and the last from Tennessee in which a Negro woman had been refused a seat in the "ladies car" of a train. All but the Tennessee case were criminal prosecutions.

The fact that three of the cases came from the West and North, another from a border state, and the fifth from the upper South was evidence both of the widespread character of racial discrimination and the failure of enforcement in the Deep South. Many Northerners, it appeared, would approve invalidation of the legislation. Significantly, none of the defendants in the criminal cases bothered to appear by counsel in the Supreme Court, indicating that all were fairly well convinced that the Court would take their side. The government was represented by the Solicitor General, while private counsel appeared only in the Tennessee railroad case, where both sides had conceded the validity of the act in the trial of the lawsuit.

The Solicitor General, in effect, rested the government's case on two supporting theories that, it was argued, gave Congress the power to legislate. The first contention was that Congress had power to enact the law under the Thirteenth Amendment. Slavery, that argument ran, was all-pervasive, and racial discriminations were incidents and badges of servitude. At bottom, this view rested on the proposition that all free men, as such, were possessed of all rights and privileges inherent in a state of freedom. The Thirteenth Amendment had conferred freedom on Negroes and vested Congress with power to enforce that article by appropriate legislation: the Civil Rights Act was appropriate to that end. Secondly, the government pointed to the Fourteenth Amendment with its command for due process and equal protection of the laws by the states. Congress, it was said, as the primary organ for the implementation of those rights had the duty and responsibility of choosing the methods by which those rights were to be vindicated where the states had failed to provide complete equality before the law.

Justice Joseph Bradley, chosen to write the opinion for the eight-to-one majority of the Court, had once seemed to entertain the views espoused by the government. In correspondence with Circuit Judge Woods, he had expressed the view that the Fourteenth Amendment "not only prohibits the making or enforcing of laws which shall abridge the privileges of the citizen; but prohibits the states from denying to all persons within its jurisdiction the equal protection of the laws." [3] He went on to say that "Denying includes inaction as well as the omission to pass laws, for protection of the laws includes the omission to protect as well as the omission to pass laws for protection." In the *Slaughter House Cases* in 1873, he had insisted that the Fourteenth Amendment "was an attempt to give voice to the strong national yearning for that time and that condition of things in which American citizenship would be a sure guaranty of safety, and in which every citizen of the United States might stand erect in every portion of its soil, in the full enjoyment of every right and privilege belonging to a free man. . . ."

The nub of Justice Bradley's majority opinion in the *Civil Rights Cases* was that the Thirteenth Amendment was not applicable and that the Fourteenth Amendment interdicted discriminatory action only by the states and not by private persons. Under those views, Congress had no constitutional warrant to enact the legislation under review. Therefore, he held squarely, Sections 1 and 2 of the act were unconstitutional and void.

Reflecting on slavery, Justice Bradley agreed that the institution had its inseparable incidents, such as compulsory labor, disability to make contracts or to sue or be sued, and "such like burdens and incapacities." But he said, with some poetic license, during slavery there were thousands of free Negroes who enjoyed all the essential rights of life, liberty, and prosperity the same as white citizens: "Yet no one, at that time, thought it was any invasion of his personal status as a freeman that he was not admitted to all the privileges enjoyed by white citizens, or because he was subjected to discrimination in the enjoyment of accommodations in inns, public conveyances or places of amusement."

It did not strike him that the argument that white citizens, *as white citizens,* enjoyed a higher range of rights than Negro freemen was both a tacit affirmation of the Taney "indelible marks" doctrine and grist for the mill of those who argued that freedom had no real meaning unless all free men possessed the same rights. In any event, he argued, the rights assured by the act were "social rights of men and races in the community," again emphasizing, without acknowledging, the Dred Scott formula that the Constitution, even as amended, recognized racial distinctions. He finally disposed of the whole matter summarily: "It would be running the slavery argument into the ground to make it apply to every act of discrimination which a person may see fit to make as to the guests he will entertain, or as to the people he will admit into his coach or cab or car, or admit to his concert or theatre, or deal with in other matters. . . ." He was unabashed by the fact that the act had no reference to "guests [a man] will entertain" or that coaches, cars, cabs, concerts, and theaters catered to the public.

Having satisfied himself that "Mere discrimination on account of race or color" was not a badge of slavery, Justice Bradley arrived at the conclusion that "If . . . the enjoyment of equal rights . . . has become established by constitutional enactment, it is not by force of the Thirteenth Amendment but by force of the Fourteenth and Fifteenth Amendments. . . ." He did agree that "Positive rights and privileges are undoubtedly secured by the Fourteenth Amendment . . ." but, he said, those rights and privileges "are secured by way of prohibition against state laws and state proceedings." Congress, therefore, could legislate only against state action. This, of course, was amplification of the rulings in the Cruikshank and Harris cases, and Justice Bradley put the holding plainly: "It is proper to state that civil rights such as are guaranteed by the Constitution against state aggression, cannot be impaired by the wrongful acts of individuals, unsupported by state authority in the shape of laws, customs, or judicial or executive proceedings. The wrongful act of an individual unsupported by any such state authority, is simply a private wrong, or a crime of that individual; an invasion of the rights of the injured party, it is true, whether they affect his person, his property or his reputation; but if not sanctioned in some way by the State, or not done under state authority, his rights remain in full force, and may presumably be vindicated by resort to the laws of the State for redress."

The last remark was pure fiction. If judges know as judges what they know as men, Justice Bradley and his colleagues of the majority knew full well that southern Negroes could not turn to their states for redress of their wrongs. What he was saying was that the disadvantaged Negro must fend for himself in the midst of an increasingly hostile social situation, in which the Court was giving the states power to regulate civil rights. He put the matter baldly, and somewhat brutally: "When a man has emerged from slavery, and by the aid of beneficent legislation has shaken off the inseparable concomitants of that state, there must be some stage in the progress of his elevation when he takes the rank of a mere citizen, and ceases to be the special favorite of the laws, and when his rights, as a citizen or a man, are to be protected in the ordinary modes by which other men's rights are protected." Justice Bradley could not foresee that, ninety years later, Congress would find it necessary to re-enact the very legislation that he had stricken down. Justices are sometimes as blind as justice.

Justice John Marshall Harlan began his lonely, and great, dissent with the melancholy lament that he could not "resist the conclusion that the substance and spirit of the recent Amendments of the Constitution have been sacrificed by a subtle and ingenious verbal criticism. . . . Constitutional provisions, adopted in the interest of liberty, and for the purpose of securing, through national legislation, if need be, rights inhering in a state of freedom, and belonging to American citizenship, have been so construed to defeat the ends the people desired to accomplish, which they attempted to accomplish, and which they supposed they had accomplished by changes in their fundamental law."

He noted that the Court had been able to imply congressional power to legislate for return of fugitive slaves when it was confronted with the fact that Congress was given no express power to do so, and contrasted the Court's zeal in that case with its refusal to admit the right of Congress to legislate in the interest of freedom when it was given that express power. The right of Congress to legislate, he said, "ought not now be abandoned when the inquiry is not as to an implied power to protect the master's rights, but what may Congress, under power expressly granted, do for the protection of freedom and rights necessarily inhering in a state of freedom."

Reviewing the Dred Scott case, Justice Harlan reminded his colleagues that Chief Justice Taney had laid great stress on the status of the Negro and his inferiority as a reason for his bondage and lack of rights. He pointed to general agreement that the Thirteenth Amendment "did something more than to prohibit slavery as an institution, resting upon distinctions of race and upheld by positive law. . . . Was nothing more intended than to forbid one man from owning another as property?" He thought much more was intended. "Was it the purpose," he asked, "simply to destroy the institution, and then remit the race, theretofore held in bondage, to the several States for such protection, in their civil rights . . . as those States, in their discretion might choose to provide? Were the States . . . to be left free, so far as national interference was concerned, to make or allow discriminations against that race, as such, in the enjoyment of those fundamental rights which by universal concession, inhere in a state of freedom?"

The answers to those questions were plain to him, and he added that, even if the Thirteenth Amendment had not included the clause giving Congress the power to enforce the article by appropriate legislation, it "would have had that power, by implication, according to *Prigg v. Commonwealth. . . .*" The argument was a telling one. He added that he did not intend to say that the Thirteenth Amendment gave Congress complete authority to define and regulate the entire body of civil rights, but he did "hold that since slavery . . . was the moving or principal cause of the adoption of that amendment and since that institution rested wholly upon the inferiority, as a race, of those held in bondage, their freedom necessarily involved immunity from, and protection against, all discrimination against them, because of their race, in respect of such civil rights as belong to freemen of other races."

Congress, Justice Harlan asserted, had power under the Thirteenth Amendment to remove "burdens which lay at the very foundation of the institution of slavery as it once existed." These burdens were the targets of the Civil Rights Act and, unless they were removed, "a freeman is not only branded as one inferior and infected, but . . . robbed of some of the most essential means of existence; and all this solely because they belong to a particular race which the nation has liberated." That conclusion was strengthened for him because, it was apparent, Congress had sought to interdict discrimination by "such individuals and corporations as exercise public functions and wield authority under the state." He included in that classification corporations and persons operating public conveyances, inns, and places of public accommodation catering to the public: "The colored race is part of that public. The local government granting the license [to public places] represents them as well as all other races within its jurisdiction."

Justice Harlan was equally certain that the Civil Rights Act was justified under the Fourteenth Amendment, which "presents the first instance in our history of the investiture of Congress with an affirmative power, by legislation, to enforce an express prohibition upon the states." The power to enforce the amendment, he stressed, was given to Congress, not the judiciary: "It is not said that the judicial power of the Nation may be exerted for the enforcement of that Amendment. No enlargement of the judicial power was required." For it was clear to him that if the amendment had not conferred power on Congress to legislate, "the judiciary could have stricken down all state laws and nullified all state proceedings in hostility to rights and privileges secured or recognized by that Amendment."

He went on to emphasize the fact that the amendment created a new national right, that of "exemption from discrimination, in respect of civil rights," and reminded the majority that "It has been the established doctrine of this court during all its history, accepted as essential to the national supremacy, that Congress, in the absence of a positive delegation of power to the State Legislatures, may, by its own legislation, enforce and protect any right derived from or created by the National Constitution." Under that doctrine, it was plain that the Fourteenth Amendment *did* permit Congress to enact legislation controlling individual, as well as state, action in the sphere of civil rights.

In any event, Justice Harlan said, it was for "Congress, not the judiciary, to say what legislation, is appropriate; that is, best adapted to the end to be attained." Justice Harlan was correct, unless, as he aptly phrased it, "the recent amendments be splendid baubles, thrown out to delude those who deserved fair and generous treatment at the hands of the nation." [4] He had an oblique answer to those who would remit the Negro to the states for redress of their grievances: "It was perfectly well known that the great danger to the equal enjoyment by citizens of their rights as citizens, was to be apprehended not altogether from unfriendly state legislation, but from the hostile action of corporations and individuals," and for this reason the amendment had clothed "Congress with power and authority to meet that danger."

Alone among the members of the Court, Justice Harlan foresaw what the future held for the nation in event of the invalidation of the Civil Rights Act. He caught a vision of the color-caste system that was bound to arise and warned that "If the constitutional amendments be enforced, according to the intent with which, as I perceive, they were adopted, there cannot be, in this republic, any class of human beings in practical subjection to another class, with power in the latter to dole out to the former just such privileges as they may choose to grant."

The dissent closed on a gloomy note: "I may be permitted to say that if the recent Amendments are so construed that Congress may not, in its own discretion, and independently of the action or non-action of the States, provide by legislation of a direct character for the security of rights created by the National Constitution; if it be adjudged that the obligation to protect and fundamental privileges and immunities granted by the 14th Amendment to citizens . . . rests primarily, not on the Nation, but on the States . . . we shall enter upon an era of constitutional law, when the rights of freedom and American citizenship cannot receive from the Nation that efficient protection which heretofore was unhesitatingly accorded to slavery and the rights of the master."

Justice Harlan had riddled the logic and the pretexts of the majority, but he had not disturbed the arithmetic of the Supreme

Court vote. The first two sections of the Civil Rights Act of 1875 were still invalid by a vote of eight to one.

The fact that the Supreme Court of 1883 found the public accommodations sections of the 1875 Civil Rights Act invalid, while the Court of 1964 declared almost identical sections of the 1964 Civil Rights Act constitutional deserves an anticipatory word of explanation here. In the first place, the truth is that time has vindicated Justice Harlan. The Fourteenth Amendment did empower Congress to enact public accommodations legislation. However, the 1964 Congress relieved the Supreme Court of the burden of having to reverse its predecessors of 1883 by placing Congess's power to enact public accommodations sections on the congressional right to regulate interstate commerce, as given by the original Constitution. Congress did not resort to its power to regulate interstate commerce in the 1875 Act, because neither proponents nor opponents doubted its right to act under the War Amendments. When the Supreme Court entertained such doubts, it should have looked to the commerce clause on its own motion, because the power to declare a congressional act invalid is one that should never be exercised unless there is no possible alternative. The duty is on the Court to *save*, not destroy, the congressional will. The unavoidable truth is that the Court's decision rested on a view that the Civil Rights Act of 1875 was unwise.

It may seem at first blush that an inordinate amount of time and space has been given to invalidation of a rather simple law that, after all, only prohibited discrimination against Negroes in places of public accommodation. But there was more to it than that, much more. The Court had sapped the Thirteenth Amendment of all vitality, except to abolish slavery and enforce servitudes; it had narrowed the scope of the Fourteenth Amendment to make it operative only against discriminatory practices sanctioned by the states through legislative, judicial, or executive action. It had decided that individuals or corporations were free to practice racial discrimination at their own whim, even when engaged in operating places of public accommodation, so long as they did not call upon the states for assistance. Without acknowledging that it was doing so, the Court had taken a long step backward, with an implicit holding that the amended Constitution tolerated, and protected, racial distinctions between citizens, by ruling that Congress lacked power to interdict racial discrimination in the use of facilities catering to the public.

In effect, the Court had decided that there was a white public, and a Negro public of which the Constitution took cognizance; the supreme law validated the conduct of an individual who chose to discriminate against a freeman and a citizen who was a member of the Negro public. Caste lines could be drawn; the Supreme Court would recognize them in law. There was a privileged class—of whites—born into perfect freedom, with power to dole out to Negroes "just such privileges as they may choose to grant." Congress could not curb, but the Court would protect, the arrogance of that privileged class.[5] Most important of all, the decision meant that the Court had arrogated to itself the power to determine what was, or was not, "appropriate legislation" to effectuate the purposes of the War Amendments. Congress must defer to its judgments.

The purposes of the amendments had been reduced to a very narrow compass. The *Civil Rights Cases* approved the doctrine of the *Slaughter House Cases* that there were two categories of citizens: national and state; that national citizenship rights were very limited; that civil rights were under the protection of the states, and that Congress could not vindicate such rights under the privileges-and-immunities clause of the Fourteenth Amendment. The Court had now made explicit that Congress could not protect civil rights against individual infringement under the due-process and equal-protection-of-the-law clauses of the amendment; it could intervene only if a state denied, or sanctioned denial of, a civil right. The states were as firmly in control of civil rights as they had been prior to the Civil War. A Negro seeking protection in the area of civil rights would have to "resort to the laws of the State for redress."

There were certain limitations as far as civil rights were concerned, and Justice Bradley took some pains to point them out. There were no constitutional protections for discriminatory private conduct; the states were perfectly free to interdict racial discrimination if they chose to do so; they could enact and enforce public accommodations statutes; no bounds were set on state authority to pass equalitarian legislation. Moreover, individual discrimination must be "unsupported by state authority in the shape of laws, customs, or judicial or executive proceedings" in order to escape constitutional interdiction. Such discrimination must not be "sanc-

tioned in some way by the State, or done under state authority."
There was more in the same tenor; a later Court found nineteen
instances in which Justice Bradley insisted that the private person
must not call upon the state for aid or assistance in pursuing discriminatory purposes.[6] He was insistent that all discrimination by
state law or state officials under color of state authority, even in
violation of state laws, offended the Fourteenth Amendment. These
very important exceptions had consequences of their own; they increased a Negro's dependence on the Supreme Court for the exercise of ordinary rights and privileges.

If it was true, as the Court said, that the Fourteenth Amendment
forbade discriminatory conduct only when such conduct was the
product of "state action" through legislative, executive, or judicial
proceedings, the Court must define state action within a dozen-and-
one different contexts. Was state action present when a state court
enforced a private contract against sale of property to Negroes?
Was there state action when a political party closed its rolls to Negroes? Did the state act when it gave public funds to a library and
that library excluded Negroes? If a state subsidized a housing project and that project excluded Negroes, what was the extent of state
action? Negroes could get the answers to these and a half-hundred
kindred questions only through long and expensive litigation. Only
the Supreme Court, the Negro's guardian, could give definitive answers.

What was the scope of congressional power to legislate for enforcement of the Civil War Amendments? Could Congress make it
a crime for a sheriff to beat a Negro prisoner to death? Could Congress enact an antilynching law? Or an antipoll tax statute? Or a
fair employment law? Only the Supreme Court had the final answers; Congress could only surmise, no matter if the amendments
did give it enforcement power through a right to enact appropriate
legislation. Again, the Negro suppliant would have to ask his guardian justices.

During the course of the *Civil Rights Cases* decision, Justice
Bradley had referred to the use of public accommodations as a "social right." What was a "social right," as distinguished from a political or a civil right? The Supreme Court would have to offer a definition, but Supreme Court definitions are given only in actual cases
and controversies, and the Negro ward would have to file a suit and
wait until the Guardian Court answered the intricate inquiry.

In actual practice, the answers to many of what seemed to be pressing problems were delayed for decades, simply because disadvantaged Negroes lacked funds and skill to pursue their constitutional inquiries. In many instances, the Court vindicated a claimed right that had been denied for years to the tune of great rejoicing, but that vindication was small comfort to those who had suffered the long denial. A right denied today is forever lost.

The sophisticated problems of constitutional interpretation raised by the decision in the *Civil Rights Cases* were only dimly perceived at the time. Their solution lay in the future; the immediate consequence was that racial discrimination increased by leaps and bounds. Americans tend to regard as moral and permissible that which is said to be constitutional. Private persons and corporations—north, east, south and west—drew increasingly rigid color lines in the exercise of what they came to regard as their constitutionally protected right to discriminate at will. State protection of civil rights dwindled even in the North; it became nonexistent in the South. The Supreme Court held fast to only one creed of the War Amendments. It consistently struck down persistent attempts of the states to enact or enforce discriminatory legislation.

Justice Bradley spoke about the "beneficent legislation" which, he said, protected Negroes, while Justice Field asserted in the jury cases that "the ballot being assured them," Negroes had an "effectual weapon against unjust legislation." As justices of the Supreme Court, both had sat, and would sit, on cases involving the Fifteenth Amendment and the legislation enacted under it. It was true that the right to the ballot was an effectual weapon in the hands of Negroes—if that right was effectively protected. It is time to inquire into the effectiveness of federal protection of the right to vote without restraint as to race or color.

◄{ 10 }► *The Law Is Good*

*But we know that the law is
good, if a man use it lawfully.*

I TIMOTHY 1:8

Queried as to the purpose and effect of the Fifteenth Amendment,
the average college student would answer quickly that it was intended to and did give Negroes the right to vote. That common-
sense answer would merit a low grade from the Supreme Court of
the United States.

"The Fifteenth Amendment," the Court said early and has reiterated many times, "does not confer the right of suffrage upon anyone. It prevents the States, or the United States, however, from
giving preference, in this particular, to one citizen of the United
States over another on account of race, color or previous condition
of servitude. Before its adoption this could have been done. It was
as much within the power of a State to exclude citizens on account
of race as it was on account of age, property or education." [1] The
wording of the amendment seems to lend some weight to this judicial formulation. It provides: "The right of citizens of the United
States to vote shall not be denied or abridged by the United States
or any State on account of race, color or previous condition of servitude."

The words are not as limiting as they appear, when constitutional
style is borne in mind and when the circumstances that led to the
enactment and ratification of the amendment are examined. A constitutional negative often evokes an affirmative right, as Justice William Strong pointed out when he construed Fourteenth-Amendment language prohibiting any state from denying due process or

equal protection of the law. "The words of the Amendment, it is true, are prohibitory," he observed, "but they contain a necessary implication of a positive immunity, or right, most valuable to the colored race. . . ." [2] The same observation may be made of the prohibitory words of the Fifteenth Amendment; they imply a positive immunity, or right: that of Negroes to vote on the same footing with other Americans. In that sense, the college student's answer that the Fifteenth Amendment confers the right of suffrage on the Negro is correct; the Supreme Court's all-too-technical restriction of that meaning has led to all sorts of difficulties for Negroes in their long struggle to cast their ballots. Like the Thirteenth and Fourteenth Amendments, the Fifteenth ended with a clause giving Congress the "power to enforce this article by appropriate legislation." It was ratified on March 30, 1870, and Congress promptly legislated in 1870 and in 1871, while the purposes of the amendment were fresh in the minds of many of the very men who had proposed it.

Constitutional amendments are not proposed and ratified or laws enacted in a social vacuum. They are aimed to cure specific ills or achieve particular goals. Courts agree that they should be interpreted in light of what they are intended to accomplish. Congress had originally sought to persuade, or coerce, the states into abandoning all restrictions on the Negro's right to vote through the second section of the Fourteenth Amendment, providing that state representation in Congress should be reduced in direct proportion to denial of the right to vote except for participation in rebellion or commission of a crime. If a state denied Negroes the right to vote, it would lose seats in Congress. Two years later, Congress decided to tackle the problem directly and proposed the Fifteenth Amendment. Prior to its ratification, as Justice Ward Hunt put it: "A higher privilege was yet untouched; a security, vastly greater than any thus far given to the colored race was not provided for, but on the contrary, its exclusion was permitted. This was the elective franchise—the right to vote at the elections of the country, and for officers by whom the country should be governed." [3] The states acquiesced in the congressional judgment and ratified the amendment.

When the Fifteenth Amendment was proposed and ratified, Congress and the ratifying states were deeply disturbed at rising efforts in the South to keep Negroes from voting by terror, open intimida-

tion, and violent assaults on them, and by the conduct of state election officials who refused to receive and count the votes of Negroes
through various evasive practices. The Ku Klux Klan was active, so
much so that the Enforcement Act of 1871 was known as the Klan
Act.

The immediate threat to the exercise of the franchise by Negroes
did not lie in state laws restricting the Negro's exercise of the right
to vote but in wholesale lawlessness intended to keep him from the
polls, in bribery and intimidation that would corrupt his vote, and
in the obstructive conduct of election officials. Congress wanted
constitutional power to meet these evils. As soon as the amendment
was approved, it enacted a series of measures aimed at penalizing
election officials and other individuals who interfered with the right
bestowed by the amendment. The passage of that legislation is eloquent evidence of the congressional understanding that the power
to enact "appropriate legislation" as provided in the amendment
included the power to proscribe individual lawless conduct and to
regulate and control all other interference with the Negro's right to
vote in elections for local, state, and federal officials, and that it was
not limited to legislation forbidding *state* interference with that
right.

The first Supreme Court case involving the Fifteenth Amendment, decided in 1873, was *United States v. Reese*.[4] The defendants were indicted under the first four sections of the Enforcement
Act of 1870, which was entitled "An Act To Enforce the Right of
Citizens of the United States To Vote." Section 1 stated that the
right to vote should not be abridged on account of race or color;
Section 2 required that equal opportunity to vote should be accorded to all races and provided for a levy of civil damages or
criminal penalties on officials who violated the provision; Section 3
imposed penalties and provided that where a citizen had been prevented from complying with election procedures "for the reasons as
aforesaid," he should be entitled to vote on showing that he had
tried to comply; Section 4 provided for the punishment of any person who by force, bribery, threats, intimidation, or other unlawful
means "for the reasons aforesaid" hindered or delayed a citizen's
attempt to vote. The final issue for Supreme Court resolution was
the validity of Sections 3 and 4 of the act.

William Garner, a Negro, wanted to vote in an election in Lexington, Kentucky, and offered to pay the capitation tax required for

that privilege. His offer to pay was refused. When election time rolled around, he went to the polls and filed his affidavit showing his offer to pay the required tax. Election officials who refused to let him vote were indicted. Mr. Garner's case was disposed of by the Supreme Court on a higgling interpretation of the language of the third and fourth sections, an action that drew a withering blast of dissent from Justice Hunt for what he regarded as a pettifogging evasion of the real issue.[5] Obscurity of language in the majority opinion written by Chief Justice Morrison Waite led the official court reporter to note that the Court had simply decided that "Congress has not as yet provided by 'appropriate legislation' for the punishment of said offense." In later decisions, however, the Court insisted that it had found the two sections unconstitutional.

The fundamental issue, elaborately briefed and argued, was the scope of the Fifteenth Amendment, that is, the extent to which Congress was empowered to legislate under the amendment. The government argued that Congress had entire power to regulate and control *all* interference with the right of a citizen to vote, whether for local, state, or federal officials. That was the view taken by Congress.

Chief Justice Waite disagreed. He began by announcing the doctrine that the Fifteenth Amendment did not confer the right of suffrage on anyone. He conceded that "the Amendment has invested the citizens of the United States with a new constitutional right which is within the protecting care of Congress. That is exemption from discrimination in the exercise of the elective franchise on account of race, color or previous condition of servitude." Therefore, he said in effect, Congress was limited to passage of legislation protecting the citizen "from discrimination in the exercise of the election franchise" by the states. It could not regulate or control *all* interference with a citizen's right to vote. The third and fourth sections of the Enforcement Act were disapproved, because the Court held that Congress went too far and penalized *all* interference with Mr. Garner's right to vote in the Kentucky election.

The point made by the Chief Justice is a fine one but very important in practical application. As a Negro spokesman later complained, it meant that a Negro must show "that the *state* had abridged or denied his right to vote, or that persons who had prevented him from voting had done so because of his *race, color, or previous condition of servitude*. So unable to prove that the com-

mittee which had met him at the polls with shotguns was actuated
by any such base and unconstitutional motives, he found his case
thrown out." [6]

Justice Hunt dissented from that narrow and restrictive interpretation of the amendment and the rigid restraints it laid on Congress. He was certain that Congress did have the power to regulate
and control *all* interference with the Negro's right to vote in all
elections. That power existed because the Negro was a citizen and,
as he pointed out, the right protected by the amendment "is in
behalf of a particular class of persons; to wit, citizens of the United
States. The limitation is to the persons concerned, and not to the
class of cases in which the question shall arise. The right of a citizen
of the United States to vote, and *not the right to vote at an election
for United States officers*, is the subject of the provision. The person
protected must be a citizen of the United States and whenever a
right to vote exists in such person, the case is within the amendment. This is the literal and grammatical construction of the language."

It is hard to dispute the logic of Justice Hunt's pronouncement
and he pursued it to its relevant conclusion: "I hold therefore that
the Fifteenth Amendment embraces the case of elections held for
state, or municipal as well as federal officers. . . ." He reviewed
the history that lay back of the amendment and the reason Congress had decided to legislate on behalf of Negroes. "The existence
of a large colored population in the Southern States, lately slaves
and necessarily ignorant was a disturbing element. . . . It confronted us always and everywhere," he wrote. "Congress determined to meet the emergency by creating a political equality. . . ."
As he saw it, the Fifteenth Amendment not only created that
equality but gave Congress the power to determine what was appropriate legislation: "In adopting the Fifteenth Amendment it was
ordained 'The Congress shall have power to enforce this article by
appropriate legislation.' This was done to remove doubts, if any
existed" as to congressional power to determine what was needed
in the circumstances.

Armed with the power to protect *citizens* in their right to vote on
a plane of equality, Justice Hunt argued, Congress had the power
to protect the voting rights of citizens who happened to be Negroes. "If Congress, being authorized to do so, desires to protect the
freedmen in his rights as a citizen and a voter, and against those

who may be prejudiced and unscrupulous in their hostility to him and his newly conferred rights, its manifest course would be to enact that they should possess that right . . . and [provide] for punishment of those who interfere with that right," he explained.

It was apparent to him that Congress had entire power to legislate concerning all interference with a Negro citizen's right to vote and that it was not limited to the narrow case where official conduct interfered with the right to vote on account of race or color. He reminded the Court that in the case of fugitive slaves, "Congress from time to time passed laws providing not only the means of restoring the escaped slave to his master, but inflicting punishment upon those who violated the master's right." The Supreme Court had approved those laws.[7] Justice Hunt also called attention to the fact that "The clause protecting the freedman, like that sustaining the right of the slaveholder, is found in the Federal Constitution only." Congress, therefore, was armed with enforcement "authority, through fines and imprisonment, in the Federal courts and here, as there, the national govennment is bound, through its own departments, to carry into effect all the rights and duties imposed by the Constitution."

Justice Hunt was not troubled by the issue of *state* action in the Reese case, because the election officials were state agents and "When the Constitution speaks of a State and prescribes what it may or what it may not do, it includes, in some cases, the agencies and instrumentalities by which the State acts." He rejected the argument that the Negro complainant should be left to pursue civil remedies under other sections of the act. "The arrest, conviction and sentence to imprisonment of one inspector, who refused to count the vote of a person of African descent on account of his race would more effectively secure the rights of the voter than would any number of civil suits," he said. He feared that if there was no "protection to the ignorant freedman against any hostile legislation and personal prejudice other than a tedious, expensive and uncertain course of litigation . . . he has practically no remedy."

Unhappily for Negroes and fortunately for the defendants, Justice Hunt's correct exposition of the law was only a dissenting opinion. The defendants were neither fined nor imprisoned.

Nobody knows whether Mr. Garner's vote would have made any difference in the election results in Lexington, but his attempt to cast his ballot resulted in a landmark decision, as important in the developing history of the Fifteenth Amendment as the Slaughter House, Cruikshank, and Civil Rights cases were in respect of the Fourteenth Amendment. For it foreshadowed restrictive decisions that would wind up with the southern Negro virtually barred from the polling places in his states for more than half a century.

The case of *United States v. Cruikshank,* decided at the same time as the Reese case, has been previously considered because its prime importance lay in questions resolved under the Fourteenth Amendment.[8] The Court held in that aspect of the case that there were two categories of citizenship, state and national, and that the privileges-and-immunities clause of the amendment protected only national citizenship rights. It also held that the due-process and equal-protection-of-the-law clauses were restrictions on state, and not on individual, action. But the case also concerned the Fifteenth Amendment, because one count of the indictment charged interference with the right to vote. The Court then repeated the Reese case formula that the "right of suffrage is not a necessary attribute of national citizenship but exemption from prohibited discrimination comes from the United States." It went on to say that the conviction could not be upheld, because there was no charge in the indictment that it was the intent of the defendants to prevent Negroes from exercising the right to vote *because* of their race. The fact is that the section involved was largely aimed at individual interference with the Negro's right to vote, and the Court's decision crippled efforts to make the Fifteenth Amendment meaningful.

Congress tried to bolster the supposed weakness of the sections of the Enforcement Act of 1870 involved in the Cruikshank case by changes and modifications in the Enforcement Act of 1871, the so-called Klan Act. The Klan had embarked on a wholesale campaign of intimidation and violence in an effort to prevent Negroes from exercising citizenship rights claimed under both the Fourteenth and Fifteenth Amendments. A very definite aspect of that campaign was to make Negroes afraid to go to the polls. The sixth section of the act made it a crime to conspire "for the purpose of depriving . . . any person or class of persons of the equal protection of the laws, or equal privileges under the laws." That section was held invalid in *United States v. Harris,* decided in 1883, as not warranted by either the Thirteenth, Fourteenth, or Fifteenth Amendments.[9] The decision said that only states, and never individuals, could deny equal protection of the laws. Justice Harlan, as we have seen, dissented without a written opinion in the Harris case, but in a later case involving violence against Chinese he explained his disagreement with the Cruikshank and Harris decisions that there was no denial of equal protection of the laws when lawless individuals prevented a Negro from exercising constitutional rights.[10]

"It seems to me," said Justice Harlan, "that the main purpose of giving power to Congress to enforce, by *legislation,* the provisions of the [Fourteenth] Amendment was that the rights therein guarded or guaranteed might be guarded or protected against lawless combinations of individuals, acting without the sanction of the state. The denial of equal protection of the laws to persons within its jurisdiction may arise as well from the failure or inability of the state authority to give that protection, as from unfriendly enactments." He did not say so but that was the viewpoint of the framers of the amendment.

"If Congress, upon looking over the whole ground, determined that an effectual and appropriate mode to secure such protection was to proceed directly against combinations of individuals who sought, by conspiracy or violent means, to defeat the enjoyment of rights given by the Constitution, I do not see upon what grounds the courts can question the validity of legislation to that end," he remonstrated to no avail. In retrospect, it is apparent that if Congress lacked power to suppress the mob violence of the Klan directed against all exercise of constitutional rights, it could not effectively safeguard the Negro's right of franchise. Terrorized and frightened Negroes were made as fearful of trying to vote as of holding meetings or protesting other injustices.

Having put down congressional attempts to protect Negroes against individual wrongdoing in elections for state and local officers, the Court was left with the question of what Congress could do in the case where there was individual interference with the right to vote for federal officials. That issue reached it in 1883, in the case of *ex parte Yarborough*.[11] Jasper Yarborough, his brothers, and a group of friends gave Barry Sanders, a Negro, a good whipping for his temerity in trying to vote in an election for a congressman. They were indicted for violation of two sections of the Enforcement Act of 1871 which forbade a conspiracy to "injure, oppress, threaten, or intimidate any citizen in the free exercise of any right or privilege secured to him by the Constitution or laws of the

United States" and penalized conspiracies to prevent a citizen from "giving his support or advocacy . . . toward or in favor of the election . . . of a person . . . as a Member of Congress." Mr. Yarborough and his friends promptly claimed that the sections were unconstitutional. They were rebuffed by the Court, speaking by Justice Miller.

"Can it be doubted," asked Justice Miller, "that Congress can by law protect the act of voting, the place where it is done, and the man who votes, from personal violence or intimidation and the election itself from corruption and fraud?" He was sure Congress had that right as far as election of members of Congress was concerned, in light of the provision in the original Constitution that Congress had power to "make or alter" state legislation prescribing the times, places, and manner of holding elections for Congress. He was equally certain that the Fifteenth Amendment "by its limitation on the power of the States . . . to prescribe qualifications of voters in their own elections . . . clearly shows that the right of suffrage was considered to be of supreme importance to the national government, and was not intended to be left within the exclusive control of the States." He went far enough to say that while in the ordinary case it was true that the amendment did not confer the right of suffrage on anyone, as said in the Reese case, it was "easy to see that under some circumstances it may operate as the immediate source of a right to vote." That was the situation where, for example, the amendment struck down white voting provisions of state laws, and in such cases "the [Fifteenth Amendment] does . . . substantially confer on the Negro the right to vote, and Congress has the power to protect and enforce that right" in federal elections. Jasper Yarborough and his friends were sent back to jail.

The elaborate structure of Supreme Court decisions meant that in the realm of voting a state couldn't pass a law, or interpret or administer its laws, to prevent a Negro, as such, from voting for local or state officials; that if it desired to do so, Congress could pass laws regulating elections in which federal officers were chosen, and that only the states could penalize mob violence which might result in frightening or preventing a Negro from voting, unless the mob went on a rampage to deprive a Negro of a right directly guaranteed by the federal Constitution or laws. In short, the states were back in the saddle as far as the franchise went, except for their inability to draw a color line. The Supreme Court had substituted its judgment for that of Congress as to the scope of the Fifteenth Amendment and the power of Congress to enforce the amendment by appropriate legislation.

The single most crippling Supreme Court ruling in the whole series of cases respecting the Fifteenth Amendment was that the amendment did not empower Congress to legislate against individual wrongdoing in interference with voting rights in state and local elections. It had jumped to that conclusion very early in its consideration of the issue and finally made its implicit rule very explicit in *James v. Bowman.*[12] In that case Justice David Brewer held that the "amendment relates solely to action by the 'United States or by any State' and does not contemplate wrongful individual action." He explained that "It is in these respects similar to [the due-process and equal-protection] clauses in the Fourteenth Amendment." The analogy was a false one, entirely lacking in substance.

Even if it is assumed that the Court was completely correct in its decisions that the Fourteenth Amendment did not vest Congress with the power to punish an "individual invasion of an individual right," it does not follow that Congress lacked such power under the Fifteenth Amendment. Justice Miller had noted in the Yarborough case that, "while it may be true that acts which are mere invasions of private rights, which acts have no sanction in the statutes of a state, are not within the scope of the Fourteenth Amendment, it is quite a different matter when Congress undertakes to protect the citizen in the exercise of rights conferred by the Constitution of the United States essential to the healthy organization of the government itself."

The rights asserted by Negroes under the Fourteenth Amendment existed prior to its adoption, and the question before the Court was whether they had been assigned to protection of the federal government or remained under state control. The Court held that such rights were still under control of the states, where they had always resided. On the other hand, the right to equality in the exercise of the franchise stemmed directly from the Fifteenth Amendment. The national government had created that right; its protection surely lay with its creator. The correct view was, and is, that Congress had power to proscribe and punish all interference with that federally created right in all elections and whether by individuals, state officials, or states.[13] The Court's contrary holding was simply a judicial accommodation to the rising clamor against centralization of power in the federal government, and in consummation of the Compromise of 1876, returning power to the southern states to deal with the so-called Negro question as they saw fit.

The absurd lengths to which holding that the Fifteenth Amendment related solely to state action drove the Court is well illustrated by the facts in *James v. Bowman*.[14] Bowman and others were indicted for a violation of what had been Section 5 of the Enforcement Act of 1871, which set punishment for persons who hindered, controlled, or intimidated another from "exercising the right of suffrage, to whom that right is guaranteed by the Fifteenth Amendment" by bribery, economic pressures, or other means. Bowman was charged with bribery in an election in which a congressman and state officers were chosen. Congress, Justice Brewer said for the seven-to-two majority, had no power to enact such a law inhibiting individual conduct, because the law did not strike at *state* action alone. Justices William Day and Harlan dissented without opinion.

Withdrawal of federal troops from the South, atrophy of the congressional will to act, Supreme Court decisions sapping the vitality of equalitarian legislation enacted by Congress, and indifference, or worse, of federal prosecutors—all attendant on the settlement of the Hayes-Tilden election—combined to leave Negro voters defenseless in the southern states. They fell prey to the determined violence and intimidation of the Ku Klux Klan, and by the 1880's whites were in control of the legislative and constitution-making power in those states. White supremacy had been re-established.

Violence had served its purpose, and the time had come for more genteel methods of disfranchising Negroes.[15] One after another, the southern states passed laws or amended their constitutions to proscribe Negro voting. As William Jennings Bryan, titular head of the Democratic party and its three-time presidential nominee, put it in a speech at Cooper Union in New York in 1908: "The white man in the South has disfranchised the Negro in self-protection, and there is not a white man in the North who would not have done the same thing under the same circumstances. The white men of the South are determined that the Negro will and shall be disfranchised. . . ."[16] The problem was how to make that disfranchisement constitutionally palatable.

Mississippi led the way in 1890, with a constitution that, by the confession of its own supreme court, "swept the circle of expedients to obstruct the franchise by the Negro race. . . ." [17] Among the most widely used of those expedients were the imposition of onerous registration statutes easily interpreted to apply only to Negroes, poll tax payments, stiff educational requirements again easily waived for white voters, disfranchisement for criminal offenses believed to comprehend a disproportionate number of Negroes, and the setting of arbitrary dates for registration with provisos that all who were on the rolls prior to the date would remain qualified while those who sought to register afterward were required to pass very difficult tests. Whites were then enrolled prior to the critical date, while Negroes were made to wait until they had to take tests under which few whites or Negroes could qualify.

A test of some of these practices got to the Supreme Court in an oblique manner in *Williams v. Mississippi*[18] in 1890. Mississippi law required a juror to be a voter, and as a consequence the disfranchisement laws disqualified Negroes as jurors. Williams, a Negro, complained that he was indicted and tried by all-white juries, resulting from both direct operation of the constitutional provisions and the manner in which they were administered. The Supreme Court, speaking through Justice Joseph McKenna, made short shrift of his complaint. Justice McKenna took due note of what the Mississippi Supreme Court had said about the state's "sweeping the circle of expedients" to bar Negroes from the ballot but held that the state constitution and codes "do not, on their face, discriminate between the white and Negro races, and do not amount to a denial of equal protection of the law, secured by the Fourteenth Amendment . . . and it has not been shown that their actual administration was evil but only that evil was possible under them."

Only a bold and imaginative Court, determined to curb racial injustice—the like of which the nation would not see for another sixty years—could have, or at least would have, cut through the procedural difficulties to tackle the voting problem laid bare in *Williams v. Mississippi*, but the issue cropped up directly in *Giles v. Harris*[19] in 1903. Encouraged by Mississippi's example and emboldened by its success, Alabama amended its constitution in 1901 for the openly proclaimed purpose of disfranchising Negro voters. Some new expedients were dredged up. Veterans of all wars and their descendants, including those who had served the Confederacy, were made eligible to vote. A deadline was set, and all voters registered prior to that time were permanently enfranchised. Those who registered after that date were required to pass difficult tests. Whites were registered prior to the date, while registration of Negroes was stalled. The Democratic party told white voters that "under the operation of the registration feature of the new Constitution no white man who can now vote will be disfranchised." It also promised that "The registration will be conducted by three reputable and suitable persons in each county, appointed by three Democratic State officials. When the party's pledge not to disfranchise any white man is remembered, it is easy to see that the above plan will effectuate it." There was more in the same vein; everybody in the country knew what Alabama was up to.

William Giles, a Negro who had been voting for twenty years, filed a suit in federal court, in which he charged that his native state had hatched a plot to disfranchise Negroes in plain violation of the Fifteenth Amendment. He detailed the various evasive devices, explained how they worked to discriminate against qualified Negroes while they permitted any white person to register, and asked the court to order his registration and that of five thousand other Negroes in whose behalf he said he sued. The federal Circuit Court passed the issue along to the Supreme Court. The Court couldn't say that *state* action was absent, nor could it hide behind the claim that there was no allegation that the scheme was not a direct attempt to deprive Negroes of the vote on "account of race, color or previous condition of servitude." Nevertheless, it evaded a direct ruling by a six-to-three vote.

Justice Oliver Wendell Holmes, lately come to the Court and a New England Brahmin who had served the Union in the Civil War, spoke for the majority in the chilly and detached, almost cynical, manner that would be his trademark whenever civil rights were considered during his long service on the Court. He found two difficulties "which we cannot overcome." The first, he said, "is this: The plaintiff alleges that the whole registration scheme is a fraud upon the Constitution . . . and asks us to declare it void. But of course he could not maintain a bill for a mere declaration in the air. He does not try to do this but asks us to be registered as a party under the void instrument. If then we accept the conclusion which it is the chief purpose of the bill to maintain, how can we make the court a party to the unlawful scheme by accepting it and adding another voter to its fraudulent list?" The plaintiff had a ready answer to that question: If all Negroes were ordered registered by the Court on a parity with white persons, the attempted fraud would be cured. Justice Holmes was not swayed by that common-sense plea.

"It is not an answer to say that if all the blacks who are qualified according to the letter of the instrument were registered, the fraud would be cured," he replied in formal legal language. "In the first place there is no probability that any way is now open by which more than a few could be registered, but if all could be the difficulty would not be overcome. If the sections of the constitution concerning registration were illegal in their inception, it would be a new doctrine in constitutional law that the original invalidity could be cured by an administration which defeated their intent." Successful fraud would bring its own reward, he had said. He gilded the lily by offering the second reason why the Court was powerless to act.

"The other difficulty," said Justice Holmes, "is of a different sort and strikingly reenforces the argument that equity cannot . . . enforce political rights. . . . One of the first questions is what it can do to enforce any order it may make. The bill imports that the great mass of white population intends to keep the blacks from voting. . . . If the conspiracy and the intent exists, a name on a piece of paper will not defeat them. Unless we are prepared to supervise voting in that State by officers of the Court it seems to us that all plaintiffs would get from equity would be an empty form. . . . Relief from a great political wrong . . . by the people of a State and the State itself must be given by them or by the legislative and political department of the government of the United States." A state, he had said, could paralyze the federal courts if it could muster majority opposition to a "political" right cemented into the Constitution and guaranteed against state impairment.

The invitation to a resort to the "legislative and political departments" of the federal government for redress of the wrong was an astounding, almost shocking, pronouncement for a Court that had consistently and persistently nullified federal laws and hamstrung Congress and the executive when they had sought to do the very thing he now proposed. Justices Henry B. Brown, Brewer and, of course, Harlan dissented on the ground that the courts did have power to act.

In the course of his opinion, Justice Holmes tendered the hint

that Mr. Giles might find some relief in a suit for damages if he
could sustain his claims, and the complainant trudged back to the
Alabama courts, where he sued the offending voting registrars for
damages and asked the courts to put him and those for whom he
sued on the voting lists. The Alabama courts threw his suit out and
justified its action on state law. In due course, Mr. Giles asked the
Supreme Court in 1904 to undo the Alabama decision that was an
ingenious paraphrase of the first "difficulty" found by Justice
Holmes in the original suit.[20] Alabama courts were quite within
their rights as to the damage aspects of the suit, Justice Day said, in
their determination that "conceding the allegations of the petition
to be true, and the registrars to have been appointed and qualified
under a constitution which had for its purpose to prevent Negroes
from voting and to exclude them from registration, no damage has
been suffered by the plaintiff because no refusal to register by a
board thus constituted in defiance of the Federal Constitution
could have the effect to disqualify a legal voter, otherwise entitled
to exercise the elective franchise. In such a decision no right, immunity or privilege, the creation of Federal authority, has been set up
by the plaintiff." Sophistry of that dimension has rarely been accorded judicial sanction, but it won Supreme Court approval.

Justice Day then turned to Mr. Giles's demand to be registered.
In that portion of his suit, the complainant had asked that the registration boards, which he had previously attacked as being unlawfully constituted, be required to enroll him and those on whose
behalf he sued. Justice Day agreed with the contention of the Alabama courts that no valid claim for relief had been, or could be,
stated "because there would be no board to perform the duty
sought to be compelled by the writ and no duty imposed on which
the petitioner (Giles) can avail himself in this proceeding, to say
nothing of his right to be registered." Neither the Alabama courts
nor Justice Day took notice of the fact that the boards were registering white men every day, that as a result of such registration
white voters were casting their ballots, and that the only way Mr.
Giles could vote was by being registered. Presumably, Justice Harlan noted that fact. He dissented without opinion.

Virginia embarked on a wholesale disfranchisement scheme at
about the same time as Alabama. Its constitutional convention was
enlivened with a frank statement by Carter Glass, who would become a United States senator and later Secretary of the Treasury

under Woodrow Wilson, that the purpose of the new constitution
was to discriminate against Negro voters to the very limit of the
law. Hopeful Negroes challenged an election held under Virginia's constitution in two suits that found their way to the Supreme
Court, *Jones v. Montague* and *Seldon v. Montague*.[21] Both were
dismissed on the technical grounds that the elections had been held
between their filing and the time for decision. The same fate had
overtaken a suit to test elections under a South Carolina constitution in 1895.[22]

Negroes had lost the battle for the franchise.

In the first phase of the struggle, they had been driven from the
polls by open intimidation and violence; in the second phase, they
had been barred from voting by evasive and cynical state laws and
registration procedures, confessedly devised to disfranchise them.
The Supreme Court had connived at the results in both instances,
in the first by narrow constructions of the Fourteenth and Fifteenth
Amendments leading to invalidation of federal legislation enacted
to protect Negroes from mob violence and safeguard franchise
rights, and in the second, by abdicating its responsibility to afford
judicial protection to Negroes who tried to assert their rights under
the Fifteenth Amendment. Negro registration dropped catastrophi-
cally, and voteless Negroes were overwhelmed by a tide of custom
and practice and a spate of Jim Crow laws consigning them to an
inferior status.

Southern outcries against recent judicial decisions and laws striking down segregation statutes have given the impression that Jim
Crow laws have always been the rule in the South. The truth is
otherwise; the South's Jim Crow laws are of comparatively recent
origin beginning about 1890 and, more amazing, an import from
the North.[23] There was no need for segregation laws under the slave
system, and free Negroes in the South were not assertive enough to
invoke the need for legislation. Jim Crow laws were designed to
keep restive Negroes, demanding equality, in their place, as the
phrase goes. As long as Negroes shared political power and were
able to vote freely in the South, enactment of Jim Crow legislation
was a political impossibility. After Reconstruction failed and as the
Negro lost the ballot, segregation laws blossomed against considerable resistance by former slaveholders whose mores they offended
and who needed Negroes as a makeweight against rising discontent and economic radicalism among poor whites.

Southern reformers seized on racism as a device to unify poor whites in their cause and began a frenzied campaign of proposing both disfranchisement and segregation laws. The southern reform movement became a political Typhoid Mary, spreading social reform and segregation sentiment as it sought political power and translating its promises into Jim Crow laws as it succeeded. Southern conservatives joined the hue and cry, in an effort to hold on to old privileges. Each side tried to outbid the other, and southern poor whites, traditionally at the bottom of the heap, found huge psychological satisfaction in their legally guaranteed superiority.

During the course of the first quarter of a century of decisions construing the Civil War Amendments, the Supreme Court clung resolutely to the doctrine that the amendments did not tolerate state-imposed racial distinctions. It insisted time and again that the states could not sanction or support the individual racial discrimination which it found permissible under the equal-protection clause of the Fourteenth Amendment. Proponents of Jim Crow laws agreed that state sanction of discrimination was forbidden, but they insisted that equal protection of the law was satisfied through the requirement of equal and separate facilities for Negroes in segregation legislation.

As such state laws increased in number and scope, a Supreme Court test became inevitable. A test case reached the Court in 1896, in a challenge to the constitutionality of a Louisiana law requiring racial separation of railroad passengers traveling within the state. The man who made the challenge was Homer A. Plessy, who was a Negro only by courtesy of popular and unscientific belief that there is a peculiar potency in African blood. The cold and lifeless law books which tell his story say that he was seven-eighths white and that his one-eighth "colored blood was not discernible." [24]

⊰{ 11 }⊱ *Instruments of Wrong*

Out upon you, that enact ill decrees,
and draw up instruments of wrong; and
refuse redress to humble folk. . . .

ISAIAH 10:1 (Douay Version)

The law books don't tell us how the conductor knew that Homer A. Plessy, whose colored blood was not discernible, was violating Louisiana's Jim Crow law by taking a seat in the "white" railroad coach that was running between New Orleans and Covington, Louisiana, on June 7, 1892. All we know is that he ordered Mr. Plessy, who held a first-class ticket, to ride in the "colored" coach and that Mr. Plessy staged a nineteenth-century sit-down. He refused to budge. The conductor summoned police officers, who removed the obstinate passenger and filed a criminal complaint, as required by Louisiana's 1890 statute.

Judge John L. Ferguson was all set to hear the case, but the resourceful Mr. Plessy sought a writ from the state's higher courts—a writ of prohibition, as the lawyers call it. He alleged that Louisiana's segregation law was unconstitutional because it violated the Thirteenth Amendment and in particular because it denied him that equal protection of the laws guaranteed by the Fourteenth Amendment. He asked the higher courts to prohibit Judge Ferguson from holding the trial.

The case of *Plessy v. Ferguson* had been born.[1]

In due season, the Lousiana supreme court upheld the law on the ground that racial classification of citizens was reasonable under the circumstances and decided that a state law ordering racial separation of passengers on a railroad train did not offend the equal-

protection clause of the Fourteenth Amendment, as long as equal
facilities were provided for both whites and Negroes. The dissatisfied Mr. Plessy then asked the Supreme Court to intervene and save
him from Judge Ferguson's judicial wrath. When the Court agreed
to examine the issue, the stage was all set for a decision that would
shape American race relations for a long time to come and, incidentally, rescue Mr. Plessy and Judge Ferguson from the obscurity that
would otherwise have been theirs.

If opponents of Jim Crow laws wanted a Supreme Court decision
that would settle the issue of constitutionality of state-imposed racial segregation, they chose the worst possible test case. The Supreme Court that decided the case was composed of six justices
who had served as lawyers for railroads or corporations closely al-
lied with railroads, of Justice Stephen Field who had had a long
judicial love affair with the Southern Pacific Railroad and of Justice
John M. Harlan. Justice David Brewer, the ninth justice, did not
participate in the case. The seven justices who had old ties with
railroads were all honorable men, but it is not remarkable that they
should entertain some sympathy with public carriers which had
troubles enough with state regulation without championing the
cause of Negroes who were neither large shippers nor lucrative
passengers.

There was also the very practical consideration that railroads
could furnish equal accommodations—they could in fact provide
identical facilities for whites and Negroes. Added to all that was
the circumstance that the Court had come dangerously close to approving Jim Crow laws for railroads in prior decisions. Public carriers had been one of the first targets for Jim Crow laws, probably
because they had traditionally provided two classes of service for
passengers, and had almost universally assigned Negroes to their
second-class facilities. It was easy to graft segregation laws onto
the first- and second-class accommodations that were offered. Mr.
Plessy's chances of success were not bright.

The Court had been shadowboxing with the issue of separate
racial transportation accommodations for almost two decades. In
1877 it had decided *Hall v. De Cuir*,[2] which concerned the validity
of an 1869 Louisiana law giving common carriers the power to
make rules and regulations regarding passenger service within the
state, "provided said rules make no discrimination on account of
race or color." Mrs. De Cuir, a Negro woman, tried to buy a first-

class ticket on an interstate boat operating between New Orleans and another Louisiana city. Refused first-class accommodations, she bought a second-class ticket and promptly took possession of a first-class cabin set apart for whites. She was ejected, and sued for damages. A Louisiana jury awarded her damages in the sum of $1000, and the Louisiana courts upheld the verdict. The very fact that Louisiana prohibited racial segregation in 1869 by public carrier and required it in 1890 is a thumbnail history of the rise and fall of equalitarian sentiment and of Negro political power in that state, a course matched throughout the South. Equally significant is the circumstance that segregation was accepted as "discrimination" in 1869 and touted as equality under the equal-and-separate doctrine in 1895 by the Louisiana courts.

The Supreme Court, speaking through Chief Justice Waite, reversed Mrs. De Cuir's state court victory, on the narrow ground that the law was a regulation of interstate commerce. "While [the statute] purports only to control the carrier when engaged within the state, it must necessarily influence his conduct to some extent . . . throughout his voyage," the Chief Justice said. "A passenger in the cabin set apart for the use of whites without the states must, when the boat comes within, share the accommodation . . . with" colored passengers. "If," he added, "the public good requires such legislation, it must come from Congress and not from the states." [3]

Mississippi took the opposite tack in 1888 and passed a law requiring railroads operating within the state to maintain separate accommodations for white and Negro passengers and to separate such passengers by race. The Louisville, New Orleans and Texas Railway was prosecuted and fined by Mississippi for refusal to obey that section of the law requiring it to provide separate accommodations.[4] Obviously, the legal situation was exactly the same as that presented in Mrs. De Cuir's case as far as interstate commerce was concerned: if the requirement of nonsegregation was a regulation of interstate commerce in her case, the requirement of segregation was also such a regulation in the Mississippi case. Nevertheless, the Court majority, in an opinion written by Justice Brewer, was able to find a way to uphold the Mississippi law. Justice Harlan dissented: "I am unable to perceive," he said, "how the [Louisiana law] is a regulation of interstate commerce and the [Mississippi law] is not." Justice Bradley agreed with him.

Justice Brewer professed to find the difference in the circumstance that the Mississippi courts had held that its law was applicable only to travel within the state, a distinction without a difference, in lawyers' language. In the course of his opinion, he was at some pains to point out that the issue of whether the use of the required Jim Crow accommodations "is to be a matter of choice or compulsion does not enter into the case. . . . All that we can consider is whether the state has power to require . . . separate accommodations for the two races." The states did have such power, he said. The decision meant that the Court had determined that a state could compel a railroad to maintain Jim Crow accommodations within a state, but that it had ducked the question of whether or not Negro passengers had to use the separate facilities and submit to segregation imposed by law or railroad regulations. Mr. Plessy's case would supply the answer as far as state law was concerned.

As almost any lawyer could have predicted upon a reading of its railroad decisions, the Supreme Court spent little time—and precious little law for that matter—in disposing of Mr. Plessy's complaint. There was a distinct air of impatience in Justice Brown's seven-to-one majority opinion. "A statute," he wrote, "which implies merely a legal distinction between the white and colored races—a distinction which is founded on the color of the races, and which must always exist so long as white men are distinguished from the other race—has no tendency to destroy the legal equality of the two races. . . ." This facile generalization entirely neglected the very obvious truth that Mr. Plessy, whose colored blood was not discernible, was not "distinguished from the other race" by color. More important and ominous, it was a throwback to Chief Justice Taney's dictum that the "unhappy black race were separated from the white by indelible marks."

Justice Brown remarked in passing that he did not "understand that the Thirteenth Amendment was strenuously relied on" and hurried on to a consideration of the Fourteenth Amendment. He agreed that the object of that amendment "was undoubtedly to enforce the absolute equality of the two races before the law," but he was sure that "in the nature of things it could not have been intended to abolish distinction based on color, or to enforce social, as distinguished from political equality, or a commingling of the two races upon terms unsatisfactory to either." He added that "Laws permitting, and even requiring separation [of the races] in places where they are liable to be brought into contact do not necessarily imply the inferiority of either race to the other and have been generally, if not universally, recognized as within the competency of the state legislatures in the exercise of their police power." He bolstered that argument with a reference to eight state cases in which separate schools had been approved, the most important of which had been decided *before* the Fourteenth Amendment. Justice Brown was entirely mistaken, or worse, as to the purport and impact of the Fourteenth Amendment; it was entirely clear from debates and history and from prior decisions of the Court itself that the major purpose of that amendment was to abolish all legal distinctions based on race.

Having reduced the Fourteenth Amendment to little more than a pious goodwill resolution, Justice Brown decided that as far as a "conflict with the Fourteenth Amendment is concerned, the case reduces itself to the question of whether the statute of Louisiana is a reasonable regulation and with respect to it . . . the legislature . . . is at liberty to act with reference to the established usages, customs and traditions of the people and with a view to the promotion of their comfort, and the preservation of the public peace and good order." That test was in direct conflict with the Court's own rulings; even in the very limiting decision in the *Civil Rights Cases*, Justice Bradley had been very careful to say that the states could not sanction or support privately imposed discrimination. Congress had also proceeded on a diametrically opposite assumption in every instance from passage of the Civil Rights Act of 1866 to that of 1875. Where the Court had invalidated congressional laws, it had done so only because the legislation prohibited private discrimination not supported or sanctioned by a state. The vice in the Plessy case was the fact that the state had imposed the discrimination.

Finally, Justice Brown pounced on what he said was the fallacy in Mr. Plessy's complaint. "We consider the underlying fallacy of the plaintiff's argument to consist in the assumption that the enforced separation of the two races stamps the colored race with a badge of inferiority. If this be so, it is not by reason of anything found in the Act, but solely because the colored race chooses to put that assumption upon it." What he had said was that if the Negro would cheerfully accept his place, he would not find it degrading. Having advised the Negro to accept his place with equanimity, Justice Brown had a word of advice on the virtues of humility. He warned against the assumption that "social prejudices may be overcome by legislation" and charged Mr. Plessy with seeking an "enforced commingling of the two races." He had no difficulty in demolishing the strawman he had erected: "If the two races are to meet on the terms of social equality, it must be the result of natural affinities, a mutual appreciation of each other's merits, and a voluntary consent of individuals."

Justice Brown finally put the stamp of judicial approval on Professor William Graham Sumner's dogma that law ways cannot change folkways. "Legislation," he intoned, "is powerless to eradicate racial instincts based upon physical differences, and the attempt to do so can only result in accentuating the difficulties of the present situation. If the civil and political rights of both races be equal, one cannot be inferior to the other civilly or politically. If one race be inferior to the other socially, the Constitution of the United States cannot put them upon the same plane." He had smuggled Social Darwinism into the Constitution and had armed future generations of segregationists with the cherished doctrine that they could protect racial discrimination *through law* while preserving it against change with the fiction that *law* could not function in that sphere of human affairs!

Justice Harlan was as eloquent and lonely—and as correct—in dissent as he had been in the *Civil Rights Cases*. He scorned the rationalization that the equal-and-separate law was passed with any concern for the rights of Negroes. "Everyone knows," he said, "that the statute . . . had its origin and purpose, not to exclude white persons from railroad cars occupied by blacks. . . . The thing to accomplish was, under the guise of equal accommodations for whites and blacks, to compel the latter to keep to themselves while traveling in railroad passenger coaches. No one would be so wanting in candor as to assert the contrary." The effect of the law, he said, was that "it interferes with the personal freedom of citizens." He reminded the Court of the essential purpose of the Civil War Amendments.

"These notable additions to the fundamental law were welcomed by friends of liberty throughout the world," Justice Harlan wrote. "They removed the race line from our governmental system. They had, as this Court has said, a common purpose . . . to secure to [Negroes] 'all the civil rights that the superior race enjoy.' They declared . . . 'that the law in the states shall be the same for the black as for the white; that all persons whether colored or white, shall stand equal before the laws of the states. . . .'" He called the Court's attention to the fact that it had declared that the "words of the Amendment . . . contain a necessary implication of a . . . right to exemption from unfriendly legislation against [Negroes] . . . exemption from legal discriminations, implying their inferiority in civil society. . . ." He could see clearly that in "the view of the Constitution, in the eye of the law, there is in this country no superior, dominant ruling class of citizens. There is no caste here. Our Constitution is color-blind, and neither knows nor tolerates classes among citizens."

Justice Harlan pursued the constitutional doctrine of equality before the law to its relentless conclusion. "The law," he said, "regards man as man, and takes no account of his . . . color when his civil rights as guaranteed by the supreme law of the land are involved. It is therefore to be regretted that this high tribunal, the final expositor of the fundamental law of the land, has reached the conclusion that it is competent for a state to regulate the enjoyment by citizens of their civil rights solely upon the basis of race. In my opinion, the judgment this day rendered will, in time, prove to be quite as pernicious as the decision made by this tribunal in *The Dred Scott Case*. . . ."

He reviewed the Dred Scott case and reminded his judicial brethren that the case had rested upon the proposition of racial inequality and the unbridled right of the white majority to deny Negroes all rights under the Constitution: "The recent amendments, it was supposed, had eradicated these principles from our institutions," he said. But, he said reproachfully, "it seems that we have yet in some of the states a dominant race—a superior class of citizens, which assumes to regulate the enjoyment of civil rights, common to all citizens, upon the basis of race."

Justice Harlan accurately foresaw that the separate-but-equal doctrine would not be confined to railroads, but he could not forecast the lengths to which it would be carried. "Why," he asked with obvious sarcasm, may not the legislature "punish whites and blacks who ride together in street cars . . . ? Why may it not require sheriffs to assign whites to one side of the court room and blacks to the other? And why may it not also prohibit the commingling of the two races in the galleries of legislative halls or in public assemblages convened for consideration of the political questions of the day?" The answer given to these inquiries "at the argument," he said, "was that regulations of the kind they suggest would be unreasonable, and could not, therefore, stand before the law."

Even Justice Harlan could not predict that the time would come when streetcar segregation would be the universal rule in the entire South, to be abandoned only after a sensational Negro boycott in Montgomery, Alabama—first capital of the Confederacy—had pricked the national conscience and prodded another Supreme Court to nullify such laws almost 65 years later.[5] Nor could he foresee that a vice-presidential candidate would be arrested in 1948 for violating a Jim Crow law requiring separation of the races "in public assemblages convened for consideration of the public questions of the day." [6] And it was a melancholy fact that his grandson would be sitting on the Supreme Court when that high tribunal invalidated court rules requiring sheriffs to assign "whites to one side of the court room and blacks to the other." [7]

What Justice Harlan did foresee with uncanny accuracy was that "the present decision . . . will not only stimulate aggressions, more or less brutal and irritating, upon the admitted rights of colored citizens, but will encourage the belief that it is possible, by means of state enactments, to defeat the beneficent purposes which the people . . . had in view when they adopted the recent Amendments of the Constitution. . . . The destinies of the two races in this country are indissolubly linked together, and the interests of both require that the common government of all shall not permit the seeds of race hate to be planted under sanction of law. What can more certainly arouse race hate . . . than state enactments which in fact proceed on the ground that colored citizens are so far inferior and degraded that they cannot be allowed to sit in public coaches occupied by white citizens? That, as all will admit, is the real meaning of such legislation as was enacted in Louisiana. . . ." History would bear out Justice Harlan's prognosis.

He had a final word for those who insisted that segregation statutes would assure racial harmony. The Negro, he said, "objects, and ought never to cease objecting, to the proposition that citizens of the white and black races can be adjudged criminals because they sit, or claim the right to sit, in the same public coach, on a public highway. . . . The thin disguise of 'equal' accommodations for passengers in railroad coaches will not mislead anyone, or atone for the wrong this day done."

But the wrong was done.

It would be compounded many times over in the flood of Jim Crow statutes that would deluge the South in its wake.[8]

Although the immediate and intended effect of the Plessy decision was that it sanctioned Jim Crow laws, it cut far deeper than that. It grafted a color-caste system onto the amended Constitution, a result achieved by vesting the states, and presumably the national government, with power to classify their citizens and residents on the basis of race. The power to classify in law is exercised in order to differentiate in the treatment of citizens or persons. If a state has the power to classify a group, it can exercise power to pass special legislation affecting that classified group. Minors are classified in distinction to adults in order that the states or the national government may protect them against exploitation through passage of child labor laws and other protective legislation. Women workers are classified apart from other workers in order to validate laws prescribing hours and working conditions for their benefit. These and many other classifications are beneficent in design.

The other side of the coin is that classification may be undertaken to impose disabilities. Thus, persons convicted of crime are put in a special class and denied the right to vote or hold office; persons with communicable diseases are classified so that they may be quarantined or isolated. Southern states asserted the right to classify Negroes on a racial basis—to make them a distinct class—in order to exclude them from accommodations or facilities provided for white citizens. Negro railroad coaches, Negro schools, Negro parks, Negro playgrounds, Negro army units, Negro libraries —the whole paraphernalia of separate institutionalism—could be created and could exist only as long as the governmental unit which ordered them had power to classify persons on a racial basis. In the final analysis, all that a law, or judicial decision or executive order, does when it forbids racial segregation by a state is to deny the state the right to classify persons on a racial basis. Such a law or decision or order compels the state to be "color-blind" and to regard "man as man" in Justice Harlan's searching phrases.

The Court's discovery of constitutional recognition and approval of the color-caste system by the amended Constitution in its Plessy decision extended its dominion over the Negro's exercise of civil rights. As has been pointed out, that dominion was asserted in the *Slaughter House Cases,* with their ruling that there were two

classes of citizenship rights—national and state—and that the
Court had sole power to determine whether a particular right was
dependent on national or state citizenship; in the Cruikshank and
Harris cases, which decided that Congress could not legislate to
protect Negroes against mob violence in the absence of state sanction; and in the *Civil Rights Cases,* where it was held that Congress
could not interdict individual invasion of individual rights and that
the Court must determine whether or not state action, sufficient to
invoke protection of the Fourteenth Amendment, was involved
when a Negro's rights were invaded or denied.

In the jury cases the Court held that arbitrary exclusion of Negroes from grand and trial jury panels by state jury commissioners
in violation of the fourth section of the 1875 Civil Rights Act simply
gave the Negro a right to challenge his own indictment or conviction, and saddled him with the burden of proving racial discrimination. The Supreme Court was the final arbiter of that claim.

The Negro's right to the exercise of the franchise was also dependent on the Supreme Court's adjudication. In the case where he
was excluded from the polling place by a mob or his vote refused
by arbitrary action of the election judge in state elections, he would
have to prove to the Court's satisfaction that the interference or
refusal was undertaken because of his race or color. Moreover, the
Court held, Congress lacked power to legislate in his behalf against
individual wrongdoing in state elections; it could move only when
there was state action to deprive him of the vote because of his race
or color. Where the state imposed restrictions on registration and
consequent voting through laws that were fair on their face, the
Negro would have to satisfy the Court that the law was an evasive
attempt at disfranchisement because, the Court said, the Fifteenth
Amendment did not confer the franchise but only prohibited discrimination in the exercise of the voting privilege. But, strangely
enough, the Court held in the Giles case that it could not, or would
not, intervene to protect the Negro against wholesale disfranchisement through an evasive scheme because the right was "political"
in nature and its protection dependent on congressional protection.
The Court had the final say-so as to when a right was political in
the sense in which it used the term.

The Plessy case added another condition of Negro dependency
on the Supreme Court. The right to common use of state facilities
or public utility accommodations with white persons was denomi-

nated a "social right," and not a civil right. What was a "social right"? Only the Court could answer. What was equality within the purview of the separate-but-equal doctrine? Again, only the Court could answer.

This long and necessarily tedious recital may seem only a set of abstractions, but it had a very practical meaning when the everyday life of a white American was contrasted with that of his Negro neighbor, who belonged to the same economic category or social group, in the situation where both were residents of a southern state after the overthrow of Reconstruction governments and rendition of the Supreme Court decisions we have just considered.

With only his color as a touchstone, the white American could enjoy all rights and privileges afforded by federal and state constitutions and laws. It made no difference to him whether the right he wanted to exercise flowed from his national or his state citizenship. If it arose out of national citizenship, the federal government would protect him; if it came from state citizenship, the state would shield him.

With his color as a badge, the Negro faced all manner of difficulties. Assaulted and beaten by a Klan mob intent on keeping him in his place, he might seek redress through laws passed by Congress to put down Klan violence; if so, he would ultimately be told by the Supreme Court that the laws on which he depended were void, because the right he claimed was not an attribute of his national citizenship, but of his state citizenship. He would also be told that the Fourteenth Amendment did not empower Congress to protect rights flowing from state citizenship and that he must turn to his state for protection. In practice, the hostile state would not protect him; 231 Negroes were lynched in 1892—the yearly average between 1882 and 1901 was 150. Congress could do nothing under the Supreme Court ruling. The Negro would have to bow to the mob's dictates.

If the white American was charged with an act of aggression against his Negro neighbor, his case would be referred to a grand jury, more often than not composed of white citizens, from which all Negroes had been excluded in plain violation of the Civil Rights Act of 1875. The probabilities of indictment were slim, but if by some fortuitous circumstance an indictment was preferred, trial would be set before an all-white trial jury, also selected in violation of the Civil Rights Act. Conviction was improbable.

If the Negro was charged with an aggression against his white neighbor, that same all-white grand jury would be quick to indict and the all-white trial jury as quick to convict. True enough, the Negro could contest the issue of Negro exclusion from those juries and get the indictment thrown out or his almost certain conviction reversed, if he could prove that Negroes had been excluded from the juries on the basis of race and color. Proof was difficult indeed in hostile state trial and appeals courts. If the Negro persisted all the way to the Supreme Court of the United States, he would certainly get a resounding opinion inveighing against the evil of jury discrimination, but all too often he would learn that his proof of discrimination was not particular enough or that errors in procedure foreclosed relief in his case. Meanwhile, all-white juries chosen in violation of federal law would settle disputes on contracts or land boundaries or issues of debt that arose between the white American and his Negro neighbor. "The law belongs to the white man," the Negro would say with bitterness—and with truth.

When election rolled around and it was time to select state lawmakers, the judges, and sheriffs, and jury commissioners, the white American could vote without let or hindrance.

Barred from the polls by a mob or cheated out of his vote by the refusal of the election judge to receive or count his ballot, the Negro who appealed to the Supreme Court would learn that the Fifteenth Amendment had not conferred the right to vote on him but that it was only designed to protect him against racial discrimination in the casting or counting of his ballot. He would have to prove more than that the mob had barred him from the polling place or that the corrupt judge had refused to accept or count his ballot in state elections; he would have to *prove* that the wrong done him had been done because of his race or color.

The white American had easy and open access to hotels, inns, restaurants, and other places of public accommodation.

His Negro neighbor, assured the same right by the Civil Rights Act of 1875, would be told by the Supreme Court that the act was void and that he must suffer discrimination and exclusion—unless his state assured that right. The Fourteenth Amendment, the Court would say, did not empower Congress to proscribe individual invasion of individual rights, although it did prohibit state sanction or support of racial discrimination through legislative, executive, or judicial action. The white American did not need to be concerned about state action in furtherance of racial discrimination against him. There would be none. On the other hand, his Negro neighbor would have to engage in long, expensive, and tedious litigation in an effort to discover and prove that state action had been exerted against him, if he hoped to enjoy the protection of the Fourteenth Amendment in his attempt to use places of public accommodation. If the state stood aside and did nothing except let popular prejudices take their toll, the white man would continue to have easy and open access to hotels, inns, and restaurants. The Negro would be barred, branded as a pariah, solely because of his race.

The Plessy case validated segregation in schools, where it had existed even prior to the decision. And always the question would occur, what was equality? Ordinarily—almost always—the answer would be that equality consisted of the use of whatever accommodations were provided for the voteless by those who controlled the lawmaking power. Sometimes it meant a one-room, one-teacher school for the Negro's children, contrasted to a graded school for his white neighbor's children; sometimes it meant a park for the white American and the mere promise of a future park for his Negro neighbor. At other times it meant barring the Negro from swimming in the ocean, if only one beach was available. The Negro had his remedy in law—a hazardous and expensive suit to compel the state to provide a facility equal to that provided without question for his white neighbor. These disabilities, by fiat of the Supreme Court, satisfied that equal protection of the law guaranteed by the Fourteenth Amendment.

The short of the matter was that a white American, by the circumstance of color, could and did exercise the common garden variety of personal rights without question and without—indeed, with no thought of—resort to law. His Negro neighbor, citizen of the United States and of the state wherein he resided, was required to pay his way through the courts, often to the highest court in the land, to beg the same boon.

The gap between what the framers of the Civil War Amendments had intended and Congress had sought to achieve through equalitarian legislation and what the Supreme Court had arrived at through interpretation of the amendments and construction of that legislation was wide and deep. The framers and the lawmakers had envisaged a color-blind Constitution regarding "man as man" and taking "no account of his . . . color," in the words of Justice Harlan. They believed that the amended Constitution tolerated only one category of citizens and citizenship rights, with all civil rights under the protection of the federal government. The framers vested Congress with power to enforce the equalitarian amendments by "appropriate legislation." Congress believed it had acted in such a manner that "hereafter in all of our legislation there shall be no such words as 'black' or 'white' but that one shall speak only of citizens," as Charles Sumner put it when he introduced the Civil Rights Act of 1875.

By 1900, three short decades after the ratification of the last of the amendments, the Supreme Court, in the words of a southern professor of law, had made itself, "and not Congress, the major organ for the enforcement of the Fourteenth Amendment, contrary to the expectations of its framers and clear meaning of its text." That transfer, he points out, was a "major triumph for the South, which was given a free hand in the control of race relations. . . . Although the South had lost the war it had conquered constitutional law." [9] It was by the Court's action in making itself the major organ for the enforcement of the amendment that the Court made the Negro its dependent.

In reducing the Negro to dependence on it for the exercise of his personal rights, the Supreme Court had revived some of the dogmas of the Dred Scott case. The Court renewed the doctrine that Negroes were a special class of beings in a constitutional sense, attributed to the amended Constitution a complete scheme defining the special relationship of Negroes, as Negroes, to the federal government and to the states, and asserted for itself the exclusive power to determine the nature, character, and extent of those relationships. It emasculated the privileges-and-immunities clause of the Fourteenth Amendment and decided that the Negro's civil rights were under regulation and control of the states, "where they had always been." It restored dual citizenship, national and state, with national citizenship rights alone subject to federal protection, in complete agreement with Chief Justice Taney's viewpoint. It then took the next step by deciding that the federal government could not protect the Negro from individual aggression: Congress was as powerless as it had been before the Civil War to protect the Negro from mob violence in the face of state complacency and indifference; it could not safeguard him against discrimination by places of public accommodation or, indeed, shield him from any individual invasion of his individual rights. The Court was equally careful to decide that the Fifteenth Amendment did not confer the right to vote on the Negro and that the states retained the right to determine qualifications for voters in state elections. Finally, the Court held in the Plessy case that the amended Constitution acknowledged and approved racial distinctions between citizens, just as the original Constitution had done and, as a consequence, it asserted the power of the states to classify residents on the basis of race. For better or for worse, the Court had made the Negro its unwilling ward again.

In harking back to the dogmas of the Dred Scott case in its decisions, the Supreme Court did not justify its rulings on the underlying philosophy of that case or refer to it as a precedent. It consistently ignored the charges of dissenting justices, particularly Justice Harlan, that it was doing so. What the Court did was to ignore revolutionary changes in constitutional law effected by the Civil War Amendments in putting civil rights under the protection of the federal government and proceed as if the original Constitution had not been profoundly altered. The Court clung to states' rights doctrines developed prior to the Civil War in respect of civil rights, which gave the Dred Scott case whatever validity it had in that area of race relations. It persisted in acting, and deciding civil rights issues, as if the victors in the Civil War had not accomplished their purpose in proposing and securing ratification of amendments, openly proclaimed by their framers as designed to reverse and eradicate every vestige of the Dred Scott decision.

This stubbornness reflected a genuine belief that Congress had gone too far in centralization of power in the federal government, as far as protection of civil rights was concerned. In that respect the Court was reflecting a substantial body of public opinion, but that does not alter the fact that it was substituting its own judgment for that of Congress and the states which ratified the amendments. That the Court had its way was due to the growth and national acceptance of judicial supremacy; that is, the power of the Court to determine constitutional meaning and to invalidate federal and state laws that it found to be in conflict with the meaning it attributed to the Constitution. It had triumphed over the protests of Thomas Jefferson and Andrew Jackson that "the Supreme Court . . . must not . . . be permitted to control the Congress or the Executive." [10] The Supreme Court had taken control, and Congress and the Executive bowed to its will. Of course, the Court did not deny the efficacy of the Civil War Amendments in all particulars. Rather, it restricted and narrowed their meanings to fit its own collective judgment as to how far Congress *should* have gone in framing the amendments and in passing legislation for their enforcement. It rationalized its views as to how far Congress should have gone by ruling that Congress had only gone that far. Judges, like other mere mortals, often see that which they expect to see, or want to see—in their lovers, or on the printed page.

In the Supreme Court's narrow view, the Thirteenth Amendment had abolished slavery; the Fourteenth Amendment conferred citizenship on the Negro and restrained the states and the national government from making or enforcing laws in an unequal, hostile, or oppressive manner but did not prohibit state statutes imposing racial segregation; and the Fifteenth Amendment prohibited racial restrictions on the right to vote. Otherwise, the Civil War Amendments had changed little, as far as the Negro's constitutional rights were concerned.

The Negro, under the Court's guardianship, was reduced to a despairing second-class citizenship: voteless in the South; helpless in the face of constant and brutal aggression; indicted by all-white grand juries and convicted by all-white trial juries; denied access to places of public accommodation; represented in public office by those whose very elections were dependent on their promise to white voters to double and redouble his disabilities; forced to scrounge and cadge for an education; segregated in every phase of his life; condemned to separate and unequal schools and public facilities of every kind; and with no place to turn for redress of his grievances except to the Court that had approved the devices used to reduce him to his helpless and almost hopeless degradation.

In the North the Negro fared a little better, just as he had prior to the Civil War. There, at least, he voted freely and his children had access to public schools. But the long shadow of Jim Crow fell athwart him there, too. Existing public accommodations laws were indifferently enforced.

Voluntary associations, taking their cue from the national mood, barred the Negro from, or segregated him in, labor unions, trade and professional groups, and that vast array of organizations that shape our lives in our pluralistic society.

Responding to pressure of disproportionate southern political power, made possible by Negro disfranchisement and the resulting one-party system, the federal government bowed to segregationist demands and confined the Negro to segregated Army units led by white officers, excluded him from all but the menial branch in the Navy, barred him from the Marine Corps and the Coast Guard, and generally restricted him to the lower reaches of the federal civil service. As southern pressure increased, the federal government finally Jim Crowed Negro employees in government offices in the capital of the nation.[11]

It would be a gross error to lay all these ills to the Supreme Court's undoing of the high purpose of the Civil War Amendments and its persistent sabotage of congressional attempts to carry out the mandates of those amendments. Congress itself bore a share of the blame; it did little, all too little, to provide a sound economic base for the pauperized Negro freedman that would have enabled him to resist encroachment on his civil and political rights.[12] Some congressional legislation was imperfectly conceived, and Congress was all too ready to abandon legislative attempts to achieve its stated purposes. After the Compromise of 1876, indifferent Chief Executives and slothful Attorneys General showed neither zeal nor imagination in pressing for enforcement of Reconstruction legislation left untouched by the Court.[13]

With all of that, the harsh truth remains that it was the Court that dulled the cutting edge of the Civil War Amendments and pulled the teeth of equalitarian legislation. The dissents in the landmark Slaughter House, Reese, Harris, Civil Rights, Plessy, and Giles[14] cases demonstrate how much farther the Court could have gone to protect and preserve the Negro's civil and political rights through a different constitutional interpretation. The temper of the times was such that the Negro would have had a hard row to hoe, even if those dissents had become the law of the land. They would have been widely disregarded initially, but they would have been loaded weapons ready for use and would have served as powerful deterrents. As it was, the Court's every narrowing decision whetted the appetite of opponents of civil rights for additional concessions and delayed historically inevitable change. If, for example, the Court had sustained the public accommodations sections of the Civil Rights Act of 1875, its enforcement and observance would have begun long before enactment of virtually duplicate sections in the Civil Rights Act of 1964. Or had the Court accepted Justice

Harlan's dissent in *Plessy v. Ferguson* as its prevailing opinion, informal racial segregation would not have persisted until 1954, when the Court finally deprived the separate-but-equal ruling of all validity.

However, there are no second guesses in history, and the purpose here is to chronicle the story of the Supreme Court and the Negro. For the first three decades of the twentieth century, the Court decided cases involving the Negro's civil rights within the stultifying framework it had created from 1873 to 1900. The story is, in the main, a depressing one.

PART THREE

Through a glass, darkly

For now we see

through a glass, darkly . . . ☀ I CORINTHIANS 13:12

The wall's too high,
You can't get over it,
Too low, you can't get under it,
Too wide, you can't go 'round it.
You must come in at the gate.

NEGRO SPIRITUAL

As the Supreme Court turned to a practical application of the rules announced from 1870 to 1900 in its interpretation of the Civil War Amendments and implementing legislation, race relations seemed stable, almost immutable, in the South and fairly well settled in the rest of the nation. The last of the Negro Reconstruction congressmen left the House at the turn of the century and, although he predicted that other Negroes would soon return, his prophecy had the ring of unrealism. Booker T. Washington, slave-born educator, who appeared to speak for all Negroes, reassured an eagerly listening nation that "The wisest among my race understand that the agitation of social equality is the extremest folly, and that progress in the enjoyment of all privileges that will come to us must be the result of severe and constant struggle rather than of artificial forcing." He made the statement at the Atlanta Exposition of 1895, with its separate "Negro department," and he was careful to tell his listeners that "In all things that are purely social we can be as separate as the fingers. . . ." [1]

By 1900, the Democrats were in firm control of the one-party South, and Republicans had virtually ceased demanding voting rights for Negroes except in run-of-mine resolutions in party platforms every four years. The United States as a rising world power established its own colonial system in the aftermath of the Spanish-American War and accepted the judgment of the western world that lesser breeds without the law needed the firm guiding hand, and the chastening rod, of the White Man to assure stability in Asia, in Africa, and in the Islands of the Seas. It was increasingly apparent to the opinion makers of the North that Negroes of the South, as domesticated savages, also needed the overlordship of beneficent White Men who understood them.[2] Sociologists, novelists, essayists, anthropologists, and philosophers of all kinds ground out treatises and learned articles not only proving that Negroes were inferiors but also that they were both better off and happier in their subordinate status.[3] The plantation system with its sharecropping and tenancy features was hailed as a near perfect answer to the needs of landowners for a stable supply of agricultural laborers and equally effective and desirable to meet the complementary need of shiftless and unthinking Negroes for a way to earn an honest living.

Most of the old abolitionists were dead, or their voices were stilled by age; many of their prosperous children had renounced the equalitarian heresies of their ancestors. The judgment of *Plessy v. Ferguson*[4] that the "law is powerless to eradicate racial instincts or to abolish distinctions based upon physical differences" was accepted not only as the law of the land but as an almost inspired statement of eternal truth. In translation, it meant that correction of racial injustices was left to what was called the "long, slow process of education" and "a change in the hearts and minds of men." Civil rights legislation fell into disuse in the North.

There were dissents, of course. Negroes themselves were voting against the plantation system with their feet; since 1890, they had embarked on an inexorable and irrevocable trek to the cities. W. E. B. Du Bois, an acid-tongued Negro graduate of Harvard and of German universities, cried out in 1900 that "The problem of the Twentieth Century is the problem of the color line" and opposed his strident voice to the calm pronouncements of the respected Booker T. Washington on domestic racial policies. He was little heard, and as little heeded. Justice John M. Harlan persisted in his disagreement with Supreme Court restrictions of the Civil War Amendments, but he was a prophet with little honor in his own court—so little that a later justice would brand him an eccentric, even as the Court gradually made his dissents the law of the land.[5]

The original Ku Klux Klan was remembered in song and story for what was hailed as its noble role in driving Negroes and their carpetbag and scalawag allies from the fleshpots of power in state governments and in restoring that power to white men, to whom it rightfully belonged.[6] (In time a novel would be written to extol its virtues and Hollywood would glorify it in a great film, "Birth of a Nation.") The Klan's work was done by 1900, but its bastard progeny, the lynch mob, continued the terror it had spawned. On average, 150 Negroes a year were burned at the stake, tortured, and killed from 1890 to 1902; after that year, the average declined to about 100. Southern states professed inability to cope with this lawbreaking, and the federal government could not act because the Supreme Court had found that civil rights, including the personal security of the individual, were left under the control of the states by the Civil War Amendments and that federal legislation directed against individual invasion of individual rights was unconstitutional.

Depradations of lynchers were quite generally excused on the ground that they were roused to their fierce passions by violations of the Sanctity of White Womanhood, but there were many other occasions on which mobs functioned to enforce the unwritten code of race relations.[7]

Berry Winn and seven other Arkansas Negroes entered into labor contracts with a lumber company and had hardly begun to work before a mob of white men, in the stilted language of the law, moved "in a body to and against the place of business . . . armed with deadly weapons, threatening and intimidating said workmen . . . compelling them to quit work." [8] Members of the mob were indicted for violating Section 5508 of the United States Code, which made it a crime for two or more persons to conspire "to injure, oppress, threaten, or intimidate any person in the free exercise of any right or privilege secured to him by the Constitution or laws of the United States." By another section of the Code, originally enacted in the Civil Rights Act of 1866, Mr. Winn and his fellow workmen were given "the same right in every State and territory to make and enforce contracts . . . as is enjoyed by white persons. . . ." A jury found the defendants guilty of conspiring to intimidate and injure the Negro workmen "in the free exercise of" their right to "make and enforce contracts." The defendants took their case to the Supreme Court in 1905 in a case called *Hodges v. United States.*

The government attorney saw the issue before the Court as the rather simple one of whether or not a "colored citizen [had] a right secured to him by the Constitution . . . to work . . . free from injury, oppression, or interference on the part of individual citizens when the motive . . . arises solely from the fact that such laborer is a colored person. . . ." He argued that the right flowed from the Thirteenth Amendment. Prior to the passage of that amendment, everybody agreed, a slave had no right to make or enter into a contract, a lack that was one of the badges and incidents of slavery. Before ratification, Congress could not have enacted a law bestowing the right to make or enforce contracts on any Negro, free or slave, but after addition of the amendment to the Constitution, Congress could legislate under the clause giving it power to enforce the article by appropriate legislation. It could punish individuals who transgressed rights secured by the amendment. The case seemed to be complete.

Justice Brewer, nephew of Justice Field and son of missionary parents, would have none of that simple explanation. He did agree that one of the incidents of slavery was a "lack of power to make or enforce contracts." He had authored a Supreme Court opinion in which he had said that "It is not open to doubt that Congress may enforce the Thirteenth Amendment by direct legislation. . . ." [9] He escaped his apparent dilemma by asserting that, "while the inciting cause of the [Thirteenth] Amendment was the emancipation of colored race, yet it is not an attempt to commit that race to the care of the Nation." The amendment, he said, bestowed freedom on all Americans, not Negroes alone. That led him to the conclusion that it had no particular reference to Negroes, or to wrongs done to Negroes as Negroes. Therefore, he reasoned, the amendment did not empower Congress to enact legislation designed to protect the rights of Negroes as such. And, he said, "nowhere in the record does it appear that the parties charged to have been wronged have ever themselves been slaves, or were the descendants of slaves."

Congress, Justice Brewer insisted, could no more legislate against individual conduct designed to injure or oppress Negroes in the making of contracts than it could to protect a white man from comparable wrongdoing. What he was saying was that only the states could enact laws to protect the Negro workman against mob violence interfering with his right to earn a living. The assertion that the Thirteenth Amendment had no particular reference to the protection of Negroes flew in the face of remembered history and what every school boy knew, and affronted what the Court itself had said time and time again. But six other members of the Court agreed with Justice Brewer's obscurantist reasoning, with its repudiation of history.

Nor could Justice Brewer find any warrant in the Fourteenth Amendment for the protection of the Negro's right to work under a labor contract. "At the close of the Civil War," he said, "when the problem of the emancipated slaves was before the nation, it might have left them in alienage or established them as wards" of the government, as was the case with Indians. Instead, he pointed out, Negroes were given citizenship. Whether or not the grant of citizenship, he said, "was or was not the wiser way to deal with the great problem is not a matter for the courts to consider." All the courts could say, he insisted, was that, having been granted citizenship, Negroes must "take their chances with other citizens in the States where they make their homes." The proposition that the grant of citizenship in the Fourteenth Amendment had stripped Congress of all power to protect or conserve the rights of Negroes was at complete variance with everything that was said in congressional debates by friend and foe alike when the meaning of the amendment was under discussion; it ran counter to the Court's own studied opinion that the "one pervading purpose" of the Civil War Amendments was "the freedom of the slave race, the security and firm establishment of that freedom, and the protection of the newly made freeman from the oppression of those who had formerly exercised dominion over him." [10]

Harking back to the position he had taken on many occasions, Justice Harlan—joined on this occasion by Justice Day—repeated what everybody knew. The Thirteenth Amendment, he reminded his colleagues, "destroyed slavery and all its incidents and badges and established freedom." Moreover, it "invested Congress with power . . . to enforce that right." Thus "it became competent for Congress" to protect the rights of Negroes and to proscribe individual conduct designed to "subject anyone to the badges or incidents of slavery. . . ." Since the Court agreed that Section 5508 was a valid exercise of congressional power, it seemed plain to Justice Harlan that Congress could punish members of a mob who interfered with a right conferred by the Thirteenth Amendment.

Justice Harlan also pointed to the Court's rhetoric in *Allegeyer v. Louisiana,* in which it had said that the liberty mentioned in the due-process clause of the Fourteenth Amendment embraced "the right of the citizen . . . to live and work where he will; to earn his livelihood by any lawful calling; . . . to enter into all contracts which may be proper, necessary and essential. . . ." He regretted that the Court had departed from that concept "so as to deny to millions of citizens—laborers of African descent . . . the right to appeal for National protection against lawless combinations of individuals who seek, by force, and solely because of the race of such laborers, to deprive them of the freedom established by the Constitution—so far as that freedom involves [their] right . . . to earn a living . . . and to dispose of their labor by contract." His regrets were unavailing.

The use of labor contracts with individual Negro workmen was often an attempt to adapt features of the peonage system to the labor needs of southern employers and plantation owners. Peonage, permissible under Spanish law and widespread in New Mexico, was just a cut above slavery: the state compelled the workman to serve the landowner or employer to whom he had become indebted. After ratification of the Thirteenth Amendment, Congress passed sweeping legislation nullifying all state laws protecting peonage and punishing individuals who attempted its practice. The validity of such legislation insofar as it purported to punish individuals reached the Court in 1905, in the case of *Clyatt v. United States.*[11]

Mose Ridley and Will Gordon received an advance and hired out to do some work for Samuel Clyatt, D. T. Clyatt, and H. H. Tift but reneged on their contract and skipped out to Florida. The irate Mr. Clyatt, in the words of Justice Brewer, "went to Florida and caused the arrest of Gordon and Ridley on warrants issued by a magistrate in Georgia; but there can be little doubt that these criminal proceedings were only an excuse for securing the custody of Gordon and Ridley and taking them back to Georgia to work out a debt." [12] Clyatt was indicted for violation of the federal statute abolishing peonage and making it a criminal offense to "hold, arrest, return or cause to be held, arrested or returned [any person] . . . to a condition of peonage." The indictment charged the defendant with "returning" Ridley and Gordon to peonage and he was convicted and given four years at hard labor. Justice Brewer's scrutiny uncovered the technical objection that "there was not a scintilla of testimony that Gordon and Ridley were ever theretofore in a condition of peonage" and that hence they could not be "returned" to that condition. The defendant had made no such objection at his trial and had not raised the point in any manner, but Justice Brewer held that the trial court had erred in not directing a verdict for the defendant. Clyatt went scot free, while Justice Harlan pointed out that there was some evidence of prior peonage and lamented that "it is going very far to hold in a case like this disclosing barbarities of the worst kind against these Negroes that the trial court erred in sending the case to the jury." [13] It was, indeed, in light of the rule of law that a defendant cannot assert on appeal a right he has not claimed at his trial. But whatever its other shortcomings, the case settled the issue that congressional legislation punishing individuals for holding others in a state of peonage was valid. No man could compel another to work out a debt.

Southern states tried to lift the onus of peonage from employers and plantation owners through legislation that made it a crime for a person to break a labor contract with an intention to defraud the other party while he was still indebted to the employer or landowner. The practice was for the employer to make a small advance to the laborer or farm hand and to provide that it be repaid in small installments over a year's period, during which the employee was paid a monthly wage. If the workman walked off the job at any time within the year without first repaying the advance, he could be charged with what amounted to theft by trickery. If found guilty, he could be fined double the amount he still owed, plus court costs, and one half of the fine would be paid to the employer or plantation owner, with the other half accruing to the state. At his trial the workman could not testify that he had no intent to defraud his employer: his intention to cheat the boss was presumed from the fact that he had received the money and was still indebted when he quit work.

Obviously, an impecunious workman, almost universally a Negro, who had been reduced to signing one of these dead-end labor contracts would seldom have the money to pay the fine and court costs levied on him for breaking his agreement. The lawmakers had thought of that, too. Another person, called a surety, could come in

and offer to pay a fine and costs in any criminal case. If that arrangement was agreeable to the defendant, he could then, in open
court, sign another installment contract approved by the judge
agreeing to repay the surety, and thereupon he would be released
to his new boss until he had repaid the new debt. Of course, almost
any arrangement suggested by a judge was agreeable to a Negro
caught in the toils of the law in the Deep South, especially in light
of the fact that if he didn't come to the terms with the surety, he
could be leased out to that person, or somebody else, until the state
had collected the fine and costs.[14]

Lonzo Bailey, an illiterate Alabama Negro, got a $15 advance
from the Riverside Company and agreed to "work and labor . . .
as a farm hand" from December 30, 1907, to December 30, 1908,
at the rate of $12 a month. He also agreed to repay the $15 at the
rate of $1.25 a month. After working a month, he walked off the job
still owing $13.75 and was promptly arrested and held for trial. Mr.
Bailey's lawyers claimed the law was invalid under the Thirteenth
Amendment and the congressional statutes against peonage, and
asked the Alabama supreme court to free him on a writ of habeas
corpus. Unfortunately for him, the Alabama court could see nothing wrong with the law, and in 1908, Bailey had to take his
case to the Supreme Court of the United States, where, in the case
of *Bailey v. Alabama*,[15] he repeated his contention that the Alabama
law was unconstitutional and violative of federal antipeonage statutes.

Justice Holmes, as cool and detached as he had been in the Alabama voting cases, told Bailey that he had been in too much of
a hurry to reach the nation's highest tribunal. "The trouble with the
whole case," he said, "is that it is brought here prematurely by an
attempt to take a short cut. . . ." Inherent in his decision was the
ruling that the law was perfectly valid and that Bailey could
get relief only if he could prove that it was unequally applied to
Negroes. Justice Harlan entered a dissent, saying in effect that the
law was unconstitutional and that the Court should say so without
further ado. "It is a curious condition of things," he said with asper-
ity, "if this Court must remain silent when the question comes before it regularly, whether the final judgment of the highest court of
a State does not deprive a citizen of rights secured to him by the
Supreme Law of the Land." It might have been curious, but it was

the law because the eight-to-one Court majority said it was, and Bailey had to go to trial in Alabama. He was fined.

There had been some changes in personnel by the time Bailey came back to the Court three years later in another case also called *Bailey v. Alabama.*[16] By that time he had been tried and duly convicted, and the Alabama supreme court had renewed its decision that the law was perfectly valid. On January 3, 1911, Justice Charles Evans Hughes—he would be a presidential candidate in 1916 and ultimately a Chief Justice of the Court—delivered an opinion striking down the Alabama statute as it was applied to Bailey's case. Because the "law of the State did not permit [Bailey] to testify that he did not intend to injure or defraud . . . he stood, stripped by the statute of the presumption of innocence, and exposed to conviction for fraud upon evidence only of breach of contract and failure to pay," Justice Hughes said. He added that the "essence of peonage is compulsory service in payment of a debt." It seemed apparent to him and six other justices that "What the State may not do directly it may not do indirectly. If it cannot punish the servant as a criminal for the mere failure to serve without paying his debt, it is not permitted to accomplish the same result by creating a statutory presumption which . . . exposes him to conviction and punishment." That precise legal issue could as well have been determined in 1908 when Bailey was first before the Court, just as Justice Harlan had said.

Justice Holmes hadn't changed his mind since 1908, and he said so in an acidulous dissent, in which he was joined by Justice Horace Lurton. "We are all agreed," he wrote, "that this case is to be decided in the same way as if it arose in New York or Idaho. . . . The fact that in Alabama it mainly concerns the black does not matter." It didn't strike him that no such case had arisen in New York or Idaho because neither of those states was encumbered by a history of slavery, and that Alabama was trying to reduce "the blacks" to a condition as close as possible to the condition of servitude outlawed by the Thirteenth Amendment. He said irrelevantly that "the Thirteenth Amendment does not outlaw contracts for labor" and was vehement in his protest that "obtaining money by fraud may be made a crime as well as murder or theft." And, he argued, all the law "purports to punish is fradulently obtaining money by a false pretense of an intent to keep the written contract in consideration of which money is advanced." He thought "the matter may well be left to a jury" and was certain that a "fair jury would acquit if the only evidence were departure [of the workman] after eleven months work" or another reasonable service, rather than the short period of labor by Bailey. Apparently, he knew almost nothing about the white jury system of the Deep South or the proclivities of such juries.

In any event, Bailey was finally free after three years of litigation and two trips to the U. S. Supreme Court. Most illiterate southern Negroes who couldn't repay a $13.75 debt couldn't have laid out the cash for attorney fees and costs entailed in two appeals to a state supreme court and another pair to the nation's highest court. There are no available statistics on how many of them simply bore up under what Justice Hughes found to be peonage in Bailey's case, or how many were reduced to that state between December, 1908, when his first appeal was heard to the Court, and January, 1911, when the case was decided in his favor. It later turned out that Bailey wasn't as affluent as the appeals indicated; he had been financed by Booker T. Washington and other interested persons.[17]

The Bailey case had not involved the situation where a surety paid a fine and costs in a criminal case and subsequently entered into a court-approved contract with a defendant. That aspect of the Alabama law was before the Court in 1914 in two cases decided together—*United States v. Reynolds* and *United States v. Broughton*. Ed Rivers was convicted of petty theft, fined $15, and assessed $43.75 in court costs.[18] Under Alabama law, he would have had to serve ten days under the fine and could have worked out the costs at the rate of 75 cents a day and thus would have been free in about 68 days. Mr. Reynolds showed up, however, and offered to become a surety for the total of $58.75 fine and costs, on condition that Mr. Rivers agree to work as a farm hand for 9 months and 24 days at the monthly rate of $6. Rivers wasn't too well versed in arithmetic, and he put his "X" on the agreement on May 4, 1910. The trial judge approved the contract in open court, but Rivers apparently had second thoughts after he got on the job. He quit on June 6, 1910, and Reynolds promptly had him arrested, as the law provided, for failing to keep his bargain. Back in the same court, Rivers was fined *one cent* and assessed $87.05 in court costs, which would have netted him about 75 days in jail. But his arithmetic failed him again, and he agreed to work out the $87.06 for another surety, Mr. Broughton, for 14 months and 15 days at the going rate of $6 per month. A United States grand jury finally stopped the merry-go-round by indicting Reynolds and Broughton for peonage.

Broughton meanwhile was busy rounding up other laborers under his surety system. E. W. Fields was fined $50 for selling mortgaged property, and his costs amounted to $69.70. Broughton was right on hand with an offer to discharge the debt on condition that Mr. Fields work for him for 19 months and 29 days at the usual $6 per month. Fields couldn't read or write either, and his mathematics were as inadequate as those of Rivers. He signed the proposed contract on July 8, 1910, and the obliging judge approved it. He walked off the job on September 14, 1910, but the grand jury indictment halted proceedings in his case.

An Alabama federal district judge could find no fault in the law and dismissed the indictments against Reynolds and Broughton. Alabama's attorney general had appeared to defend the statute, and it may be that the federal district judge was beguiled by his argument, also presented in the Supreme Court, that "The statute is a humane one. If the convict does his duty according to his contract, there is no reminder of his convict-state, save at the end of the month when his wage is withheld. He is practically a free man and the law delights in the liberty and happiness of the citizen." The Supreme Court wasn't impressed. It reversed the lower court and ordered trials for Rivers and Broughton.

"Under this statute," Justice Day said, "the surety may cause the arrest of the convict for violation of his labor contract. He may be sentenced and punished for this new offense, and undertake to liquidate the penalty by a new contract of a similar nature, and if again broken may again be prosecuted, and the convict is thus kept chained to an ever turning wheel of servitude." Even Justice Holmes gave grudging assent to the majority opinion. "There seems to me nothing in the Thirteenth Amendment or the Revised Statutes that prevents a State from making a breach of contract . . . a crime," he said in repetition of his Bailey dissent. "But," he added, "impulsive people with little intelligence or foresight may be expected to lay hold of anything that affords a relief from present pain even though it will cause greater trouble by and by. The successive contracts, each for a longer term than the last are inevitable. . . ." With that in mind, he said he was "inclined to agree that the statutes in question disclose the attempt to maintain the service" forbidden by the antipeonage statute.

Statutes similar to the Alabama law were in effect and were being enforced in all the states of the Deep South and, as we shall see, the identical issue thought to have been disposed of in the Bailey case was before the Court in 1942 in a Georgia case and again in 1944 as a result of a Florida statute passed in 1943! [19]

The Court's refusal to countenance federal prosecution of mob members who interfered with the attempt of Negroes to fulfill labor contracts, as set forth in the Hodges case, appears in a curious light in view of the underlying reason for these contracts. But the Court was not concerned with the inherent evil in labor contract statutes in the Hodges case; what it did there was to restrict the scope of the Thirteenth Amendment with the ruling that mobs could drive Negroes from employment without fear of federal intervention and with full knowledge that the states would not intervene. When it was directly confronted with state statutes enacted to bolster peonage, the Court struck them down despite the strong and influential dissent and questioning attitude of Justice Holmes. Its only dereliction lay in its refusal to declare the Alabama statute invalid in the Bailey case of 1908 as it did in the Bailey case of 1911, a failure directly attributable to Justice Holmes's judicial blind spot in the area of civil rights.

The existence, and persistence, of state statutes encouraging peonage cannot be laid at the Court's doorstep, however, in the same sense that it bears responsibility for the overthrow of the 1875 public accommodations law in the *Civil Rights Cases* or the approval and encouragement it gave racial segregation statutes in the Plessy case. State laws favoring peonage were politically possible because the Court had fallen flat on its face in the voting cases—a voteless people is a helpless people in a democratic society. Convictions of Negroes charged with violating labor contracts were obtained easily, because the Supreme Court had stopped short in its construction of federal laws designed to further integration of Negroes into the jury systems of southern states. The climate of southern opinion which tolerated peonage was a partial derivative of the Plessy decision with its invidious sanction of racial discrimination, bearing out Justice Harlan's prophecy that the ruling would "stimulate aggressions, more or less brutal and irritating upon the admit-

ted rights of colored citizens." Brooding over the whole scene was
the Court's resignation of civil rights to the care of the states, in
plain contradiction to the command of the Fourteenth Amendment,
and the correlative doctrine that the federal government could not
protect its citizens against mob violence when the states were unable or unwilling to do so. The Court's attempt to protect the rights
of Negroes in the area of peonage was encouraging and valuable;
the difficulty was that it had helped create a milieu in which that
attempt was foredoomed to partial failure and almost endless evasion.

Meanwhile, racial segregation grew by leaps and bounds after
the decision in *Plessy v. Ferguson.* In upholding the separate-but-
equal doctrine announced in that case, Justice Brown placed great
reliance on the supposed fact that segregation laws were permissible because they accorded with the "established usages, customs
and traditions of the people and with a view to the promotion of
their comfort." He added that "If the two races are to meet together on terms of social equality, it must be the result of natural
affinities, a mutual appreciation of each other's merits and a voluntary consent of individuals." The "commingling" of the two races,
he said, must not be undertaken "on terms unsatisfactory to either."
The hollow character of these justifications was thrown in bold relief by a 1906 case, styled *Berea College v. Kentucky.*[20]

A little band of Christians, interested in "promoting the cause of
Christ" as they put it, established Berea College in the Kentucky
mountains in 1854. Its charter began with the words "God hath
made of one blood all nations that dwell upon the face of the
earth," and after the Civil War it admitted students without reference to race or color. By 1904, it had 753 white and 174 Negro
students, who found its doctrines acceptable; it was a private institution, attended only by those who subscribed to its tenets, and it
neither sought nor accepted state aid or assistance. Over its an-
guished protests and in the face of pleas by its students and faculty
for a chance to practice Christianity as they understood that religion, the Kentucky legislature enacted a statute, effective July 15,
1904, forbidding the maintenance of any "school, college or institution where persons of the white and Negro races are both received
as pupils for instruction." The college clung to its principles and, as
a corporation, was indicted, convicted, and fined one thousand dol-

lars for violation of the law. Kentucky's court of appeals upheld the statute, and Berea took its case to the nation's highest court.

What happened to Berea College in the Supreme Court of the United States is one of the most remarkable episodes in American jurisprudence.

◄{ 13 }► *No Yards To Measure*

The law's our yardstick, and it measures well
Or well enough when there are yards to measure.

STEPHEN VINCENT BENÉT, *John Brown's Body*

The right of American citizens to associate together for innocent
purposes is so fundamental that it is taken for granted. The very
suggestion that it was open to question or subject to prohibition or
regulation by law would have shocked the Founding Fathers. But
there was a disturbing exception, the more disturbing because it
was concealed beneath the verbiage of the Constitution. Free Negroes of the South were subject to restraints on their innocent associations, together or with white Americans. Chief Justice Taney explained that riddle in Dred Scott's case. Free Negroes, he had said,
were not national citizens and could claim no privilege of free association, because "It would exempt them from operation of special
laws and from police regulations . . . it would give them full liberty of speech in public and private upon all subjects . . . to hold
public meetings upon political affairs . . . inevitably producing
discontent and insubordination among them. . . ." The Fourteenth
Amendment had cut the ground from beneath that rationalization;
Negroes were citizens by its definition and shielded against denial
of equal protection and due process of state law. As free men, it
seemed that their right to innocent association was secure against
state interdiction.

The decision in the Plessy case had cast the first faint shadow of
doubt over the right of association across the color line, but the
Supreme Court had justified the restriction on the ground that
"commingling of the races" could be prohibited by law because the

need to use a common carrier threw the races together against their will. Segregated public schools were similarly justified because of compulsory attendance. But in each instance, equal facilities for Negroes were required. There was no taint of enforced commingling in a private school such as Berea College, which taught only those who voluntarily attended. The framers of the Fourteenth Amendment would have been shocked at the suggestion that a state could penalize voluntary interracial association of students at a private school.

Kentucky's statute forbidding teaching of white and Negro students at the same school at the same time was a broad one, applying to "any person, corporation, or association of persons" maintaining or operating "any school, college or institution." Under the law, an institution of learning could teach both races only if it maintained a "separate and distinct branch thereof, in a different locality, not less than twenty five miles distant, for the education exclusively of one race or color." The law levied a fine of $1000 on an offending school and $100 for each day's violation, imposed identical punishments on instructors in such a school, and provided for a fine of $50 a day on its students.

Berea College was incorporated under Kentucky law in 1859 and had changed its corporate charter, the last time in 1899, to provide that it was established for the purpose of "promoting the cause of Christ" and of giving general and nonsectarian instruction to "all youth of good moral character." Under Kentucky practice, the legislature could change or amend the terms of a corporate charter by law but could not "defeat or substantially impair" such a charter.

The supreme court of Kentucky held that the provision for a 25-mile distance between branches of a school teaching Negro and white students was unreasonable and invalid but sustained the statute in all other respects. It spurned the argument that citizens had a right to make a choice as to their interracial associations, on the ground that the law was "aimed at something deeper and more important than choice. . . ." That something, it said, was the "preservation and purity of the races. . . ." The court was certain that there was an "antipathy between the races" and that "God has made them dissimilar." Any interracial association "at all, under certain conditions, leads to the main evil, which is amalgamation," the judges said, and added that "from social amalgamation it is but a step to illicit intercourse, and but another to intermarriage." It was apparent to the Kentucky court that "following the order of Divine Providence human authority ought not to compel these widely separated races to intermix. The right . . . to be free from social contact is as clear as the right to be free from intermarriage." It ignored the fact that there was no compulsion involved at Berea, although everybody knew the law was aimed at that school.

The Kentucky justices found no barrier in the Fourteenth Amendment, because the law, they said, "applies equally to all citizens. It makes no discrimination against either race." As an afterthought, they said, "Besides, [Berea College], as a corporation created by this state, has no natural right to teach at all. Its right to teach is such as the state sees fit to give it. The state may withhold it altogether, or qualify it." That statement was made to bolster the claim that Kentucky, which had approved the corporate charter according Berea the privilege of giving instruction to "all youth of good moral character," could change the charter to limit the scope of the college's teaching activities. The assertion was accurate enough, but it had no relevance to the issues. The U. S. Supreme Court had long since decided that a corporation, as an artificial person, was entitled to due process of law and equal protection of the laws under the Fourteenth Amendment. Since Berea College was permitted to continue its teaching function as a corporation, the real question was whether or not Kentucky could forbid it to teach white and colored Kentucky citizens at the same time in the same classrooms, when the college voluntarily chose to instruct them. At issue was the right of voluntary association for an innocent purpose, a fact recognized by the Kentucky court and denied by it on purely racial grounds.

When the case got to the U. S. Supreme Court, Justice Brewer, speaking for himself and four other justices, evaded the real issue by seizing on the pretext that the only question before the Court was the applicability of Kentucky law to changes in corporation charters and the corollary question of whether the state statute merely amended Berea's charter, as was permissible under state law, or defeated or substantially impaired it.

Pointing out that the Kentucky court had invalidated the provision that places of instruction for Negroes must be 25 miles distant from places where white students were taught, Justice Brewer argued that the Kentucky court had decided in effect that the statute did not prohibit Berea from teaching students of different races at the *same* place at *different* times or teaching them at *different* places at the *same* time. He agreed that under its 1899 charter, Berea had formerly had the right to teach both white and colored students at the same place at the same time, but, he said, the purport of the Kentucky statute was to take away that privilege while leaving the college free to teach both whites and Negroes—at the same place at different times or at different places at the same time. "Now," he said, "an amendment to the original charter, which does not destroy the power of the college to furnish an education to all persons, but which simply separates [students] by time or place of instruction cannot be said to 'defeat or substantially impair the terms'" of its charter giving the corporation the right to instruct "all youth of good moral character." What he had said was that there was nothing in the Constitution to prohibit a state from forcing corporations chartered by it to interdict voluntary interracial association for innocent purposes by citizens of the United States.

As limited by Justice Brewer, the Kentucky statute was upheld only as to corporations, but the law itself proscribed teaching of both races at the same time in the same school by "any person, corporation, or association of persons." The Kentucky court had not drawn the distinction made by Justice Brewer. It had upheld the law as applied to all persons and associations of persons, and had not intended to limit its ruling to corporations. Justice Brewer sidestepped that difficulty by holding that if the provisions of the law were "separable," it might be upheld as to corporations, without reference to whether it was valid as to persons or associations of persons. A provision of a statute is said to be separable if it is determined that the legislature would have enacted that particular provision even if other provisions were unconstitutional. He found the provision separable. "The act itself," he said, "being separable is to be read as though it in one section prohibited any person, in another any corporation and in another section any association of persons to do the acts named." He had arrived at what was obviously his goal; he stopped there and upheld the Kentucky court. Of course, he had merely begged the question. He had not dealt with the great constitutional issue before the Court, that of whether or not a state could classify its citizens on the basis of race and forbid their voluntary association for innocent purposes on the basis of that racial classification.

Four justices agreed with Justice Brewer in his evasive approval of a law that, in the final analysis, had to stand or fall on the racist justification of the Kentucky court. Two justices—William Moody and Holmes—agreed with the result but not with Justice Brewer's thin reasoning. Palpably, they were committed to the doctrine that the states could forbid voluntary interracial association if the legislature chose to do so, even if justification were placed on racist grounds by state legislators and judges. The state, they obviously believed, could make its own choice, regardless of the Fourteenth Amendment.

Justice Harlan stood his ground. "Have we," he asked his colleagues, "become so innoculated with prejudice of race that an American government, professedly based on the principles of freedom, and charged with the protection of all citizens alike, can make distinctions between such citizens in the matter of their voluntary meeting for innocent purposes simply because of their respective races?" The statute, he said, was "cruel . . . and . . . inconsistent . . . with the great principle of the equality of citizens before the law." Nobody answered his rhetorical question. Justice Day also dissented but wrote no opinion.

Turning to Justice Brewer's assertion that the provisions of the statute as to persons, corporations or associations of persons were "separable," Justice Harlan pointed out that its title was "An Act To Prohibit White and Colored Persons" from attending the same school. "It is absolutely certain," he said, "that the legislature had in mind to prohibit the teaching of the two races in the same private institution, at the same time by whomsoever that institution was conducted. It is a reflection on the common sense of the legislators that they might have prohibited a private *corporation* from teaching . . . and yet left individuals and unincorporated associations entirely at liberty [to do so]. . . . It was the teaching of the two races together . . . which the legislature sought to prevent." He insisted that the Kentucky court's reference to powers of corporations was "merely incidental . . . or a make-weight" to its decision, which rested on its racial views. The Supreme Court, he insisted, "should directly meet and decide the broad question presented" and should adjudge "whether the statute . . . is or is not unconstitutional in that it makes it a crime against the state to maintain or operate a private institution of learning where white and black pupils are received, at the same time, for instruction.

"If pupils of whatever race—certainly if they be citizens—choose with the consent of their parents or voluntarily to sit together in a private institution of learning . . . no government, whether Federal or state, can legally forbid their coming together for such an innocent purpose," he said heatedly. And he warned that Kentucky would regard the decision as a blanket endorsement of the principle that "the teaching of white and black pupils, at the same time, even in a private institution, is a crime against that Commonwealth," no matter whether the school was conducted by a corporation or by a private person or association of persons. He was right. All interracial teaching ceased in Kentucky schools, and in due season other southern states strengthened or passed laws of the same import and applied them to persons and corporations.[1]

Berea College did the best it could. In the fall of 1905, it bore transportation expenses of more than a hundred of its 174 Negro students to Negro schools, and its white students addressed a sorrowful letter to them:

> Friends and Fellow-Students: As we meet for the first time under new conditions to enjoy the great privileges of Berea College, we think at once of you who are now deprived of these privileges. Our sense of justice shows us that others have the same rights as ourselves, and the teaching of Christ leads us to "remember them that are in bond as bound with them."
>
> We realize that you are excluded from the class rooms of Berea College . . . by no fault of your own, and that this hardship is a part of a long line of deprivations under which you live . . . Because you were born in a race long oppressed . . . heartless people feel more free to do you wrong . . . Even good people sometimes fear to recognize your worth, or take your part in a neighborly way because of the violence and prejudices around us.
>
> We hope never to be afraid or ashamed to show our approval of any colored person who has the character and worth of most of the colored students of Berea.

Ultimately, Justice Harlan's dissent became the law of the land, and Negro students returned to Berea. But that was a half-century after passage of the Kentucky law.[2]

The Berea College case is ordinarily regarded solely as a part of the developing law of segregation in schools. It was that and much more. In his dissent, Justice Harlan was careful to say that the decision he proposed was not necessarily applicable to public schools, a recognition of the fact that the impact of the case fell far more heavily in other aspects of the law than on public school segregation.

The principle that it grafted onto the Constitution was that the states might forbid voluntary interracial association for innocent purposes. States and cities took the cue and tumbled over themselves to pass laws and ordinances prohibiting innocent association of Negroes and white persons in pool halls, taxicabs, restaurants, hotels, barber shops, hired automobiles, ball parks, theaters, yards, auditoriums, toilet facilities, domino or checker contests, card games, or in almost any conceivable place where association might occur. In many instances in which Negroes and whites were permitted to attend the same gatherings, laws required separate seating, separate exits, and separate entrances. Negro and white friends could not associate for the limited purpose of entering or leaving a meeting together.

Laws forbidding common use of a facility by both white persons and Negroes are commonly supposed to stem from the decision in *Plessy v. Ferguson*. That is only part of the constitutional story. The essential contribution of the Plessy case was its sanction of state classification of citizens on a racial basis. But there was nothing in that case that even hinted that Negroes could be wholly excluded by law from use of a facility open to the public. It was concerned with state sanction of racial segregation, and such segregation was approved on the theory that the constitutional command for equal protection of the law was satisfied when separate and equal facilities were provided for Negroes. There was no such saving clause in the Berea case, which not only approved racial classification by the states but also permitted them to command overt racial discrimination by ordering exclusion of a Negro from a place to which he had been extended a welcome. Neither the state nor any private individual was under any duty to provide separate facilities equal, or even comparable, to those from which he had been excluded because of race, whether in private schools, barber shops, restaurants, taxicabs, or any other place serving the general public. State law could command private persons or corporations to treat the Negro as a pariah.

Racial exclusionary laws forbidding innocent association that trailed in the wake of the Berea College case were pieces of color-

caste legislation, designed to thwart all voluntary interracial association. Those statutes penalized the restaurant keeper, for example,
who wanted to serve Negroes and whites alike, as well as Negroes
and whites who wanted to lunch together. They were justified on
the ground that they were necessary to preserve the public peace
and were permissible under the police power of the states. This
illicit harvest of color-caste legislation was the direct result of a
complete disregard of constitutional principles, particularly the
equalitarian command of the Fourteenth Amendment, as expressed
in its privileges-and-immunities, due-process, and equal-protection
clauses.

The framers of the Fourteenth Amendment and their contemporaries believed that it vested them with power to prohibit all racial
distinctions in places of public accommodation and amusement, as
evidenced by the passage of the 1875 Civil Rights Act, eight years
after the ratification of the amendment. When the Supreme Court
invalidated the Civil Rights Act in 1883, it was extremely careful to
say that racial discrimination by individuals must be "unsupported
by state authority in the shape of laws, customs, or judicial or executive proceedings" in order to escape constitutional interdiction,
and that it must not "be sanctioned in some way by the State, or
done under state authority." The Berea College case, by supporting, even commanding, racial discrimination, jettisoned the limited
protection of the *Civil Rights Cases*. Kentucky's statute and other
such laws and ordinances proscribing voluntary interracial association were throwbacks to the Black Codes enacted prior to the
Fourteenth Amendment; their constitutional ancestor was Chief
Justice Taney's dictum that the "unhappy black race were separated from the white by indelible marks." In the area of voluntary
association, these laws veered dangerously close to the Dred Scott
doctrine that a Negro "had no rights which a white man was bound
to respect."

The upsurge of this species of legislation, and judicial tolerance
of it, can be understood only through an understanding that the
South was in the grip of a paroxysm of racism that would have no
counterpart until the rise of anti-Semitism in the Germany of the
1930's and 1940's and the apartheid of South Africa. There is no
time to detail it here; a few examples will have to suffice. When
President Theodore Roosevelt lunched with Booker T. Washington
in 1903, he threw the white South into a rage. The *Memphis Scimi-*

tar said, "The most damnable outrage which has ever been perpetrated by any citizen of the United States was committed yesterday by the President, when he invited a nigger to dine with him at the White House." Senator Benjamin Tillman of South Carolina said, "Now that Roosevelt has eaten with that nigger Washington, we shall have to kill a thousand niggers to get them back to their places." Georgia's governor was sure that "no Southerner can respect any white man who would eat with a negro." The ultimate obscenity was sponsored by Governor James K. Vardaman of Mississippi, in his newspaper: "It is said that men follow the bent of their geniuses, and that prenatal influences are often potent in shaping thoughts and ideas in after life. Probably old lady Roosevelt, during the period of gestation, was frightened by a dog, and that fact may account for the qualities of the male pup that are so prominent in Teddy. I would not do either an injustice, but am disposed to apologize to the dog for mentioning it." There was more, much more, in the same scurrilous vein by newspapers, officeholders and southern politicians.[3]

Lynching found its defenders in high places and low in the early years of the twentieth century. A coroner's jury in Charlotte, North Carolina, said that members of a mob which killed a Negro "would have been recreant to their duty as good citizens had they acted otherwise." A Jacksonville, Florida, minister thought that the only check on mob violence was that the "mob be certain 'beyond a reasonable doubt.'"[4] The historian Albert Bushnell Hart noted that railroads ran special trains in order to carry parties of lynchers and that "the burning at the stake of Negroes has been advertised by telegraph."[5] It was his opinion that "the whole fabric of defense of lynching . . . in some cases and for some crimes is justified by the large majority of white men and women in the South. . . ."[6] A doctor of philosophy who wrote a volume devoted to *The Truth About Lynching* was convinced that when "proper restraint is removed from the Negro he gets beyond bounds . . . hence lynching to hold in check the Negro in the South."[7] Senator Tillman was fond of boasting that he had killed Negroes as a mob member and of asserting that he stood ready to lead other lynchers on the proper occasion.

Resistance to Negro participation in government and insistence on his disfranchisement pervaded the entire South. President Roosevelt's appointment of a Negro woman as postmaster in Indianola,

Mississippi, in 1903 roused so much fury that she was forced to flee the town and the post office was closed. The *New Orleans Daily States* called the appointment a "determination to cram an insult down the throats of white men of the South," and its contemporary, the *New Orleans Press*, warned that Roosevelt's "negro appointees will be killed just as the negro appointees of other Republican Presidents have been killed." The *Atlanta Journal* put it that Negroes "are unacceptable as officeholders to the white people of the Southern States," and its competitor, the *Atlanta News*, said that the basis for the objection was that "it gives the negro a hope that he shall continue as a political factor." The ever bloodthirsty Senator Tillman shouted, "There might be no alternative for the Southern people but to kill negroes to prevent them from holding office. There are still ropes and guns in the South." As late as 1919, the Jackson, Mississippi, *Daily News* said that the "door of hope is forever closed to the Negro, in so far as participation in politics is concerned, and there is no appeal from that decree." [8]

Opposition to Negro voting was universal and all-encompassing. "I am opposed to Negro voting," Governor Vardaman of Mississippi told his constituents in 1908; "it matters not what his advertised moral and mental qualifications may be. I am just as much opposed to Booker T. Washington as a voter, with all his Anglo-Saxon reinforcements, as I am to the coconut-headed, chocolate-colored, typical little coon Andy Dotson, who blacks my shoes every morning. Neither is fit to perform the supreme functions of citizenship." [9] William Jennings Bryan, three-time Democratic presidential aspirant, approved disfranchisement.

These repressive attitudes were bottomed on an almost fanatic belief in the inferiority of the Negro and on the necessity for keeping "white blood" pure and untainted. Even Professor Hart, essentially favorable to the Negro's cause, said in 1910, "that the Negro is inferior to the Whites among whom he lives is a cause of apprehension to the whole land." Southern scholars went much further.

William Benjamin Smith, a Tulane University professor, wrote a widely circulated book, *The Color Line, a Brief for the Unborn*, in 1905, devoted to the thesis that the South "is entirely right in keeping open at all times, at all hazards, and at all sacrifices an impassable social chasm between white and black. This she *must* do in behalf of her blood, her essence, of the stock of her Caucasian race." Race mixture, he said, was the ultimate in disaster for the

South: "Flood and fire, fever and famine, and the sword—even ignorance, indolence, and carpet-baggery—she may endure and conquer while her blood remains pure; but once taint the wellspring of her life, and all is lost. It is this immediate jewel of her soul that the South watches with such a dragon eye, that she guards with more than vestal vigilance, with a circle of perpetual fire." Why? He had a ready answer; it was "proof" shown "craniologically and by six thousand years of planet-wide experimentation" that the "Negro is markedly inferior to the Caucasian." Education and civilization, he said, are "weak and beggarly as over against the omnipotence of the transmitted germ plasma. Let this be amerced of its ancient rights, let it be shorn in some measure of its exceeding weight of ancestral glory, let it be soiled in its millennial purity and integrity, and nothing shall ever restore it; neither wealth, nor culture, nor science, nor art, nor religion—not even Christianity itself." The line must be held at all costs and at all levels, for, he said, "if the best Negro in the land is the social equal of the best Caucasian, then it will be hard to prove that the lowest white is higher than the lowest black." [10] As we have seen, Kentucky's highest court echoed these sentiments in its Berea decision.

Chief of the popularizers of this blood doctrine was the Reverend Thomas Dixon, Jr., of North Carolina, whose paean of praise to the Ku Klux Klan was made into the movie "Birth of a Nation," in 1915. Nothing was too extreme for him. "My deliberate opinion of the negro is that he is not worth hell-room," he wrote; "If I were the devil I would not let him in hell." He was certain that education was wasted on the Negro. "Education!" he sneered, "Can you change the color of [the Negro's] skin, the kink of his hair, the bulge of his lips, the spread of his nose, or the beat of his heart with a spelling book? The negro is a human donkey." The *Saturday Evening Post* opened its pages to Dixon; Hollywood glorified his dogmas.

On the political front, Senator Tillman and Governor, later Senator, Vardaman, were the most vocal exponents of white supremacy. They had a thousand pigmy imitators. In 1908, Governor Vardaman urged the Mississippi legislature to strike out all appropriations for Negro schools. "Money spent for the maintenance of public schools for Negroes is robbery of the white man and a waste upon negroes. It does him no good, but it does him harm," he said. Governor Hoke Smith of Georgia chimed in to argue that it was "folly to tax the people of Georgia for the purpose of conducting a plan of education for the Negro which fails to recognize the difference between the Negro and the white man. . . . Negro education should have reference to the Negro's future work . . . it is practicable to make that education really the training for farm labor." [11]

The literate and articulate John Temple Graves, still remembered as something of a southern oracle, seriously proposed that special courts be set up for Negroes convicted of rape. "Upon conviction of his crime," he wrote, "[the Negro] would cross a 'Bridge of Sighs' and disappear into a prison of darkness and mystery from which he would never emerge and in which he would meet a fate known to no man save the Government and the executioners of the law. . . ." These proposals, of course, ran counter to the Constitution but, as spokesman for their protagonists, the governor of Mississippi said blandly in 1908 that "There are certain things that must be done for the control of the negro. . . . In spite of the provisions of the federal constitution the men who are called upon to deal with this great problem must do that which is necessary to be done. . . ."

There was southern opposition to this orgy of racism, and there were plenty of Northerners who decried it. The "best" people, it was said, did not approve the racist demagogues. But the fact remains that Negroes *were* denied the ballot. Negro officeholders *did* disappear in the South. Negro schools *were* obviously inferior; Negro pupils received but a fraction of per capita expenditures made for whites. By 1912 the average yearly per capita school expenditure for Negroes was $1.71; that for white students was $15.00. Lynchers were *not* arrested, let alone prosecuted. Negroes *were* excluded from grand and trial juries. Segregation laws *grew* in intensity and volume. In the fullness of time, Oklahoma provided for separate telephone booths! When the Democrats took over the White House and Congress in 1912, "liberal" southern congressmen and senators of the stripe of John Sharp Williams of Mississippi joined with their demagogic colleagues in proposing a spate of Jim Crow laws for the District of Columbia. "Liberal" administrators, such as Secretary of Treasury Carter Glass of Virginia and Secretary of Navy Josephus Daniels of North Carolina, instituted racial segregation in their departments with the approval of the scholarly President Woodrow Wilson. The "best people," it appeared, may not have approved the tactics of their more racist colleagues, but they agreed with the ends.

This recital does not mean that the justices of the Supreme Court agreed with, or even sympathized with, southern demagogues, nor does it signify that they approved racist laws enacted in response to demagogic pressure and upheld by the Court. What had happened was that the Court had opened a Pandora's box by its earlier decisions resigning civil rights to regulation and control of the states. Those decisions served as precedents for the Court, and it was not easy for the justices to repudiate recent pronouncements and fly in the face of almost monolithic southern pressure and northern apathy. It was difficult to admit so quickly that Justice Harlan had been correct in his monumental dissents that the only security for civil rights lay in their protection by the federal government, under which the Fourteenth Amendment had placed them. And even if the Court had been willing to admit error, the executive and legislative branches of the federal government were no longer suffused with equalitarian sentiment or willingness to act. The Court had played its part—a very important part—in helping to create a climate of opinion in which legislative and executive wills had atrophied.

In that atmosphere, whatever doubts remained as to the power of the states to require racial segregation in public schools were regarded as dispelled by the Berea case. That assumption did not necessarily follow. All that the Court had professed to decide in the Berea case was that a state could restrict a private corporation from teaching Negro and white students at the same time in the same place if it chose to do so, by exacting such a limitation in the corporation's charter. But public schools were themselves instrumentalities of the states, and everybody agreed that at a very minimum the Fourteenth Amendment required equality in the use of state facilities. Assuming the state's power to classify citizens on a racial basis, the ultimate issue in the case of public schools was whether or not state-imposed racial segregation visited inequality on Negro pupils.

Curiously enough, the Supreme Court did not directly confront or decide that issue for half a century—until 1954 in the school segregation cases. Even more curious is the fact that the long-standing practice of racial segregation in public schools—without direct Supreme Court adjudication as to its permissibility—was seized upon by the Court to justify racial classification by the states when it upheld state-required segregation on railroads under the separate-but-equal doctrine in the Plessy case. In that case, Justice Brown had said that "the establishment of separate schools for white and colored children . . . has been held to be a valid exercise of the legislative power. . . ." He then referred to eight cases, seven of which had been decided by state courts and one by a lower federal court. One of the state cases had been decided before the Civil War. He also pointed out that Congress had established segregated schools in the District of Columbia, that its power to do so had not been questioned in litigation, and that similar state legislation had gone unchallenged.

After the existence of racial segregation in public schools had been relied upon to justify segregation laws in the case of public carriers under the separate-but-equal rule, the Plessy case was, in its proper turn, seized upon as a precedent for justification of such segregation in public schools. This bootstrap-lifting operation was accepted and permitted to obfuscate the fundamental constitutional issue, partially because of the rather confusing history that lay back of the growth of separate school systems.

There had been one case, *Roberts v. City of Boston*,[12] in which the Massachusetts supreme court had upheld school segregation in 1849 under its state constitution. In that case, Charles Sumner argued that school segregation violated a state constitutional clause providing that all men were created free and equal. "Free and equal," he asserted, meant that all men were entitled to equal protection of the law, and equal protection, he said, forbade racial classification and consequent segregation. Massachusetts later changed its law to prohibit segregated schools. After, or pending, the ratification of the Fourteenth Amendment, all states made provisions for education of Negro children. Some provided for segregated schools, others abolished separate schools, and still others followed the prior practice of segregated or nonsegregated schools, whatever it had been. Congress set up a separate school system in the District of Columbia, where it had legislative control and where the Fourteenth Amendment was not applicable.

At war's end, white missionairies, principally from New England, swarmed over the South setting up schools for Negroes. These schools attracted adults as well as children; their primary purpose was the eradication of the almost total illiteracy of former slaves.

The Freedmen's Bureau also established schools designed to root out Negro illiteracy and likewise attended by adults and children. Schools founded by missionaries and the Freedmen's Bureau were schools *for* Negroes, rather than *Negro* schools of the kind established under segregation statutes, but they helped bolster a climate of opinion already favorable to racial separation in education.

When Sumner proposed the 1875 Civil Rights Act, he included a provision forbidding separate schools, but that clause was omitted from the final bill on policy grounds. There was little doubt at that time that Congress had power to prohibit segregation in public schools, but that agreement did not extend to, or settle, the issue of what the courts could do, a question dependent on whether or not the Fourteenth Amendment by its terms proscribed racial segregation in the use of state-supplied public facilities. That question was raised in the Supreme Court in respect of schools in 1899, three years after the decision in the Plessy case but it went unanswered for technical reasons in the case of *Cummings v. Board of Education.*[13]

In the Cummings case, a Georgia county closed its Negro high school in order to use funds expended on it for Negro grade schools. Negroes sued to close down the white high schools until a high school was provided for Negroes. The Georgia supreme court refused to approve such an order. Justice Harlan, as spokesman for a unanimous Supreme Court, observed that when the case reached that Court, "It was said at the argument that the vice in the common school system of Georgia was the requirement that white and colored children of the state be educated in separate schools." But, he said, "we need not consider that question in this case. No such issue was made in the pleadings." That answer tells us nothing except that the Court was unwilling to embrace the larger issue, premised on a close following of its rules that a constitutional question cannot be considered unless it was raised in the initial proceedings and that the Court decides only questions before it.

Technically, the Court decided that closing down of schools for white pupils was an inappropriate remedy for failure to maintain comparable school facilities for Negroes. In the course of his opinion, Justice Harlan observed that "the education of pupils in schools maintained by state taxation is a matter belonging to the respective states, and any interference on the part of Federal authority with the management of such schools cannot be justified except in the case of a clear and unmistakable disregard of rights secured by the supreme law of the land. We have here no such case to be determined." The Court had not only evaded a ruling on the validity of the separate-but-equal doctrine in public schools but had also failed to define a standard of equality in the case where separate schools were in existence. The ruling in the Cummings case, although evasive, was widely regarded as Supreme Court approval of separate schools.

The practical result was that lower federal and state courts fashioned a separate-but-equal formula for schools out of the Plessy, Cummings, and Berea cases, and in time the fiction grew that the Supreme Court had considered and determined that issue with finality, whereas the truth was that it had only skirted around the question and had spoken only by evasions and indirection. Lower courts were then faced with the question of what constituted equality within the confines of the doctrine they had expounded.

As has been pointed out, it was physically possible for railroads to furnish absolutely equal, even identical, facilities for white and Negro passengers and thus satisfy the equal equation in the separate-but-equal formula devised in the Plessy case. No such matching of facilities was possible in the case of public schools. There was no way to measure equality when one school was compared with another. Matching buildings, for example, were impractical and unnecessary when a school district had 1500 white pupils and 100 Negro students; curricular identity was next to impossible in such schools because of varying pupil needs. Disparate per capita expenditures as between white and Negro pupils were sure indications of some sort of malady, but they were not absolute guides—costs per pupil might depend on necessary extensiveness of curricula, required size of buildings or playgrounds or equipment. The separate-but-equal school formula was plainly unworkable, unless the courts fell back on the wry doctrine that some people were more equal than others. They did just that by transmuting the requirement of equality into the formula of "substantial equality," which was impossible of definition. In practice, voteless southern Negroes got less and less, as school boards responded to the pressure of white voters and applied the doctrine of white supremacy. There came a time when everybody who had given the matter the slightest thought knew that Negro schools were inferior to white schools in every particular.[14] Among those who had given it some thought were Gong Lum and his daughter, Martha Lum, who lived in Mississippi.

As her name suggests, Martha Lum was Chinese, but Mississippi's constitution provided that "Separate schools shall be maintained for children of the white and colored races." Miss Lum professed no objection to separate schools in her suit. She argued that the word *colored*, as used in the constitution, meant "Negro" and insisted that she had a right to attend "white" schools since she was not a Negro. The Mississippi court disagreed; it said that everybody who wasn't white was "colored," under the definition intended in the state constitution. When her case, *Gong Lum v. Rice*, got to the Supreme Court in 1927, Chief Justice and former President William Howard Taft, who spoke for a unanimous court, agreed with Mississippi that Miss Lum was colored in the eyes of the law.[15] He said that her "case then reduces itself to the question of whether a state can be said to afford a child of Chinese ancestry, born in this country, and a citizen of the United States, the equal protection of the laws by the opportunity for a common school education in a school which receives only colored children. . . ." He cited the Cummings case as determining that public school education was solely a matter of state concern.

The Chief Justice then went on to say that if the issue of separate schools was "a new question it would call for very full argument and consideration." But, he said, "we think that it is the same question which has been many times decided to be within the constitutional power of the state legislature to settle without intervention of the federal courts under the Federal Constitution." He buttressed his point by citing fifteen federal and state cases upholding the separate-but-equal rule in schools. None of those cases had been decided by the Supreme Court, but Chief Justice Taft bridged that gap by asserting that in the Plessy case, the Court had in effect approved separate schools by approving the 1849 Massachusetts decision embodied in *Roberts v. Boston*. He was inaccurate. The Roberts case had arisen twenty years before the ratification of the Fourteenth Amendment, and at most the Plessy case had cited it only as some evidence that "custom, usage and practice" justified racial classification by the states. It was true, however, that the fifteen state and lower federal court cases listed by the Chief Justice did apply the separate-but-equal rule to schools. He ended on a weak note by upholding the Mississippi court through *assuming* "the [fifteen] cases above cited to be rightly decided." Again, the Court had been evasive, but that didn't matter very much. Miss Lum's case was seized upon as added proof that the Supreme Court approved separate schools and was totted up with the Plessy, Cummings, and Berea cases to bolster the argument that such schools afforded Negro pupils that equal protection of the law commanded by the Fourteenth Amendment.

In the first three decades of the new century, the Court's course in reference to school segregation had been weak and inconclusive. It had not faced the problem squarely, but its evasions bolstered the widely held lay and legal belief that such segregation squared with the requirements of the equal-protection clause of the Fourteenth Amendment. States were encouraged to pursue separate school policies and practices. The ruling in the Berea College case was indefensible. It put the great seal of Supreme Court approval on racist legislation that was patently proscribed even under the most restrictive interpretation of the amendment and, in doing so, institutionalized racial segregation and the color-caste system. The Court's Negro wards had fared ill at its hands.

Meanwhile, southern politicians were on the prowl for new devices to strengthen and perpetuate Negro disfranchisement, which undergirded their ability to keep the Negro in that subordinate position to which he had been condemned by the rising tide of racism. The politicians' early, and continued, successes emboldened them to believe public opinion would tolerate, and the Supreme Court would approve, any evasive scheme that stopped short of affronting the literal text of the Fifteenth Amendment.

Southern segregationists fastened on the idea that if racial ancestry could be used as a means of obstructing Negro access to the polling place and if the primary election could be made white and kept white, their purposes could be served. Negroes resisted and waged a thirty-year judicial war against the "grandfather clauses" and the white primary.

⊰ 14 ⊱ *There Came Darkness*

*When I looked for good, then evil
came . . . and when I waited for light,
there came darkness.*

JOB 30:26

When Congress was importuned to revise Reconstruction legislation, initially embodied in the Enforcement Acts of 1870 and 1871,
a House committee took a survey of the scene and urged wholesale
repeal of voting sections of the act in 1894.

"Let every trace of the reconstruction measures be wiped from
the statute books," the committee reported, "let the States of this
great Union understand that the elections are in their hands, and if
there be fraud, coercion or force used they will be the first to feel it.
Responding to a universal sentiment throughout the country for
greater purity in elections, many of our States have enacted laws to
protect the voters and purify the ballot. These, under the guidance
of State officers, have worked efficiently, satisfactorily, and benefi-
cently; and if the Federal statutes are repealed that sentiment will
receive an impetus which, if the cause still exists, will carry such
enactments in every State in the Union." Congress responded by
repealing ten sections of the act.[1]

The committee's report was, of course, a case of special pleading
for states' rights, and repeal was the work of a Democratic Congress in the second Cleveland administration. In retrospect, it is
easy to see that repeal cleared the way for sweeping changes in
southern constitutions and statutes designed to disfranchise Negroes. But it must be borne in mind that, in 1894, Negroes were still
on the voter rolls in the South, although all Reconstruction govern-

ments had been overthrown and government was firmly in the hands of so-called Redeemers. Only Mississippi had fashioned a constitution in 1890, shot through with devices that could be used to bar the Negro from the ballot box. And even in that state, Democratic and Republican politicians had a working arrangement under which some Negroes cast their ballots and a small share of minor state and county offices were apportioned to Negro favorites who went along with those who controlled the state. There were still Democratic fears that the Supreme Court might not approve Mississippi's facile subversion of the Fifteenth Amendment.

In 1898, the Court indirectly approved Mississippi's 1890 constitution, while noting that it was an instrument that "swept the field of expedients" to disfranchise Negroes.² As we have seen, a veritable tornado of change soon swept through the South. One after another, southern states amended their constitutions to add literacy tests, good-character clauses, reading-and-understanding provisions, and poll tax requirements as prerequisites for registration and voting. Proponents of these provisions said openly that the purpose was to deprive the Negro of the vote. These were fair-on-their-face provisions that could be utilized to deny registration to Negroes but could also be applied in such a manner as to extend the voting privilege to white applicants. Their efficacy may be gauged from the fact that Louisiana amended its constitution in 1898, and that its Negro voter registration dropped from 130,334 in 1896 to 1324 in 1904; 99 out of every 100 Negro voters were lopped off.

The forerunners of the grandfather clauses exempted war veterans and their lineal descendants from compliance with the onerous and tricky prerequisites for registration and voting. Confederate veterans were included. In some cases, such persons, permitted to register prior to a given date, became permanent registrants thereafter. Obviously, these clauses weighted the scales in favor of white voters—the intended result. Louisiana added a new gimmick in 1893: it gave the right of permanent registration to any person who was *entitled* to vote in any state on January 1, 1867, and to the sons or grandsons of such a person. Outside of a few New England states, Negroes were universally denied the ballot on that critical date; only white persons were *entitled* to vote.

Oklahoma's constitution contained no grandfather clause when it was admitted to the Union in 1908, but hard on the heels of admission its constitution was amended to provide that "no person shall be registered . . . or allowed to vote, unless he be able to read and write any section of the constitution" of the state. It had set a net to catch Negro applicants with a mesh wide enough to permit registrars to put white persons on the voter rolls. But Oklahoma left nothing to chance, or to the honesty of the registrar. An escape clause provided that "no person who was, on January 1, 1866, or at any time prior thereto, under any form of government, or who at that time resided in some foreign nation, and no lineal descendant of such preson shall be denied the right to vote because of his inability to read and write sections" of the state constitution.

Election judges Guinn and Beal obeyed the Oklahoma law and refused a Negro the privilege of voting because he did not qualify under the grandfather clause. They were indicted and convicted for a conspiracy to deny a citizen the "free exercise of any right or privilege secured to him by the Constitution or laws of the United States," as provided in what had been a section of the Enforcement Act of 1871 and was later codified as Section 5508 of the revised federal statutes.[3] Their Supreme Court hearing in 1914 involved the constitutionality of the grandfather clause, the state law upon which they relied to excuse their conduct. Chief Justice Edward White spoke for eight justices of the Court in an opinion invalidating the clause in *Guinn v. United States*.[4] Justice McReynolds did not sit.

The Chief Justice said that, while it was true that the Fifteenth Amendment "gives no right of suffrage, it was long ago recognized that in operation its prohibition [against racial discrimination] might measurably have that effect." It seemed to him that there was no escape from the conclusion that the amendment operated to strike down Oklahoma's grandfather clause. Otherwise, he insisted, the amendment could be rendered "inapplicable by mere forms of expression embodying no exercise of judgment and resting on no discernible reason other than the purpose to disregard" its prohibition. "Certainly," he added, "it cannot be said that there was any peculiar necromancy in the time named which engendered attributes affecting the qualification to vote. . . ." Because the grandfather clause was such an integral part of the constitutional provision, the whole article was held void.

There was another significant fact relating to the decision which was little noted at the time. Moorfield Storey, a distinguished Boston lawyer and one-time secretary to Charles Sumner, appeared as a "friend of the court" to urge the unconstitutionality of the Oklahoma law. He appeared on behalf of a five-year-old organization, The National Association for the Advancement of Colored People —the NAACP as it would soon become known.

At the same term, the Court considered civil suits filed by three Annapolis, Maryland, Negroes seeking damages against a state official who had denied them ballots in a municipal election held in their city. Anderson, the state official, had excused his conduct by a statute which provided that those eligible to vote in the election were: (1) taxpayers owning property valued at $500; (2) duly naturalized citizens; (3) male children of duly naturalized citizens; and (4) "All citizens who, prior to January 1, 1868, were entitled to vote in the State of Maryland, or any other state of the United States at a state election and lawful male descendants of" such persons. "No other person," the statute provided, "not coming within one of the three enumerated classes shall be registered as a legal voter of the City of Annapolis or qualified to vote at the municipal elections. . . ." Basing his decision largely on what he had said in the Guinn case, Chief Justice White declared the Maryland statute invalid.

The grandfather clause was dead.

The Supreme Court took another step toward protecting the Negro who sought to exercise his privilege of voting for federal officials, in *United States v. Moseley* decided at the same term as the grandfather cases.[5] Moseley and another election judge were indicted for refusing to count the vote of a Negro cast in a congressional election. Again the indictment was based on the section of the Enforcement Act, 5508, which had been involved in the Guinn case. Moseley argued vigorously that the section was unconstitutional as applied to election officials and that, while the right to vote without discrimination as to race or color was a "right or privilege secured . . . by the Constitution or laws," the *counting* of the vote was not such a right or privilege.

That quibble was too much for Justice Holmes. He replied brusquely that the law was constitutional and added that "We regard it as equally unquestionable that the right to have one's vote counted is as open to protection by Congress as the right to put a ballot in the box."

Justice Joseph R. Lamar dissented on the ground that the only section of the Enforcement Act under which Moseley could have been prosecuted had been repealed in 1894. "Revised Statute 5508 has been in force for forty-five years," he said. "During those forty-five years no prosecution has ever been instituted under it against a state election officer. That non-action but confirms the correctness of the construction that it was never intended to apply to offenses by state election officers." His was a curious, almost certainly unintended, statement that Moseley's offense had been a common one. That was certainly true, in Justice Lamar's own Mississippi and in other southern states.

Taken together, the three cases offered evidence that the Court had decided to call a halt to outright evasive aggressions against the Fifteenth Amendment. Oklahoma repaired some of the damage that had been done to its lily white voting system by enacting a 1916 law bestowing permanent registration status on those who had voted in the general election of 1914 under the invalid grandfather clause law and giving "others" (generally excluded Negroes) who were of voting age at the time just twelve days to get their names on the voter rolls or be disfranchised for life—a law that would not be challenged in the Supreme Court for more than twenty years.

One of the reforms impressed on the South during the course of and in the aftermath of Agrarian and Populist uprisings was the direct primary election, an especially important reform in that one-party section because it gave voters their only real opportunity to make a choice between candidates and took their selection away from party conventions dominated by vested interests. The movement began in South Carolina in 1896, and by 1907 ten southern states had established primary elections. North Carolina was the last to adopt the device, in 1915. That period was roughly contemporaneous with wholesale Negro disfranchisement, and the comparatively few Negroes left on the voter rolls were Republican in politics. It was not until the Woodrow Wilson campaign of 1912 that a substantial number of Negroes, North or South, broke the ties that had bound them to the party of Abraham Lincoln; in that year even the truculent W. E. B. Du Bois advised Negroes to give their votes to the Democratic presidential candidate.[6] The South had a new problem: that of barring Negro participation in the selection of Democratic candidates. Democrats first tackled the problem by party resolutions excluding Negroes from party primaries.

A Supreme Court decision that had nothing to do with Negroes or Negro voting opened up a new vista in 1921. Truman Newberry, a Michigan senatorial candidate, and a number of his followers were indicted for violation of the Federal Corrupt Practices Act for excessive expenditure of funds in a primary election.[7] In the course of a long and unclear decision, marked by dissents, the Court held that primary elections were not a part of the election process in a significant enough manner to give Congress the right to limit expenditure of funds. Texas seized on the decision to enact the first white primary law in 1923. The statute was simple and to the point. "In no event," it provided, "shall a negro be eligible to participate in a Democratic party primary election in the State of Texas. . . ." A challenge was not long in coming. Significantly, the plaintiff was a member of the rising Negro middle class, Dr. A. L. Nixon of El Paso, Texas, and the lawyers in his Supreme Court case were easily identifiable as members and supporters of the NAACP. Moreover, one of them was a Negro. The case, *Nixon v. Herndon*,[8] was decided by the Court in 1927.

Dr. Nixon's argument, as advanced by his lawyers, was the straightforward one that "Casting a ballot in a primary election established and regulated by state law is an act of voting within the meaning of the Fifteenth Amendment." That amendment, as he pointed out, said in so many words, "The right of citizens of the United States to vote shall not be denied or abridged by the United States, or by any State on account of race, color, or previous condition of servitude." The case seemed complete: the state of Texas had forbidden a Negro "to participate" in an "*election* in the State of Texas. . . ." Participation in an election meant only one thing: *voting* in that election. The Supreme Court declined that simple solution of the problem. Speaking through Justice Holmes, it based its ruling on the Fourteenth Amendment.

"We find it unnecessary to consider the 15th Amendment," Justice Holmes wrote, "because it seems to us hard to imagine a more direct and obvious infringement of the Fourteenth. That Amendment . . . was passed, as we know, with a special intent to protect blacks from discrimination against them." He paid his judicial respects to the purposes of the amendment. "States," he said, "may do a good deal of classifying that it is difficult to believe rational, but there are limits, and it is too clear for extended argument that color cannot be made the basis of a statutory classification affecting the right set up in this case."

Wittingly or unwittingly, Justice Holmes had fallen into a trap. He had reached the right result for the wrong reason and upon the basis of the wrong amendment. One of his most ardent admirers says that at the close of reading his opinion, he remarked in an aside to members of the Court, "I know that our good brethren, the Negroes of Texas, will now rejoice that they possess at the primary the rights which heretofore they have enjoyed at the general election." [9] That cruel quip had meaning because Justice Holmes and his colleagues knew that Texas Negroes "enjoyed" almost no rights in general elections. It was a callous tip-off Justice Holmes expected no more of the current decision. In any event, all that the Court decided under Justice Holmes's opinion was that states could not classify citizens on the basis of race and exclude them from party membership, with its concomitant right to vote in Democratic primary elections, on that basis. He had not resolved the real issue of the right of a Negro to vote in an election conducted by the state. The decision sent a wave of dismay through the South. But there was an escape hatch. Texas Democrats noted that Justice Holmes had limited his opinion to state action; he had not said that the party itself could not bar Negroes.

In 1927 the Texas legislature moved to solve the problem by providing that "every political party in this State through its State Executive Committee shall have power to prescribe the qualifications of its own members and shall in its own way determine who shall be qualified to vote or otherwise participate in such political party." The Democratic Executive Committee promptly confined the right to vote in primary elections to "all white Democrats who are qualified under the consitution and laws of Texas." Dr. Nixon was right back where he had started in 1925. Abetted by the NAACP, he promptly sued the new registrar. The new case, *Nixon v. Condon*,[10] was decided in 1932.

The Court was sharply divided this time, five to four, with Justice Benjamin Cardozo, Holmes's successor, speaking for the majority and invalidating the new racial proscription on the narrow ground that the action of the State Executive Committee was "state action within the meaning of the Fourteenth Amendment." Dr. Nixon's argument that a "vote at a primary election is a vote within the intendment of the Fifteenth Amendment," which forbade racial restrictions on the "right to vote at 'any election' " was passed over, as was his claim that detailed regulation by the state transformed the Democratic party into an instrumentality of the state.

All of the justices seemed to agree that racial discrimination was permissible by a private organization unless it was imposed or sanctioned by state law, an agreement that limited the immediate issue in the case to the question of whether or not the action of the Executive Committee was "state action." Justice Cardozo pointed out that the "State Executive Committee . . . is a . . . Committee and nothing more" and that it had no power except that conferred by the state. That being so, he said, the committee's power to exclude Negroes from the primary election "is statutory. If the State had not conferred it, there would hardly be any color of right to give a basis for its exercise." Having determined that state action was present, Justice Cardozo found the voting restriction a denial of equal protection of the laws. "The Fourteenth Amendment," he explained, "adopted as it was with special solicitude for the equal protection of members of the Negro race, lays a duty upon the Court to level by its judgment these barriers of color." Justices Hughes, Louis Brandeis, Harlan Stone, and Owen Roberts agreed with him. Dr. Nixon had re-established his right to vote in the Texas Democratic primary election.

Justice McReynolds, former Attorney General under President Wilson, spoke for the dissenters. His argument was the simplistic one that the Democratic party was an organization of private individuals with the same right to exclude Negroes, or any other unwanted person or group of persons, as any other private organization. "Political parties," he said, "are fruits of voluntary action . . . citizens may create them at will and limit their membership as seems wise. The State may not interfere. White men may organize; blacks may do likewise; a woman's party may exclude males. This much is essential to free government." He saw no constitutional significance in the fact that a "private organization," such as the Democratic party of Texas, chose its candidates for public office in a primary election minutely regulated by the state, for, he said, "the primary is conducted largely under party rules. Expenses are borne by the party." Nor was he troubled by the circumstance that the Executive Committee had limited the right to vote in a Democratic primary to those "who are qualified under the constitution and laws of Texas." It was plain to him that the "act now challenged withholds nothing from any Negro; it makes no discrimination. It recognizes power in every political party, acting through its Executive Committee, to prescribe qualifications for membership. . . ." The Texas election officials, he said, had "inflicted no wrong on Nixon." Justices Willis Van Devanter, George Sutherland, and Pierce Butler agreed.

Dr. Nixon had won two battles for the right to vote, but the portent was that he had lost the war. Implicit in the decisions announcing his victories was tacit agreement of the entire Court that a political party, as a private organization, could exclude Negroes from membership and from voting in its primary election. Justice Cardozo had issued a thinly disguised warning to that effect. "Whether the effect of the Texas legislation has been to work so complete a transformation of the concept of a political party as a voluntary organization we do not now decide," he wrote. "Nothing in this opinion is to be taken as carrying with it an intimation that the Court is ready or unready to follow [Dr. Nixon] that far. As to that, decision must be postponed until decision becomes necessary." Decision would soon become necessary.

The ink was hardly dry on the law books reporting the second Nixon decision before the Texas Democratic convention met on May 24, 1932, and solemnly resolved "that all white citizens of the State of Texas who are qualified to vote under the constitution and laws of the state shall be eligible to membership in the Democratic party and as such entitled to participate in its deliberations." The phrase *participate in its deliberations* plainly meant voting in the party primary.

William Grovey, a Negro, went to County Clerk Townsend of Harris County, Texas, and demanded an absentee ballot for the July 28, 1934, Democratic primary election. Mr. Townsend read the convention resolution and refused to give Mr. Grovey the ballot to which he was entitled except for the fact that he was a Negro. Grovey retaliated by suing the clerk for ten dollars in the justice court. He lost the case and then took his troubles to the Supreme Court which handed down its decision on April 1, 1935 in *Grovey v. Townsend*.[11] The court spent no time on the applicability of the Fifteenth Amendment; its major premise was that a political party was a private association or organization; its sole concern was whether or not the actions of that private organization—the Democratic party of Texas—constituted state action within the meaning of the Fourteenth Amendment. The answer, as formulated in a unanimous opinion by Justice Roberts, was a resounding no. It held in effect that a political party, any political party, in any or all states of the Union, having laws such as the Texas primary statutes, could exclude Negroes from party membership and prohibit them from voting in party primary elections!

Grovey pointed out in minute detail that Texas required a primary election, that state law had originally established the primary system, that party officials were required by state law to permit voting by all persons, except Negroes, who qualified as voters under state statutes, that the only qualified voters who could be denied the right to vote in a primary election were Negroes, and that state law defined and regulated the conduct of party officials. He demonstrated that Texas demanded the same qualifications for voters in primary elections as in general elections, that the state required use of an official primary ballot, that the number of ballots was prescribed by state law, that the same guard rails, voting booths, and ballot boxes were used in both primary and general elections, that the ballot boxes had to be delivered to county clerks, and that primary contests were decided by state judges in the same manner as general election contests. That impressive recital, Grovey argued, showed that the state had regulated primary elections as fully as general elections and had made those who managed the primaries state officers, subject to state direction and control. He had, he insisted, demonstrated state action and state involvement within the meaning of the Fourteenth Amendment.

Justice Roberts was unmoved. He answered that while it was "true that Texas has by its laws . . . provided for the expression of party preferences as to nominees, has required that preference to be expressed in a certain form of voting and has attempted in minute detail to protect the suffrage of the members of the organization against fraud, it is equally true that the primary is a party primary." He added that primary expenses and ballots were provided by the Democratic party, that votes were counted and returns made by the party to the county clerk, and that Texas itself recognized the state convention as the organ of the party for formulation of policies.

Grovey's added contention that the Democratic state convention which adopted the lily white resolution was a creature of the state and that it could no more impose a racial restriction than its creator was brushed aside with the crisp statement that the Court was not "prepared to hold that in Texas the state convention has become a mere instrumentality or agency for expressing the voice or will of the state." Nor was Justice Roberts impressed by the argument that nomination by the Democratic party was tantamount to election in Texas. "That argument," he explained, "is that as a negro may not be denied a ballot at a general election on account of his race or color, if exclusion from the primary renders his vote at the general election insignificant and useless, the result is to deny him the suffrage altogether." He did not refute the logic of the argument but rejected it on the ground that "so to say [it] is to confuse the privilege of membership in a party with the right to vote for one who is to hold public office." He stuck to his naïve view that the suit concerned party membership alone and would not lift his eyes to see that the real issue was not party membership, *per se,* but with party membership as a device to disfranchise Negroes.

Justice Roberts finally disposed of the entire matter by concluding that "the state need have no concern" with party membership and was only concerned with the general election, "for the general election is a function of state government and [racial] discrimination by the state . . . is prohibited by the Federal Constitution." He could find no ground for holding that County Clerk Townsend "has in obedience to the mandate of the law of Texas discriminated against [Grovey] or denied him any right granted by the Fourteenth and Fifteenth Amendments." The reassurance was pleasant enough, but the reality was that somebody had denied Grovey the privilege of voting in an election minutely regulated, and required, by the state of Texas.

What the Supreme Court had decided was that Negroes could be deprived of an effective voice in the election of local and state officials and of United States senators and representatives by the device of the white primary! The one-party white South had nullified the 65-year-old Fifteenth Amendment; other sections of the nation could do likewise, whenever states chose to model their laws on Texas statutes and political parties decided to follow the example of Texas Democrats. It is remarkable that there was no dissenting justice to cry judicial shame on his colleagues, as Justice Harlan had done in comparable situations.

The Court had distorted the question before it from the very beginning. From the outset, the fundamental issue, never faced by the Court, was the scope of the Fifteenth Amendment and its command that "The right of citizens to vote shall not be denied or abridged by . . . any State on account of race. . . ." Of course, primary elections were unknown when the amendment was framed and approved. It is likewise true, as the Court later pointed out, that the Founding Fathers did not foresee "the application of the commerce clause to interstate telephone, telegraph or wireless communication. But in determining whether a provision of the Constitution applies to new subject matter, it is of little significance that it is one with which the framers were not familiar." For, as Chief Justice Marshall said in 1819, ours "is a constitution intended to endure for ages to come, and consequently, to be adapted to the various crises in human affairs." [12] And as another Chief Justice explained, the words of the Constitution are to be read "not as we read legislative codes . . . subject to continuous revision . . . but as the revelation of the great purpose . . . intended to be achieved by the Constitution as a continuing instrument of government." [13] At a very minimum, the "great purpose" of the Fifteenth Amendment was to strike down every state restriction on the Negro's right to vote on a plane of equality in the election of local, state, and federal officials. Application of that principle in the first Nixon case would have aborted twenty years of litigation and two decades of practical disfranchisement of southern Negroes. For, as we shall see, the principle was finally applied in 1944. But that is anticipation.

The fact that the Court went astray in the first Nixon case and pitched its decision on the Fourteenth Amendment, instead of the Fifteenth, did not justify its decision in the Grovey case. In the landmark *Civil Rights Cases,* in which the Court held that individual invasion of individual rights was not proscribed by the Fourteenth Amendment, Justice Bradley said over and over again that the Fourteenth Amendment did not permit the individual to call upon the state to assist him in his discrimination. Individual discrimination, he said, in effect, was permissible only so long as it was "unsupported by State authority in the shape of laws, customs, or judicial or executive authority" or not protected by "some shield of State law or State authority."

The Court had interpreted Justice Bradley's language as meaning that wherever there was *state action* that furthered or assisted individual discrimination, the Fourteenth Amendment was violated. Thus, even assuming that the Democratic party of Texas was a private organization, the question to be decided was whether there was *state action* in support of the discriminatory purposes of that organization. By today's Supreme Court standards, Grovey's long and admittedly correct recital of the manner in which Texas law dovetailed with and supported the efforts of the Democratic party to deprive Negroes of a voice in a state-regulated election, which eventuated in the election of local, state and federal office-holders, was ample proof there was state action, and a consequent violation of the Fourteenth Amendment. The 1935 Court's vision was less clear.

The Newberry case, upon which Texas had seized to justify the statute in the first Nixon case, had no significance in the white-primary cases. Its purport was that the primary election was not an integral part of the state election process, insofar as a criminal prosecution under the Federal Corrupt Practices Act was concerned, although only four justices were in specific agreement on that point. But that was as far as the case went, at best or at worst. It did not involve voting rights in a primary election or composition of or membership in a political party. The case was not referred to or specifically depended upon by the Court in any of the white-primary cases.

In the final reckoning, white-primary statutes and practices were Jim Crow laws and devices, and the Supreme Court's reluctance to invalidate them was a facet of the Court's hesitancy to interfere with the segregation system it had condoned and nourished in the Plessy, Berea College, and similar cases. Having given its consent to the doctrine that states could classify their citizens on the basis of race and could legislate to protect such classification by private persons or groups, the Supreme Court found it difficult to depart from its rule, even in the case of political parties. Its difficulty was compounded by the fact that it had resigned civil rights to state regulation and control, on the assumption that the states would protect Negroes in the exercise of those rights. It was only where the states sanctioned or imposed or supported racial discrimination—that is, where there was state action—that the Court insisted that it would, or could, intervene in response to the Fourteenth-Amendment command for equal protection of the laws.

The assessment of what was or was not state action presented problems of its own. For example, in the white-primary cases, Texas legislation became increasingly fair on its face, and Texas courts rendered an elaborate series of opinions, somewhat contradictory, but holding that political parties were private organizations and that no state action was involved in voting rules and regulations. Reviewing those cases and taking them at face value, Justice Roberts said in the Grovey case that, "in light of the principles" announced in those cases, "we are unable to characterize . . . any action" taken by Democratic party officials as "state action." There was a certain judicial naïveté in such trusting dependence on state judges elected under laws challenged in their own courts. Later Supreme Court justices found it appropriate to decide such issues for themselves, and it came as no shock to sophisticated lawyers when they observed disparities between what state judges found and what Supreme Court justices discerned. Human experience is that it is often difficult for the man in the midst of the woods to distinguish between the forest and the trees.

In all fairness, it must also be borne in mind that neither Congress nor United States Attorneys General, as the legislative and executive arms of the federal government, and as such charged with concern for the rights of citizens under the Fifteenth Amendment, offered the slightest help to the Court or the slightest objection to the white primary.

In review, the Court did little between the turn of the century and the mid-1930's to protect or conserve the Negro's right to vote. To its credit, it invalidated the offensive grandfather clause. It marched bravely up the hill to strike down an obviously discriminatory state statute in the first Nixon case and marched, or slid, as bravely down that same hill to approve white-primary restrictions on Negro voting in the Grovey case, largely because it had taken the wrong upward path in the first instance. After all was said and done, southern Negroes were almost as completely and effectively disfranchised in 1935 as they were in the early 1900's, by administration of statutory literacy tests, reading-and-understanding clauses, poll tax requirements and finally by white-primary practices, all of which had received Supreme Court approval.

The southern Negro's lack of the vote was reflected in other phases of his life. Separate but equal accommodations, including schools, were certainly separate, rarely equal. Elective law enforcement officials cut the cloth of the law to fit the pattern of the color-caste system. All-white juries were the rule; they measured civil and criminal justice by the yardstick of their own prejudices. Understandably and predictably, the Negro got precious little due process of law in the courts when he could not vote for, or influence the selection of, sheriffs, police officers, prosecutors, jury commissioners, judges, mayors, governors, or legislators. In many instances, there was little to choose from between the crudities of lynch law and the summary character of justice as dispensed in rural courts.

By the second decade of the century, however, stirring social forces brought the hope of some amelioration of the southern Negro's lot. Total illiteracy was on the decline, even if it was too often replaced with only a low-level ability to read and write. The tide of early twentieth-century racism had begun to recede by the time of World War I. The air was filled with the talk of democracy. Negroes continued their steady, plodding march to the cities, where the racial atmosphere was a little less polluted with prejudice, and that march climbed to record proportions during and after World War I. The Negro middle class kept growing and kept strengthening its chosen instrument, the NAACP, for the fight for civil rights. Thousands of young southern Negroes marched, or were marched, off to war and to Europe, where they caught a new glimpse of freedom—and a new militancy that was offensive to their white neighbors. Social conflict, the certain forerunner of reform, flared in race riots, North and South.

One of those conflicts, in Arkansas, shed a blinding light on practices that were all too common in rural courts when the Negro was charged with a crime that affronted southern mores. When state judicial conduct in the trial of Negroes involved in the Arkansas conflict was examined in the Supreme Court, it resulted in a new interpretation of the due-process-of-law clause of the Fourteenth Amendment.

◄ 15 ► *The Ruling Passion*

The ruling passion, be it what it will,
The ruling passion conquers reason still.

ALEXANDER POPE, *Moral Essays*

Phillips County, Arkansas, offered an almost classic example of the way of life in the South's 221 Black Belt counties in 1919, with their total Negro population of 3,251,440 and their white population of 1,815,245.[1] It bordered on the Mississippi river. Phillips County's total population was about 44,500 persons, of whom 32,929—73.9 per cent—were Negroes. More than 75 per cent of this Negro population was described in census reports as rural; Negro tenant farmers outnumbered Negro farm owners by about nine to one; farm ownership was on the decrease; farm tenancy was growing. The average Negro tenant farmed about 24 acres of land valued at some $1200 and owned $43 worth of machinery. Cotton was king.

The urban population was concentrated in Helena, which had a white population of 4249 and a Negro population of 4863, and its companion city of West Helena, four miles distant, with a white population of 1982 and a Negro population of 4244. About 15 per cent of its Negro children between the ages of seven and ten did not attend school. The Negro population more than ten years old was 19.2 per cent illiterate. The illiteracy rate for comparable white persons was about 10 per cent. There were 18,000 Negroes of voting age in Phillips County in 1919. Very few voted. All local, county, and state officials were white. No Negro had served on either a grand jury or a trial jury in 30 years. Phillips County Negroes were poor, restive, and discontented. All too many white persons lived close to or below the poverty line, thanking God that they were not as their inferior Negro neighbors were.

Some time in 1919 a 26-year-old Negro war veteran, Robert L. Hill, founded a "fraternal order" with the high-sounding name of The Farmers Progressive Household Union of America, replete with passwords and secret ritual, the real object of which was to demand reforms in accountings between farm owners and Negro tenants. Its avowed purpose was to "advance the interests of the Negro, mentally and intellectually, and to make him a better citizen and a better farmer." Fear-ridden whites charged that the organization was storing up arms and ammunition for an insurrection and a massacre of white persons. On the night of September 30, 1919, while the union was meeting, as was its custom, at a Negro church near the village of Hoop Spur, Deputy Sheriff Charles Pratt and another white man said to be a special agent for the Missouri Pacific Railroad stopped their automobile near the church. They said it broke down. The church was riddled with gunfire and later burned. A battle ensued, in which "some" Negroes were killed and in which Pratt was killed and Adkins severely wounded. The next day fighting resumed, and another white man, Clinton Lee, and additional Negroes were killed. Pandemonium broke loose. Newspapers "discovered" a plot "of more than a local nature, possibly planned for the entire South."

The sheriff swore in 300 white deputies. The governor called for United States troops, and 500 were dispatched, who, the *Arkansas Gazette* of October 6 reported, "appeared anxious to get into battle with the blacks." After seven bloody days, during which Negroes later claimed more than 25 Negroes and at least five white men were killed, peace of a sort descended on Phillips County. The governor appointed an investigating "Committee of Seven," and on October 7 it charged that trouble resulted "from a deliberately planned insurrection of the negroes against the whites . . . for the purpose of banding negroes together for the killing of white people." The committee noted sadly that ringleaders included "the oldest and most reliable . . . Negroes . . . of the past fifteen years." A mob organized, but disbanded when the troops showed resistance and after the Committee of Seven promised that the leaders would be executed in the form of law. In keeping with that promise, an all-white grand jury, which included one member of the

Committee of Seven, met on October 27 and indicted the alleged ringleaders on October 29.

Six prisoners were taken to Court on November 3 and a lawyer appointed for them. A white attorney, O. S. Bratten, who had gone from Little Rock to Helena to confer with the union, was arrested on October 1 and locked up on a murder charge. He was unable to represent the men, because he was held in jail until October 30, then indicted for barratry on a charge of stirring up useless litigation, escorted to West Helena and told to get out of the county or run the risk of being killed. The appointed lawyer did not confer with his clients before the trial. No witnesses were called for the defense, and the trial of the first man, Frank Hicks, charged with the murder of Clinton Lee, lasted 45 minutes. An all-white jury returned a verdict of first-degree murder in five minutes. The *Memphis Commercial Appeal* reported on November 4 that the record for speed in Hicks's case "was broken in the gathering darkness when a jury retired at 5:32 to decide the fate of five other Negroes charged with the murder of Lee. Seven minutes later they returned a verdict finding the defendants guilty, sending them to the electric chair." Before the orgy was over on November 5, six other Negroes had been tried in the same shorthand manner and condemned to death. Another 36 Negroes had pleaded guilty to second-degree murder, in order to escape the summary fate that had overtaken their friends and neighbors. Evidence in the cases had been supplied by arrested Negroes who had been beaten and whipped with chains to make them confess and by two white men who later recanted their testimony.

This is just a barebones outline of the allegations of a petition for habeas corpus, sworn to by a convicted defendant, Frank Moore, and filed in the U. S. District Court after the Arkansas supreme court had ultimately upheld the convictions. His legal contention rested on the claim that he had been denied due process of law as guaranteed by the Fourteenth Amendment, because the trial was a farce, dominated by a riotous mob. No juror, he said, could have voted for an acquittal and continued to live in Phillips County, and if any prisoner had been acquitted by the jury, he could not have escaped the mob. The district judge dismissed the petition on the ground that he had no jurisdiction to grant a hearing after a trial and an appeal to the state supreme court and after the U. S. Supreme Court had declined to review the convictions. The appeal from the district judge's refusal to hear the petition for habeas corpus reached the Supreme Court in 1923, in a case styled *Moore v. Dempsey*.[2]

Justice Holmes, who had no passion for civil rights but who did have a concern, a deep concern, for the right to a fair trial, spoke for a seven-to-two majority of the Court and ordered the district judge to hold a hearing and inquire into the truth of the charges recited in Moore's affidavit. "If in fact a trial is dominated by a mob, so that there is a departure from due process of law," he said, "and . . . if the state, supplying no corrective process, carries into execution a judgment of death or imprisonment based upon a verdict thus produced by mob domination, the state deprives the accused of his life or liberty without due process of law." The Court had taken a long step forward in a direction previously advocated by Justice Holmes. It had cut through fiction and faced the reality of the situation too often confronting a southern Negro who had been condemned after conformity with the ritual and forms of the law.

The rule announced in the Moore case was one Justice Holmes had advanced in complete form in *Frank v. Mangum*[3] in 1915. That case involved a young New York Jew who was tried for murder in Atlanta in an atmosphere of complete hostility and near-hysteria. After his conviction and after the Georgia supreme court had held there were no errors requiring reversal, Frank sought a writ of habeas corpus and, upon refusal, asked the Supreme Court to require the court to examine his claim that his trial had been so dominated by mob spirit that he had been unable to get a fair trial. The Court turned him down by a seven-to-two vote, but Justice Holmes wrote a dissent, joined by Chief Justice Hughes, in which he said "it is our duty to act . . . and to declare lynch law as little valid when practiced by a regularly drawn juror as when administered by one elected by a mob intent on death." He argued vigorously that mere observance of the forms of law from indictment and trial through appeal did not preclude federal courts from probing beneath the surface in habeas corpus proceedings to determine whether or not the trial had been mob-dominated. The pervasiveness of the mob spirit was later demonstrated. Frank was seized and lynched before his sentence could be carried out.

With the majority on his side in the Moore case, Justice Holmes made his views very explicit. He agreed that mere errors of law occurring during trial could not be corrected through habeas corpus proceedings but must be examined on appeal. "But," he said, "if the case is that the whole proceeding is a mask—that counsel, jury and judge were swept to the fatal end by an irresistible wave of public passion, and that the state courts failed to correct the wrong, neither perfection in the machinery for correction nor the possibility that the trial court and counsel saw no other way of avoiding an immediate outbreak of the mob can prevent this court from securing to [the Arkansas Negroes] their constitutional rights." His reference to "an immediate outbreak of the mob" was to the fact that the Helena American Legion Post, backed by the Helena Rotary and Lions clubs, had protested later leniency to the prisoners on the ground that "a solemn promise was given to leading citizens of the community that if the guilty parties were not lynched, and let the law take its course, that justice would be done and the majesty of the law upheld." Five members of the Committee of Seven joined in a statement implying that they had forestalled a lynching on the promise that the prisoners would be condemned to death by the courts after trial. Justice Holmes's final word on the matter was that if the allegations in Moore's petition were true, "they make the trial utterly void."

Justice McReynolds, joined by Justice George Sutherland, dissented. He remarked that the Court had refused to review the original convictions and said that he could not agree that "the solemn adjudications of a great State, which this Court has refused to review, can be successfully impeached by mere affidavits made upon the information and belief of ignorant convicts joined by two white men—confessedly atrocious criminals." He upbraided his colleagues for departing from the ruling in the Frank case and said "I cannot agree now to put [the Frank case] aside and substitute the view expressed by the minority of the Court in that case. . . . The fact that [the Arkansas Negroes] are poor and ignorant and black naturally arouses sympathy; but that does not release us from enforcing principles. . . ."

Justice McReynolds's dissent harked back to the rigid concept of state regulation, control, and protection of civil rights that experience had shown was ineffectual against the realities of race relations in the South. In the Frank case, where religious prejudice was at play, Georgia not only failed to accord the prisoner a fair trial but was unable, or unwilling, to protect him from a mob. In the

Moore case, where much stronger racial prejudice was the determinant, Arkansas was unable or unwilling to afford the defendants a trial that was more than a farcical spectacle to appease the mob. The farcical nature of the trial may be gauged from the fact that the defendants were never retried. Most of them were simply turned loose and left the state. Sentences of others were commuted. The court's decision had saved them from state-contrived mob violence. Unfortunately, and despite the great importance of the decision, the Court was only treating symptoms. The deep-seated cause of the malady was left untouched.

The conduct of the Moore case, which Justice Holmes condemned so heartily, was but the poison fruit of a poison tree. When all was said and done, prosecution success rested on the attitude of the all-white grand jury, so ready to indict, and the all-white trial jury, so eager to convict. Both were spawned by the systematic exclusion of Negroes from such juries, a system which had flourished in Phillips County for thirty years, in open defiance of federal law and the Fourteenth Amendment. Within that thirty-year period, the Court had reversed two convictions on claims that Negroes had been excluded from juries—after a consideration of twelve such contests. By way of contrast, it reversed ten convictions on a similar claim in the next thirty-year period, during which it heard fourteen cases.[4]

In every jury case, the Supreme Court reiterated the rule that systematic exclusion of Negroes from juries on the basis of race offended the Fourteenth Amendment but insisted that the Negro complainant must prove with particularity that the absence of Negro jurors was due to specific discriminatory action by state officials. Its attitude was epitomized in a Texas case in which it said that jury discrimination "cannot be established by merely proving that no one of defendant's race was on either of the juries."[5] Long-continued absence of Negroes from all juries in a county did not meet the Court's test. In the almost universal situation where all officials concerned with jury selection were white, the burden thus laid on the Negro was well nigh insurmountable.

In other situations, as we have seen, states frankly disfranchised Negroes through various evasive schemes and then confined jury service to voters, a device that also drew early Supreme Court approval.[6] Pink Franklin, a South Carolina Negro, tried another challenge to this practice, in a case decided by the Court in 1910.[7] A congressional act of 1868 approved South Carolina's amended constitution, on condition that the state would never deprive any citizen of the privilege of voting except for the commission of a crime. Later, South Carolina amended its constitution to confine suffrage to those who could read or write any section of the document submitted by the registrar or meet certain property qualifications. Registrars used the reading-and-writing provision to exclude Negroes from registration, and the state confined jury service to voters. The South Carolina court decided that the change in constitutional qualifications for voters did not offend the congressional act of 1868 and upheld Franklin's first-degree murder conviction on the ground that the absence of Negroes from the grand jury which indicted him was not due to racial discrimination but to failure of Negroes to qualify to vote and, hence, to serve on the grand jury.

The Supreme Court approved the South Carolina decision, largely in dependence on the findings of the state courts. Reliance on state court decision as to whether or not there had been racial discrimination in jury selection was thoroughly consistent with the fiction developed in cases construing the Fourteenth Amendment that the states retained control and regulation of civil rights and could be counted upon to protect the rights of Negroes—the contention of Justice McReynolds in the Moore case. It was not until the Court finally decided in the 1930's that it would make its own determination as to whether or not there had been jury discrimination that it began upsetting a significant number of convictions. Between the turn of the century and the Moore case, the Supreme Court reversed two convictions out of seven appeals in which jury discrimination was alleged—one in 1900 and another in 1904. It did not reverse another such case for thirty years—until 1935. As a matter of fact, no jury discrimination cases came before the Court between 1910 and 1935, a tacit confession of defeat on the part of Negroes, since the all-white jury system continued to flourish.

The flourishing white jury system contributed to the kind of trials condemned in the Moore case in a tangential manner through the system's operation in civil litigation. One of the complaints made by the Phillips County Farmers Union was that Negro tenant farmers were consistently cheated by their landlords. As Moore set forth in his affidavit in the habeas corpus proceedings, plantation owners refused to give sharecroppers itemized statements of indebtedness and refused to let them dispose of their own cotton. The landlords, he recited, "sell and dispose of [the crops] at such prices as they please, and then give to the Negroes no account thereof, in this way keeping them down, poverty-stricken, and under their control." Relief could not be obtained in the civil courts, Moore charged. A white attorney—a former assistant United States attorney and the father of the lawyer who was arrested and jailed in the riots—supplied some interesting details in a statement to U. S. Senator, later Vice-President, Charles Curtis. He said he had represented a Phillips County Negro tenant farmer who was shot and crippled for life for requesting a settlement from a landlord. The prosecuting attorney declined to prosecute, but the Negro tenant sued for damages, and the facts were so plain that a federal jury had to return a verdict in his favor. He was awarded $100. The prosecuting attorney for Phillips County served as defense lawyer for the planter in the civil trial! [8]

The federal statute which proscribed racial discrimination in the summoning of citizens for jury service applied to civil as well as criminal jury panels, but, as we have seen, that proscription of discrimination went unheeded, except in the situation where a particular Negro defendant in a criminal proceeding raised the issue in his own case. That result flowed partially from the fact that the Supreme Court had insisted on regarding the illegally drawn all-white juries as competent to function and their verdicts as valid in all situations, unless a Negro defendant charged and could prove systematic exclusion under the Court's restrictive rules. When it had been presented early opportunities to do so, the Court passed up the chance to hold that a grand jury from which Negroes had systematically and illegally been excluded was without competence to indict or such a trial jury disabled from sitting in either a civil or a criminal trial. And, as we have also noted, Attorneys General simply did not try to enforce federal law prohibiting jury discrimination. The only prosecution undertaken in the 90 years that the statute has been in force occurred in 1877, and it was successful at least to the extent that the government secured an indictment. This lassitude and indifference has amounted to federal sanction of jury discrimination in light of the fact that such discrimination was a matter of common knowledge and that Negro defendants have proved it on numerous occasions.

Of course, the Supreme Court cannot be held directly responsible for the derelictions of U. S. Attorneys General in this area of the law, but vigorous comment, even by way of dictum, might have jogged the conscience of law enforcement officials. The Court's particular responsibility lay in its reduction of the federal statute against jury discrimination, and the safeguards of the Fourteenth Amendment for equal protection of the law, to a limited separate-but-equal device available only to a Negro defendant in his own trial. Beyond that is the fact that the strength and weakness of the jury system is that the jury mirrors the attitudes of the community in which it sits.

Southern jurors knew full well that they were selected on a racially discriminatory basis; it would have been more than a miracle if their verdicts had not reflected the discrimination exercised in their own selection. They were equally aware that Jim Crow practices had the active support and sanction of what we have come to call the power structure in their communities and in their states and that in its proper turn the color-caste system had received the approval of the courts, ranging from the lowest justice court to the Supreme Court of the United States. As momentary participants in the judicial system, southern white jurors were as zealous to keep the Negro in his place as the judges who had played their role in assigning that subordinate place to the Negro. As Justice Holmes explained it in the Frank case, "Any judge who has sat with juries knows that in spite of forms they are extremely likely to be impregnated by the environing atmosphere."

A part of the total "environing atmosphere" in which southern jurors sat in judgment on Negroes in civil and criminal cases was the helplessness of the Negro, attendant upon his lack of the vote and consequent inability to play a part in the selection of local, state, and federal officials. Elective and appointive officials alike, more often than not, owed their positions to their promises made to the white electorate, from which juries were chosen, to compound and intensify discrimination against Negroes. It seemed to the white juror that his own well-being depended upon his willingness to play his assigned part in upholding the segregation system, at no matter what cost to his oath.

Through its restrictive interpretations of the Civil War Amendments and subsequent equalitarian legislation, the Supreme Court had played a significant part in the creation and protection of the color-caste system, and to that extent it bore a share of the responsibility for the mock justice afforded the defendants in the Arkansas cases. The Court's intervention in that farce by its decision in the Moore case was only the beginning of an obvious determination on its part to lift the trials of Negroes out of the muck and mire of racism, as we shall see. That task was tremendously complicated and difficult, and could not be achieved without change and reform in other aspects of race relations. Under the segregation system, justice, too, would remain separate—and never equal.

Meanwhile, there was little indication in the first 30 years of the century that the Supreme Court was ready to call a halt to racial segregation, or indeed to ameliorate it in any particular. The separate-but-equal doctrine seemed to be rigidly fixed in the constitutional firmament. Within that span, a series of cases came to the Court regarding segregation in interstate travel and before it was through, it had extended the scope of the ruling it had first made in *Plessy v. Ferguson.*

These cases had no great importance in and of themselves and announced no startling new principles of law, but the circumstance that the separate-but-equal doctrine was first approved in a railroad case gave them symbolic value and significance. The Chesapeake and Ohio Railway Company was indicted for refusal to maintain a Jim Crow car in compliance with what was a plain attempt of the Kentucky legislature to require segregation of passengers in interstate travel. The railroad complained that state regulation of interstate commerce was impermissible, but the Kentucky court answered that if "it were conceded (which it is not) that the statute is invalid as to interstate passengers, the proper construction would then be that the legislature . . . intended it to apply to transportation within the state. . . ." The Supreme Court upheld the Kentucky court in a 1900 decision, in which Justice Brown thought it would be "scarcely courteous to impute to a legislature the enactment of a law which it knew to be unconstitutional." The practical effect of the case was to require the railroad to maintain Jim Crow cars on its interstate passenger lines.

Forced to maintain Jim Crow cars on its interstate lines, the Chesapeake and Ohio Railway adopted regulations requiring Negro passengers to leave their previous seats and ride in the Jim Crow car when they reached Kentucky soil. J. Alexander Chiles, a Negro lawyer, bought a ticket from Washington, D.C., to Lexington, Kentucky, and was ordered into the Jim Crow car at Ashland, Kentucky. After a great deal of sparring around, he was forced into the Jim Crow car and later sued the railroad on the ground that he was an interstate passenger. His case was decided by the Supreme Court in 1910.[9] The railroad justified its action on the ground that it was entitled to establish reasonable rules and regulations of its own and disclaimed all reliance on Kentucky law. Justice McKenna described the separate accommodations as equal. He said the train had four coaches: a baggage coach; a coach divided into three sections, with one "set apart for colored passengers [sic]," another for colored persons who smoked, and a third for white persons who smoked; a third "passenger car for the use of white ladies and gentlemen [sic]," and a sleeper. Interstate passengers, he said, could be segregated by the railroad by regulation in any state in the absence of congressional law. "Regulations," he said, "which are induced by the general sentiment of the community for whom they are made and upon whom they operate, cannot be said to be unreasonable." Justice Harlan again dissented in frustrated silence.

Mrs. Emma Butts bought a first-class ticket from Boston to Norfolk, Virginia, and return on a coastal steamer, operated by the Merchants and Miners Transportation Company. Because she was a Negro, she was refused service at regular meal times and forced to wait for a second call to meals, and denied a cabin on the first deck. When she got back home, she sued under Sections 1 and 2 of the 1875 Civil Rights Act. She pointed out that the Court had said in 1883, when it held the sections unconstitutional as applied to states: "We have discussed the validity of the law in reference to cases arising in the States only; and not in reference to cases arising in the territories or the District of Columbia." Mrs. Butts argued that the act was still in force in the District of Columbia and in the territories and, also, on the high seas in which Congress had jurisdiction to legislate as it chose. It specifically forbade racial discrimination in "public conveyances on land or water. . . ."

The Court, speaking through Justice Van Devanter, rejected her claim on the ground that because it was a criminal statute, the provisions of the act were not separable. Its ruling as to separability was in marked contrast to the similar ease with which it had found a Kentucky law separable in the Berea case, when it eagerly upheld a segregation statute imposing criminal penalties. At any rate, Sections 1 and 2 of the 1875 Civil Rights Act were dead beyond hope of resurrection. Justice Harlan had died and there was no dissenting voice.[10]

Oklahoma, admitted to the Union long after the Civil War, had all of the earnest zeal of a convert in the cause of racial segregation. As we have seen, it had enacted a sweeping grandfather clause to harass Negro voters, had provided for separate-but-equal telephone booths, and had polished up almost every other conceivable kind of Jim Crow statutes. It also enacted a sweeping transportation segregation statute, under which Negroes were segregated in all kinds of travel and which exempted railroads from furnishing Pullman and dining cars for Negroes because there was little demand for such service. Five Negro Oklahomans sued to restrain the Santa Fe and four other railroads from observing the law.[11] Their suits were dismissed on technical grounds in 1914, but Justice Hughes, who spoke for five justices, approved the separate-but-equal rule in railroad travel. However, he said that if railroads furnished Pullman and dining car accommodations for white persons, they must also furnish such accommodations for Negroes, regardless of the fact that there was little demand from Negroes as a class for such services. He announced the important principle that the Oklahoma law had tried to make "the consitutional right depend upon the number of persons who may be discriminated against, where the essence of the constitutional right is that it is a personal one." What he had said was that a constitutional right inhered in a person as an individual and not as a member of a group. Justices White, Holmes, Lamar, and McReynolds agreed with the dismissal but not with Justice Hughes's opinion, obviously because they believed that Oklahoma could relieve the railroads from furnishing Pullman and dining car accommodations to Negroes where there was no profit in such services.

The Court wound up its pre-1935 transportation cases with a holding that Kentucky could require an interurban line running from Cincinnati, Ohio, to Covington, Kentucky, to maintain a Jim Crow section and herd Negroes into it as long as they were on the Kentucky side of the Ohio river. That requirement, it said, did not burden interstate commerce! Justice McKenna wrote the opinion with the concurrence of Justices White, Holmes, Brandeis, John Clarke and, of course, McReynolds. Justice Day wrote a dissent for himself and Justices Van Devanter and Mahlon Pitney.[12]

Relatively unimportant in themselves, these cases illustrate the Court's complete subscription to the separate-but-equal doctrine and approval of the color-caste system. Taken together, they closed almost every possible loophole and made railroad travel in the South wholly Jim Crow. Moreover, they set the tone, and created a climate of judicial opinion in which lower federal and state courts hastened to give their judicial blessings to racial segregation in almost every phase of national life. Segregation imposed by state law was much more rigid and widespread in 1930 than in 1900, and it was growing in scope and intensity. Challenges in the Supreme Court to such segregation were not undertaken, because there was general agreement that there was little prospect of success or for important dissents after Justice Harlan's death in 1911. Supreme Court liberals, whatever that term may mean, had come to terms with the segregation system.

With sporadic exceptions on the part of each, Justices Day, Brandeis, Cardozo, and Hughes seldom dissented in segregation cases. Their concern was not with civil rights but with civil liberties, where their dissents and decisions made judicial history. They spoke out only in the aggravated cases where segregationists over-reached themselves, as in the grandfather clause cases or in the first and second Nixon voting cases, but were easily assuaged when segregatory devices were overlaid with constitutional sophistry, as in the Grovey case. Justice Holmes, who was impatient with equalitarian sentiment and believed that the demand for equality was only a species of envy, offered no leadership in the arena of civil rights; as the fabled Great Dissenter of his time, he found himself in agreement with his colleagues in the most restrictive of their civil rights decisions. Where an issue of fair trial arose, Justice Holmes spoke out, but his underlying philosophy was that, despite history and the great purpose of the Fourteenth Amendment, the states were as free to experiment in racial matters as he contended they were in economic and other social issues.

Within the context of expanding segregation and with snail's-pace relief from restrictions on voting rights and jury service, the Negro's chance for fairness in trials as demanded in the Moore case was limited. But there was a social change in the South that promised more by way of relief from oppressive rural justice than did judicial intervention. As the Negro continued his trek to the cities, southern segregationists sought new ways to keep him in his place. Characteristically, they turned to, and sought to expand, legal segregation.

Baltimore enacted a racial zoning ordinance on May 15, 1911, limiting and defining Negro residence within its boundaries. The state of North Carolina, Wilmington, Atlanta, and New Orleans followed suit, as did some smaller cities. These ordinances were based on the separate-but-equal formula approved by the Supreme Court and refined by state and lower federal courts. Twentieth-century southern American cities were turning back to the ghetto of the Middle Ages. The alarmed Negro middle class girded for the battle; such segregation was plainly intolerable. The test came in the case of a Louisville, Kentucky, ordinance that had been carefully tailored and enacted in 1914 to meet judicial specifications that were said to conform to the requirements of the Fourteenth Amendment. The question got to the Supreme Court in 1917, with the NAACP and southern cities locked in battle.

His Castle and Fortress

*The home of every one is to him as his castle and
fortress, as well for his defence against
injury and violence as for his repose.*

LORD COKE, *Semayne's Case*

The municipal segregation ordinances that flowered in the South
after 1910 were not the first attempts at racial zoning. San Francisco deserves whatever honor is due for pioneering in that field.
California's 1879 constitution clothed cities and towns with the authority to exclude Chinese or segregate them within city limits, and
San Francisco responded with a segregation ordinance. A federal
court promptly invalidated the measure in 1890, on the ground that
it denied Chinese the equal protection of the law demanded by the
Fourteenth Amendment.[1]

Louisville's 1914 ordinance, designed as a model, was artfully
drawn in an attempt to square it with constitutional requirements.
It was entitled an "ordinance to prevent conflict and ill-feeling between the white and colored races . . . to preserve the public
peace and promote the general welfare by making reasonable provisions requiring . . . the use of separate blocks for residence,
places of abode and places of assembly by white and colored people respectively." After its effective date, Negroes were forbidden
to use or occupy places of residence or assembly in blocks where
the majority of inhabitants were white and, conversely, white persons were prohibited from using or occupying places of residence
or assembly in blocks where the majority of residents were Negroes. If a building was used by, or sold or rented as a place of
public assemblage to, whites after the passage of the ordinance, it

could not thereafter be used by Negroes; if a building was used by, or sold or rented as a place of assemblage to, Negroes after the passage of the ordinance, it could not thereafter be used by white persons. In short, every restriction imposed on Negroes was also imposed on white persons. The ordinance did not apply to residential uses enjoyed prior to its passage. A Negro or a white person could buy property anywhere, but the purchaser, white or Negro, had to comply with the terms of the ordinance as far as racial use or occupancy were concerned. Violation of its provisions was made a criminal offense.

The careful balancing of restrictions, with every restraint imposed on Negroes duplicated by an identical restraint imposed on white persons, had two purposes. First, it was believed to avoid the fatal constitutional flaw in the San Francisco ordinance which was directed against Chinese as a single racial group. Second, it embodied the curious concept that the Fourteenth Amendment's command for equal protection of the law was satisfied if both Negroes and white persons were equally discriminated against in the same statute. That ingenious interpretation was first announced by the Court in an opinion written by Justice Field in 1883, upholding an Alabama statute which punished adultery for both participants more severely when one of the adulterers was white and the other colored than when both were members of the same race.[2] He said that since the punishment was the same for both white and Negro offenders, there was no denial of equal protection. That same concept was believed to justify laws which prohibited "white" hotels from receiving Negro guests and "Negro" hotels from catering to white guests. The provision that Negroes, or white persons, were perfectly free to buy or own property anywhere, subject to racial restrictions on use or occupancy, was an obvious attempt to fend off the possibility of a successful attack on the ordinance on the ground that it interfered with the highly cherished right of free ownership of land.

Negroes and white opponents of the ordinance did not wait for a test of its validity through a challenge to the arrest and conviction of some witting or unwitting violator. They attacked it head-on through a carefully contrived civil case. Robert Buchanan, a white man who owned a lot in a block in which there were eight white and two Negro residents, entered into a sales agreement with William Warley, a Negro. The agreement contained a clause in which

Mr. Warley recited that "I am purchasing the . . . property for the purpose of having erected there on a house which I propose to make my residence. . . . I shall not be required to accept a deed . . . or pay for said property unless I have the right under the laws of the State of Kentucky and the City of Louisville to occupy said property as a residence." Both of them, and their lawyers, knew perfectly well that Warley couldn't build a house on the lot and occupy it as a residence if the segregation ordinance was valid, because the majority of residents in that block were white persons.

In due season, Buchanan demanded the purchase price and offered to deed the property to Warley, who at once professed legal pain and surprise. He told Buchanan he wouldn't pay and wouldn't accept the deed, because the agreement said he didn't have to pay or accept the deed unless he had a right to build and occupy a residence on the lot. He reminded Buchanan that the ordinance prohibiting his residence was still in full force and effect. It was now Buchanan's turn to profess pain and surprise. His answer was that the ordinance was invalid and obnoxious to the Constitution and that Warley knew it. To prove his point, he sued Warley to make him accept the deed and fork over the purchase money. Louisville's attorneys took up the cudgels for Warley—perhaps they didn't trust him to defend his own suit properly. When the case got to Court, it presented the strange spectacle of the white plaintiff, Buchanan, contending that a segregation ordinance was unconstitutional and of the Negro defendant, Warley, apparently fighting tooth and nail to uphold racial segregation. The ways of lawyers, like the ways of Providence, sometimes appear inscrutable.

The trial judge impatiently threw Buchanan's case out of court, saying that of course the ordinance was constitutional and that Warley didn't have to accept the deed or pay a single dime. Buchanan patiently appealed to Kentucky's highest court, where he repeated his argument that the ordinance was unconstitutional and asked the judges to compel Warley to accept the deed and pay the purchase price. He fared no better than he had in the lower court and was given a stern lecture on racial purity and integrity in the bargain.[3]

The Kentucky court of appeals reminded the litigants that in the Berea case voluntary association of the races had been prohibited, partly, it said, "in recognition of the peril to race integrity induced by mere propinquity." The judges added that they would "not close their eyes to the fact" that there was as much if not "a greater association of children of white and colored inhabitants living side by side than there would be in mixed schools. . . ." The state, they said, could exercise "the police power of government to prevent the mixing of the races in cross breeding." To the complaint that residential segregation would compel Negroes to live in less desirable sections of the city, the court returned the answer that Negroes could beautify their section of the city just as whites had done. Finally, it said, municipal segregation would compel more fortunate Negroes to stay with and assist "their less fortunate fellows . . . and thus in the end, it will justify that enlightened civic spirit by which it is demanded."

The skeptical Buchanan took his case, entitled *Buchanan v. Warley*,[4] to the U. S. Supreme Court, where, to nobody's surprise, he was represented by attorneys for the NAACP. Justice Day spoke for a unanimous Court in 1917, holding that the Louisville ordinance was unconstitutional. "It is the purpose of such enactments," he said, "to require by law . . . the compulsory segregation of the races on account of color. Such action is said to be essential to the maintenance of the purity of the races. . . ." Justice Day rejected the racist argument of the Kentucky court of appeals with the blunt statement that "The case does not deal with an attempt to prohibit the amalgamation of the races. . . ." He saw the question as that of whether or not the Fourteenth Amendment was applicable and said validity of the ordinance also depended on one of the provisions of the original Civil Rights Act of 1866, re-enacted after passage of the Fourteenth. That section provided, "All citizens of the United States shall have the same right in every state and territory as is enjoyed by white citizens thereof to inherit, purchase, lease, sell, hold and convey real and personal property."

Justice Day, who had dissented in the Berea case, said that decision was no precedent in the Buchanan case, because it merely concerned the power of the Kentucky legislature to amend a corporation's charter. He was quite willing to admit that "there exists a serious and difficult problem arising from a feeling of race hostility which the law is powerless to control and to which it must give a measure of consideration . . . ," but he said, "its solution cannot be promoted by depriving citizens of their constitutional rights and privileges. . . ." The concrete question before the Court, he said is,

"May the occupancy, and, necessarily the purchase and sale of property of which occupancy is an incident be inhibited by the States, or by one of its municipalities, solely because of the color of the proposed occupant of the premises?"

The justice had an answer to his own question. "Colored persons," he wrote, "are citizens of the United States and have the right to purchase property and enjoy the use of the same without laws discriminating against them solely on account of color. . . . The Fourteenth Amendment and these statutes enacted in furtherance of its purpose operate to qualify and entitle a colored man to acquire property without state legislation discriminating against him solely because of his color." Louisville's lawyers then advanced the argument that Buchanan was a white man and couldn't claim the protection of the Fourteenth Amendment under the circumstances of the case. Justice Day was not impressed. "The right which the ordinance annulled was the civil right of a white man to dispose of his property as he saw fit to a person of color, and of a colored person to make such a disposition to a white person." Buchanan, he said, would be denied due process of law if he could not complete the sale.

The social arguments advanced to bolster the ordinance did not daunt Justice Day. He noted that it "is urged that this proposed segregation will promote the public peace by preventing race conflicts. Desirable as this is . . . this aim cannot be accomplished by law or ordinance which deny rights created or protected by the Federal Constitution. It is said that such acquisitions by colored persons depreciate property owned in the neighborhood by white persons. But property may be acquired by undesirable white neighbors, or put to disagreeable though lawful uses with like results."

Everybody but Louisville, other southern cities, and segregationists, North and South, was happy: the NAACP, because it had established the great principle that states and cities could not impose residential segregation by law or ordinance; Buchanan, because he had won, and Warley, because he had lost. There were sporadic attempts to evade the ruling, but the Supreme Court stuck to its guns and invalidated two other ordinances by mere reference to its holding in the Buchanan case.[5] News of Supreme Court civil rights decisions often travels slowly in the South, however, and as late as 1949, Birmingham enacted a racial zoning ordinance which was quickly invalidated by lower federal courts in 1950.[6] Other laggard southern municipalities enforced such ordinances in plain defiance of the Supreme Court.[7]

Amid the general rejoicing over the victory in the Buchanan case, a cloud no larger than a lawyer's pen rose on the housing horizon. State courts began enforcing racially restrictive covenants.

The racially restrictive covenant was a simple device imposed by the deed of the subdivider or by recorded neighborhood agreements, providing that the parcels of land belonging to the signer or signers should not thereafter be owned or used or occupied by Negroes, or Orientals, or Jews, or other prescribed members of an unpopular minority. In case a Negro bought or occupied property covered by a racial covenant, a white property owner in the tract could file suit. The court would then issue an injunction nullifying the sale or ordering the offending Negro to vacate the property. If he failed to obey the order, he could be jailed for contempt of court. Negroes took up arms against this new sea of troubles with the argument that a decree of a state court in issuing an injunction was the action of the state and violated the equal-protection clause of the Fourteenth Amendment, which provided that no *state* should deny any person equal protection of its laws.

That argument had been effective in an 1892 California case, when a lower federal court had held that judicial enforcement of racial covenants was indeed state action and violative of the Fourteenth Amendment.[8] The steady migration of Negroes to cities and the Supreme Court invalidation of racial zoning ordinances in 1917 exacerbated the demand for some means of imposing residential segregation. The 1892 case was disregarded.

Proponents of racial covenants argued that they had a right to have their contracts enforced in the courts. The principle of equal protection of the laws was met, they said, by the fact that Negroes were equally free to create and enforce restrictive covenants against ownership, use, or occupancy of their property by white persons. Besides, they added, the Fourteenth Amendment did not prohibit discrimination by private persons. A Louisiana court of last resort examined the legal question in 1914 and found that judicial enforcement of racial covenants was permissible under the Fourteenth Amendment. "Since the days of the *Civil Rights Cases*," it said, "it has been settled that the provisions of the Fourteenth Amendment [apply] to legislative acts of the state rather than to individuals." The Louisiana court was mistaken. The Supreme

Court had repeatedly held that the amendment applied to judicial and administrative actions of the state as well as to legislative acts. California appeals courts agreed with Louisiana in 1917.[9] Missouri's highest tribunal, echoing *Plessy v. Ferguson*, fell in line in 1918, with the observation that residential segregation did not offend constitutional guarantees, because "For instance, the law providing for segregation of Negroes in separate passenger coaches from those occupied by whites has been held lawful." [10] Michigan's highest court in 1922 upheld judicial enforcement of racial covenants with the knowing dictum—borrowed from the Plessy case— that "The law is powerless to eradicate racial instincts or to abolish distinctions which some citizens draw on account of racial difference in relation to matters of purely private concern. . . . The discrimination against Negroes has been recognized by the courts in other matters where their presence has been objected to for reasons similar to those advanced here." [11] In 1925, a federal trial court in the District of Columbia upheld court enforcement of such an agreement. The next year, the Court of Appeals for the District agreed and held that "segregation of the races, whether by statute or private agreement that does not amount to the denial of fundamental constitutional rights, cannot be held to be against public policy. Nor can the social equality of the races be attained either by legislation or by the forcible assertion of assumed rights." [12] The Supreme Court reviewed the case, *Corrigan v. Buckley*, in 1926.

In 1921, John J. Buckley, Mrs. Irene Corrigan, and 28 other white persons signed an agreement covering 25 parcels of land then owned by them in Washington, D.C. That agreement provided that "no part of these properties shall ever be used or occupied by, or sold, leased or given to, any person of the negro race or blood." In 1922, Mrs. Corrigan entered into an agreement to sell her lot to Mrs. Helen Curtis, wife of a prominent Negro physician.

Mr. Buckley sued Mrs. Corrigan and Mrs. Curtis, and asked the court to nullify the sale on the ground that it violated the terms of the restrictive covenant signed by Mrs. Corrigan. Mrs. Curtis filed a motion to dismiss the suit, urging that the covenant itself was "void" because it attempted to deprive her of property without due process of law, abridged her "privileges and immunities," and denied her equal protection of the law in violation of the "Fifth, Thirteenth and Fourteenth Amendments." She also insisted that racially restrictive covenants violated the public policy of the District of

Columbia and were of a kind that the courts of the District should not enforce. The trial court dismissed her motion and held that Buckley was entitled to a judgment nullifying the sale of the property. The Court of Appeals agreed, as we have seen.

In the appeal to the Supreme Court, the by-now familiar NAACP attorneys sought to broaden their attack. They reiterated the charge made in the trial court that the covenant itself was "void," and they also stressed the contention that a court decree ordering enforcement of a racial covenant was governmental action to impose residential segregation. As they put it, "These decrees have all the force of a statute. They have behind them the sovereign power. In rendering these decrees, the courts which have pronounced them have functioned as the law making power." The purpose of that argument was apparent: the Court had decided in the Buchanan case that residential segregation could not be imposed by law. If Mrs. Curtis's lawyers could convince the Court that a decree ordering enforcement of a segregation agreement had "all the force of a statute" and that in issuing such a decree the trial court had "functioned as the law making power," they hoped that the Supreme Court Justices would hold that a court could no more issue a decree enforcing a segregatory agreement than a city council or state legislature could enact an ordinance or a law enforcing residential segregation.

The unanimous Supreme Court opinion written by Justice Sanford began by severely limiting the issue before it. "The only constitutional question involved," he wrote, "was that arising on the motion to dismiss" on the ground that the covenant itself was "void." He was of the opinion that "This contention is entirely lacking in substance or color of merit." The Thirteenth Amendment, he said, only abolished slavery; the Fifth was a restriction on the federal government, and the Fourteenth simply prohibited racial discrimination by the states. "It is obvious," he insisted, "that none of these amendments prohibited private individuals from entering into contracts respecting the control and disposition of their own property." Nor could he find any comfort for Mrs. Curtis in civil rights laws enacted by Congress, giving Negroes the same right "as is enjoyed by white citizens . . . to inherit, purchase, lease, sell, hold and convey real . . . property." Such laws, he said, "do not in any manner prohibit or invalidate contracts entered into by private parties in respect to control and disposition of their own property."

What he had said was that the racial covenant itself was not void.

Justice Sanford then turned to the claim that the trial court decree was a species of lawmaking. "It was further urged in this Court," he said, "that the decrees of the court below in themselves deprived defendants of their liberty and property without due process of law in violation of the Fifth and Fourteenth Amendments." He asserted that this contention came too late to be effective and could not serve as the basis for an appeal, because "it was not raised by the petition for the appeal or by assignment of error, either in the Court of Appeals or in this Court." But, he added, that contention "is likewise lacking in substance." His meaning was clear: the claim that court decrees were lawmaking devices came too late and in addition was groundless. Justices Holmes, Sutherland, Brandeis, Van Devanter, Taft, Roberts, Stone and Butler all agreed with Justice Sutherland. The case was dismissed for "lack of jurisdiction."

From a strictly legal and technical point of view, all that the Court had decided was that a racially restrictive covenant was not void in and of itself, that property owners were entirely free to enter into such agreements and abide by them if they chose to do so, and that a court would not hold them void on the complaint of a Negro who wanted to buy the land. It said it had no jursidiction to decide any other issue. By that reckoning it had not decided the crucial question of whether or not judicial decrees ordering enforcement of such agreements were akin to municipal zoning ordinances and hence violative of constitutional guarantees. However, the Court's assertion that such a contention was "likewise lacking in substance" was seized upon by state courts as a settlement of the constitutional question, and for the next two decades they repeated almost endlessly that the issue had been settled by the Supreme Court. Federal housing agencies acted on the same assumption from 1934 to 1948. The Court lent color to that interpretation by subsequent refusal and failure to clarify its declaration when it had opportunities to do so. Despite a later disclaimer, it is apparent that the Supreme Court had given effective sanction to the proposition that judicial enforcement of racial covenants squared with constitutional requirements.

Just as the Buchanan case was a great victory for Negroes, so the Corrigan case was a major disaster. The proposition that courts could enforce racial covenants weakened the prior ruling that mu-

nicipal segregation ordinances were invalid, and opened the flood-
gates for residential segregation, North and South. Voters who
could not impose such segregation by legislation could and did do
so through private agreements enforced by the judicial arm of government. The ruling came on the eve of an upsurge of Negro immi-
gration to cities and on the threshold of widespread governmental
involvement in housing. The dogma that private property owners
had a constitutional right to insist upon exclusion of Negroes from
urban communities and neighborhoods was woven into the warp
and woof of governmental housing policies, practices, and procedures, even to the extent that the Federal Housing Administration
later furnished a model racial covenant for builders and developers
and insisted upon its use as a condition for the grant of mortgage
insurance.[13] Negroes were shut up in the decaying centers of cities,
while new suburbs became lily white.

Ultimately, courts of last resort in 19 states and the District of
Columbia gave their assent to the doctrine that judicial enforcement of racial covenants was compatible with the Fourteenth
Amendment. That was not quite the whole story; the doctrine was
accepted and acted upon even in states where there was no final
adjudication of the question. Enforcement was nationwide. Dependence on the Supreme Court's decision in the Corrigan case
encouraged and stimulated state court decisions and armored the
segregatory policies of governmental housing agencies against
criticism and attack.

The Negro ghetto planted by racial covenants and rooted in the
segregation system flourished and grew in the warm sunlight of
Supreme Court approval.

Gifted as we are with the perfect vision of 20-20 hindsight, we
can see quite clearly that in the years from 1900 to 1930, or there-
abouts, the Supreme Court had failed its Negro wards in some significant respects and had aided them materially in fewer situations.
On the debit side of the ledger, it had restricted federal protection
of the individual Negro in the Hodges case, where a mob had
driven Negroes from a job; it had spurred the growth and intensity
of racial segregation by its decisions in the Berea College case, the
transportation decisions regarding railroad travel, and in the Gong
Lum case involving schools; it had bolstered disfranchisement by
its ultimate resolution of the white primary dispute; it had left un-
checked the flourishing all-white jury system, and it had encour-

aged the rise of the Negro ghetto in the Corrigan case. That its lapses in every one of these situations was not due to constitutional impediments, but rather to myopic interpretations of the Constitution, will become apparent when it is seen later that the Court found remedies in a changed interpretation of the requirements of the Fourteenth Amendment.

On the credit side of the ledger during that same period, the Court had called a halt to peonage practices in the Bailey cases; it had vitiated the grandfather clauses; it had nullified municipal racial zoning ordinances in the Buchanan case, and it had frowned on mob-dominated trials in the Moore case. In later years, every one of these cases would be found efficacious to bolster and broaden the Negro's citizenship rights.

What the Supreme Court had done in respect of the rights of Negroes in the years from 1900 to 1935 flowed logically enough, almost inexorably, from its rulings in the Slaughter House, Cruikshank, and Civil Rights cases, Reese and other voting cases, *Neal v. Delaware* and other jury cases, and finally from *Plessy v. Ferguson.* It had held, successively, in those decisions that the Fourteenth Amendment had left untouched the Dred Scott formula that there were two classes of citizenship rights—state and federal—and that the privileges-and-immunities clause of the amendment had left civil rights under the regulation and control of the states; that the federal government had no power to protect Negroes from mob violence in the absence of state assistance to the mob, unless the mob conspired to deny a Negro a right guaranteed by the Constitution or federal law; that the Fifteenth Amendment did not bestow the franchise on Negroes nor vest Congress with power to regulate and control all interference with the Negro's right to vote in all elections, but that it simply prevented the states and the federal government from infringing on the right to vote on racial grounds; that neither the Thirteenth nor the Fourteenth Amendment empowered Congress to proscribe individual invasion of individual rights, and that the Fourteenth Amendment was effective against racial discrimination only when the state imposed or sanctioned racial discrimination; that neither the Fourteenth Amendment nor federal legislation passed under it nullified all proceedings of illegally summoned all-white grand or trial juries, that they provided only that the individual Negro defendant had a right to complain of systematic exclusion of Negroes from grand jury or trial jury panels on the basis of race and that systematic racial exclusion must be proved by the Negro complainant; and that the states could classify Negro citizens on the basis of race and exclude them from use of public and public-utility facilities, as long as they were provided separate and equal facilities.

Long-continued adherence to such principles bred the popular belief that they were immutable. But a Supreme Court such as ours charged with responsibility of interpreting our kind of a written constitution cannot long neglect the fact, noted by Chief Justice Marshall, that such a constitution is "intended to endure for ages to come, and consequently, to be adapted to the various crises in human affairs." [14] The nation was at crisis in the early 1930's, a crisis that had been touched off with the stock market crash in the fall of 1929, that intensified the Negro's problem.

After the crash, the great American industrial plant slowed down, leaving without work its tens of thousands, then its hundreds of thousands, and finally its millions. Last-hired Negroes were the first fired. The agricultural depression festering since the early 1920's burst into a running sore. Already impoverished Negro sharecroppers and tenant farmers plunged deeper into economic misery. The hard-hit American upper middle class discharged and laid off Negro menials and servants. Negro professional men found to their dismay that their out-of-work clients had no money for fees.

The smell of change hung heavy in the political air.

The agricultural South hard-hit as a region, the white American urban worker jobless and standing in soup lines, and Negroes hardest-hit because farthest down in the social scale forged an uneasy political alliance, each distrusting the other, each with no place else to turn. A master politician, Franklin D. Roosevelt, led them together into the promised land of the New Deal.

There were other changes and rumors of change as far as the Negro was concerned. In 1929, a Negro was elected to Congress, the first since 1899; he came not from the South but predictably from a seething black belt in a northern city, in this case Chicago. And in 1930, NAACP-led Negroes supplied the balance-of-power pressure sufficient to prevent the confirmation of Judge John J. Parker as a Supreme Court justice because he had supported a grandfather clause for North Carolina's constitution and had said in 1920 that the "participation of the Negro in politics is a source of evil and danger to both races."

Scientists and anthropologists had exploded shallow notions of racial superiority and inferiority; the extravagant claims for racial purity and integrity were thereafter reserved for southern politicians, cadging votes on appeals to ingrained prejudice.

Communists, serving their own selfish purposes and hacking away at their opponents, were crying out against America's racial discrimination wherever it was expedient for them to do so in Europe, Asia, and Africa.

A new generation of Negro writers, poets, and artists had arisen. They called themselves The New Negro and their work The Negro Renaissance. They were heralds of a New Era, and their voices were strong in the land.

The National Association for the Advancement of Colored People had reached the age of majority. The NAACP was 21 years old in 1930, under the able and clever leadership of Walter White, a master salesman of equality cast in the mold of Madison Avenue. The urban Negro middle class was solidly enlisted under its banner and its influence and reached down into the ranks of the more privileged workmen. Negro newspapers, now widely read, rallied their readers behind the NAACP program, and the organization had branches in every important city and town in the nation.

In 1930, the NAACP made a historic decision, hardly noticed at the time. It decided to launch a "large-scale, widespread, dramatic campaign to give the Southern Negro his constitutional rights, his political and civil equality . . . and to give the Negroes equal rights in the public schools, in the voting booths, on the railroads and on juries in every state where they are at present denied them, and the right to own and occupy real property." There was nothing new in those objectives. What was new and very important was the decision to use the courts to achieve the objectives and to put major emphasis on planned and orderly litigation. Nathan Margold, later solicitor for the Department of Labor, was named to blueprint the campaign.

Details of that dramatic program would be spelled out in the Supreme Court of the United States, down through our own times.

❖{ 17 }❖ *Taken at the Flood*

There is a tide in the affairs of men,
Which, taken at the flood, leads on to fortune.
SHAKESPEARE, *Julius Caesar* [Act IV, Scene 3]

The decision of the NAACP to utilize the courts as the major weapon in its intensified campaign for equality was not a whimsical one. The program was national in scope and purpose, and Congress was so thoroughly dominated by southern Democrats through the seniority system for committee chairmanships in both houses and the filibuster privilege in the Senate that there was no hope for passage of civil rights legislation. A Democratic chief executive could, or would, undertake only a minimum of racial reforms, in light of the political necessity of keeping southern Democrats pacified and willing participants in the delicately balanced South-Labor-Negro political alliance upon which his power rested. Republican Presidents were so beguiled with the hope of breaking the Solid South that they, too, were unwilling to favor the Negro's demands. There was practically no place to turn except to the courts.

Beyond the practical considerations lay the fact that the Negroes had never abandoned the belief that the Civil War Amendments had made them free men and that all that was needed to restore that freedom was Supreme Court enforcement of those amendments according to their original intent and purpose. Reconstruction was fancifully remembered as a Golden Age, and the constitutional problem was assayed as that of inducing the Supreme Court to recant the errors that had led to the undoing of Reconstruction and into which it had been led by evil men. The Great Dream was that the Court by a process of interpretation could restore the Thirteenth, Fourteenth, and Fifteenth Amendments to their pristine glory and thus strike off the shackles of second-class citizenship.

Parenthetically, it is well to observe here that the NAACP did not abandon its work at state and local levels, or its nonlegal tasks. Increased political power in northern and western cities and states meant that Negro councilmen and legislators, representing ghetto constituencies, joined by liberal and labor counterparts, pressed for and secured reforms in ordinances and statutes. In southern states, where there was little chance for more than amelioration of the worst aspects of the Jim Crow system, the NAACP kept up a drumfire of equalitarian propaganda, as it did in the areas of the North and West where legal change was impossible.

Inextricably interwoven with the belief and hope that the Supreme Court could restore the Civil War Amendments to their meaning and efficacy was the knowledge that, for better or worse, the Negro was the ward of the Court and that the prospect for immediate relief lay in inducing it to grant relief from the more onerous restrictions it had laid on his exercise of constitutional rights. There was the additional fact that the Court was under heavy attack by liberals and labor leaders, both professing friendship with the Negro's aspirations. The Court was being derided as a collection of nine old men, most of whom were out of step with their times. The NAACP calculation was that the Court was on the eve of change in both personnel and attitude on social issues. Negro leaders hoped that during the process of that change they could press their own case and secure some of the changes they desired.

Another circumstance of inestimable importance was the rise of a corps of talented and resourceful young Negro lawyers, social scientists, and educators—all chafing under racial discrimination and ready to contribute their learning and skill to an assault on the restrictions that hemmed them in. When Margold left the NAACP in 1933 to take a government post, he was replaced by Charles H. Houston, Harvard-trained, second-generation Negro lawyer, a man of vast creative skill and ability. He expanded and improved Margold's original blueprint for legal action and recruited Negro lawyers from all over the nation to assist in the assault on segregationist bastions. As Dean of the Howard University Law School, he turned that law school into a laboratory for civil rights which trained new classes of militant Negro lawyers. Working closely with him was the erudite William H. Hastie, his cousin, as militant as he was learned in the ways of the law.

One of the Howard Law School trainees was Thurgood Marshall, who ultimately replaced Houston as the NAACP's special counsel and head of its legal program. A bluff and brilliant trial lawyer, he was to translate the "impractical" theories of intellectual lawyers and social scientists into effective courtroom tactics. He expanded the NAACP legal committee to take in more and more gifted lawyers and established liaison with law school professors throughout the nation who were willing to help with research into intricate constitutional problems.

A new day dawned, in which southern attorneys general and lawyer-spokesmen for segregationists everywhere found themselves matched against opponents of superb legal skill and determination. Their names would become bywords in constitutional law, and their pleadings would be accorded great judicial respect. In time, these Negro lawyers and social scientists would become judges, diplomats, college and university presidents, legislators, and men high in the echelons of government.[1]

Changes in legal and constitutional interpretations are not wrought by skilled advocacy alone, nor solely through depth of preparation or new insights into problems. These are but the tools without which opportunity may be lost or frittered away. Without them, little is possible; even with them, little may be gained. There are other factors. Judicial interpretations change as the social climate changes. Vast changes, far beyond the ability of any man to foresee in 1930, were to sweep over the United States, and the world, in the area of race relations, in the swift-moving decades after 1930. Old ideas perished, and new and revolutionary concepts replaced them. An appreciable part of the genius of the NAACP lawyers lay in their acute perception of the depth and direction of these changes, and their ability to take them at their flood and translate them into constitutional concepts palatable to Supreme Court justices, who were at once propelled in new directions by social change and architects of that change. NAACP lawyers could not have won the constitutional victories that lay ahead of them without their technical and legal skills, even in the context of the changing climate of the times. But with the greatest of skill and preparation, they could not have prevailed in an unchanged climate or in a closed society.

The NAACP was not always able to follow its legal blueprint. There were setbacks and defeats. Sometimes events moved too fast, sometimes too slowly. On other occasions, aggressive segregationists acted before the NAACP was ready for the fray. There was an ebb and flow in the generally favorable climate of public opinion that required adjustment and readjustment. But it is hard to overestimate the tactical advantage that lay in the fact that, beginning in the 1930's, Negroes were on the offensive, whereas they had been on the defensive prior to that time. Their lawyers could and did exploit every advantage that lies with having the initiative.

It is against this background that we must examine the story of the Negro and the Supreme Court of the United States as it unfolded after the early 1930's.

PART FOUR

The welcome table

*I'm gonna sit at the welcome
table one o' these days. . . .* NEGRO SPIRITUAL

For, lo, the winter is past,
the rain is over and gone.

THE SONG OF SOLOMON 2:11

The historian can supply the date when Columbus reached the New World or when the armies clashed at Gettysburg, but there is no certain date marking the time when the Industrial Revolution began or when the Renaissance reached its flower. Nor is there any day or hour or minute when the Supreme Court of the United States turned away from its restrictive interpretation of the Civil War Amendments and Reconstruction legislation and began to put a new and more equalitarian meaning on the language of those amendments and statutes. We can read that change into a reported case or into a series of reported cases and trace a trend thereafter to defend our choice, but the selection must always be somewhat arbitrary and there will be others to challenge us. A part of the difficulty lies in the fact that every case presents its own peculiar state of facts on which the Court must rule, and another part arises from the circumstance that the Court's course is rarely a straight-line march. It zig-zags forward, and sometimes it "zigs" when it seems it should "zag" or "zags" when it could be expected to "zig." The course of the court-made law, like the course of true love, seldom runs smoothly.

If we choose to date the Court's change from its decisions in a series of cases involving the arrest and prosecution of nine Negro youngsters in Alabama for the rape of two young white women in the early 1930's, there will be some to dispute us but none to prove us wrong. Three separate cases involving the incident reached the

Supreme Court—*Powell v. Alabama*[1] in 1932, and *Norris v. Alabama*[2] and *Patterson v. Alabama* in 1935. The Scottsboro case, as it came to be called, was a near-perfect mirror of its troubled times and an almost complete exposition of the manner in which the legal processes of the Deep South functioned when a Negro was charged with a crime which also offended southern racial taboos, in this case the strongest of them all. The case approached perfection in these particulars so closely and so clearly that if it had not occurred, some sociologist or historian would have had to invent it in order to illustrate a lecture on the changing times and southern race relations.

On March 25, 1931, a dozen Negro youngsters, ranging in age from 13 to 19, were bumming a ride on a freight train southbound from Chattanooga, Tennessee, near Stevenson in Jackson County, Alabama. Riding on that same freight were a half-dozen or so young white boys and men, two of them accompanied by 21-year-old, twice-married and twice-divorced snuff-dipping Victoria Price, who had always used her maiden name, and 17-year-old Ruby Bates. Victoria Price and Ruby Bates, who were wearing overalls on the train, were poor whites, thrown out of textile employment in Huntsville, Alabama, by the deepening economic crisis. The boys, Negro and white alike, were also unemployed and out-of-school youths, wandering somewhat aimlessly in search of stability and jobs. Everybody later agreed that during the course of a racial clash, some of the Negroes chased, or threw, all but one of the white boys off the train before it reached Stevenson. Some of the defeated white boys told law enforcement officers that the Negroes had attacked them and the white women, and the train was ordered stopped at Paint Rock, where the nine Negro youngsters then remaining on it were removed and lodged in the Jackson County jail at Scottsboro. Victoria Price and Ruby Bates were also removed and, after having been jailed, told a harrowing tale of forcible rape by six of the arrested nine Negroes. Confronted with this story, the prisoners told conflicting stories, with some admissions saddling others with the crime but with none admitting that he had participated in the rape. The six white boys were all held in jail until after the trial, although only one of them was called as a witness.

A mob barged into Scottsboro the next day, but the governor of Alabama responded to the sheriff's plea for assistance, and the prisoners were protected and later taken to another county for safekeeping. On March 30, Circuit Judge James A. Hawkins convened a special grand jury—all white—and on March 31 it returned indictments charging all nine youths with forcible rape, a crime punishable by death at the option of the trial jury. Trial was set for April 6, and the judge appointed the six members of the Scottsboro bar to represent the defendants at arraignment. At that juncture, a Chattanooga white lawyer, who said he had been hired but not paid by that city's Negro Inter-Denominational Ministerial Alliance, showed up and asked to participate in the case. His ambiguous request was granted.

On April 6, approximately 10,000 white persons swarmed into Scottsboro (population 2300) for the trial. National guardsmen were stationed around the courthouse. A brass band or an advertising calliope furnished music for the crowd's entertainment. A jury panel of one hundred white men was summoned. The judge refused to remove the trial to another county, and Clarence Norris and Charlie Weems went on trial first. The prosecution presented eight witnesses, including the alleged victims, in a perfunctory trial; only one of the white boys, Victoria Price's friend, testified. The case went to the jury the next day, and after less than two hours deliberation, the jury found Norris and Weems guilty and fixed their punishment at death. The crowded court roared its approval; the judge threatened to clear the courtroom, and national guardsmen removed a few persons.

Meanwhile, Haywood Patterson had been placed on trial on April 7, and his case went to the jury on the morning of April 8. While his jury was out, another five—Ozie Powell, Andy Wright, Eugene Williams, crippled Willie Roberson, and the near-blind Olen Montgomery—were put on trial, with defense counsel protesting in vain that the fifteen-year-old Williams was subject to juvenile court jurisdiction. On the afternoon of April 8, Patterson was found guilty and his penalty assessed at death. The next day, a jury found the other five guilty and fixed punishment at death. The thirteen-year-old Roy Wright fared better: the prosecution forbore to ask the death penalty because of his extreme youth, but some of the jurors held out for death anyhow, and a mistrial was finally declared. On April 9, 1931, the judge lined them up and pronounced sentence of death on the eight convicted Negroes. That night, they rioted in their cells, tore up their bedding, and shouted imprecations on the court, their prosecutors, and whites in general. Exactly two weeks had elapsed since the fateful fight on the freight train on March 25!

In the early stages of the trial, the judge received a telegram from the International Labor Defense, a Communist-oriented defense organization, "demanding" a fair trial for the defendants. At its close there was a larger crop of telegrams protesting the conduct of the trial, and on April 11, Governor B. M. Miller began receiving similar messages demanding that he free the defendants. Protest meetings sprang up like mushrooms across the land crying "frame-up," and worse, and in short order, demonstrators showed up at American consulates and embassies around the world clamoring against Alabama justice and linking the defendants with the "Communist struggle for the working class."

In an appeal to the Alabama supreme court, attorneys, supplied by the International Labor Defense, argued vigorously that the defendants had been denied due process of law as required by the Fourteenth Amendment because they had not been given adequate time to secure counsel and prepare their defense and that there had been systematic exclusion of Negroes from the grand jury that had indicted them. Over the strong dissent of its chief justice, the Alabama court held that there had been adequate representation by counsel. It could find no sufficient evidence of exclusion of Negroes from the juries but did reverse Williams's conviction because of his age. The U. S. Supreme Court agreed to review the proceedings and handed down its decision on November 7, 1932.

The world was in ferment by then: the Supreme Court was under heavy fire, sneered at as the bastion of special privilege, its justices derided as nine old men. Franklin Delano Roosevelt was on the eve of his assumption of the presidency; the restless unemployed were clamoring for more than doles and soup kitchens; a brilliant military tactician, General Douglas McArthur, had cleared the Bonus Army out of Washington, as its tents and shacks went up in flames; stocks were plunging downward, and factories were closing their gates everywhere; embattled midwestern farmers were defying the law to prevent foreclosures; Communists were fishing in the troubled waters of race relations; a psychotic Austrian house painter named Adolf Schickelgruber, passing under the alias of Hitler, was flying the flag of anti-Semitism and preparing to seize power in Germany; Gandhi was preaching the doctrine of nonviolence and, although few perceived it, the sun was preparing to set on the British Empire in Asia and in Africa. There was no hint of these momentous events in the tempered and measured prose of Justice George Sutherland, who spoke for a seven-to-two majority of the predominantly conservative Supreme Court Justices, reversing the convictions of the Scottsboro Boys.[3] The very fact that the ultra-conservative Justice Sutherland wrote the opinion was indicative of the shift in the Court's attitude and direction. He had been one of the two justices who dissented in the Arkansas riot cases in 1923.

Justice Sutherland reviewed the haste with which the Scottsboro trial was held and the slipshod manner in which the trial judge had gone through the motions of appointing counsel for the defendants. He had no doubt that the "action of the trial judge in respect of appointment of counsel was little more than an expansive gesture." That observation, he said, was "borne out by the fact that . . . a leading member of the local bar accepted employment on the side of the prosecution," after he had been named as one of counsel for the defendants at their arraignment.

Under the circumstances of the case, he wrote, "the necessity of counsel was so vital that the failure of the court to make an effective appointment of counsel was likewise a denial of due process within the meaning of the Fourteenth Amendment," and it seemed to him that "in a capital case, where the defendant is unable to employ counsel, and is incapable of making his own defense because of ignorance, feeble mindedness, illiteracy, or the like, it is the duty of the court, whether requested or not, to assign counsel for him as a necessary requisite of due process of law. . . ." Justices Hughes, Van Devanter, Brandeis, Stone, Roberts, and Cardozo agreed. Alabama was ordered to hold new trials for the seven convicted defendants.

Justice Pierce Butler of Minnesota dissented, out of concern for the right of the states to order their own affairs. He pointed out that the Alabama supreme court had carefully and painstakingly reviewed the case and had held that state laws had been observed. The Supreme Court decision, Justice Butler said pointedly, was "an extension of federal authority in a field hitherto occupied exclusively by the several states." Justice McReynolds agreed with him.

When the cases went back to Scottsboro, they were removed to adjoining Morgan County for trial. More internal trouble flared out in a bitter contest between the International Labor Defense and the NAACP over who would furnish counsel and conduct the case. Clarence Darrow, Arthur Garfield Hayes, and a distinguished Birmingham lawyer had been employed by the NAACP to appeal the cases on the first occasion when the defendants had indicated their desire for new counsel, but after changing their minds a half-dozen times, the defendants decided to stay with the Labor Defense. When the case was set for retrial, the NAACP tried again to participate, with the proviso that the Communist-oriented Labor Defense be ousted. The defendants refused, and at the second trial, defense counsel were headed by the brilliant Samuel Leibowitz of Brooklyn, who refused to accept a fee for his services or payment of his costs.

On March 30, 1933, Alabama put Haywood Patterson on trial, and on the fourth day a bombshell burst. Ruby Bates appeared to testify for the defense that she had not been raped and had seen nobody rape Victoria Price. In fact, she said, she and Lester Carter, one of the white riders on the freight train, and Victoria Price and Orville Gilley, another of the white hoboes, had spent the night before the incident at lovemaking in Chattanooga. Victoria Price, she insisted, had told her what to say at the first trial and had told some of the white boys that, unless they backed her up, they might get in trouble for violating the Mann Act. Lester Carter agreed with Ruby Bates; Orville Gilley didn't testify. One of the prosecution attorneys asked the jurors "if justice . . . is going to be bought and sold in Alabama with Jew money from New York." The all-white jury found Patterson guilty and fixed his punishment at death. The other trials were postponed after Leibowitz was charged with having made a violent verbal attack on the jurors. Trial Judge James E. Horton duly sentenced Patterson to death, but on July 22 suddenly granted a new trial in a 22-page opinion, in which he said that the prosecution proof was inadequate and that, in fact, the evidence preponderated on the side of the defense. Two years later he was defeated for re-election.

The third trial finally got under way on November 20, 1933. Again, Patterson was put on trial first and, on December 1, was again found guilty. Clarence Norris went on trial the next day and was also found guilty. Both were sentenced to death on December 6, 1933. The other trials were then postponed to await a ruling on the fundamental issue raised in the two cases: exclusion of Negroes from the grand and trial juries.

That the probability of a fair trial for a Negro charged with a crime offensive to southern mores demanded something more than adequate counsel, time for preparation of the defense case, and adherence to procedural safeguards was demonstrated by the verdicts in the second and third trials, where the outcome was the same as that in the perfunctory first trial. A critical factor was the white jury system, with its built-in guarantee of a quick indictment of the accused Negro by the grand jury and the near certainty of conviction by the trial jury. In both instances, the juries simply acted out the hostility of the white community against the Negro defendant and gave it a legal coloration. They enforced the unwritten code of the color-caste system. Southern states tried to armor racial discrimination in the selection of juries against successful judicial attack by fair-on-their-face laws that lent themselves to discriminatory administration, just as they had done in the case of voting statutes.

Alabama law, for example, vested jury selection in commissioners, who were directed to "place on the jury roll and in the jury box all male citizens who are generally reputed to be honest and intelligent men, and are esteemed in the community for their integrity, good character and sound judgment." They were required to exclude males under 21 and over 65, habitual drunkards, men convicted of offenses involving moral turpitude, those "afflicted with a permanent disease or physical weakness" making them "unfit to discharge the duties of a juror," and persons who could not read English. But the commissioners were admonished that "If a person cannot read English and has all other qualifications described [in the law] and is a freeholder, his name may be placed on the jury roll and in the jury box." Alabama courts then held that jury commissioners were vested with absolute discretion in the selection of jurors who met the statutory qualifications. Their judgments could not be questioned. They exercised that discretion to exclude Negroes and met all complaints with the bland explanation that they had complied with the law to the best of their ability.

Defense attorneys showed that Jackson County had a total population of 36,881 of whom 2688 were Negroes. They proved that no person could remember when a Negro had served on a grand jury

—one of the witnesses to that effect was a man 76 years old. Court attachés agreed. Morgan County, where the second and third trials were held, had a total population of 46,176, of whom 8311 were Negroes. Again, no person, including a 76-year-old witness, could remember when a Negro had served on a Morgan County trial jury. In both instances, the defense and prosecution agreed that there were Negro freeholders, school board members, farmers, and others with apparent qualifications for jury service.

Jury commissioners protested, however, that they had not deliberately excluded Negroes. They testified under oath that race had not been a factor in jury selection. One commissioner testified: "I do not know of any Negro in Morgan County over 21 and under 65 who is generally reputed to be honest and intelligent, and who is esteemed in the community for his integrity, good character and sound judgment, who is not an habitual drunkard, and who isn't afflicted with a permanent weakness which would render him unfit to discharge the duties of a juror, and who can read English, and who has never been convicted of a crime involving moral turpitude." In short, he was saying that there was not a single Negro in the entire county who met the requirements for jury service. The trial judge and the Alabama supreme court agreed that under the circumstances there had been no proof of deliberate exclusion of Negroes in either Jackson County, where the indictment had been returned, or in Morgan County, where the trial was held. The Supreme Court reviewed the issue and handed down its decision in the Norris and Patterson cases on April 1, 1935.[4]

Alabama argued that the issue of deliberate jury exclusion was one of fact and that where a state court had found as a fact that there had been no such exclusion, the question was settled. Chief Justice Hughes spoke for eight members of the court in the Norris case, rejecting that contention. "That the question is one of fact does not relieve us of the duty to determine whether in truth a federal right has been denied," he said. "When a federal right has been specially set up and claimed in a state court, it is our province to inquire not merely whether it was denied in express terms but also whether it was denied in substance and effect. If this requires an examination of the evidence, that examination must be made. Otherwise, review by this court would fail of its purpose in safeguarding constitutional rights."

The Chief Justice then proceeded to examine the evidence. He was not impressed by the jury commissioner's testimony that no Negro in Morgan County possessed the qualifications for a juror under Alabama law. "We find it impossible to accept such a sweeping characterization of the lack of qualifications of Negroes in Morgan county," he wrote. He turned to the evidence concerning the long history of the absence of Negroes from Jackson County grand juries and Morgan County trial juries. Looking through form and examining substance, he pronounced the judgment of the Court: "For this long-continued, unvarying and wholesale exclusion of Negroes from jury service, we find no justification consistent with the constitutional mandate." In a specific reference to the lack of Negro grand jurors in Jackson County, the Chief Justice said, "We are of the opinion that the evidence required a different opinion from that reached in the state court. We think that the evidence that for a generation or longer no Negro had been called for service on any jury in Jackson county, that there were Negroes qualified for jury service . . . that no names of Negroes were placed on the jury roll . . . established the discrimination which the Constitution forbids." The Jackson County grand jury indictment was ordered set aside, and Alabama was directed to lay the Norris case before another grand jury from which Negroes were not deliberately excluded. After clearing a technical hurdle, the Court entered the same judgment in the Patterson case. In substance, the decision meant that the prosecution must begin all over again as far as all defendants were concerned.

Despite its former protests, the prosecution was able to find two Jackson County Negro farmers with grand jury qualifications, and one of them sat on the grand jury that returned a new indictment on November 13, 1935, charging the prisoners with the same offense as that alleged on April 1, 1931. With new trials imminent, a new quarrel sprang up between the NAACP, the Labor Defense, and other organizations over who should conduct the defense. Leibowitz charged that the Communists had used the case as a "meal ticket" for years and demanded that they withdraw from all connection with it. That issue was finally settled with the formation of a nonpartisan Scottsboro Defense Committee, with Leibowitz listed as chief defense counsel but with a southern lawyer in actual command of the trial. Alabama again chose Patterson as its first target, and his fourth trial got under way on January 20, 1936. Morgan County jury commissioners, who had not been able to find a

qualified Negro juror within the memory of a living witness prior to
1931, discovered an even dozen with proper qualifications for the
hundred-man trial panel, but none served; one was called for interrogation, and the judge ordered him seated on a chair outside the
jury box. Patterson went on trial before another all-white jury,
which found him guilty on January 23 after eight hours' deliberation. There was one significant difference on his fourth conviction:
his punishment was fixed at 75 years' imprisonment instead of
death. Trials of other defendants were postponed after illness in the
family of one of the jurors.

Meanwhile, the Scottsboro case had become a worldwide *cause
célèbre*. A steady stream of articles, books, and pamphlets poured
out denouncing the prosecution; a fairly successful Broadway play
harped on the same theme. Domestic and foreign demonstrations
denounced the trials as examples of American racism, and cried
shame on the nation. One of the defendants was shot by a deputy
sheriff while handcuffed in an automobile. While both sides were
proclaiming that they would fight to the bitter end, they were nego-
tiating backstage, and the whole matter wound up in a practical
lawyer's compromise under which defendants entered various
pleas. Within a short period, all but Patterson were released on
parole or on termination of their sentences. All lives had been
saved. The Scottsboro case had come to an inconclusive end as far
as guilt or innocence of the defendants was concerned, but it had
set off a chain reaction in constitutional law.

By its decision in the first of the cases, the Supreme Court had
returned to the concept of the framers of the Fourteenth Amendment that the federal government had assumed at least a limited
supervisory function to assure due process and equal protection of
law to Negroes where the states had failed to do so, either through
unjust laws or through unfair administration of their laws in a criminal case. Justice Butler's dissent that the decision was an "extension
of federal authority in a field hitherto occupied exclusively by the
several States" was true only to the extent that the Court had failed
to heed the command of the Fourteenth Amendment; it had always
had that authority and duty. It had failed to exercise its responsibility, a failure attendant upon its early and disputed rulings that civil
rights remained under exclusive control and supervision of the
states after passage of the Civil War Amendments and upon its

consequent failure to look behind form and distinguish the fiction of fair trial from the reality of discriminatory treatment for Negro defendants. The decision put the states on notice that the Court would no longer accept at face value state court determinations that apparently fair statutes had been administered in an impartial manner but would decide for itself whether or not a Negro defendant had been accorded a fair trial in reality as well as in theory.

The jury decisions in the second Scottsboro case also marked a change in Supreme Court outlook, although the Court was careful to give the impression that it was simply following precedent. Here, too, the most important shift was the Court's assertion that it would not be bound by state court findings that no racial discrimination had been exercised in jury selection but would insist upon determining whether "in truth a federal right had been denied" and would examine the evidence upon which the findings rested. Moreover, its summary rejection of Alabama court findings that there had been no discrimination was an eloquent warning to the states that the Supreme Court would insist upon exercising its function under the Fourteenth Amendment of asserting a substantial measure of federal control and supervision of civil rights. That, too, was a return to the original intent of the framers of the Fourteenth Amendment. The Court re-enforced its changed attitude by giving critical weight to a long-continued absence of Negroes from grand and trial juries as a species of proof that there had been systematic racial exclusion. That same contention had been subtly rejected in a Mississippi case in 1896 and in Florida and South Carolina cases in 1903.[5]

The importance of the Scottsboro cases lay in the fact that they marked the end of a trend begun in the *Slaughter House Cases* in 1873 of resigning complete control and supervision of civil rights to the states. The Supreme Court had indicated that it was prepared to assume at least some of its responsibility under the Fourteenth Amendment for federal primacy to assure a Negro defendant a fair trial and due process and equal protection of the law when he was accused of crime. But that assurance was more implied than expressed in the cases, and 70 years of Court retreat before aggressive and successful state assault on the federal prerogative had taken their toll. The once robust doctrine of federal protection of the Negro's civil rights had been starved to skin and bones. Much remained to be done to flesh out the intent of the framers of the Civil War Amendments.

The swift tempo of the times and the rising clamor of Negroes for "first-class citizenship" would give the Supreme Court no rest for the next three decades.

᪥ 19 ᪥ *Can These Bones Live?*

And he said unto me, Son of man,
can these bones live?

EZEKIEL 37:3

Strictly construed, the first Scottsboro case decided only that a defendant was denied due process of law within the meaning of the Fourteenth Amendment when he was not afforded adequate counsel in a capital case and was not given sufficient time to prepare his defense. The essence of the matter was that a defendant must be given a fair trial in these respects and that the Supreme Court would examine the proceedings and determine that issue for itself, no matter what the state courts had done in a particular case. While the decision was a significant step toward restoration of federal supervision of civil rights, as the framers of the Fourteenth Amendment had intended, it did not hold that the Supreme Court had assumed entire control of state trials. One of the questions left open was that of the use of confessions in state trials where the defendant claimed he had been coerced into admitting guilt.

The use of involuntary confessions was a critical issue in the South, where the entire law enforcement machinery was in the hands of white persons, indifferent at best, hostile at worst, to Negroes who had run afoul of the law, especially in the situation where they were charged with an offense against a white person. The Court was called upon to determine whether the use of a coerced confession in a state trial denied due process of law, as that phrase is used in the Fourteenth Amendment, in 1936 in *Brown v. Mississippi*,[1] a case as classic in the sphere of confessions as the first

Scottsboro case was in the right to counsel and time for preparation of a defense.

Yank Ellington, an impoverished and ignorant Negro, was suspected of the murder of Raymond Stewart, a white man. The murder was discovered on March 30, 1934, at about 1:00 P.M. That night, Deputy Sheriff Dial and some of his civilian cronies went to Ellington's home, accused him of the murder, took him to Stewart's home, and demanded that he confess. When he refused, they hanged him on a tree limb, let him down, hanged him again, and beat him. Upon his continued protest that he was innocent, he was released, but the deputy and other civilians returned the next day, seized Ellington, and on their way to an adjoining county jail, they went through Alabama, where, after a severe beating, Ellington finally confessed. The next day, Ed Brown and Henry Shields, two other near-illiterate Negroes, were also taken to the adjoining county jail, where they were stripped, laid over chairs, and beaten by deputies and civilians until "their backs were cut to pieces with a leather strap with buckles on it." Ultimately, they made the kind of a confession that was desired. On April 2, the three men were taken before the sheriff of the county in which the crime had been committed, and repeated the confessions. Those confessions, the sheriff later testified, were voluntary, although he did admit that one of the men complained of the whippings.

On April 3, 1934, the circuit judge summoned a special, and all-white, grand jury, which returned an indictment on April 4 at 9:00 A.M. Late that afternoon, the prisoners were arraigned. The court appointed counsel for them, and they went on trial on April 5, with Deputy Dial on duty as bailiff of the court. Ellington, Brown, and Shields took the witness stand in turn and detailed the stories of the beatings and brutalities which led to the confessions. Each repudiated his confession and testified that he had confessed only to escape further torture. In rebuttal, deputy sheriffs also took the witness stand and admitted the whippings—one of the deputies explained that he had whipped the defendants "not too much for a negro; not as much as I would have done if it were left to me." The rope burns on Ellington's neck were clearly visible.[2]

Mississippi law forbade the use of confessions which were not freely and voluntarily made, but the trial judge admitted all of them into evidence after a hearing on their admissibility, on the specious ground that the confessions to the sheriff were voluntary.

Without the confessions, the judge would have been required under state law to order an acquittal. The jury returned a guilty verdict, and the three men were sentenced to death on April 6, one
week after Stewart's killing.

The Mississippi supreme court upheld the trial court over the
dissent of two justices, who pointed out that "The facts of the confessions were not only undisputed, they [were] admitted to have
been done by officers of the state, in conjunction with other participants, and all of this was definitely known to everybody connected
with the trial, and during the trial, including the state's prosecuting
attorney and the trial judge presiding."

The Mississippi court majority said that the issue before it was
purely a question of procedure and that all procedural requirements had been met by the trial court's decision that the confessions were voluntary. It answered the argument that use of
confessions obtained by force violated the privilege against self-
incrimination guaranteed in the Fifth Amendment of the federal
Constitution, by holding, in effect, that the Bill of Rights was a
restriction on the federal government and not on the states. Nor was
the court impressed with the argument that the due-process-of-law
clause of the Fourteenth Amendment required a trial, fair in fact as
well as in form. It added that the men's lawyers had made a fatal
mistake in not bolstering their proof of the manner in which the
confessions had been procured with a formal motion to exclude
them from evidence. The court majority assured the prisoners that
"All litigants of every race or color are equal at the bar of this court
and we would feel deeply humiliated if the contrary could justly be
said" and that "Nothing herein said is intended to even remotely
sanction the method by which these confessions were obtained."

Chief Justice Hughes spoke for a unanimous Supreme Court in
reversing the convictions. "The rack and the torture chamber," he
said, "may not be substituted for the witness stand." He reminded
the Mississippi supreme court that it had previously held that "The
duty of maintaining constitutional rights of a person on trial for his
life rises above the rules of procedure, and whenever the court is
clearly satisfied that such violations exist, it will refuse to sanction
such violations and will apply the corrective."

"In [this] case," the Chief Justice wrote, "the trial court was fully
advised by the undisputed evidence of the way in which the confessions had been procured. The trial court knew that there was no

other evidence upon which sentence and conviction could be based. Yet it proceeded to permit conviction and pronounce sentence. The conviction and sentence were void for want of essential elements of due process and the proceeding thus vitiated could be challenged. . . . It was challenged before the Supreme Court of the State by the express invocation of the Fourteenth Amendment. The court entertained the challenge, considered the federal question . . . but declined to enforce [the prisoners'] constitutional right. The court thus denied a federal right fully established and especially set up and claimed." The case was sent back for a new trial.

Again, the Supreme Court had returned to the original intent of the framers of the Fourteenth Amendment: it had assumed its responsibility of protecting civil rights of Negroes in a criminal case by expressly overruling a state court finding that court procedure was within the exclusive control of the state. It was now more than ever apparent that the Court was ready to look over the shoulder of state trial and supreme courts and inquire into substance; it would no longer be beguiled by the form of law. Incidentally, the prisoners were never retried. They later made what amounted to a farcical "escape" and were never apprehended.

The decision had significance beyond cases in which racial prejudice and discrimination were issues and foreshadowed an extension of the Fourteenth Amendment's due-process-of-law clause in the protection of individual liberties. Laymen, and many lawyers, constantly blur over the fact that the guarantees of the Bill of Rights were not binding on the states when added to the Constitution. That much was decided with finality by the Supreme Court under Chief Justice Marshall in 1833; thus, any state could deny trial by jury, freedom of speech or assemblage, or any other so-called fundamental right without offending the federal Constitution. The question of whether or not the Fourteenth Amendment made the guarantees of the Bill of Rights binding on the states has been in dispute ever since passage of the amendment. Robert Bingham, the father of the Fourteenth, always insisted that it did. The Supreme Court has never agreed. It held in a series of cases, not involving Negroes, that the states could alter the jury system at will, that they need not initiate prosecutions through indictment by grand juries, and could abolish at least some aspects of the privilege against self-incrimination.[3]

In another series of decisions, the Court ultimately held that some guarantees of the Bill of Rights bound the states, because they were integral aspects of that due process of law which the states were forbidden to deny by the express language of the Fourteenth Amendment. What was, or is, due process within this context? Nobody yet knows the full answer; the concept is constantly growing through Supreme Court definition and redefinition. It was certain after the first Scottsboro case and the Brown case that the right to counsel in a capital case, the right to adequate time to prepare a defense, and the right to be free from self-incrimination through the use of forced confessions were included.

It was plain enough after the Brown case that a confession extorted by force could not be used to convict a defendant. What about confessions secured by long and exhaustive questioning that ultimately broke the prisoner's will and led him to admit what the police wanted to hear? The Court began to deal with that question in *Chambers v. Florida* in 1940, another case involving ignorant Negroes charged with an incendiary crime against a white person.[4] The prisoners were questioned almost continuously for six days outside the presence of lawyers, families, or friends and finally confessed. On a trial and a retrial, two Florida juries expressly held that no force was used and that the confessions were voluntary. Nevertheless, the Supreme Court held through Justice Hugo Black that "Due process of law commands that no such practice as that disclosed by this record shall send any accused to his death."

A spate of cases involving confessions got to the Court after 1940, so many that they cannot be dealt with individually here.[5] Most of them involved southern Negroes, because, as Justice Black observed in the Chambers case, "they who have suffered most from secret and dictatorial proceedings have almost always been the poor, the ignorant, the numerically weak, the friendless and the powerless." In the process of examining these cases, the Court constantly widened the scope of its rule against the use of confessions secured even by slight force or by persistent and secret questioning. Increasingly, it brushed aside the claim that states were free to establish their own procedural rules in criminal cases. Justice Felix Frankfurter asserted in 1949 that "Although the Constitution puts protection against crime predominantly in the keeping of the States, the Fourteenth Amendment severely restricts the States in their administration of criminal justice."[6] Certainly, Thaddeus

Stevens would have approved that observation. The erudite Charles Sumner would have nodded agreement with Justice Frankfurter's 1957 comment in an Alabama case that "the Due Process Clause of the Fourteenth Amendment has placed limitations upon the discretion, unbridled for all practical purposes, that belonged to the States prior to its adoption and, more particularly, confines their freedom of action in devising criminal procedure." [7]

By 1960, Chief Justice Earl Warren could say, "this Court, in a line of decisions beginning in 1936 with *Brown v. Mississippi* . . . and including cases by now too well known to bear citation has established the principle that the Fourteenth Amendment is grievously breached when an involuntary confession is obtained by state officers and introduced into a criminal proceeding. . . ." [8] He pointed out that the Court would reverse such a conviction, whether the confession, extorted by force or exhaustive and unfair questioning, was true or false and whether or not there was other evidence to sustain the conviction. "The Fourteenth Amendment," he said, "forbids fundamental unfairness in the use of evidence whether true or false . . . we have rejected the argument that introduction of an involuntary confession is immaterial where other evidence establishes guilt. . . ."

The rope burns on Yank Ellington's neck had set the Court on a course that led back toward the original meaning and intent of the Fourteenth Amendment. Every Negro walked a freer man in courtrooms, in the South and all over the land, and the rules evoked to safeguard rights of Negroes protected other Americans as well. Ultimately, the Court pronounced the judgment that the due-process-of-law clause of the Fourteenth Amendment precluded the use in state prosecutions of evidence obtained by unlawful searches and seizures, a ruling that also traced back to the Brown case. [9] Finally, in 1964, three decades after Ed Brown and Henry Shields were flogged into confessions, it held that a prisoner on whom suspicion had centered was denied due process of law unless he was advised by interrogating officers of his right to counsel and that whatever he said might be used against him at his trial. [10]

The right to counsel in capital cases, announced in the first Scottsboro case, bore fruit of its own. After a long and zigzag course, the Supreme Court decided in 1963 in a case called *Gideon v. Wainwright* that the due process clause required the states to furnish lawyers for every impecunious defendant charged with a felony.[11] And that same year, it said in *Douglas v. California* that the states must likewise provide counsel for penniless defendants who sought to avail themselves of regular appellate procedure.[12] Neither Gideon nor Douglas was a Negro, yet each owed an enormous debt to the National Association for the Advancement of *Colored* People, which had played so large a part in the development of the law that redounded to his benefit.

There were ironic footnotes to these landmark cases that assured Negroes a larger measure of fairness in southern courts. Practices almost trivial in themselves but revealing in the light they shed on judicial attitudes and practices fell under a judicial ban. Ford Johnson had to travel all the way to the Supreme Court in 1963 to halt racial segregation of witnesses and litigants in a Virginia traffic court. "State compelled segregation in a court of justice is a manifest violation of the State's duty to deny to no one the equal protection of its laws," the Court told Virginia in *Johnson v. Virginia.*[13] Mary Hamilton refused to answer questions when an Alabama prosecutor insisted on calling her "Mary" while she was on the witness stand. She was fined fifty dollars and given a five-day jail sentence for contempt of court in 1964—one hundred years after Emancipation! She, too, had to go all the way to the Supreme Court to vindicate her right to be treated with respect, rather than contemptuous familiarity. The Court voided her fine and jail sentence in *Hamilton v. Alabama,*[14] and she became a person in a court of law: Miss Hamilton.

As the confession cases reveal, Negro defendants in the South were often subjected to violence to make them confess or, even worse, to visit extrajudicial punishment on them for what law enforcement officers regarded as their reprehensible conduct in insisting on their rights. The states almost never punished such conduct, even when death resulted. Bobby Hall had a reputation in Baker County, Georgia, for being a troublemaker because of his militancy. On January 29, 1943, Sheriff Claude Screws, with a local police officer and a deputy sheriff "fortified themselves at a near-by bar . . . resisted the bartender's importunities not to carry out the arrest" and arrested Hall on a charge of tire theft. They handcuffed him and "took him to the court house yard and there beat him to death" with a tire iron[15] in full view of Negro and white spectators.

The local prosecutor took no action, although the case smacked of murder under Georgia law. Sheriff Screws was ultimately indicted by a federal grand jury under a law enacted as one section of the first federal Civil Rights Act of 1866 and amended in 1870, 1874, and 1909. That law made it a crime punishable by a thousand dollar fine or a year in jail, or both, when a person "under color of law, statute, ordinance, regulation or custom wilfully subjects . . . any inhabitant of any state, territory, or district to the deprivation of any rights, privileges or immunities secured or protected by the Constitution. . . ." Sheriff Screws, the indictment charged, had deprived Mr. Hall of his right to due process of law as provided in the Fourteenth Amendment. A federal jury convicted the sheriff, and his case got to the Supreme Court in 1945 as *Screws v. United States*.[16]

The sheriff's lawyers argued that their client had been unjustly convicted, because the statute was unconstitutional; they insisted that it was too vague and indefinite to define the rights, privileges, or immunities that were protected by the Constitution and denied by the sheriff. They added that whatever Sheriff Screws had done was a crime under the laws of Georgia and that he had not acted "under color of law" because his actions ran directly contrary to Georgia law. Congress, they said, had no constitutional authority to legislate in the field unless state law *required* the wrongdoing. What they were saying was that there was no "state action," as that term had been defined in the Civil Rights Cases of 1883, and other cases.

Four members of the Court, Justices William O. Douglas, Hugo Black, Stanley Reed, and Harlan F. Stone, brushed aside the argument that the sheriff had not acted "under color of law"; they said that whatever he had done as a law enforcement officer of the state was the action of the state and that he could not escape the consequences of his conduct by the nimble argument that his action was contrary to state law. They did agree that the statute itself was somewhat vague and indefinite but insisted that the vagueness and indefiniteness would have been cured had the trial judge instructed the jury that the prosecution must prove that Sheriff Screws's conduct was a "willful" denial of rights guaranteed by the Constitution. Because the trial judge had failed to give such an instruction, they agreed that the case must be sent back for a retrial, with a directive to the judge to instruct the jury that it could not convict unless it found that the sheriff had acted willfully.

At the other end of the spectrum, three members of the Court,

Justices Felix Frankfurter, Owen Roberts, and Robert H. Jackson, agreed that the law was indeed unconstitutional. First, they said, the statute was vague and indefinite and, secondly, they argued that Congress had no authority to punish Screws's conduct, no matter how reprehensible. The dissenters assailed the law under which the sheriff had been prosecuted as one "born of that vengeful spirit which to no small degree envenomed the Reconstruction era," during which, they said, Congress had enacted much legislation that was "clearly unconstitutional," such as the Civil Rights Act of 1875. They had learned nothing and forgotten nothing that had happened in the seventy critical years from 1875 to 1945.

The other two members of the Court, Justices Wiley Rutledge and Frank Murphy, took a position in the middle of these conflicting opinions. They viewed the statute as constitutional and saw no need for the restrictive instruction as to willfulness. As Justice Rutledge put it, "The position urged is it is murder [the defendant has] done, not the deprivation of a constitutional right. Strange as the argument, is the reason. It comes to this, that the abuse of state power creates immunity from federal power." He pointed out that Sheriff Screws and his lawyers were arguing that "whatever state officers may do in abuse of their official capacity can give [the federal] government no concern. This, though the prime object of the Fourteenth Amendment and [the statute in question] was to assure these fundamental rights against wrongful denial by the exercise of the power of the states." But because the issue had to be resolved, Justice Rutledge cast his vote to send the case back for a retrial in which the trial judge would instruct the jury that the prosecution must prove that Sheriff Screws had acted willfully.

The statute had been rescued from unconstitutionality and had been restored to a posture in which it could be used to prosecute lawless state officials. But the requirement that "willfulness" must be proved laid a burden on the prosecution. In Sheriff Screws's case, that burden proved a boon to the defense. A white federal jury found him not guilty, and he went scot-free as far as the federal government was concerned. His acquittal in federal court was no bar to state prosecution. In their dissent, Justices Roberts, Frankfurter, and Jackson had laid great stress on the sheriff's violation of state law; they insisted that the federal prosecutors had "deflected" Georgia's responsibility. "We should leave to the States the enforcement of their criminal laws," they said, and not "relieve states of the responsibility for vindicating wrongdoing. . . ." Their naïve faith was misplaced. Georgia did not prosecute the sheriff for violation of state law. A few years later, Claude Screws was elected to the Georgia senate by his Baker County neighbors.

Lying at the root of Georgia's abysmal failure to punish the wrongdoing in Bobby Hall's case was the white jury system: no state white grand jury would have indicted Sheriff Screws in Baker County; no state white trial jury would have convicted him. There would have been none with standing to complain if Baker County had summoned an all-white grand jury to consider an indictment of the sheriff, nor, in the unlikely event of an indictment, nobody with standing to complain if an all-white trial jury had been summoned to try him.

After the second Scottsboro case in 1935, however, the Court steadily broadened its protection of Negro defendants who complained of exclusion of Negroes from jury panels. A veritable torrent of such cases—far too many to consider here one by one—reached the Court thereafter. In the thirty-year period between 1935 and 1965, the Court heard at least twenty cases in which Negroes complained of exclusionary jury practices. It found the complaints justified in eighteen of them, over the protest of state trial and appellate courts! But that is not quite the whole story.[17]

The Supreme Court is not required either by law or its own rules to review every case which it is asked to consider; in many instances, it may simply decline to issue the proper writ of review and thus leave effective a state decision or a decision by a court of appeals or a specially constituted three-judge federal court. It followed that procedure in a number of cases in which subordinate federal courts had determined that there had been discrimination in the selection of grand and trial juries. In still other cases in which subordinate federal courts found exclusionary practices, the Court was not even asked for a writ of review.[18]

The magnitude and widespread character of jury exclusionary practices in our own times is reflected in the number of cases in which the Court reversed state court determinations that there had been no transgression of the law, in the cases in which it denied review where subordinate federal courts had found exclusion, and in cases where exclusion was found by federal courts and no request for Supreme Court review was made. But in 1960, the U. S.

Commission on Civil Rights found eleven Black Belt counties in which no Negro had ever served on either grand or trial juries.[19]

The Supreme Court began broadening the jury exclusion rule it had initiated in the second Scottsboro case in *Hale v. Kentucky* in 1938. A Negro indicted for murder filed affidavits asserting that there were 48,000 persons in McCracken County, of whom 8000 were Negroes; that 6000 whites and 700 Negroes were eligible for jury service, and that 600 white persons, and no Negroes were named to the grand jury panel which indicted him. The affidavits were not controverted, but the trial court denied the motion to set aside the indictment. The defendant was convicted, and on appeal the court clerk mistakenly failed to include the motion to set aside the indictment in papers filed with the appellate court. The state court of appeals then held that there was no proper record before it in the absence of the motion and affirmed the conviction. The Supreme Court cut through that procedural rigmarole and ordered a reversal.

The Hale case was followed by *Pierre v. Louisiana*[20] in 1939, a case in which the trial court found discrimination in the selection of the panel from which both the grand and trial juries were drawn but held that absence of Negroes from the grand jury was not a ground for setting aside the indictment. It did order a new trial jury panel on which Negroes were included, only to be reversed by the state supreme court. Justice Black spoke for a unanimous Supreme Court in ruling that systematic exclusion of Negroes from an indicting grand jury denied equal protection of the law. The Court laid new stress on the fact that unexplained long-continued absence of Negroes from jury service must be taken as proof of systematic exclusion and that it was the Court's "solemn duty to make independent inquiry of the disputed facts" and determine for itself the issue of exclusion, even in opposition to determinations by state courts.

Some states tried a new tack, highlighted in *Eubanks v. Louisiana*,[21] decided by the Supreme Court in 1958. Negroes constituted one third of the population of a Louisiana parish, but only one Negro had served on a grand jury prior to 1936, and he was apparently named because the jury commissioner thought he was white. From 1936 to 1954, six Negroes were placed on each grand jury list, but of the 432 Negroes thus named, only one actually served. Justice Black spoke for the Court which reversed the conviction and state court findings that there had been no systematic exclusion. "We are reluctantly forced to conclude," he wrote, "that the uniform and long continued exclusion of Negroes from grand juries shown by the record cannot be attributed to chance, to accident, or to the fact that no sufficiently qualified Negroes have ever been included in the lists. . . ." Georgia tried another innovation: names of Negroes drawn for jury service were written on cards of one color, whites on cards of another color. The Supreme Court reversed a conviction where there was no Negro on the jury panel but no direct proof that discrimination had resulted from this color scheme.[22] It found the device an open invitation to exclusion of Negroes and saw in the absence of Negroes the fruits of that invitation.

The unwilling states shifted tactics again. Under Texas law, jury commissioners chose sixteen persons, from which twelve were selected as grand jurors for a current term of court. In *Akins v. Texas*,[23] decided in 1945, jury commissioners named one Negro, and no more, to each panel, a proportion roughly equivalent to that of Negroes to the total population. The Court forbore to decide the question as to whether or not "a purposeful limitation of jurors by race to the approximate proportion that the eligible jurymen of the race to the total eligibles is invalid under the Fourteenth Amendment." Over the dissents of Chief Justice Stone and Justices Murphy and Black, it held, in essence, that there had been no intentional discrimination and let the conviction stand. As spokesman for the majority, Justice Reed said there "must be a purpose to discriminate." Justice Murphy posited his dissent on the fact that "Clearer proof of intentional and deliberate limitation on the basis of color would be difficult to produce. The commissioner's declaration that they did not intend to discriminate . . . fade into insignificance beside the obvious and admitted fact that they intended to and did limit the number of Negroes on the jury panel. By limiting the number to one, they thereby excluded the possibility that two or more Negroes might be among the persons qualified."

Without saying so, the Court seemed to recognize the validity of Justice Murphy's dissent in the Akins case in *Cassell v. Texas*,[24] decided five years later in 1950. Jury commissioners, using the same formula of one Negro to every sixteen-member panel in another Texas county, testified that they chose only persons whom they knew and that they knew no additional eligible Negroes. Justice Reed, speaking for the Court, found systematic exclusion in their professed ignorance. "The statements of jury commissioners that they chose only whom they knew, and that they knew no eligible Negroes in an area where Negroes made up so large a proportion of the population, prove the intentional exclusion that is discrimination in violation of [defendant's] constitutional rights," he wrote. Justice Frankfurter added the observation, "The prohibition of the Constitution against discrimination because of color does not require in and of itself the presence of a Negro on a jury. But neither is it satisfied by Negro representation limited to one. . . . The basis of selection cannot consciously take color into account. . . ."

By the 1960's, the Court had made it plain that its guiding philosophy was, "It is a right to which every colored man is entitled that, in the selection of jurors to pass upon his life, liberty or property, there shall be no exclusion of his race, and no discrimination because of their color," a formulation expressed by Justice Black in the Pierre case. There was nothing new in that statement; it stemmed back to the earliest jury cases. What the Court had done was to give it substance by disregarding the facile dodges of state trial and appellate courts and by cutting through onerous state procedural requirements imposed to clog the exercise of the right. But the Court continued to insist that the presence of Negroes on a grand or trial jury indicting or trying a Negro was not required; the state's duty was done if it laid no color or racial restriction on the selection of grand or trial jurors and tolerated no such restriction on the administration of its jury system. "Once that restriction upon the State's freedom in devising and administering its jury system is observed, the States are masters in their own household," Justice Frankfurter said in the Cassell case. "If it is observed they cannot be charged with discrimination by color, no matter what the composition of a grand jury may turn out to be." Within that context, the Court upheld a North Carolina ruling that a Negro could not complain of discrimination where state law confined jury service to registered voters.[25]

The rule in the North Carolina case was workable enough where there were some Negroes on the voter rolls; it ran into trouble in a Mississippi county where there were no Negro registrants. Robert Lee Goldsby was indicted and convicted for a murder that occurred on September 4, 1954.[26] Both juries were all-white, although the population of Carroll County was 57 per cent Negro. There was not a single registered Negro voter in the county, and since Mississippi confined jury service to registered voters, there was no Negro eligible to serve either on the grand or trial jury. After a long and intricate series of legal manuevers, the Court of Appeals for the Fifth Circuit reversed Mr. Goldsby's conviction, on the ground that Negroes had been systematically excluded from jury service. It ordered him freed, unless he was indicted and tried by juries from which Negroes were not excluded within eight months after its decision, or in the event of appeal, after Supreme Court action in upholding its ruling. The Supreme Court refused to review, thus leaving the Court of Appeals decision in force.[27] The Court has always insisted that its action in refusing review does not necessarily hold or imply agreement with lower court action, but its refusal in a case of the magnitude of the Goldsby ruling must be read as an indication that the states cannot restrict jury service through limiting such service to registered voters and then preventing Negroes from registering, by one device or another.

Supreme Court insistence that there must be no purposeful and systematic exclusion of Negroes from jury panels apparently left the states free to determine the manner in which fairness could be achieved. The ideal answer was, and is, that all eligible persons be liable for jury duty, and the presence or absence of Negroes left to chance. Under the law of probabilities, pursuit of that ideal would, of course, result in the presence of Negroes on all juries, including those where no racial conflict was involved, a situation that obtains in the average northern state with a Negro population of any consequence. The white jury system, as an institution, would be in peril under that practice. In order to obviate that danger, some southern counties summoned all-white grand juries and then hastily and deliberately summoned Negroes to the panel when a Negro was accused of an incendiary crime, if they believed that the jury exclusion issue would be raised. Although Supreme Court opinions are studded with statements to the effect that jurors "should be selected as individuals, on the basis of individual qualifications and not as members of a race" and that "selection cannot consciously take race into account," [28] the Court has never met the issue of deliberate *inclusion* of Negroes for jury service *as Negroes* head-on. In 1965, however, it refused to review another Court of Appeals decision involving a Negro, which held that deliberate *inclusion* of

Negroes offends the equal-protection clause of the Fourteenth Amendment.[29]

In the course of grappling with jury exclusion after the second Scottsboro case, the Court was confronted with almost every possible scheme that could be devised to evade the necessity of including Negroes on jury panels. It toppled them one by one. Fortunately, the Court's intransigence on the issue has prodded many state courts, on both trial and appellate levels, into adopting its example. Federal courts of appeal and district courts have followed the Supreme Court's ruling.

There can be no doubt that the Court's jury decisions since 1935 have substantially increased the *probability* that a Negro accused of a crime against a white person in the South will receive a fair trial. That probability is diminished by the rule that there is no requirement that a Negro actually sit on the indicting grand or the trial jury. What the Court has done has been to strengthen its early establishment of a separate-but-equal rule for Negro defendants, with the Negro in a position to claim a kind of separate treatment through the demand that Negroes be included on jury panels concerned with his case but with no provision for implementing the equality that supposedly flows from having other Negroes sit in judgment on him.

The shortcomings of the Supreme Court's jury rules were graphically illustrated in *Swain v. Alabama*,[30] decided on March 8, 1965. Robert Swain, a 19-year-old Negro, was indicted and sentenced to death in Talladega County for the alleged rape of a 17-year-old white girl. Negroes did sit on the grand jury which indicted him, and there were Negroes on the trial jury *panel*, all of whom were removed from the trial jury by objection of the prosecutor through the exercise of what is commonly called a peremptory challenge, that is, an objection to a particular juror for which no reason need be given. It appeared that Negro males constitute about 26 per cent of the county's population and that some 10 to 15 per cent of the persons placed on trial jury *panels* have been Negroes in recent years; however, no living person could remember when a Negro actually *served* on a trial jury. They were all eliminated either by agreement of the prosecutor and defense lawyers or through exercise of peremptory challenges by the prosecutor. A six-to-three majority of the Court, speaking through Justice White, could find no fault with this facile system in Swain's case and upheld the conviction. Justice Harlan made it plain, however, that he was not passing on the constitutionality of complete exclusion through exercise of peremptory challenges but was assenting on procedural grounds. Justice Black agreed only with the result.

On his part, Justice White speaking for himself and Justices Clark, Stewart, and Brennan took a half-step backward by limiting the impact of recent cases in which the Court had held that long-continued absence of Negroes from juries was a species of proof of systematic exclusion. He insisted that such absence must be coupled with proof on the defendant's part that absence was a result of the state's choice, and he could find no such proof in the record. As for peremptory challenges, Justice White was certain that their exercise by the prosecutor, even to the extent of assuring an all-white jury, raised no constitutional issue.

Justice Goldberg wrote a dissenting opinion for himself, Justice Douglas, and Chief Justice Warren. The important point for the three dissenters was the fact that "no Negro within the memory of persons now living has served on any petit (trial) jury in any civil or criminal case tried in Talladega county, Alabama." Such long-continued absence of Negroes, coupled with the prosecutor's practice of agreeing to remove Negroes from juries and his use of peremptory challenges, persuaded them that the defendant had proved systematic exclusion. They agreed that removal of Negroes by peremptory challenge, standing alone, did not constitute systematic exclusion. At worst, Talladega County's ingenuity had apparently found a way to go through the motions of complying with constitutional rules against discrimination in jury selection and service while retaining the white jury system, even where Negroes were on trial. At best, the Swain case reimposed a burden on the Negro defendant when he sought to prove jury exclusion. He could no longer rest his case on the absence of Negroes from jury service, as long as the state could show that it placed Negroes on jury panels, no matter how long it failed to put them on trial juries.

The Supreme Court rules offer no comfort to the Negro victim of white aggression; his assailant need have little fear of indictment by a white grand jury and less fear of conviction by a white trial jury. For example, a Georgia grand jury did indict three white men for the wanton and senseless murder of a Negro army officer in 1964. An all-white trial jury acquitted them. Neshoba County, Mississippi, refused even to indict the murderers of three student leaders of a Negro registration drive in another 1964 case. The white jury system will remain intact for a long time, unless the Court finds, or seizes, an occasion to hold that an all-white jury constituted in defiance of the Constitution and federal law is a spurious jury, whose verdicts are as illegal as its composition, in both civil and criminal cases. It may be that the Court has followed an old path too far and too long to retrace its steps through the procedural maze it would have to unravel to achieve that result, but forthright recognition of and comment on the problem might galvanize the Attorney General into action and lead to the prosecution of jury commissioners who insist on violating constitutional commands and statutory requirements forbidding discrimination in the summoning and selecting of jurors.

It would be a grave mistake to minimize what the Supreme Court has done in the past 35 years to secure for Negroes the fair trial enjoined directly by the due-process clause of the Fourteenth Amendment and by the command for equality that permeates the entire amendment. Within that three-and-a-half decades, it has required the states to furnish counsel for needy defendants and to afford them time and opportunity to prepare an adequate defense; it has interdicted the use of confessions wrung from defendants by force or by overreaching interrogation; it has required the inclusion of Negroes on grand and trial jury panels, where a Negro is a defendant; it has revitalized federal laws designed to punish and deter police lawlessness; it has clothed Negro witnesses and litigants with dignity when they appear in courtrooms.

The Court had no legislative help and precious little assistance from the executive branch of government, as it made this long trip back to the fundamental purposes of the Civil War Amendments. It was fought every step of the way by southern states, to whom its predecessors had surrendered its prerogatives in these areas. Its task was made more difficult, much more difficult in respect of the franchise, by prior Court decisions construing the Fifteenth Amendment. For in the long run, a voteless people is an almost helpless people. And southern Negroes were almost voteless. As it strove to assure Negroes the rudiments of fair trial, the Supreme Court also hacked at the bonds of disfranchisement prior justices had helped to forge.

✦{ 20 }✦ *Tumbling Walls*

Joshua fit the battle of Jericho,
And the walls came tumbling down.

NEGRO SPIRITUAL

The single most effective instrument used to prevent Negroes from
playing a significant role in southern elections after the 1920's was
the white primary. By rule or resolution, southern Democratic parties prohibited Negroes from voting in their primary elections, in
which local, state, and federal officials were nominated. Nomination was tantamount to election in the one-party South, and the
exclusion of Negroes meant that they were disfranchised for all
practical purposes. As we have seen, the Supreme Court struck
down state laws excluding Negroes from voting in primary elections but upheld the authority of political parties to exclude Negroes from primaries as constitutional in a unanimous decision in
Grovey v. Townsend in 1935. The Grovey case was an anomaly.
Wrongly decided and out of step with its times, it rested on shop-
worn concepts of state action under the Fourteenth Amendment,
whereas the issues involved arose under the Fifteenth Amendment.
The opportunity to attack the case came after the Supreme Court
reversed a prior ruling and held in 1941, in a case not involving
Negroes, that party primaries were an integral part of the election
process.

Lonnie Smith filed a suit against S. E. Allwright, a Texas election
judge, in which he sought damages because he was not permitted
to vote in the 1940 Democratic primary election. Lower courts dismissed the action, relying on the Grovey holding that the Texas
Democratic party was a private organization with a right to limit its

membership on the basis of race. The case reached the Supreme Court in 1943 and was decided in 1944.[1] Speaking for an eight-to-one majority, Justice Reed did not quibble or try to distinguish the facts from those in the Grovey case. "The statutes of Texas," he said, "relating to primaries and the resolution of the Democratic party of Texas extending the privilege of membership to white citizens only are the same in substance and effect today as they were when *Grovey v. Townsend* was decided by a unanimous court. The question as to whether the exclusionary action of the party was the action of the state persists as the determinative factor." Nor was he deterred by the fact that Texas courts had held that "the exclusion is produced by private or party action. . . ."

"Federal courts," he said, "must for themselves appraise the facts leading to that conclusion. It is only by the performance of this obligation that a final and uniform interpretation can be given to the Constitution, the 'supreme law of the land.'" Justice Reed then examined Texas election laws and concluded, "We think this statutory system for the selection of party nominees for inclusion on the general election ballot makes the party which is required to follow these legislative laws an agency of the state insofar as it determines participants in a primary election. . . . This is state action within the meaning of the Fifteenth Amendment." He felt called upon to comment on the fact that the Court had repudiated the Grovey case so quickly. "We are not unmindful of the desirability of continuity of decision in constitutional questions. However, when convinced of former error, this Court has never felt constrained to follow precedent. In constitutional questions . . . this Court . . . has freely exercised its power to re-examine the basis of its constitutional questions. . . . *Grovey v. Townsend is overruled.*"

Justice Roberts, who had written the Grovey opinion, filed a petulant dissent in which he insisted that "my concern is that the instant decision, overruling that announced about nine years ago, tends to bring adjudications of this tribunal into the same class as a restricted railroad ticket, good for this day and train only. I have no assurance . . . that the opinion announced today may not shortly be repudiated and overruled by Justices who deem they have new light on the subject." Thus far his fears have remained groundless.

The white primary was dead. South Carolina tried to revitalize the corpse by repealing all state laws governing primary elections and by leaving conduct of the primaries to the entire discretion of political parties. The Democratic party then barred Negroes from the primary election. Trial Judge Waites Waring, a native South Carolinian, rejected this transparent device, and the Court of Appeals for the Fourth Circuit sustained him saying, "the fundamental error . . . consists in the premise that a political party is a mere private aggregation of individuals like a country club and that the primary is a mere piece of party machinery"—a significant statement, because it embodies the precise concept that had beguiled the Supreme Court in the Grovey case. The appeals court added, "Even though the election laws of South Carolina be fair on their face, yet if they be administered in such a way as to result in persons being denied any real voice in government because of race or color, it is idle to say that the power of the State is not being used in violating the Constitution." The Supreme Court, apparently satisfied with the result, refused to review the case.[2]

South Carolina tried again, with a new law vesting control of primary elections in private clubs which barred Negroes. Negroes were not excluded from primary elections but were required to take an oath that they believed in the "social and educational separation" of the races and were "opposed to the proposed Federal so-called F.E.P.C. laws."[3] Remarking acidly that it was time South Carolina rejoined the Union, Judge Waring voided that device, and the Court of Appeals sustained him. The discouraged clubs did not attempt to secure review from the Supreme Court.

The final chapter in the white primary controversy was written by the Supreme Court in 1953 in *Terry v. Adams*.[4] Democrats in Fort Bend County, Texas, concocted an organization in 1889 called the Jaybird party, that was a cross between a political machine and a private club from which Negroes were barred but which included all white voters. The Jaybirds held a primary of their own to select and endorse nominees for the Democratic party for state and local offices in primary elections. These endorsed nominees were almost universally successful in winning nomination in Democratic primary elections at which Negroes could, and did, vote. John Terry and three other Negroes claimed a right to vote in the Jaybird elections and, upon rejection, sued on the claim that the Jaybird machinery was a thinly disguised attempt to escape Supreme Court decisions outlawing the white primary. There were three opinions for the eight-to-one majority that found the scheme unconstitutional. Justice Black had no doubt that the Jaybird-primary election device was evasive and that it was a violation of "the Fifteenth Amendment for a state, by such circumvention to permit within its borders the use of any device that produces an equivalent of the prohibited [white primary] election." Justice Frankfurter wrote that the state was linked to the Jaybirds, because county officials gave their "aid in this subversion of the State's official scheme of which they are trustees, by helping as participants in the [Jaybird] scheme and by condoning it." Justice Tom Clark, a Texan, reduced the issue to the simple proposition that "the Fifteenth Amendment as the Fourteenth 'refers to exertions of state power in all forms.'" Justice Minton dissented: he could see no state involvement.

It is noteworthy that the Jaybird case was the first in which the Court lifted a prohibition against Negro participation in an election for state offices only. Justice Black stressed the fact that the Fifteenth "Amendment includes any election in which public issues are decided or public officials" are chosen. Of course, that was the obvious intent of its framers, but that intent had been clouded in earlier cases when the Court seemed almost obsessed with a determination to find ways and means of restoring state supremacy in the area of civil rights. The stress on the applicability of the amendment to all elections was another indication of the Court's return to the original meaning of the Civil War Amendments, as was the fact that in the Smith case it had deliberately overruled an interpretation of the Texas statutes by state courts and insisted that it would make its own determination as to the scope and reach of white primary laws. Clearly, the Court was done with upholding legal barriers to Negro voting, no matter how ingeniously contrived. It had said as much in an earlier case involving a hangover from the grandfather clause cases.

After the Court invalidated Oklahoma's grandfather clause in 1915, the state legislature enacted a law in February, 1916, providing that all citizens qualified to vote in 1916 who failed to register between April 30 and May 11, 1916, would be perpetually disfranchised, except eligible voters in 1914. The effect was that white citizens who were on the voting list in 1914 by virtue of the grandfather clause were kept on the voter rolls, while Negroes, kept from voting by that clause, would remain voteless unless they registered during the limited twelve-day period. Robert Lane was qualified to vote in 1916 but failed to register in the critical twelve days. His case reached the Supreme Court as *Lane v. Wilson.*[5]

"The practical effect of the 1916 legislation was to accord to the members of the Negro race who had been discriminated against . . . not more than twelve days within which to re-assert constitutional rights . . . improperly taken from them," Justice Frankfurter wrote for the six-to-two majority. "We believe that the opportunity thus given Negro voters to free themselves from the effects of discrimination to which they should never have been subjected was too cabined and confined." The law was invalidated, with Justices McReynolds and Butler dissenting and Justice Douglas taking no part. The number of persons affected was not large, but the significance of the case lay in Justice Frankfurter's tart comment that the Fifteenth "Amendment nullifies sophisticated as well as simple-minded modes of discrimination. It hits onerous procedural requirements which effectively handicap exercise of the franchise by the colored race although the abstract right to vote may remain unrestricted as to race."

In 1932, there were approximately 100,000 registered Negro voters in the white primary states. By 1947, that number had risen to some 645,000; by 1952, it exceeded a million, and in 1964 had risen to more than two million. Not all of the accretion could be attributed to Supreme Court invalidation of the white primary. Increased education and militancy of Negroes and a diminution of white resistance played a significant role, as did new federal legislation in 1957. But it is also true that increased militancy of Negroes and the diminution of white resistance were influenced by favorable Court decisions and by the fact that Negro voters were factors that had to be reckoned with by realistic politicians. By 1964, Negro Democrats had appeared in many local offices, in Democratic party organizations, and in the state legislatures of Georgia, Tennessee, and Oklahoma—occurrences that were unthinkable under the white primary system. But there were other restraints on Negro voting. One of them was the requirement to a poll tax as a prerequisite to casting a ballot.

The poll tax is a burden only on the poor, but because Negroes were at the bottom of the economic heap, it hit them hardest. But poor whites also complained, and a challenge to the tax came from a white voter in *Breedlove v. Suttles* in 1937. Justice Butler spoke for a unanimous Court in saying that "To make payment of poll taxes a prerequisite for voting is not to deny any privilege or immunity protected by the Fourteenth Amendment. Privilege of voting is not derived from the United States, but is conferred by the state. . . ." [6] The issue has become moot as far as election of federal officials is concerned through enactment of the Twenty-fourth Amendment. Only four states retain it as a condition for voting in state elections: Alabama, Texas, Mississippi, and Virginia.

More effective than payment of a poll tax as a device to disfranchise Negroes in southern states were the literacy tests, the reading-and-understanding clauses, and the good moral requirements of state constitutions and statutes of the states in the Deep South. All of them traced back to Mississippi's successful attempt to bar Negroes from the polls by constitutional amendments in 1890 when, as its supreme court said, it "swept the circle of expedients to obstruct the exercise of the franchise by the Negro race. . . ." The Supreme Court put its stamp of approval on what Mississippi had done in *Williams v. Mississippi* in 1898, in which it held that the state's obstructionist constitution and laws "do not, on their face, discriminate between the white and Negro race, and do not amount to a denial of the equal protection of the law . . . and it has not been shown that their actual administration is evil but only that evil was possible under them." As we have seen, state after state soon followed the Mississippi example, with spokesmen for constitutional and statutory changes openly proclaiming that their intent was to disfranchise Negroes. The Court bumbled away its opportunities to crack down on these sophisticated disfranchisement statutes in the Giles and Teasley cases in the early 1900's, and its every refusal to act to protect Negro voters was taken as a warrant to impose added disabilities. [7]

The increasing thrust of these discriminatory devices was to lodge ever more power in local registrars to determine whether or not Negroes met literacy requirements, could read and understand sections of the state or federal constitution, or met the good-morals test imposed as a qualification for registration. In some counties, an applicant for registration was required to produce an already registered voter to "vouch" for him. [8] No white person would dare to do so, and where there were no registered Negro voters, there was nobody to vouch for the Negro, no matter what his qualifications. Local boards or registrars readily found highly educated Negroes unable to pass literacy tests and just as readily registered illiterate or semiliterate whites. When all else failed, local registrars resorted to slow-downs, in which one or two Negroes per day were permitted to take tests, or suddenly resigned, leaving no registration machinery available.

In the face of what everybody knows, the Supreme Court long exhibited a reluctance to look behind the façade of fairness and invalidate these racial restrictions on the franchise. In this area at least, it belied its brave words that the Constitution "nullifies sophisticated as well as simple-minded modes of discrimination," perhaps out of reluctance to overrule earlier major precedents. As late as 1958, it upheld literacy test provisions of a North Carolina law, although the real purpose of the tests was made plain through the fact that they had originally been intertwined with a recently repealed grandfather clause.[9] In 1960, the U. S. Commission on Civil Rights found eleven Black Belt counties—counties in which Negro population exceeded whites—with not a single Negro voter; in 35 other such counties less than 3 per cent of eligible Negroes were registered, and 41 others had fewer than 10 per cent of Negro eligibles on their voter rolls. All lay within states with involved voter laws on their books, giving registrars wide areas of discretion.

Alabama finally ran afoul of constitutional safeguards when its voters approved the so-called Boswell Amendment in 1946. Among other provisions, the amendment permitted registration only of voters who could "understand and explain" any article of the federal Constitution to the satisfaction of local registrars. Predictably, it turned out in practice that almost every white person could "understand and explain" any article of that complex document, while very few Negroes had such ability. In a 1946 test of the amendment, a lower federal court took evidence of the gross disparity between numbers of white persons and Negroes registered after its enactment and in its opinion listed at some length the arguments of the amendment's proponents. "Let us be frank and honest," one of them wrote; "You and I know the people of our state are expected to adopt this Amendment in order to give the Registrars arbitrary power to exclude Negroes from voting." Another agreed: "I earnestly favor a law that will make it impossible for a Negro to qualify, if that is possible." The official slogan of the proponents of the Boswell Amendment was "VOTE WHITE—VOTE RIGHT—VOTE FOR AMENDMENT NO. 4."

These sentiments were mere echoes of what had been said in the disfranchising conventions of the late 1890's and the early 1900's, and the results were the same that had flowed from the actions of earlier years, but the three-judge trial court was not as naïve as its predecessor courts. It held that the Boswell Amendment was a discriminatory device designed to escape the stricture of the white primary decisions and invalid under the Fifteenth Amendment. The Supreme Court affirmed the lower court judgment in *Davis v. Schnell* [10] in 1949. Alabama then amended its constitution using more refined language and extending the ballot to all applicants who could read and write "any article of the Constitution of the United States in the English language, which may be submitted to them by the board of registrars," who were of "good character," and who "embrace the duties and obligations of citizenship under the Constitution of the United States and under the constitution of the State of Alabama." It had swapped the devil for the witch: the discriminating registrars were back in the saddle, and the new language had passed Supreme Court scrutiny in earlier decisions.

Macon County, Alabama, presents a near-perfect example of the manner in which registrars can, and did, control voting in that state and in other states determined to maintain white supremacy at the polls. In 1950, the total population of the county was 30,661— 4777 white and 25,784 nonwhite; in 1958, it had 3081 whites of voting age and, miraculously, 3102 registered white voters; it had 14,539 Negroes of voting age and 1218 registered Negro voters. Tuskegee, the county seat, is the home of Booker T. Washington's famed Tuskegee Institute and a regional Veterans' Hospital. Together they attract a large number of obviously qualified Negro voters. It became apparent in the 1950's that it was only a question of time until Negro voters would outnumber white voters in the city, despite every effort to prevent their registration, since three fourths of its 6700 residents were qualified Negroes. In order to forestall that possibility, the Alabama legislature unanimously altered the city boundaries in 1957, putting all but four or five Negro voters outside the city, and changing the city map from a 4-sided to a 28-sided figure resembling a paralytic sea horse.

G. C. Gomillion, a Tuskegee professor, sued Mayor Lightfoot and in effect asked the courts to restore the city's former boundary lines, on the ground that the Alabama legislature had disfranchised the Negro city voters in violation of the Fifteenth Amendment. Lower federal courts denied relief, holding that there were no federal restraints on the state's resorting to gerrymander of political districts, that courts could not inquire into the motives of legislators, and that in any event the federal courts could not decide political issues.

Quoting Felix Frankfurter, one of his favorite authorities, Justice Frankfurter reminded Alabama that the Fifteenth Amendment "nullifies sophisticated as well as simple-minded modes of discrimination." Seven justices agreed with him in *Gomillion v. Lightfoot,* decided in 1960, that "the Alabama legislature has not merely redrawn the Tuskegee city limits with incidental inconvenience to [Negroes]; it is more accurate to say that it has deprived [them] of the municipal franchise and consequent rights, and to that end has incidentally changed the city's boundaries. While in form it is merely an act of redefining metes and bounds . . . the inescapable effect of this essay into geometry and geography is to despoil colored citizens, and only colored citizens, of their theretofore enjoyed voting rights." [11] What he has said was that where racial discrimination was the moving factor in a gerrymander, the federal courts did have authority to correct it, that under that circumstance, the federal courts could look into the intent of the legislature and that the state could not insulate racial discrimination by calling its exercise a mere "political" issue. What he had done was to reassert federal primacy in protection of Fifteenth-Amendment rights. Justice Charles Whitaker agreed with the result but would have placed the decision on Fourteenth-Amendment grounds.

Meanwhile, Congress, prodded into action by the national conscience which had been partially aroused by long-continued Supreme Court decisions laying bare and correcting racial injustice, had enacted the 1957 Civil Rights Act, its first affirmative legislation in that field since 1875. The new act strove to undo some of the damage done by the wholesale repeal of federal voting statutes in 1894. It established a federal Civil Rights Commission, with authority to inquire into denials of civil rights in all areas.

One of the provisions of the 1875 Act left untouched by the 1894 repeal reads:

> All citizens of the United States who are otherwise qualified to vote at any election by the people in any State, Territory, district, county, city, parish, township, school district, municipality or other territorial subdivision shall be entitled to vote at all such elections, without distinction of race, color or previous condition of servitude; any constitution, law, custom, usage, or

regulation of any State, Territory or by or under its authority
to the contrary notwithstanding.

The provision was left untouched probably because, despite its
lofty tone, it was sterile in practice; it provided no remedies and
extended no protection. Congress amended it in the 1957 Act to
provide that, under certain conditions, "the attorney general may
institute for the United States, or in the name of the United States,
a civil action or proper proceeding for preventive relief, including
an application for a permanent or temporary injunction, restraining
order, or other relief." Such an action, the act provided, might be
brought when "any person has engaged or there are reasonable
grounds to believe that any person is about to engage in any act or
practice which would deprive any other person of any right or privilege" secured by the original act.

The Attorney General sued James Raines and other election officials of Terrell County, Georgia, alleging that they had engaged in
a long series of discriminatory acts designed to prevent registration
of Negroes. A federal district judge found the 1957 Act unconstitutional in 1959, insofar as it purported to give the Attorney General
the right to bring an action against the registrars. The district judge
placed primary reliance on the ruling of the Supreme Court in
United States v. Reese,[12] the initial case in which the Court had
gutted Reconstruction voting legislation. Technically speaking, he
was correct, if the Reese case had been rightly decided. For it was
in that case that the Court had held that the Fifteenth Amendment
applied only to wrongful action of state officials and that Congress
was not authorized to penalize private conduct interfering with the
exercise of the franchise. The statute overthrown in the Reese case
in effect penalized the conduct of "any person," just as the 1957
Act did.

Having decided that the Fifteenth Amendment did not authorize
Congress to proscribe individual conduct, the Court in the Reese
case was confronted with a situation in which the statute rightfully
condemned action of state officials but also included unauthorized
proscription of individual action. The Court invalidated the entire
statute, saying, "We are, therefore, called upon to decide whether a
penal statute enacted by Congress . . . which is in general language broad enough to cover wrongful acts, without as well as
within its jurisdiction, can be limited by judicial construction, so as

to make it operate only on that which Congress may rightfully prohibit and punish. . . . We are not able to reject a part and retain the remainder, because it is not possible to separate that which is constitutional . . . from that which is not."

When *United States v. Raines* was decided by the Supreme Court in 1960, six other justices agreed with Justice William Brennan that the 1957 Act was constitutional as written and that the fact that it gave the Attorney General the right to proceed against "any person" did not condemn it, even if, as he seemed to assume, Congress had authority only to proscribe discriminatory conduct of state officials.[13] Raines and the other election officials, he pointed out, *were* state officials, and their conduct could not be excused because the act might be ineffective as to private persons. He said that when the district judge found that Raines and other voting officials were state officers, he should have stopped there without speculating as to the act's impact on private persons. As for the Reese case, he said "that decision may have drawn support from the assumption that if the Court had not passed on the statute's validity *in toto,* it would have left standing a criminal statute incapable of giving fair warning of its prohibitions." And then he added significantly, "But to the extent *Reese* did depend on an approach inconsistent with what we think the better one . . . we cannot follow it here." He also noted that Raines and his fellow defendants had "urged that it is beyond the power of the United States to bring this action in support of private rights. But there is the highest public interest in the due observance of all constitutional guarantees." Negroes could call upon the federal government to vindicate their voting rights. Justice Frankfurter and the second John Marshall Harlan agreed with the result. In the interim, another federal district judge had upheld the 1957 Act, and his decision was affirmed on the basis of the Raines case, when it reached the Supreme Court as *United States v. Thomas* in 1960.[14]

Lawyers can reconcile the Reese case and the Raines case on the grounds that the former concerned a criminal statute and the latter a suit for an injunction, but that reconciliation is only word-deep. The hard-rock truth is that the Court's attitude had changed. In the Reese case it was casting about for ways to undo what it then regarded as excesses of congressional exercise of federal power and was eager to restore state control of civil rights. Time had come full circle when the Raines case was decided, and the Court was ready to restore the right of Congress to enforce the Fifteenth Amendment by what it regarded as appropriate legislation. It was giving back that which it had taken away.

The 1957 Civil Rights Act ran into heavy going on another score in *United States v. Alabama*,[15] decided on May 16, 1960. The Attorney General filed suit against the Board of Registrars of Macon County, Alabama, charging them with a wide variety of discriminatory acts against Negroes who sought to register as voters and seeking an injunction againt those tactics.

When they learned that the suit was being prepared, the two Macon County registrars resigned, leaving no persons empowered to register applicants. The Attorney General then sought to join the state of Alabama as a defendant in order to make the suit meaningful. The federal district judge dismissed the action, holding that the Board of Registrars could not be sued as a board, that the resigned registrars had no further functions to perform and could not be sued, and that the state of Alabama was not a "person" within the meaning of the law. There was no one to sue! While the case was pending undecided in the Supreme Court, Congress passed the Civil Rights Act of 1960 granting specific authority for suits by the Attorney General against the states in voting cases and also giving federal courts authority to appoint federal voting registrars where necessary to protect the rights of eligible Negroes. The Court then reversed the dismissal order in *United States v. Alabama* in May, 1960, and the district judge later issued a sweeping decree ordering some Negroes registered, forbidding slow-down tactics by registrars, and ordering registration of all Negroes who fulfilled the qualifications of the least qualified whites who had been put on the voting rolls. By 1964, two out of five elective Tuskegee city councilmen and some minor county officials were Negroes.

The Civil Rights Commission ran into troubles of its own. When it sought to investigate complaints of voter discrimination in Alabama and Louisiana, registrars and other state officials set out to obstruct its investigation in every possible manner. Some officials refused to testify, others refused to make voting records available, still others refused any kind of information. When it finally issued subpoenas for the desired records, it was met with federal court actions challenging its authority and claiming that registrars were excused from production of records by the constitutional privilege against self-incrimination.

A Louisiana federal court issued an injunction prohibiting the commission from proceeding under its rules and regulations. The Supreme Court reversed the lower court in *Hannah v. Larche*[16] on June 20, 1960, holding that the commission was authorized to proceed under its rules and that Congress was within its authority in establishing it. Chief Justice Warren spoke for a seven-to-two majority in finding that the Commission's "function is purely investigative and fact finding. It does not adjudicate. It does not hold trials or determine anyone's civil or criminal liability. It does not issue orders. Nor does it indict, punish or impose legal sanctions. It does not make determinations depriving anyone of his life, liberty, or property. . . . The only purpose of its existence is to find facts which may subsequently be used as the basis for legislative or executive action." He could find no authority for judicial interference with the investigations.

Justices Douglas and Black, inveterate opponents of all inquisitorial bodies, dissented with Justice Douglas, protesting that "When it summons a person accused under affidavit of having violated the federal election laws, to see if the charge is true, [the Commission] acts in lieu of a grand jury or a committing magistrate." The dissenters would have placed strict restraints on the commission's investigatory powers.

Every investigation by the commission turned up additional evidence of discrimination against Negro registrants in the Deep South. Louisiana struck back with a statute requiring racial labeling of candidates on state ballots. It required that the race of the candidate "whether Caucasian, Negro or other specific race" must be printed on the ballot opposite the candidate's name in type as large as his name. The state protested that there was nothing invidious in the requirement and that it did not offend the equal-protection clause of the Fourteenth Amendment because it applied equally to all races! On December 13, 1964, the Court struck down the law. "We see no relevance in the State's pointing up the race of the candidate," Justice Clark said for a unanimous Court in *Anderson v. Martin*.[17] "Obviously," he continued, "Louisiana may not bar Negro citizens from offering themselves as candidates for public office, nor can it encourage its citizens to vote for a candidate solely on account of race. And that which cannot be done by express statutory prohibition cannot be done by indirection." He saw no merit in the claim that the statute met the test of equality: "[We] view the equality as superficial," he said curtly.

After its invalidation of the white primary by party rule or resolution, the Court hewed to a consistent line of striking down evasive attempts to circumvent its decision. In the Gomillion case it served notice that it would not tolerate state use of the gerrymander to disfranchise Negroes and in the Anderson case that cynical racial designation of candidates would not be permitted. When Congress enacted new voting legislation in 1957 and 1960, the Court broke with old precedents to clear the way for executive action. It was hestitant only where its half-century-old decisions had helped institutionalize such discriminatory practices as state literacy test provisions and interpretive requirements. It moved to challenge those and similar provisions of state laws and constitutions in two decisions handed down on March 8, 1965, *Louisiana v. United States* and *United States v. Mississippi*.[18] Both cases had been filed under the authority of the 1960 Civil Rights Act and were originally heard by three-judge federal courts. Justice Black spoke for a unanimous Court in each case.

In the face of plain words of a federal statute to the contrary, the Mississippi federal court held that the United States had no authority to sue a state under the circumstances. Through a process of "ingenious verbal criticism," it also arrived at the conclusion that although a private citizen and even the government might sue a discriminatory registrar, the statute did not give the United States the right "to bring suits challenging the validity of the State's voting laws as such." Justice Black could "find no possible justification for such a construction" and found it "difficult to take seriously the argument that Congress intended to dilute its guarantee of the right to vote regardless of race by saying that a State was free to disqualify its Negro citizens by laws which violated the United States Constitution."

Justice Black reviewed Mississippi's long history of excluding Negroes from voting in the state and noted that the complaint charged that "the State of Mississippi and its officials for the past three quarters of a century have been writing and adopting constitutional provisions, statutes, rules and regulations all designed to keep the number of white voters at the highest possible figure and the number of colored voters at the lowest. It is alleged that the common

purpose . . . has been to adopt whatever expedient seemed necessary to establish white political supremacy in a completely segregated society." He saw substance for the complaint in the state supreme court's celebrated dictum that Mississippi's constitutional
convention of 1890 "swept the circle of expedients to obstruct the
franchise by the negro race." There was an edge of criticism in
Justice Black's quotation of that statement that had been entirely
absent in prior cases where it had been quoted. The district court
had dismissed the case; the Court ordered it "tried without delay."

The district court that tried the Louisiana case gave judgment
for the United States after examining a long series of historical
events in which the state had disfranchised Negroes through one
ingenious statute after another, including use of the grandfather
clause, the white primary, interpretation tests, and finally the requirement that a person seeking to register must be able to read
and explain constitutional provisions to the satisfaction of the
registrar. Justice Black noted that the evidence showed, "colored
people, some even with the most advanced education and schol-
arship, were declared by voting registrars with less education to
have an unsatisfactory understanding of the constitution of Louisiana or the United States." He remarked acidly, "This is not a
test but a trap, sufficient to stop even the most brilliant man on
his way to the voting booth."

The Supreme Court approved the district court's decree that
"the provisions of the Louisiana Constitution and statutes which
require voters to satisfy registrars of their ability to 'understand
and give a reasonable interpretation of any section' of the federal or Louisiana constitutions violate the Constitution." It further
agreed with the district court that the Constitution was violated by subjecting "citizens to such an arbitrary power as Louisiana has given its registrars under these laws." The Court also
approved the district court's decree ordering 21 parishes to retrace their steps and give Negroes the same opportunity to register that had been extended to white voters in the past.

At long last, the Court had come to grips with evasive and discriminatory voting legislation it had refused to review and condemn in the voting cases of the waning years of the nineteenth
century and the early days of the twentieth. Inestimable harm
had been done meanwhile, as Justice Black tacitly recognized in
his comment, "The need to eradicate past evil effects and to pre-

vent the continuation and repetition in the future of discriminatory practices shown to be so deeply ingrained in the laws, policies and traditions of the State of Louisiana" justified the district
court's sweeping decree. Even as the Court spoke, Congress was
considering new legislation proposed by President Lyndon B.
Johnson to wipe out state legislation and practices condemned in
the Mississippi and Louisiana cases. It is crystal clear that the
Court will now act on its own initiative or in approval of new
federal legislation to curb the abuses of registration statutes.

Congress enacted new voting legislation in August 1955, including a provision for federal registrars, and the Attorney General
ordered them into action in test countries. Even as they turned
southward, Mississippi repealed the worst features of its voting
laws. Negroes swarmed to registration offices—state and federal—
all over the South. The Fifteenth Amendment became meaningful
again for the first time since the 1890's. And this time there was no
doubt that the Supreme Court would uphold congressional legislators.

Every time the Court acted to protect a right in the late 1930's
and 1940's, Negroes were emboldened to assert another, a circumstance that flowed inevitably from their intransigent belief
that, rightly interpreted, the Civil War amendments wiped out
every vestige of inequality. That sentiment cropped up in the
field of employment, where discrimination was rampant. American involvement in World War II demanded unflagging opposition to Hitler's racism, and that opposition shed a new and
shaming light on American racism. And as the nation scraped
the bottom of the barrel to find manpower to create the weapons
of war, Negroes, and their increasing number of allies, seized
the opportunity to point a finger at discriminatory practices that
confined Negroes to agricultural labor and excluded them from
industry. They turned to the Court for relief, a consequence of
the fact that they were its wards, dependent on its interpretation
of the Constitution to achieve the equality they claimed. It is
time to turn back and take a look at what had happened in the
area of employment.

The old ark's a-moverin'
A-moverin', a-moverin'
The old ark's a-moverin'
A-moverin' along.

NEGRO SPIRITUAL

Southern resistance to the Supreme Court edict in the school segregation cases was not a spontaneous reaction to an unpopular decision. It was rooted in southern tradition. North Carolina retained, and some of its counties enforced, grandfather clauses until the 1950's, although the Supreme Court interdicted them in 1915. Birmingham enacted and enforced a racial zoning ordinance in 1949, in defiance of a Supreme Court decision of 1917. Haywood County, Tennessee, Democrats provided for a white primary in 1959, knowing that the Supreme Court had held that requirement unconstitutional in 1944. In 1911, the Court in the Bailey case held with finality that a state statute making it a crime to fail to perform the terms of a labor contract after receiving an advance offended both the Thirteenth Amendment and federal peonage statutes. In that case the Court laid great stress on the invalidity of sections of such statutes creating a presumption of guilt from the mere signing of a contract and failing to carry out the agreement to work. In the 1940's, three peonage cases reached the Court involving identical statutes, one of them passed and amended long after 1911.

Georgia indicted and convicted James Taylor in 1940 for accepting $19.50 from R. L. Hardie and of then failing to perform the promised services. Under Georgia law, Taylor could not testify as to his motives in signing and then repudiating the contract but could make an unsworn statement in explanation. The case was almost completely parallel with the Bailey case, but Taylor had to go to the Supreme Court to win his freedom in *Taylor v. Georgia,* decided in 1942. A unanimous Court reversed the conviction, with Justice James Byrnes of South Carolina writing, "The necessary consequence [of the contract] is that one who has received an advance on a contract for services which he is unable to repay is bound by threat of penal sanctions to remain at his employment until the debt has been discharged. Such coerced labor is peonage." [1]

The federal prosecuting attorney had to appeal to the Supreme Court in order to proceed with the prosecution of a Florida offender who arrested a Negro charged with violation of a labor contract. The indictment charged the defendant Gaskin with "arresting" Johnson "to a condition of peonage," in violation of federal laws making it a crime to "arrest . . . any person to a condition of peonage." Validity of the law had been upheld by the Court in 1905, but the federal district judge dismissed the indictment. Justice Roberts spoke for an eight-to-one majority reinstating the indictment in *United States v. Gaskin* [2] in 1944. Justice Murphy alone thought the statute as applied was too vague.

After promising to do some work, James Pollock got a five-dollar advance from the J. V. O'Albora corporation on October 14, 1942. He did not perform the promised services and was arrested on January 5, 1943, prosecuted under a statute almost identical with that involved in the Bailey case, pleaded guilty on the day of his arrest, and was sentenced to pay a hundred-dollar fine or serve sixty days in jail. He had no lawyer. The Florida supreme court upheld his conviction, although the law contained the obnoxious provision that a presumption of guilt arose from the mere promise to do the work and failure to do so. "We cannot doubt that the presumption provision had a coercive effect in producing the plea of guilty," Justice Robert Jackson wrote for a seven-to-two majority freeing Pollock, when the case was decided by the Supreme Court in 1944. [3] "No one questions," he said, "that we clearly have held such a presumption is prohibited by the Constitution and the Federal statute. *The Florida legislature has enacted and twice re-enacted it since we so held. . . . Since the presumption was known to be unconstitutional . . . the only explanation we can find for its persistence in the statute is its extra-legal coercive effect in suppressing defenses. . . . There was every probability that a law so recently* (1943) *enacted would be followed by the trial judge. . . ."* (Emphasis added.)

In its decision upholding Pollocks' conviction, the Florida court had said that the presumption played no role in light of Pollock's guilty plea, but Justice Jackson was not impressed: "We think that a state which maintains such a law in the face of the court decisions we have recited may not be heard to say that a plea of guilty under the circumstances is not due to pressure of its statutory threat to convict him on this presumption," he said. And he repeated the increasingly important assertion of federal primacy, with the observation that the Supreme Court was not bound by state court findings, "but under the circumstances [we] are authorized to make an independent determination." Justice Reed and Chief Justice Stone echoed the dissent of Justice Holmes in the Bailey case by arguing that the Court should not hold that "a statute which merely punishes a fraud in a contract . . . violates the provisions of the Thirteenth Amendment" or the applicable federal statute.

Peonage is ebbing away, helped to deserved extinction by forthright Supreme Court invalidation of state statutes designed to expedite its practice, and also doomed by increasing urbanization of Negroes. Peonage has no place in the urban industrial process, and by 1960 more than 70 per cent of America's Negroes were city dwellers. Urbanization did not solve the Negro's employment problem. It is one of the bitter paradoxes of his history as an American that his ancestors were imported and welcomed as a source of labor supply but that with his attainment of freedom, his never-ending problem immediately became that of finding employment. The Negro's search for jobs and ingenious efforts to thwart him have taken him to the Supreme Court on a number of occasions.

The boycott of the neighborhood merchant who refuses to employ Negro clerks has been used as a device to secure employment for many years. During such a boycott in Washington, D.C., a federal court enjoined peaceful picketing where it appeared that the picket carried a placard urging, "Do Your Part! Buy Where You Can Work! No Negroes Employed Here!" The Norris-La Guardia Act curtailed federal court injunctions in labor disputes, and the issue confronting the Court in *New Negro Alliance v. Sanitary Grocers*,[4] decided in 1938, was whether or not picketing to compel employment of Negroes was a labor dispute within the meaning of the federal statute. Justice Roberts answered in the affirmative for a seven-to-two majority of the Court. "Race discrimination by an employer," he said, "may reasonably be deemed more unfair and less excusable than discrimination against workers on the ground of union affiliation. There is no justification . . . for limiting [the act's] definition of labor disputes and cases arising therefrom by excluding those which arise with respect to discrimination in terms and conditions of employment based upon difference of race or color." Justices McReynolds and Butler dissented. But the issue was settled; federal courts may not issue injunctions to ban picketing against racial discrimination in employment.

Lucky Stores in Richmond, California, did employ a few Negroes, but Negroes organized a boycott and picketed the store because they claimed that the employment was insufficient. They carried placards demanding that the store employ Negroes in proportion to the amount of Negro customers. The local trial court issued a preliminary injunction forbidding the picketing. When picketing continued, it found some of the pickets in contempt and fined them. They asked the state supreme court to annul the contempt order but it declined to do so on the ground that a demand for proportional employment was in essence a demand *for* discrimination against already employed clerks. White clerks, it said, would be thrown out of jobs solely because of their race, and it therefore held the picketing unlawful.

The Supreme Court reviewed the controversy in *Hughes v. Superior Court*[5] and, in 1950, sustained the ruling of the California supreme court. Justice Frankfurter laid heavy stress on the sensitivity of California's courts and their consistent record in safeguarding civil rights of Negroes. He said that the Court would respect California's judgment that under the circumstances the end sought by the picketing was unlawful. There were no dissents, but Justice Douglas did not participate.

There was a measure of judicial naïveté in the Court's tender solicitude to protect white clerks from discrimination, a consideration that would have had validity in a society of equals but which left out of account the historical truth that compensatory measures were necessary to overcome the discrimination that had been practiced against Negroes for many years. Unwittingly, the decision put the stamp of judicial approval on tokenism in Negro employment.

There is no shabbier racial record in the history of organized labor than that compiled by the railroad brotherhoods. Early in their history they barred Negroes from membership by rituals and constitutions. As a result, no known Negro has ever been employed as a locomotive engineer, although many became qualified for the job through long training and experience as firemen. Barred from membership in the firemen's union, Negroes were extensively employed as firemen on southern railroads when their work was disagreeable and dirty. They were known as "nonpromotables" to distinguish them from white firemen who were styled "promotables" to indicate that as whites they could win promotion to the rank of engineer. As the fireman's task became more desirable, white firemen set out to drive Negroes from the railroads. Violence and even murder were first used, but the provisions of the federal Railway Labor Act seemed to offer a more genteel and effective weapon.

Under the act, the railroads were required to enter into collective bargaining with the union chosen by the majority of the employees in each craft. The Brotherhood of Locomotive Firemen and Enginemen, which excluded Negroes, won the election on the Louisville and Nashville Railroad, and in 1940 and 1941 entered into a collective bargaining agreement with the railroad severely limiting the number of Negro firemen, curtailing their employment, and laying the basis for their ultimate elimination. By right of seniority, Buster Steele had earned a desirable passenger run on the railroad but, as a result of the agreement, he was put on a less remunerative run and finally assigned to a switch engine. He sued the railroad and the union in the Alabama courts on behalf of himself and other similarly situated Negroes, claiming that the union as the elected representative of all firemen should not be permitted to enter into a racially discriminatory agreement against him and that the railroad could not honor the agreement. The Alabama supreme court held that the union as a private organization was under no duty to safeguard Steele's rights and could discriminate in favor of its white members if it chose to do so. The Supreme Court reviewed the case and decided it as *Steele v. L. & N. R.R. Co.*[6] in 1944.

Chief Justice Stone said that the issue presented by the case was whether the Railway Labor Act "imposes on a labor organization, acting by authority of the statute as the exclusive bargaining representative of a craft or class of railway employees, the duty to represent all the employees in the craft without discrimination because of their race, and if so, whether the Courts have jurisdiction to protect the minority of this craft or class from the violation of the obligation." He answered that "If the Railway Labor Act purports to impose on [Steele] and the other Negro members of the craft the legal duty to comply with the terms of a contract whereby the representative has discriminatorily restricted their employment for the benefit and advantage of the Brotherhood's own members, we must decide the constitutional questions" raised in the suit. However, he came to the conclusion that the suit could be decided without resolution of the constitutional issue.

"We think," the Chief Justice said, "that the Railway Labor Act imposes upon the statutory representatives of a craft at least as exacting a duty to protect equally the interests of the members of the Craft as the Constitution imposes upon a legislature to give equal protection to the interests of those for whom it legislates. Congress has seen fit to clothe the bargaining representative with powers comparable to a legislative body both to create and restrict the rights of those whom it represents but it has also imposed a corresponding duty." What he was announcing was an important new principle that where a legislature clothed a union with power to represent all members of a group of workers, that union could not enter into agreement discriminating against its Negro members. Such a union, he had said, was as bound by the principle of equal protection of the law as a state legislature. Six other justices were in complete agreement with their Chief, and Justice Black concurred in the result without comment.

Justice Murphy, also in agreement with the result, would have grounded the decision on constitutional principles. He warned that "The economic discrimination against Negroes practiced by the Brotherhood and the railroad under color of Congressional authority raises a grave constitutional question which should be squarely faced. The utter disregard for the dignity and the well-being of colored citizens shown by this record is so pronounced as to demand the invocation of constitutional condemnation. To decide the case on and analyze the statute solely upon the basis of legal niceties, while remaining mute and placid as to the obvious and oppressive deprivation of constitutional guarantees, is to make the judicial function less than it should be. . . ." Buster Steele, who got his old job back, was no doubt thankful for the statutory half-loaf given him by the majority of the Court.

Tom Tunstall, also caught in the machinations of the discriminatory agreement, made the Brotherhood his primary target in a suit filed in federal court. The Brotherhood answered that there was no federal right involved and that Tunstall should have filed his suit in a state court. Chief Justice Stone disagreed. He said that the "duty imposed by the Railway Labor Act on the Brotherhood, as bargaining representative, is a federal right implied from the statute and the policy which it has adopted. It is the federal statute which condemns as unlawful the Brotherhood's conduct." [7] Tunstall, of course, was entitled to the same relief as that accorded Steele and moreover could enforce his right in a federal court. He had established the principle that a federal law, such as the Railway Labor Act, creates a *federal* right vested in those whom it protects against discrimination.

The intransigent Brotherhood of Locomotive Firemen and Enginemen was back in the Supreme Court in 1949 in a case styled *Graham v. Brotherhood* for what Justice Jackson said was a "willful disregard of rights which this Court has said must be accorded to Negro firemen" arising out of its failure to protect the contract rights of 21 "nonpromotables," that is, Negroes. It sought to evade judicial stricture by arguing that the case was brought in the wrong federal court and that the federal district courts lacked jurisdiction to issue an injunction prohibiting its conduct, the very principle established by Tom Tunstall in his case. An impatient Justice Jackson spurned the argument. "If," he said, "there remains any illusion that . . . the federal courts are powerless to enforce these rights, we dispel it now. The district court has jurisdiction to enforce by injunction the rights to non-discriminatory representation by their statutory representative." [8]

Simon Howard had worked for the 'Frisco Railroad as a train porter for 40 years and belonged to a porter's union. Like all other Negroes classified as porters, he performed a brakeman's duties at less wages than white brakemen. On March 7, 1946, the Brotherhood of Railway Trainmen, which represented white brakemen, forced the railroad to agree to fire all porters and "fill their jobs with white men who . . . would do less work but get more pay." Howard sued to prevent the railroad and the Brotherhood from carrying out their agreement, and his case was decided as *Brotherhood of Railway Trainmen v. Howard* in 1952.[9] The Brotherhood's answer to the suit was that, unlike the union in the Steele and Tunstall cases, it did not and never had represented Howard, who was a member of a rival union. It had a right, it said, to seek jobs for its own members and was under no duty to safeguard Howard's rights. Justice Black, who spoke for a six-to-three majority of the Court, answered that "these train porters are threatened with loss of their jobs because they are not white and for no other reason." The Brotherhood had been placed in a position where it could represent the brakemen by virtue of the Railway Labor Act and, said Justice Black, "Bargaining agents who enjoy the advantages of the Railway Labor Act's provisions must execute their trust without lawless invasion of the rights of others." The decision was an important extension of Chief Justice Stone's holding in the Steele case that a labor union which availed itself of the advantages of the Railway Labor Act had to observe the requirements imposed on a legislature to refrain from racial discrimination.

The Railway Clerks Union and the Texas and New Orleans Railroad entered into an agreement under which 45 Negro members were fired under the guise of abolishing the jobs they held. As Justice Black observed, the jobs were not abolished "but instead were filled by whites as the Negroes were ousted." [10] He spoke for a unanimous Court in *Conley v. Gibson*, decided in 1957, condemning the failure of the union to protect the jobs of its Negro members. The union had a duty, he said, to prevent the unwarranted discharges.

It had been thirteen years since Buster Steele had won his case—thirteen years of unremitting effort on the part of railway labor unions to pervert a federal statute to discriminatory usage. The Court had remained steadfast, and its rulings had perforce been followed by federal district courts and courts of appeal in other cases that it had not reviewed, enforcing the rights of Negro railroad workers. Almost unnoticed, the Court had done a little more than that: it had whittled away at the doctrine announced in the *Civil Rights Cases* and enlarged in later decisions to the effect that neither the courts nor Congress could interdict discriminatory conduct of private persons or groups. It had found an important exception to that rule in the circumstance that where a private organization such as a railroad labor union had availed itself of the benefits of a federal statute, it could not practice or connive at racial discrimination with an employer to the detriment of its members or other employees of the railroad. Justice Minton, Chief Justice Fred Vinson, and Justice Reed had protested in the Howard case, where Justice Minton wrote that "I do not understand that private parties . . . may not discriminate on the grounds of race. Neither a state government nor the Federal government may do so, but I know of no applicable federal law which says that private parties may not." The majority ignored his plea to turn back the clock.

Meanwhile, Congress had enacted, and often amended, the National Labor Relations Act giving other labor unions advantages somewhat analogous to those extended to railway labor unions. Were those unions also bound by the nondiscriminatory inhibitions laid on railway unions? The answer, supplied in *Syres v. Oil Workers Union*[11] in 1955, was an apparent affirmative. The union and the employer entered into an agreement which disadvantaged Negro members by permitting segregation and providing two separate lines of seniority, one for whites and the other for Negroes, thus having the effect of retarding promotions of Negroes. John Syres assailed the agreement through a suit, but the Court of Appeals for the Fifth Circuit denied him relief on the ground that courts lacked jurisdiction in such cases. The Supreme Court reversed the decision in a summary opinion, simply citing the Howard and other railway labor cases, thus seeming to indicate that unions availing themselves of the benefits of the National Labor Relations Act could not discriminate against their members and that a member of such a union could secure judicial relief. It did not, however, spell out the details, and the retrial told little because of failure of proof as to damages. Other issues had become moot.

In the 1940's, the states, led by New York, had begun passage of fair employment laws prohibiting racial discrimination by employers and forbidding racial exclusion by labor unions. The Railway Mail Association, an organization of postal clerks working on mail trains, was infected with the racist virus that seems to be a common ailment of all railway workers. It limited its membership to Caucasians and American Indians. When New York ordered it to drop its color bars, it sought relief in state courts on the rather remarkable ground that the nondiscriminatory order violated the due-process and equal-protection clauses of the Fourteenth Amendment! In *Railway Mail Association v. Corsi*, decided in 1945, the Court, agreeing with New York, rejected that simplistic argument. "We have here," said Justice Reed for the Court, "a prohibition of discrimination on account of race, creed, or color. A judicial determination that such legislation violated the Fourteenth Amendment would be a distortion of the policy manifested in that amendment which was adopted to prevent state legislation designed to perpetuate discrimination on the basis of race or color." [12] Justice Frankfurter wrote his own concurrence to say with some scorn that "Elaborately to argue against [the union's] contention is to dignify a claim devoid of constitutional substance. . . . To use the Fourteenth Amendment as a sword against such state power would stultify the Amendment." State fair-employment statutes were valid.

Continental Airlines resisted an order of the Colorado Anti-Discrimination Commission directing it to employ Marion Green, a qualified Negro pilot, on the ground that its position as an interstate carrier and its regulation by the federal government exempted it from orders of such a state commission. The Colorado supreme court agreed, but its judgment was reversed in *Colorado Anti-Discrimination Commission v. Continental Airlines* in 1963, the Court holding in substance, through Justice Black, that an order issued by a fair employment commission to an interstate carrier was not a burden on interstate commerce or in conflict with federal laws.[13]

There are well-defined limits to effective judicial action against racial discrimination in employment, but the Court responded to every invitation extended to it from the 1930's onward to exert its power to strike down discriminatory labor practices. It administered the final death blow to state statutes which had the effect of fostering peonage; it blazed a new trail in its holdings that railway labor unions could not discriminate against Negro workmen where they were placed in a position to do so by federal statutes; it narrowed the doctrine that private organizations were free to discriminate under any and all circumstances, with the labor case rulings that where the union accepted statutory benefits, it was restrained from the exercise of racial discrimination in much the same manner as a legislature; it recognized the right of Negroes to picket against discrimination in employment and placed that right on a par with picketing rights of unions, despite an unnecessary limitation of that power in the Hughes case; it validated state fair-employment statutes and refused to limit their power to act to purely intrastate employers. Except in the case of peonage statutes, these actions were significant departures from the restrictive constitutional views taken in earlier cases.

Urbanization of Negroes not only broadened and diversified employment opportunities. It also bred housing problems of great complexity, principally because white Americans, North and South, were committed to racial segregation and were able to achieve a measure of such segregation through judicial enforcement of segregatory agreements.

⊰ 22 ⊱ *A Giant's Strength*

O, it is excellent
To have a giant's strength; but it is tyrannous
To use it like a giant.

SHAKESPEARE, *Measure for Measure* [Act II, Scene 2]

By the early 1940's, Negro migration to urban centers, which had ebbed after World War I and during the depression years, had swollen to a flood. The migrants came by the hundreds, by the thousands, by the tens of thousands, and by the hundreds of thousands, attracted northward by the demand for labor created by World War II. And as they sought shelter for themselves and their families, they soon used up the available housing supply in the well-established Negro communities. They doubled up and tripled up, for wherever they sought new areas, the courts turned them back by issuing injunctions forbidding them to violate race-restrictive covenants that said quite openly and quite simply, "This property shall not be used or occupied by any person or persons except those of the Caucasian race." Negro newcomers and old residents alike were hemmed in, penned up in racial ghettos—those sprawling black belts lying in the residentially least desirable heartlands of America's great cities.

War's end brought no surcease. The migrants kept on coming, the children kept on being born, the population kept on growing. The old black belts could no longer contain the burgeoning Negro population. The ghettos expanded slowly, sometimes because the courts chose to invalidate racial convenants on technical grounds, sometimes because frantic Negro homeseekers ignored courts and injunctions and overwhelmed adjacent neighborhoods while whites fled in panic. But there was a limit to what the courts would do or could do on technical grounds and a limit to flooding methods.

There was no hope for legislative relief; realtors and real estate boards were too powerful for that. There was no hope for congressional relief; Congress had not passed a civil rights bill since 1875, and southern lawmakers were in control of the House and the Senate. There was no hope for executive action; public sentiment posed too great a barrier. Indeed, the federal government was busy through the Federal Housing Administration requiring the imposition of racial restrictive covenants as a condition for extension of mortgage insurance for home loans. City and other planning and zoning commissions were manipulating their rules and regulations to conserve and strengthen the ghetto.

Inevitably, Negroes turned to the Supreme Court, that final expositor of the Constitution, which had taken unto itself the power to determine what the Constitution meant when it spoke of equal protection of the law—that Court which had made the Negro its ward before the Civil War and clung to its guardianship role when Congress had tried to wrest that function from it through the Civil War Amendments and equalitarian laws. All across the nation, Negro lawyers began arguing that the Negro homeseeker was denied equal protection of the law when a *court* enjoined him from using and occupying his own property.[1] Judicial action, the lawyers said, was state action inhibited by the Constitution. The odds were against them. By 1948, state courts of last resort in nineteen states and the District of Columbia had held that such judicial action was *not* state action within the meaning of the Fourteenth Amendment.[2]

The Supreme Court itself, as we have seen, had circuitously but effectively upheld judicial enforcement of racial covenants in *Corrigan v. Buckley*[3] in 1926. It clung resolutely to that rule for two decades by refusing all requests for review of cases challenging the Corrigan decision. In 1947, the Court agreed to review two cases, one from Missouri and another from Michigan, both based on the contention that judicial enforcement of racial covenants offended constitutional guarantees. Its rather sudden agreement to do so was a recognition of the fact that the situation was becoming intolerable and was a response to nationwide appeals for relief.[4] No matter how onerous the separate-but-equal rule was, it did at least recognize that there must be *some* provision for the Negro excluded from use of public facilities. Racial zoning in housing by private persons through court enforcement of racial restrictions took no account of the need of Negroes for shelter. The courts ordered an offending Negro's ouster with no thought and no responsibility for his housing, even where it was apparent that no shelter was available for his use. If he refused to move in response to an injunction, he was in contempt of court and was jailed.[5]

J. D. Shelley and his wife, Ethel Lee, bought and moved into a home in St. Louis, Missouri, on August 11, 1945. It was located in a tract of 57 parcels, and in 1911 its owner had signed an agreement under which it was restricted against use and occupancy by "people of the Negro or Mongolian Race." In the event of such use, the agreement provided that the owner who permitted it should lose all title to the property. Other tract owners, led by Louis Kraemer and his wife, Fern, sued Mr. and Mrs. Shelley, and ultimately the Missouri supreme court ordered the Shelleys out of their new home and their title forfeited because of their violation of the agreement. In 1947, the Supreme Court agreed to review the case, now known as *Shelley v. Kraemer.*[6]

Orsel McGhee and his wife, Minnie, bought and moved into a Detroit, Michigan, home on November 30, 1944. A committee of neighbors, headed by Mr. and Mrs. Benjamin Sipes, visited the Mc-Ghees in January, 1945, and demanded that they vacate because their occupancy violated a 1934 agreement signed by the then owner of the property restricting it against use and occupancy by "any person except those of the Caucasian race." When the Mc-Ghees refused to move, Mr. Sipes filed suit, and the Michigan courts ordered the McGhees out of their own home within 90 days after the decree. The case reached the Supreme Court in 1947 as *McGhee v. Sipes.*[7]

In 1909, Frederick Hodge and his wife, Lena, bought a house in Bryant Street in Washington, D.C. They were white and the neighborhood was entirely white at the time of the purchase. The homes in the neighborhood were covered with a restrictive agreement providing that none should ever be "rented, leased, sold, transferred or conveyed unto any Negro or colored person." In time Negroes did move into the neighborhood, and by 1944 it was almost one-third Negro. In that year, Mr. and Mrs. James Hurd bought a house on Bryant Street covered by the racial agreement. In 1945, three other Negro families bought restricted homes on

Bryant Street. All of the buyers were in desperate need of housing —two of them had been evicted from prior housing—and experts testified that housing was in such short supply for Negroes that many of them were braving lawsuits and defying court orders to move. District of Columbia courts ordered all the Negroes to vacate their newly found homes and the deeds to them canceled. The Supreme Court agreed to review the case, *Hurd v. Hodge*,[8] in January, 1948.

The two state cases presented the constitutional problem of the applicability of the Fourteenth Amendment but differed in the fact that in the Missouri case, the courts had forfeited the Shelleys' title, while the Michigan courts had only enjoined the McGhees from living in their home. The two cases were combined under the title of *Shelley v. Kraemer.* The Fourteenth Amendment is not applicable to the District of Columbia and relief had to be sought in the due-process-of-law clause of the Fifth Amendment or in federal statutes. Twenty-one organizations, ranging from the American Veterans Committee to the United Nations Association, filed briefs as friends of the court on behalf of Negro litigants and *The New York Times* saw the litigation as a new Dred Scott case. The briefs were filled with sociological data, detailing the enormity of the problem and the desperate need for judicial relief. The federal government filed a brief on behalf of the Shelleys, the McGhees, and the Hurds, and at argument the Solicitor General spoke out vigorously on their behalf, even quoting the State Department as concerned at the harm judicial enforcement was doing in the area of international relations.

A six-man Court heard the case, because Justices Reed, Jackson, and Rutledge felt that they were disqualified. Chief Justice Vinson spoke for the unanimous six: "It cannot be doubted," he said, "that among the civil rights intended to be protected from discriminatory state action by the Fourteenth Amendment are the rights to acquire, enjoy, own and dispose of property . . . Equality in the enjoyment of property rights was regarded by the framers of that Amendment as an essential precondition to the realization of other basic civil rights and liberties which the Amendment was intended to guarantee." The essential question for him was whether or not a judicial decree ordering enforcement of racial covenants was state action.

The Chief Justice wrote that "Since the decision of this Court in the *Civil Rights Cases,* the principle has become firmly imbedded in our constitutional law that the action inhibited by the first section of the Fourteenth Amendment is only such action as may fairly be said to be that of the States. That Amendment erects no shield against merely private conduct, however discriminatory." His conclusion was that *standing alone,* the restrictive agreements could not "be regarded as a violation of any rights guaranteed . . . by the Fourteenth Amendment." Was judicial action that kind of "state action" forbidden by the Fourteenth Amendment when judges enforced racial discrimination? He answered that it was.

After a long review of constitutional history and Supreme Court decisions, the Chief Justice said that "The short of the matter is that from the time of the adoption of the Fourteenth Amendment until the present, it has been the consistent ruling of this Court that the action of the States to which the Amendment has reference, includes action of state courts and state judicial officials." He pronounced the ultimate judgment: "We hold that in granting judicial enforcement of the restrictive agreements in these cases, the States have denied [Negroes] the equal protection of the laws and that, therefore, the action of the state courts cannot stand." Judicial enforcement of racially restrictive covenants by state courts had come to an end, but the Court was careful to say that its decision did not preclude voluntary compliance with a covenant if the signers chose to do so. Covenants were not void; they were unenforcible.

In the District of Columbia case, *Hurd v. Hodge,* the Chief Justice blandly explained, as he had in the Shelley case, that the Court had never ruled on the issue of judicial enforcement, despite what was said in *Corrigan v. Buckley* and despite the long-held assumption of lawyers and judges that it had done so. In the Corrigan case, he said, "the only constitutional issue which had been raised in the lower courts . . . and consequently the only constitutional question before this Court . . . related to the validity of the private agreements as such."

With the preliminary question out of the way, he said that the Court did not need to consider the due-process-of-law clause of the Fifth Amendment, because judicial enforcement of racial covenants by federal courts was proscribed by a law originally enacted in the Civil Rights Act of 1866, which provides that "All citizens of the United States shall have the same right in every State and Territory, as is enjoyed by white citizens thereof, to inherit, purchase,

lease, sell, hold, and convey real and personal property." His conclusion was that "the action of the District Court . . . denies rights
intended by Congress to be protected by the Civil Rights Act and
that, consequently, the action cannot stand." In any event, he
added, the public policy of the United States would not tolerate
federal courts doing what state courts were forbidden to do. Judicial enforcement of racial covenants was now outlawed in all American courts.

Justice Frankfurter concurred in the Hurd case on the ground
that federal courts could not issue an injunction to enforce a racial
convenant "when the authorization of such an injunction by the
States . . . violates the Constitution and violates it, not for narrow
technical reasons, but for considerations that touch rights so basic
to our society that, after the Civil War, their protection was . . .
safeguarded by the Constitution."

After the decisions in the Shelley and Hurd cases, those who had
exerted their giant's strength so long and so effectively in judicial
enforcement of convenants cast around for means of evading the
restraint placed on them. The Los Angeles Realty Board and the
California Real Estate Association proposed a constitutional
amendment to restore the old order, but more realistic proponents
hit upon the idea that indirect enforcement could be achieved
through damage suits by signers of the covenants against other
signers who sold restricted property to Negroes. Missouri and Oklahoma courts upheld the validity of damage suits; Michigan and
District of Columbia courts disagreed. The issue was settled by a
case that went from California to the Supreme Court: *Barrows v.
Jackson*,[9] decided in 1953.

Leola Jackson signed a racially restrictive covenant in 1944, covering real property in Los Angeles. Among the co-signers of the
agreement were Olive Barrows and M. M. O'Gara and an owner
who later sold to Richard Pikaar. After the decision in the Shelley
case, Mrs. Jackson sold her property to Negroes, and Mrs. Barrows,
Mr. O'Gara, and Mr. Pikaar sued her for some $16,000 in damages
for violation of the agreement. California courts held that a damage
suit could not be entertained and dismissed the action, saying in
effect that the damage suit was only an indirect attempt to enforce
the racially restrictive agreement and that enforcement could no
more be had through indirection than through the direct device of
injunction which had been forbidden in the Shelley case.[10] It placed

its decision squarely on the proposition that indirect enforcement would deny equal protection of the laws to Mrs. Jackson.

Mrs. Barrows's Supreme Court lawyers found a flaw, or what they thought was a flaw, in that reasoning. They agreed that the Negro buyer of Mrs. Jackson's property could not be sued, either for an injunction or for damages, and that he could continue to occupy the property. The constitutional right protected in the Shelley case, they said, was a Negro's constitutional right to "acquire, own, enjoy and dispose of" property without discriminatory action on the part of the state. But, they insisted, Mrs. Jackson was a white woman who could not excuse her violation of her contract by claiming protection of the constitutional right of a Negro to buy or rent property whenever he could find a seller or landlord willing to sell or rent to him. She had signed the agreement; she must abide by it or respond in damages, they concluded.

Justice Minton wrote the opinion for the eight-to-one majority upholding the California courts. "To compel [Mrs. Jackson] to respond in damages would be for the State to punish her for her failure to perform her covenant to discriminate against non-Caucasians in the use of her property," he said. "The result of that sanction by the State would be to encourage the use of restrictive covenants. To that extent, the State would put its sanction behind the covenants. If the State may thus punish [Mrs. Jackson] for her failure to carry out her covenant, she is coerced to use her property in a discriminatory manner, which in essence is the purpose of the covenant. Thus, it becomes not [her] voluntary choice but the State's choice that she observe the covenant or suffer damages."

Would the state action in allowing damages deprive anyone of his constitutional rights? Yes, answered Justice Minton: "If a state court awards damages for breach of a restrictive covenant, a prospective seller of restricted land will either refuse to sell to non-Caucasians or will . . . require a higher price to meet the damages. . . . Solely because of their race, non-Caucasians will be unable to purchase, own, and enjoy property on the same terms as Caucasians," he insisted.

There was one final question because of the Court's longstanding rule that "one may not claim standing in this Court to vindicate the constitutional rights of some third party." But, said Justice Minton, there are exceptions to every rule, and this case presented a "unique situation." He was of the opinion that "Under the peculiar circumstances of this case, we believe the reasons which underlie our denying standing to raise another's rights, which is only a rule of practice, are outweighed by the need to protect the fundamental rights which would be denied by permitting the damage action to be maintained." Mrs. Jackson could assert the constitutional rights of Negro buyers to excuse her violation of the agreement.

There was one dissent, and that by Chief Justice Vinson who had written the opinion in the Shelley case. His dissent was vigorous and caustic and revolved around the point that Mrs. Jackson could not avail herself of the constitutional rights of "some unnamed person in an amorphous class." He said he could not "see how [Mrs. Jackson] can avail herself of the Fourteenth Amendment rights of total strangers . . . and since I cannot see how the Court can find that those rights would be impaired in this particular case by requiring [her] to pay . . . for the injury she has brought upon [the plantiffs] I am unwilling to join the Court in today's decision."

The Barrows case marked the end of litigation over racially restrictive covenants. The issue of judicial enforcement had been settled: signers of covenants could not enforce them by injunctive proceedings, and they could not collect damages from a person who violated his agreement not to sell to a non-Caucasian.

When the federal government began construction of low-rent public housing in the early 1930's, it did so on a separate-but-equal basis. Later, it left the entire matter to local public housing authorites, most of which imposed racial segregation on what was called an equitable basis. The result was that when a "Negro project" was filled, the individual Negro applicant could not be admitted to low-rent housing when vacancies existed in "white projects" or when he was obviously in greater need, as that term was defined in regulations, than a white applicant. Applying the constitutional doctrine that a constitutional right was "personal and present" and that such a right was not measured by the satisfaction of the needs of other Negroes, California courts held in *Banks v. Housing Authority* in 1953 that segregation in public housing offended the equal-protection clause of the Fourteenth Amendment.[11] The Supreme Court refused to review that case. Its refusal was taken to mean that the separate-but-equal rule had no application to public housing and, although the Court never formally considered the issue, its silence established the rule. A dozen lower federal courts agreed with the

Banks ruling.[12] The issue became moot with the issuance of an executive order by President Kennedy in 1962, ordering the end of all segregation in public low-rent housing developments.

The Shelley and Barrows cases had done more than sound the death knell for restrictive covenants. They had expanded the concept of "state action," as that phrase had been used by the courts. Upon request, the Court was required to prohibit discrimination by virtue of the equal-protection clause of the Fourteenth Amendment where it found state action. During the course of his opinion in the Shelley case, Chief Justice Vinson pointed out that the phrase *state action* was not nearly as circumscribed as was often assumed by many lawyers and judges. After saying that "The [Fourteenth] Amendment erects no shield against merely private conduct however discriminatory or wrongful," he went on to point out that, as held in the *Civil Rights Cases*, "the Amendment makes void 'State action of every kind' which is inconsistent with the guarantees . . . contained [in the Amendment] and extends to manifestations of 'State authority in the shape of laws, customs, or judicial or executive proceedings.'" Such all-encompassing language was used "no less than eighteen times during the course of" the *Civil Rights Cases,* he said.

In truth, our increasingly complex urban society has progressively involved the state in a myriad of activities that were once matters of purely private concern. The distinction between "private" and "state" action has worn so thin that it is sometimes said that what the state tolerates, the State commands, these days.[13] As it moved forward toward giving the equal-protection clause the widest possible application in order to condemn racial discrimination, the Court has found "state action" in situations where such a claim would have been rejected out of hand a quarter of a century ago. We cannot deal with all these cases here. The case of *Burton v. Wilmington Parking Authority,*[14] decided on April 17, 1961, will serve as an example of the Court's willingness to find "state action" in close cases.

The Wilmington Parking Authority, a Delaware state agency, constructed a parking building to relieve street congestion. In order to provide sufficient funds for operation of the building, the authority leased space in the building to a restaurant, the Eagle Coffee Shoppe. Under Delaware law, a restaurant was not obliged to "furnish entertainment or refreshment to persons whose reception or entertainment . . . would be offensive to the major part of his customers, and would injure his business."

William H. Burton was refused service in the restaurant and sued on his own behalf and on behalf of other Negroes, asking a court decree declaring that such discrimination violated the Fourteenth Amendment. The trial court agreed, but on appeal the Delaware supreme court reversed the decision, holding that the restaurant was an entirely private enterprise, that its action was not that of the authority and was not state action within the meaning of the Fourteenth Amendment.

Speaking through Justice Tom Clark, the majority of the Court pointed out that the building in which the restaurant was located was publicly owned, that the area leased to the restaurant "constituted a physical and financially integral, and, indeed, indispensable part of the state's plan to operate its project as a self-sustaining unit." Therefore, Justice Clark said, there was "that degree of state participation and involvement in discriminatory action which it was the design of the Fourteenth Amendment to condemn."

In arriving at that determination, Justice Clark quoted Chief Justice Vinson's statement in the Shelley case that "imbedded in our constitutional law" is the principle that "the action inhibited by [the equal protection clause] of the Fourteenth Amendment is only such action as may fairly be said to be that of the States. The Amendment erects no shield against merely private conduct however discriminatory or wrongful." He adverted to the fact that the authority could have required the restaurant to pursue a nondiscriminatory course and that it failed to do so. "But," he said, "no state may effectively abdicate its responsibilities by either ignoring them or by merely failing to discharge them. . . . By its inaction, the Authority, and through it the State, has not only made itself a party to refusal of service, but has elected to place its power, property and prestige behind the admitted discrimination." He explained that "what we hold today is that when a State leases public property in the manner and for the purposes shown to have been the case here, the prescription of the Fourteenth Amendment must be complied with by the lessee as certainly as though they were binding covenants written into the lease itself." Justices Black, Douglas, Brennan, and Chief Justice Warren agreed.

Justice Stewart concurred in the result, on the ground that the enforcement of the state statute which gave restaurant keepers the right to refuse service to persons "whose reception or entertainment would be offensive to the major part of his customers" was violative of the Fourteenth Amendment. He justified the decision on that ground.

Justice Harlan, he whose grandfather had written the great dissent in the *Civil Rights Cases,* dissented on the ground that it was not clear to him whether or not the Delaware supreme court had based its decision on the discriminatory statute and would have sent the case back to the state court for clarification as to the grounds for its decision. The clear inference was that he was thinking that Justice Clark had gone too far in finding state action. Justice Whittaker agreed. Justice Frankfurter wrote his own dissent, agreeing that the case should be sent back to the Delaware courts for clarification, "without intimating my view . . . as to what constitutes state action."

The passage of the 1964 Civil Rights Act by Congress, prohibiting discrimination at places of public accommodation, and its subsequent approval by the Court, has settled the duty of restaurant keepers to serve all customers, white or Negro. There is no longer any question of state action. But the issue will continue to crop up in other situations where solution will depend on whether the Court takes a narrow or broad view of the meaning of the phrase. Continuance of the trend initiated in the Shelley case and broadened in the Burton case will give added content on the equal-protection clause of the Fourteenth Amendment and will make it conform more closely with the intent of the framers of the amendment to interdict all racial discrimination.

In summary, the Shelley and Barrows cases effectively eliminated the use of racially restrictive covenants as direct segregatory devices and at the same time opened new vistas of meaning for the state action concept favorable to Negro complainants. They had consequences beyond their primary impact. The Shelley decision did not forbid voluntary adherence to covenants, but a year after the decision, the FHA forbade imposition of racial restrictive agreements after 1950 on real property where an insured loan was sought for home construction on such property. The Veterans' Administration followed suit. Finally, in 1962, President Kennedy's executive order forbade all discrimination in sale or rental of federally assisted housing for which commitments were secured after that date. The decisions also cleared the way for state fair-housing statutes, now in force in a score of states. Clearly, the Court was laggard in bypassing opportunities to interdict judicial enforcement of covenants for the 22 crucial years between the Corrigan and Shelley cases.[15] During those two decades, the pell-mell migration of Negroes to urban centers had immeasurably stimulated the growth of black belts and segregated public facilities attendant on their existence. But however tardy its action, the Court finally recognized what was apparent to the authors of the 1866 Civil Rights Act that the Negro must have the same right as other Americans to enjoy all property rights if his freedom was to be more than a fiction.

As the Court moved toward implementing the equalitarianism written into the Civil War Amendments, it became increasingly clear that the separate-but-equal rule formulated in *Plessy v. Ferguson* was the major obstacle standing in the way of elimination of racial discrimination. Looking back, it is easy to see that the Court was on a collision course with the separate-but-equal formula. The manner in which the Court approached invalidity of the Plessy rule is an intriguing one. It begins with a case involving a Negro's right to attend a state law school, a case in which *Plessy v. Ferguson* was unequivocally recognized as the law of the land.

◄{ 23 }► *Wait a Little While*

Wait a little while,
And we'll sing a new song.

NEGRO SPIRITUAL

Lloyd Gaines decided, or perhaps was persuaded, that he needed a law school education. In 1936, he filed an application with the Board of Curators of the University of Missouri asking to be admitted to the University law school. A citizen of that state, he was a graduate of Lincoln University, Missouri's "separate-but-equal" institution of higher learning for Negroes, and it was admitted on all sides that, except for his race, he was eligible for admission to the state law school. Missouri had no law school for Negroes. He had some precedent on his side. In a similar situation, Maryland courts had ordered the admission of a Negro to that state's law school.[1] Mr. Gaines had no such luck.

Missouri's supreme court pointed out that under state law, Lincoln University was empowered to "open any necessary school or department," when its curators deemed it advisable. Where no necessary school or department had been provided, the state was required to pay tuition of Negro residents "at the university of any adjacent state to take any course or to study any subjects provided for at the state university of Missouri." The Missouri court said that the adjacent states of Kansas, Illinois, Iowa, and Nebraska all maintained law schools to which Negroes were admitted and that Missouri was quite willing to pay Gaines's tuition at any of them. Thus, it said, he had been accorded equal protection of law. He was denied relief, and the Supreme Court agreed to review his case. It did so in *Missouri ex rel. Gaines v. Canada*,[2] decided on December 12, 1938, with Chief Justice Hughes writing the majority opinion.

The Chief Justice remarked that "The state court has fully recognized the obligation of the State to provide negroes with advantages for higher education substantially equal to the advantages afforded to white students . . . by furnishing equal facilities in separate schools, a method the validity of which has been sustained by our decisions." He cited the Plessy case with approval and said that since Missouri did not have a law school for Negroes and was not absolutely required by state law to establish such a school, "we must regard the question whether the provision for legal education in other States of negroes resident in Missouri is sufficient to satisfy the constitutional requirement of equal protection. . . ." He answered that it was not, because "The white resident is afforded legal education within the State; the negro resident having the same qualification is refused it there and must go outside the State to obtain it." He rejected the contention that the fact that there was "but a limited demand in Missouri for the legal education of negroes" was sufficient to excuse "the discrimination in favor of whites."

Chief Justice Hughes underscored the fact that Gaines's "right was a personal one. It was as an individual that he was entitled to equal protection of the laws. . . . " His conclusion was that Gaines "was entitled to be admitted to the law school of the State University in the absence of other and proper provision for his legal training within the State."

Justices McReynolds and Butler dissented, with the former writing an opinion heatedly upholding Missouri's conduct and asserting that under the majority opinion, the state would have to either abandon its law school for whites "or break down settled practice concerning separate schools and thereby, as indicated by experience, damnify both races."

Lloyd Gaines did not enter the University of Missouri law school, or even attempt to do so. He disappeared and nobody ever saw him again. Missouri quickly opened a separate law school for Negroes, and future Negro students accepted it as equal to the law school at the state university. Presumably, the state escaped the dilemma foreseen by Justice McReynolds of having to "damnify both races."

The issue cropped up again in Oklahoma a decade later. Like Missouri, the state had no law school for Negroes. Ada Sipuel applied for admission to the University of Oklahoma law school in 1946, and after two years of legal sparring during which the Oklahoma supreme court refused to order her admittance to the state law school, her case reached the Supreme Court and was decided as *Sipuel v. Board of Regents*[3] on January 12, 1948, a mere four days after it was argued. The Court made short shrift of the matter and said in a unanimous, unsigned opinion that Miss Sipuel "is entitled to secure legal education afforded by a state institution. To this time, it has been denied her although during the same period many white applicants have been afforded legal education by the State. The State must provide it for her in conformity with the equal protection clause of the Fourteenth Amendment and provide it as soon as it does for applicants of any other group." The Plessy case went unmentioned, but Miss Sipuel didn't go to the University of Oklahoma immediately, as the Court seemed to order.

Miss Sipuel, married and as Ada Fisher, was back in the Court on January 30, 1948, in the case of *Fisher v. Hurst*[4] asking for an order directing Oklahoma courts to correct their directive to the University of Oklahoma. When the Oklahoma trial court received the Supreme Court mandate, it ordered the university to enroll her in the law school, to permit her to remain there until the state had provided a law school for Negroes, to refuse all students admission to the university law school until she was admitted, and to exclude her from the university law school as soon as it had opened a law school for Negroes. She and her lawyers argued that the Court had ordered her admission to the university law school with no strings attached. The Court disagreed and said on February 16, 1948, with Justices Rutledge and Murphy dissenting, that her original case "did not present the issue of whether a State might satisfy the equal protection clause of the Fourteenth Amendment by establishing a law school for Negroes."[5] The separate-but-equal rule was still in effect. But Oklahoma did not establish a Negro law school, and Mrs. Fisher entered the university, ultimately graduated from it, and was admitted to the Oklahoma bar.

The portent of these law school cases was that the states must provide Negro students with every educational facility available for whites and that such facilities must be available whenever a Negro requested them. The southern states were in a quandary. All of them had undergraduate colleges for Negroes, which offered courses of study that could be described as substantially equal to those available in their state universities for white students. They did not have similar graduate or professional schools, and it was extremely difficult to provide them because of very limited demand for their use. Under the Gaines case, they could not escape their dilemma by out-of-state scholarships; under the Sipuel case, they could not require Negroes to wait until they could establish the requisite graduate or professional schools. Some states tried to solve the problem by dubbing their Negro colleges "universities" and by adding courses of graduate study or by hurriedly setting up law schools for Negroes. Fourteen southern governors met in 1948 and drew up a grandiose plan for a Southern Regional Education program, under which their states would establish regional graduate and professional schools open to all students and with tuition paid by the student's native state. Events moved so fast that the plan never got off the ground, and it was not subjected to a Supreme Court test.

Hard on the heels of Miss Sipuel's initial victory, George W. McLaurin, a teacher, applied to the University of Oklahoma for admission to a graduate course not offered by Langston University, the state's Negro college. A three-judge federal court ordered his admission, and the Oklahoma legislature hurriedly enacted a statute opening graduate courses to Negroes where such courses were not offered at Negro schools, with the proviso that instruction for Negroes "shall be given . . . upon a segregated basis." Under the university's interpretation of that law, Professor McLaurin was required to sit in an anteroom adjoining the classroom for whites. He was given a desk on the mezzanine floor of the library but could not use the desks in the regular reading room, and was required to sit at a special table and eat at a different time from other students in the school cafeteria. The federal court approved these rules as complying with the separate-but-equal formula, and Professor McLaurin appealed to the Supreme Court.

In the interval between the district court hearing and the argument in the Supreme Court, the university modified its rules. First, Professor McLaurin was admitted to the classroom, where his seat was surrounded by a rail marked "Reserved for Colored," but the rail was later removed and he was assigned a seat in the classroom in a row set aside for colored students. He was assigned to a table on the main floor of the library and was permitted to eat at a special table in the cafeteria at the same time as other students. Oklahoma contended that the new restrictions were merely nominal and that they were imposed in order to comply with the state's valid separate-but-equal laws.

Chief Justice Vinson disapproved the restrictions for a unanimous Court in *McLaurin v. Oklahoma State Regents*[6] in a decision handed down on June 5, 1950. "The State," he said, "in administering the facilities it affords graduate and professional schools, sets McLaurin apart from the other students. The result is that [he] is handicapped in his pursuit of effective graduate instruction. Such restrictions impair and inhibit his ability to study, to engage in discussions and exchange of views with other students and, in general, to learn his profession."

The Chief Justice then turned to the social consequences of the restrictions imposed on the student. He noted that "Our society grows increasingly complex and our need for trained leaders increases correspondingly. [McLaurin's] case represents, perhaps, the epitome of that need for he is attempting to obtain an advanced degree in education to become, by definition, a leader and trainer of others." He rejected the argument that McLaurin "will be in no better position when these restrictions are removed for he may still be set apart by his fellow students. This we think irrelevant. There is a vast difference—a constitutional difference—between restrictions imposed by the state which prohibit the intellectual commingling of students, and the refusal of students to commingle where the state presents no such bar."

The Chief Justice's opinion concluded that "the conditions under which [McLaurin] is required to receive his education deprive him of his *personal and present* right to the equal protection of the laws. . . . We hold that under these circumstances the Fourteenth Amendment precludes differences in treatment by the state based upon race. [McLaurin] having been admitted to a state supported graduate school must receive the *same* treatment at the hands of the state as students of other races." (Emphasis added.)

The Court had impaired the separate-but-equal rule still further. It was plain now that Negroes must not only be admitted to graduate and professional schools immediately upon application, where no such separate facilities were provided for them, but that once admitted, they must be accorded the *same* treatment—not *equal* or *substantially equal* treatment, but the *same* treatment—as that accorded whites. The equal factor in the separate-but-equal equation had been freighted with qualitative meaning by weighing its effect on the individual Negro and its ultimate consequences for society. Thus weighed, the equation itself had been rejected as being unbalanced, a proposition that had been expounded at great length by Justice Harlan's dissent in the Plessy case. In reaching the conclusion that there was a "constitutional difference between restrictions imposed by the State . . . and the refusal of individuals to commingle where the state presents no such bar," the Court struck a body blow at the proposition implicit in the Plessy case that states were at liberty to codify discriminatory customs and traditions, and impose racial segregation by law in graduate and professional schools. The case also repudiated the shameful rule of the Berea College case that innocent voluntary interracial association could be forbidden by statute. The McLaurin case did not hold, however, that all state-supported separate graduate or professional schools were unequal, *per se*. A companion case involving another law school and decided that same day took a giant step in that direction.

Herman Marion Sweatt was a Texas postal clerk with a yen to become a lawyer. Texas had no law school for Negroes, and in 1945 he applied for admission to the University of Texas law school at the opening of the 1946 term. His application was denied, and he filed suit in the state court to compel his admission. That case was filed before the decisions in the Sipuel and McLaurin cases, and the trial court postponed the trial of his suit for six months in order to give the state time to supply facilities substantially equal to those offered white students at the University of Texas. In December, 1946, the trial court ruled against him on a showing that university officials had adopted an order calling for the opening of a law school for Negroes in February, 1947. Sweatt appealed.

While the appeal was pending, such a school was made available, but Sweatt refused to register. The Texas appellate court then ordered the trial court to hold a hearing and determine whether or not the law school for Negroes was in fact substantially equal to that of the University of Texas. At the trial, it developed that the University of Texas law school had a full-time faculty of sixteen members, a library of 65,000 volumes, 850 students, practice courts for its students, a law review, and a chapter of the nation's leading honorary legal fraternity. Its graduates were leaders in the Texas bar and held important positions in public service.

The proposed law school for Negroes would have had no independent faculty, and teaching would have been carried on by four members of the university faculty. Few of the 10,000 volumes ordered for its library had arrived. There was no full-time librarian. It was not accredited and was located in a basement. Nevertheless, the trial court held that the new school would offer Sweatt "privileges, advantages and opportunities for the study of law substantially equivalent to those offered by the State to white students at the University of Texas." Sweatt appealed and the appeals court upheld the trial court. The Supreme Court agreed to review the case, styled *Sweatt v. Painter.*[7]

At the trial, Sweatt's lawyers introduced extensive evidence designed to prove that a separate law school could never achieve equality with the University of Texas law school, because it would lack traditions, prestige, and opportunities for exchange of ideas with other students who would in time become judges, leaders of the Texas bar, and important officials of the state. Moreover, they said, Sweatt as a lawyer would have to practice in a situation where the majority of lawyers and judges would be white persons and that training in a Negro law school would ill prepare him for that experience. They boldly attacked the separate-but-equal rule and asked that the Plessy case be overruled.

While the case was pending in the Texas appeals courts and was under consideration by the Supreme Court, Texas opened a new law school for Negroes. At the time of the Court's decision on June 5, 1950, the new school had "a faculty of five full-time professors, a library of some 16,500 volumes, a practice court, a legal aid association and one alumnus who had become a member of the Texas bar." Sweatt refused invitations to enroll at that school.

Chief Justice Vinson again spoke for a unanimous Court in holding that "Whether the University of Texas law school is compared with the original or the new law school for Negroes, we cannot find substantial equality in the educational opportunities offered white and Negro law students by the State. In terms of numbers of faculty, variety of courses and opportunity for specialization, size of the student body, scope of the library, availability of law review and similar activities, the University . . . law school is superior." The Court had established a sound basis for its decision, but it did not stop there.

"What is more important," the Chief Justice insisted, "the University of Texas Law School possesses to a far greater degree those qualities which are incapable of objective measurement but which make for greatness in a law school. Such qualities, to name a few, include reputation of the faculty, experience of the administration, position and influence of the alumni standing in the community, traditions and prestige. It is difficult to believe that one who had a free choice between these law schools would consider the question close."

There were added considerations: "Moreover, although the law is a highly learned profession, we are all aware that it is an intensely practical one. The law school, the proving ground for legal learning and practice, cannot be effective in isolation from the individuals and institutions with which the law interacts. Few students and no one who has practiced law would choose to study in an academic vacuum," the Chief Justice wrote. "The law school to which Texas is willing to admit [Sweatt] excludes from its student body . . . 85 per cent of the population of the State and includes most of the lawyers, witnesses, jurors, judges and other officials with whom [he] will inevitably be dealing when he becomes a member of the Texas bar . . . [w]e cannot conclude that the education offered [him] is substantially equal to that which he would receive if admitted to the University of Texas Law School." The opinion concluded that the right which Sweatt sought was "personal and present," and that he could "claim his full constitutional right: legal education equivalent to that offered by the State to students of other races." He was ordered admitted to the university law school.

Chief Justice Vinson ended by saying that "we cannot, therefore, agree . . . that the doctrine of *Plessy v. Ferguson* requires affirmance of the judgment . . . nor need we reach [Sweatt's] contention that *Plessy v. Ferguson* should be reexamined in the light of contemporary knowledge respecting the purposes of the Fourteenth Amendment and the effects of racial segregation."

The Court had performed a rather remarkable feat: it had undermined and discredited the separate-but-equal doctrine of the Plessy case but it had wound up by refusing to disturb *Plessy v. Ferguson* as a precedent. But the handwriting on the wall was that it was ready to inquire into specific situations to determine whether or not the separate-but-equal rule was applicable to the facts of a particular case. The Plessy case was no longer an impenetrable shield to armor all segregation laws against successful attack. It was plain that no separate law school could meet the test of equality laid down in the Sweatt case; it was almost equally plain that other separate graduate and professional schools were in similar peril and that even Negro colleges could be found wanting. There was a melancholy footnote to the case. Herman Sweatt, who had shown so much integrity and courage in refusing all blandishments to abandon his case to enter, and almost certainly graduate from, the Negro law school, never became a lawyer. He entered and ultimately dropped out of the University of Texas law school.

True to their traditions, the states of the Deep South did not abolish restrictions against admission of Negroes to graduate and professional schools after the McLaurin and Sweatt decisions. Technically, of course, those decisions bound only the litigating parties, and the hard-core segregation states did nothing but wait in the hope that they would not be sued. Others, particularly border states, either dropped their barriers by statute or bowed to lower-court decisions.[8] Still other states met suits by interposing technical defenses or by devising ingenious rules designed to prevent Negro enrollment. Louisiana, for example, provided that no student could be admitted to a state university without a certificate of good moral character addressed to the particular university. Negro schools were furnished with such certificates addressed only to Negro institutions. A companion law provided that a teacher who performed an act to further racial integration should be dismissed and that issuing a certificate to a Negro to enter a "white" school was such an act.[9] Lower federal courts invalidated the scheme and the Supreme Court refused review.[10] In other instances, Negro applicants were rejected on grounds apparently unrelated to race, though racial exclusion was the real reason.[11]

After the Supreme Court had devised the deliberate-speed rule for desegregation of grade schools, Florida courts attempted to apply the formula to the state law school when a Negro applied. The Supreme Court rejected this attempt in *Florida ex rel. Hawkins v. Board of Control*[12] in 1956. The Court said that "decrees involving graduate study" did not "present the problems of elementary and secondary schools." It added that "As this case involves the admission of a Negro to a graduate professional school, there is no reason for delay. He is entitled to prompt admission under the rules and regulations applicable to other qualified candidates."[13] His right to be admitted to law school was *"personal and present,"* as the Court had said in prior cases.

A dozen years elapsed between the decisions in the Gaines and Sweatt cases, but events moved much faster in the 1950's. Less than four short years after the Sweatt case had been decided, the Supreme Court was ready to announce its sweeping decision in cases involving segregation in elementary and secondary schools. The quickened tempo was due to the fact that the NAACP was better organized and better equipped to press its litigation, that restless Negroes were less inclined to wait for vindication of their claimed civil rights, and that the Supreme Court's decisions favorable to the exercise of those rights had brightened the national climate of public opinion and pricked the conscience of the American people. An increasing number of Americans had looked through the separate-but-equal rule and had seen it for what it was: a device to stigmatize Negroes and fix a brand of inferiority on them. Troubled and troublesome international events played their part; the nation had assumed a stance as the defender of the free world, and all over the globe other people looked askance at the manifestations of racism in the United States.

A year after Herman Sweatt entered the University of Texas law school, cases were on file in four states and the District of Columbia asking four federal and one state court to apply the qualitative test of the Sweatt case to elementary and secondary schools, and declare that the separate-but-equal rule had no validity in the area of public education. The four states involved were Kansas, South Carolina, Virginia, and Delaware. Ultimately, the four state cases were grouped together and decided as *Brown v. Board of Education of Topeka*,[14] and the District of Columbia litigation was decided in a separate case, *Bolling v. Sharpe*.[15] All were decided on May 17, 1954.

The first of the cases to actually reach the Supreme Court was a suit by Harry Briggs, Jr., and 66 other Negro children, who sued the Clarendon County, South Carolina, School Board No. 22, in a case known as *Harry Briggs, Jr., v. R. W. Elliott*,[16] charging that Clarendon County's Negro schools were far inferior to its schools for white children. They asked a three-judge federal court to hold that South Carolina's separate school laws and constitutional provisions were invalid under the equal-protection clause of the Fourteenth Amendment. The federal judges agreed that the schools for

Negroes were inferior to those maintained for white children, and ordered the board to equalize the school systems and report back in six months as to the progress it had made. The judges also ruled that they were bound by *Plessy v. Ferguson* and that South Carolina's separate school laws were valid.[17] The Supreme Court agreed to review the case in June, 1951, but on January 28, 1952, sent it back to the three-judge court with instructions to report on what progress had been made toward equalization. Justices Black and Douglas dissented on the ground that the report was "wholly irrelevant to the constitutional questions presented" and urged that the case be set for argument. In March, 1952, the three-judge district court found that the Clarendon County board had complied with the equalization order, praised it for its compliance, and again upheld South Carolina segregation laws as valid under the Plessy case. The Supreme Court then restored the case to its docket.

Meanwhile, Oliver Brown had sued the Topeka, Kansas, Board of Education because his eight-year-old daughter was denied entrance to a white school only 5 blocks from her home and forced to travel 21 blocks to a Negro school. Kansas laws permitted but did not require cities of more than 15,000 to impose school segregation. Topeka imposed segregation in its grade schools but not in high school. On August 3, 1951, a three-judge federal court held that Topeka's Negro and white schools were substantially equal, criticized the separate-but-equal rule but decided it was bound by *Plessy v. Ferguson* and refused to invalidate Kansas laws. Mr. Brown lost his case and promptly appealed. When his appeal reached the Supreme Court in October, 1951, the South Carolina case had been sent back to the district court for the report on equalization plans. The Court agreed to review Brown's case, and thus it became number one on the list of school segregation cases set for hearing and decision. Brown won immortality of a sort by securing top billing: the school segregation cases would be forever known as *Brown v. Board of Education.*[18]

The Virginia case was heard in still another three-judge federal court in that state on March 7, 1952. Dorothy E. Davis and other high-school students sued the county school board of Prince Edward County asking that Virginia's constitutional and statutory provisions imposing segregation be declared invalid or that the county's Negro and white high schools be ordered equalized. The court granted the equalization request but also fell back on the

Plessy case to deny the plea for invalidation of the segregation requirements of Virginia's constitution and laws. The case was appealed to the Supreme Court as *Davis v. County School Board of
Prince Edward County.*[19]

The Delaware case was filed in the courts of that state, and on
April 1, 1952, Delaware Chancellor Collins J. Seitz found the Negro
schools inferior to white schools and enjoined Delaware from enforcing segregation laws because of that inequality. The chancellor
expressed his opinion that the "separate but equal doctrine in education should be rejected," but added that rejection must come
from the Supreme Court. Delaware's supreme court upheld the injunction on August 28, 1952, but seemed to say that the order
should be dissolved as soon as Negro schools were equalized. On
November 24, 1952, the Supreme Court added the case, *Gebhart v.
Bolton,*[20] to the list of school cases which it was willing to decide.

Brown v. Board of Education now encompassed the four state
cases, each of which presented the question of the application of
the separate-but-equal rule to public schools. Each of them rested
on the contention that the equal-protection-of-the-laws clause of
the Fourteenth Amendment prohibited state-imposed segregation
in tax-supported schools. Obviously, they could be argued together
and decided together. The Court made such an order.

The Fourteenth Amendment does not apply to the District of
Columbia but only to the states. Consequently, there is no equal-
protection clause for the District; however, the Fifth Amendment
like the Fourteenth, forbids denial of due process of law. Spottswood Bolling, who sued for admission to a Washington high school,
claimed that the due-process-of-law clause of the Fifth Amendment
was broad enough to forbid segregation in public schools, and he
asked the federal courts, which exercise jurisdiction in the District,
to invalidate congressional legislation requiring separate schools.
His suit was dismissed, and on November 10, 1952, the Supreme
Court granted review in his case, known as *Bolling v. Sharpe,*[21] and
set it down for argument at the same time as the four state cases.

There was more to this carefully stage-managed selection of
cases for review than meets the naked eye. The Kansas case concerned grade-school children in a northern state with a permissive
segregation statute; the Virginia case involved high-school students in a state having compulsory laws and located in the upper
tier of southern states; South Carolina represented the Deep South,

and Delaware the border states. The state cases all presented the issue of the application of the equal-protection-of-law clause of the Fourteenth Amendment, and the Court could have reached and decided that question in any one of them, but the wide geographical range gave the anticipated decision a national flavor and would blunt any claim that the South was being made a whipping boy. Moreover, the combination of cases included Kansas with its permissive statute, while other cases concerned state constitutional provisions as well as statutes with mandatory segregation requirements. Grade-school students were involved in the Kansas case; high-school students in the Virginia case, and all elementary and secondary students in the Delaware and South Carolina cases. The District of Columbia case drew due process of law into the cases as an issue, in distinction to the equal-protection-of-law clause, and also presented an opportunity for inquiry into the congressional power to impose racial segregation. The NAACP had touched all bases.

Initial arguments were made on December 9, 1952, two-and-a-half years after the Sweatt decision. But the Court reached no decision on the basis of the first briefs and arguments. On June 8, 1953, it issued an order setting the case for reargument that fall, submitting a series of questions to the litigants, and inviting the United States Attorney General to participate in the arguments.

The Court's first question asked what evidence there was that the Congress which submitted and the states which ratified the Fourteenth Amendment contemplated that the amendment would abolish school segregation. It then asked whether Congress had the power to abolish all school segregation, regardless of whether the framers or ratifying states believed that the amendment required its immediate abolition, and what was the reach of the Court's power under those circumstances. Its third inquiry was the extent of the Court's power to abolish school segregation in the event that the answers to the first two questions were inconclusive. The fourth question was that of whether a decree favoring the Negro plaintiffs would carry with it an order directing their immediate admission to state-supported schools or whether the Court could devise a gradualistic scheme for their enrollment—a very obvious, and very curious, inquiry as to whether the rights of Negro grade-school students to attend public schools were *personal and present* (as all constitutional rights are) or whether their exercise could be delayed until a more propitious time. The fifth question concerned the form the decree should take, if the Court decided on a gradualistic abolition of segregation.

Thurgood Marshall, counsel and director of the NAACP Legal Defense & Educational Fund, convoked sessions of lawyers, law school professors, and historians from all over the nation to help find answers to the Court's questions and to fashion briefs and arguments. The hard-pressed states hired John W. Davis, one-time Democratic candidate for the presidency of the United States and one of the nation's leading constitutional lawyers, to head an imposing array of counsel.

Reargument began on December 8, 1953 and continued for three days. Then the Court took all of the cases under submission for later decision.

The showdown had come; judgment day was near for *Plessy v. Ferguson* in the field of public education.

◄§ 24 ▷ *That Great Gettin'*
Up Morning

There's a better day a' comin'
Fare thee well, fare thee well,

In that great gettin' up morning
Fare thee well, fare thee well.

NEGRO SPIRITUAL

Chief Justice Earl Warren was almost through reading his opinion
for a unanimous Court in the case of *Brown v. Board of Education*
before he pronounced the fateful words: "We conclude that in the
field of public education the doctrine of 'separate but equal' has no
place. Therefore, we hold that the plaintiffs and others similarly
situated for whom the actions have been brought are, by reason of
the segregation complained of, deprived of the equal protection of
the laws guaranteed by the Fourteenth Amendment." The date was
May 17, 1954. That Great Gettin' Up Morning storied in the old
Negro spiritual had arrived.

The Chief Justice had pricked a careful path toward that conclusion. He began by referring to the history of the amendment in
reference to schools, in an effort to ascertain the understanding of
its framers, and found the evidence inconclusive at best. "The most
avid proponents of the post-War Amendments undoubtedly intended them to remove all legal distinctions among 'all persons
born or naturalized in the United States,'" he said. "Their opponents . . . were antagonistic to both the letter and spirit of the

Amendments. . . ." He thought that the low estate of public education, particularly in the South, also contributed to the inconclusiveness of sentiment in both Congress and the ratifying states in respect of separate schools.

The separate-but-equal rule, Chief Justice Warren reminded the nation, "did not make its appearance in [the Supreme] Court until 1896 in the case of *Plessy v. Ferguson,* not involving education but transportation." But, he pointed out, the Supreme "Court construing the Fourteenth Amendment [in cases] decided shortly after its adoption . . . construed it as proscribing all state-imposed discrimination against the Negro race." He then reviewed the fifty-year-old history of the application of the Plessy rule in education, beginning with the Cummings case in 1899 and ending with the Sweatt case in 1950. "In none of these cases," he said, "was it necessary to examine the [Plessy] doctrine to grant relief to the Negro plantiff."

Lower courts in cases under review in 1954, however, had either found Negro schools equal to their white counterparts or had ordered their physical equalization, and the Chief Justice remarked: "Our decision, therefore, cannot turn on merely a comparison of these tangible factors in the Negro and white schools involved. . . . We must look instead to the effect of segregation itself on public education." He insisted that in doing so the Court could not "turn the clock back to 1868 when the Amendment was adopted, or even to 1896 when *Plessy v. Ferguson* was written."

The Chief Justice then stressed the importance of public education in a democratic society. He posed the crucial question: "Does segregation of children in public schools solely on the basis of race, even though the facilities be equal, deprive children of the minority group of equal educational opportunity?" His answer was yes. He found support for his affirmative view in the findings of the Kansas and Delaware courts and made footnote references to sociological, historical, and educational data to the same effect. It was then that he pronounced the judgment of the Court.

What he had said was that the command of the Fourteenth Amendment was a command for equality and that when state laws subverted that command, they were unconstitutional and must be stricken down by the Supreme Court, even though such laws had been tolerated at some earlier historical times when their effect was not apparent. Plainly he had in mind Chief Justice Marshall's more than a century-old admonition that "ours is a constitution intended to endure for ages to come, and consequently to be adapted to the various crises in human affairs." [1]

The May 17 decision did not dispose of the cases. The Court renewed its previously made request for submission of briefs and arguments on the issues of whether invalidation of segregation statutes permitted it to devise a gradualistic formula for admission of Negro children to state-supported schools and, if so, what kind of a decree it should fashion to achieve that end. The Attorney General of the United States and attorneys general of states requiring or permitting segregation were invited to express their points of view. Hearing on those issues was set for the October, 1954, term of the Court. The Brown decision settled the segregation question for the four state cases which had come to the Court from Kansas, Delaware, South Carolina, and Virginia and which involved the Fourteenth Amendment.

Chief Justice Warren then turned to *Bolling v. Sharpe,* which had arisen in the District of Columbia. "The legal problem in the District," he said, "is somewhat different. . . . The Fifth Amendment which is applicable to the District of Columbia, does not contain an equal protection clause [as does the Fourteenth] which applies only to the States." But he found that the concepts of due process of law and equal protection of the law both stemmed from "our American ideal of fairness" and that while they were not interchangeable, it was true that "discrimination may be so unjustifiable as to be a violation of due process."

He reiterated the constitutional doctrine that "Classification based solely upon race must be scrutinized with particular care" and arrived at the conclusion that "segregation in public education . . . imposes on Negro children of the District of Columbia an arbitrary deprivation of their liberty in violation of the Due Process clause." Moreover, he said, "in view of our decision that the Constitution prohibits the states from maintaining separate schools it would be unthinkable that the same Constitution would impose a lesser duty on the Federal Government." The Bolling case was also put on the October, 1954, docket for further consideration of the proper remedy and decrees.

Reargument on the issues of gradualism and proper decrees began on April 11 and ended on April 14, 1955. Lawyers for the plaintiffs, the states directly involved, the District of Columbia, the Attorney General of the United States and attorneys general for Florida, North Carolina, Arkansas, Oklahoma, Maryland, and Texas filed briefs and participated in the arguments. Chief Justice Warren again spoke for a unanimous Court on May 31, 1955. He explained that "Full implementation of . . . constitutional principles may require solution of varied local school problems. School authorities have the primary responsibility for . . . solving these problems; courts will have to consider whether the action of school authorities constitutes good faith implementation of the governing constitutional principles. Because of their proximity to local conditions and the possible need for further hearings, the courts which originally heard these cases can best perform this judicial appraisal. Accordingly, we believe it appropriate to remand the cases to those courts." [2]

The courts to which the cases were remanded were admonished to apply equitable principles that would be fair to both the Negro children and school authorities but, he said, "it should go without saying that the vitality of these constitutional principles cannot be allowed to yield simply because of disagreement with them." The courts were also told to "require that the defendants make a prompt and reasonable start toward full compliance with our May 17, 1954 decision. . . . Once such a start has been made, the courts may find that additional time is necessary to carry out the ruling in an effective manner."

The ideal toward which the defendants were ordered to move was "good faith compliance at the earliest practicable date." The burden was put on the defendants to establish the need for additional time. "To that end," the Chief Justice said, "the courts may consider problems related to administration, arising from the physical condition of the school plant, the school transportation system, personnel, revision of school districts and attendance areas into compact units to achieve a system of determining admission to the public schools on a non-racial basis, and revision of local laws and regulations which may be necessary in solving the foregoing problems." The courts were ordered to enter "such orders and decrees consistent with this opinion as are necessary and proper to admit to public schools on a racially non-discriminatory basis with all deliberate speed the parties to these cases."

If the Court's order seems in the retrospect of ten years to be steeped in judical naïveté, in light of the fact that in 1965 Negro children had been admitted to so-called white schools in less than 25 per cent of southern school districts and that not a single Negro child involved in the cases ever attended integrated schools in Clarendon County, South Carolina, or Prince Edward County, Virginia, it must be borne in mind that the Court was carried away by its own optimism in 1955.[3] Chief Justice Warren noted with transparent pride in the second Brown decision that "substantial steps to eliminate racial discrimination in public schools have already been taken, not only in some of the communities in which these cases arose but in some of the states appearing as [friends of the Court] as well. Substantial progress has been made in the District of Columbia and in the communities in Kansas and Delaware involved in this litigation." The ink was hardly dry on the second decision before the states of the old Confederacy embarked on a program of massive resistance to the Brown decision. Compliance was orderly and meaningful only in the border states and in northern and western states with permissive segregation statutes.

The harsh truth is that the first Brown decision was a great decision; the second Brown decision was a great mistake. In the 1954 case, the Court said unequivocally that segregation of Negro children in public schools deprived them "of the equal protection of the laws guaranteed by the Fourteenth Amendment." As it had said so many times and with so much emphasis, a constitutional right is always *personal and present*. It inheres in the individual, in the *person* in constitutional language. But in the 1955 case, the Court held that a *personal and present* constitutional right could be deferred and extended gradually to those who were entitled to exercise it by virtue of a constitutional amendment. There was no constitutional warrant for such a ruling.

The notion that a Negro could be required to defer his exercise of a constitutional right was a by-product of the earlier attempts of southern states to hold fast to segregation in graduate and professional schools until they had time to construct separate-but-equal facilities. In its proper turn, the concept that a special rule could be applied to Negroes traced back to the Dred Scott dogma that free-born Negroes constituted an intermediate class of beings within the constitutional scheme who were not endowed by birth with the rights of free white persons. In the first cases construing them, the Court held that the all-pervading purpose of the Civil War Amendments was to abolish all racial distinction and put Negroes on a plane of absolute equality with white Americans. Whatever rights white men had, Negroes had; all were citizens of the nation and of their states; all were free men.

The great vice of the Plessy case lay in the fact that the Court was induced to rule that the Constitution as amended recognized racial distinctions; the corollary was that the Negro could exercise commonplace rights and privileges, vouchsafed by birth to white persons, such as using *public* parks, playgrounds, and libraries, attending *public* schools or enjoying full use of *public* utilities such as trains or boats at the *sufferance* of the white majority. The Negro was not a *free man;* he was a *freedman,* to whom rights could be doled out by those who had set him free. (The vulgar expression of this notion is reflected in commonly heard complaints that the Negro is "moving too fast" or "demanding too much" when he seeks to exercise the same rights enjoyed as a matter of course by the white complainant.)

The Court readily saw the incongruity of requests that it defer exercise of the constitutional rights it found existent in the graduate and professional school cases, and rejected those requests out of hand by reiterating the truism that a constitutional right is always *personal and present.* No American lawyer anywhere had ever supposed that the Supreme Court, or any other organ of government, could suspend the exercise of a peacetime constitutional right for a single day. The reason is simple: a constitutional right which is not exercised at the moment of the possessor's desire is forever lost. Even southern lawyers who argued for delay in the graduate and professional school cases were not really asking for the suspension of a constitutional right; their argument boiled down to the contention that the request for such instruction was so suddenly made that the states should have time to provide the facilities within the context of valid separate-but-equal statutes. Once the separate-but-equal rule was disavowed, there was no constitutional basis for delay in the exercise of constitutional rights.

When the Court temporized in the 1955 Brown decision and devised the deliberate-speed formula, it did so out of the best of motives. It was acting out its traditional role as the guardian of Negro rights and was moved by the triple belief—hope may be a better word—that a prompt start would be made toward compliance, that the federal district courts would act with firmness and dispatch, and that the enitre process would take only a short time. No doubt it wanted to assuage the white South. It was wrong on all scores; it only succeeded in opening a Pandora's box of troubles.

The deliberate-speed formula was not only a constitutional blunder but also a practical mistake of the first order. It armed the recalcitrant states with a built-in device for delay and resistance, and actually suggested delay in some quarters. The disposition of the four state cases after the Court had devised the formula was prophetic. In the Delaware case, *Gebhart v. Bolton,* the state courts had ordered admission of the Negro plaintiffs prior to the 1954 decision and that order was not disturbed. In another case, arising after the 1954 case and when it was apparent that the Court was going to issue a gradualistic order of some kind, the Delaware supreme court refused to order immediate admission of Negro pupils saying that it would delay action because the Brown opinion did not require "immediate desegregation of public schools." The 1955 Brown opinion actually delayed desegregation in that instance.

The three-judge Kansas federal court that had scored separate schools as discriminatory in its original opinion accepted the 1955 decision as an invitation for delay. When the plaintiffs requested a decree directing immediate desegregation, the judges responded by holding a hearing on the admittedly incomplete desegregation plan of the Topeka School Board. The Topeka superintendent admitted that the plan did not accomplish desegregation for the 1955-56 school year, but the judges were satisfied merely because a "good faith" start had been made.

The Virginia and South Carolina federal courts contented themselves with the issuance of meaningless decrees enjoining the boards of education from "refusing on account of race or color to admit . . . any child to enter" their schools. But the injunctions were to go into effect only after the boards had made "necessary arrangements . . . with all deliberate speed." Because their rights were not declared to be personal and present, Prince Edward and Clarendon County plaintiffs had won nothing except a semantic victory. They would never attend, or have an opportunity to attend, desegregated schools.

Only in the special case of the District of Columbia were the schools quickly desegregated. Fortunately, the District acted prior to the 1955 decision.

Of course, the Brown cases were binding only on the litigants before the Court. That is true in any case, but men of good judgment do not wait until their own conduct is condemned when they live under a government of laws and the course they have been pursuing is identical with that proscribed by the courts in another case. They put their own houses in order and thus ward off litigation. The border states of Oklahoma, Missouri, Kentucky, West Virginia, and Maryland did just that, as did the western states where segregation was permissive. But as we have seen in the peonage, confession, jury, and white primary cases, the states of the old Confederacy have never pursued any such policy in the area of civil rights. They have always depended on obstruction and defiance to preserve their old ways. They clung to that course as far as schools were concerned and waited for lawsuits, district by district, while they devised obstructionist laws and procedures. As a first step, Negroes had to apply for admission to public schools and, when refused, had to appeal to school boards for desegregation plans. If the boards refused to act, as many did, or drew up inadequate plans which were little more than legal jests, as many were, the offended Negroes had to file suit either to force the boards to act or to submit desegregation plans that were meaningful. The tragic inadequacies of the deliberate-speed formula were soon apparent.

As deliberative bodies, school boards could, and most of them did, stall for time under the pretext of considering the factors the Court had said were relevant. After they had consumed as much time as they felt was possible, their only duty was to devise a plan for desegregation. Most of the plans were shams; boards concocted evasive devices of almost every conceivable kind. Some proposed to begin with the first grade and integrate a grade a year; others offered to begin with the high schools and descend downward at the rate of a grade a year; there were proposals to integrate high schools over long periods of time and then grade schools over similar periods, or to begin with grade schools and then to proceed with high schools; elaborate pupil placement plans, fashioned to permit and conceal segregation, were presented; selective procedures were devised to prevent Negro attendance at white schools or to keep it on a token basis, or boards announced solemnly that they could do nothing because no plan could muster a majority. Legislatures entered the fray and enacted laws subtly or openly penalizing boards that did comply or other laws withdrawing state subsidies where Negro attendance occurred, or other statutes studded with procedural hurdles. Recalcitrant boards then hid behind these laws to excuse their inaction.

If a school board presented an inadequate plan or refused to present any plan, the only recourse was to file suit in a federal district court. What happened then was dependent on the good faith and temperament of the district judge. If he was hostile to the Brown decision, he could vent his hostility by taking his own good time to set and hold hearings. Many did. After such a hearing, he could approve an obviously inadequate plan. In that event the complainants could only undertake a long and arduous appeal. Many conscientious judges who disapproved the Brown decision honored their oaths and rejected inadequate plans, only to have the boards appeal and kill more time. Meanwhile, Negro children supposedly vested with a *constitutional* right to attend a public school without restriction because of race were shunted off to Jim Crow schools. By 1965, statistics showed that 2.3 per cent of southern school students were attending desegregated schools. But that figure is misleading; in many districts there was only token attendance, with most Negroes still walled off in separate schools. There was little speed in the deliberate-speed formula. The nation had reaped the fruit of the Court's refusal to declare the right to attend a public school personal and present, as it certainly was.

This is not to say that there would have been no resistance and delay had the Court not devised the deliberate-speed formula. Obviously, there would have been. Nor is it to argue that there would not have been violence, or even bloodshed, one of the evils the Court wanted to avoid. But there was violence, even bloodshed, in any event: in Little Rock; New Orleans; Oxford, Mississippi; Clinton, Tennessee. But if the Court had declared the rights of the litigants in the Brown case to have been personal and present, southern school boards could not have taken refuge in stultifying study and deliberation to clog compliance. They would have been confronted with having to make an immediate decision of either complying with the law as the Court had declared it or of facing the alternative of a lawsuit in which the only question could have been the bald issue of whether or not they had denied admission because of race or color.

The district judge before whom such a suit was presented would have had a single question for determination: Was, or was not, the denial of admission based on race or color? He could then have issued the proper writ of mandate or injunction, ordering or denying admission. He would not have had to study an elaborate "plan" or to devise one himself. True enough, he could have dragged his feet in setting the case for trial or in rendering a decision. But he could not have gone beyond that. On appeal by either side, the courts of appeals would not have had to restudy the "plan" offered by a school board or devised by the district judge, or to devise new plans; they, too, would have been confronted with a single issue. Where ingenious defenses were offered, the district judge or the judges of the courts of appeal would have been assisted by the Supreme Court's rule that the Constitution dooms "ingenious as well as simple minded modes of discrimination."

In shying away from declaring the rights sought in the Brown case to be personal and present, the Court was also undoubtedly moved by the belief that the gradualistic approach would be less offensive and more readily acceptable to the South. The sober truth is that change would have been gradual in any event. Negroes habituated to segregation would have moved slowly. As the chosen instrument of Negroes seeking change, the NAACP lacked financial resources and manpower to proceed in any other than a gradual manner, district by district, where boards of education did not act on application of Negroes. It could have, and undoubtedly would have, acted with as much dispatch as possible, but it could not have wrought a revolution. Armed, as they should have been, with a declaration that the right imbedded in the Fourteenth Amendment was personal and present, Negroes could have secured the claimed right at a much faster pace for the good of Negro children—and for the nation.

The Supreme Court could not possibly deal with every case raised under the deliberate-speed formula. It did not try to do so. It simply let stand many decisions of courts of appeal or district judges by exercising its prerogative of refusing to review. But there were some cases that it had to consider.

The Little Rock, Arkansas, School Board began consideration of desegregation plans after the first Brown case in 1954. After the second Brown decision, it decided to begin desegregation in the tenth through twelfth grades, with final desegregation to be complete in 1963. Negro parents objected, but a United States district court and the Court of Appeals for the Eighth Circuit approved the plan.[4] When nine Negro children prepared to attend Central High School on September 3, 1957, they found units of the Arkansas National Guard stationed there and learned that the school had been declared off limits to Negro students by Governor Orville Faubus. The school board asked the Negro students to refrain from trying to attend the school and asked the federal district court for instructions as to what it should do. The court answered that resistance was no reason for departure from the approved plan and ordered the school board to proceed with its desegregation program. The federal government entered the case and secured an injunction against Governor Faubus, enjoining him from preventing the attendance of Negro children and from all interference with the court-approved desegregation plan.[5] The National Guard was withdrawn, and on September 23, 1957, the children entered the school but were withdrawn when an unruly mob rioted in front of the school. On September 25, President Eisenhower dispatched federal troops to Little Rock. The Negro children then re-entered school and were protected during the remainder of the school year by the federalized National Guard.

The panic-stricken school board filed a petition in the federal district court in February, 1958, reciting that the school term had been attended by "chaos, bedlam, and turmoil," that the Negro children had been subjected to violence, that there was unrest within the school, and that local police would be unable to control the situation if troops were withdrawn. It asked for permission to return the Negroes to segregated schools and for a delay of two-and-a-half years in the desegregation program. The district judge granted its request on June 20, 1958, to take effect at the beginning of the September, 1958, school year. On August 18, 1958, the Court of Appeals for the Sixth Circuit reversed the district judge and ordered Little Rock to admit the students and proceed with its desegregation program. Upon Arkansas' request, the Supreme Court was called into special session to review the Court of Appeals decision, in view of the shortness of time before the beginning of the school term. The Court heard arguments on the case, *Cooper v. Aaron*,[6] on September 11 and on September 12, 1958, and unanimously upheld the Circuit Court. Opinions were prepared later.

Chief Justice Warren spoke for the Court. He called attention to the fact that the Brown case had settled the issue that "State support of segregated schools through any arrangement, management, funds, or property cannot be squared with the Amendment's command that no State shall deny to any person within its jurisdiction the equal protection of the laws." A state, he said, "acts by its legislative, executive, or its judicial authorities. It can act in no other way. The constitutional provision, therefore, must mean that no agency of the State or of the officers or agents by whom its powers are exerted, shall deny the equal protection of the laws." The school board was found to be a state agency. The great principle announced by the Chief Justice was that neither violence, nor threats of violence, nor disruption of a school program by opponents of integration could be used as an excuse or reason for delaying or interfering with school desegregation. Justice Frankfurter concurred specially with the observation that "Violent resistance to law cannot be made a reason for its suspension. . . ."

After the Brown decision, Arkansas had embarked on a course of defiance. The constitution was amended to command the legislature to oppose "in every Constitutional manner the un-Constitutional desegregation decisions of May 17, 1954 and May 31, 1955 of the United States Supreme Court." A pupil assignment plan had been added to the state laws, and the legislature provided that children assigned to integrated schools were exempt from compulsory attendance laws. The Chief Justice went out of his way in the Aaron case to answer what he called "the premise of the actions of the Governor and Legislature that they are not bound by our holding in the Brown case." His summary rejoinder was that "the interpretation of the Fourteenth Amendment enunciated in the Brown case is the supreme law of the land and Article VI of the Constitution makes it of binding effect on the states 'anything in the Constitution or Laws of any State to the contrary notwithstanding.'" He was anticipating arguments inherent in actions of other states and making it plain that the Court was not going to reconsider the Brown case. The Negro students returned to Central High School and ultimately graduated, some with honors.

The states of the old Confederacy enacted pupil placement statutes, setting up elaborate standards for admission of pupils and, often, complicated methods of review where an appeal was taken from a board's placement order. That these fair-on-their-face laws, with their extremely wide range of factors that a board might apply in pupil assignment, were intended to thwart desegregation is evident from the fact that they were enacted only in highly resistant states. Alabama's placement law provided that a board might consider factors ranging from available room in the school to which the pupil sought admission to the pupil's morals, conduct, health and personal standards of the pupil, effect of admission on the academic standards, adequacy of the pupil's academic preparation, possibility of breaches of the peace, and many others. When the law was challenged, a district court held that it was not unconstitutional on its face and that the issue could be determined only upon proof that it was administered in a discriminatory manner. The Supreme Court affirmed the district court decision in *Shuttlesworth v. Alabama*[7] in 1958 "upon the limited grounds on which the district court rested its decision."

The slow pace of desegregation in southern schools had reached the proportions of a public scandal by the 1960's; it was apparent that the deliberate-speed formula was being used to maintain segregation. The Supreme Court voiced its impatience in three cases and issued what was in effect a public reprimand to school boards which proposed, and district courts which approved, slow-moving desegregation plans. In *Goss v. Board of Education*,[8] decided in 1963, it said: "We are not unmindful of the deep rooted problems involved. Indeed it was consideration for the multifarious local difficulties and 'variety of obstacles' which might arise in this transition that led this Court eight years ago to frame its mandate in *Brown* in such language as 'good faith compliance at the earliest practicable date' and 'all deliberate speed.' Now, however, eight years after this decree was rendered and over nine years after the first *Brown* decision, the context in which we must interpret and apply this language to plans for desegregation has been significantly altered." A similar warning had been sounded in *Watson v. City of Memphis*,[9] also decided in 1963, and was re-issued in *Calhoun v. Latimer*,[10] decided in 1964 by quoting the language of the Goss case. The Court spelled out what it meant in *Griffin v. County School Board*[11] in 1964, when it said in waspish language that "There has been entirely too much deliberation and not enough speed in enforcing the constitutional rights which we held in *Brown v. Board of Education* had been denied. . . ." Plainly, the Court was tiring of evasion and delay.

The Griffin case, in which the Court found "too much deliberation and not enough speed," was the same case under a new name that had been considered as one of the four state cases in the first

Brown decision. It was originally filed as *Allen v. County School Board* [12] in 1951, and thirteen years after its filing, Prince Edward County, Virginia, had not budged an inch: there had been no desegregation and the high-school children involved had long since been graduated. Some of them had school-age children themselves. All public schools in the county had been closed since 1959, in order to forestall desegregation. It was back in the Court to test the issue of whether or not a state could close its public schools when desegregation was ordered and educate white children at "private" schools through tuition grants and rebatement of taxes.

The threat to close public schools rather than integrate them was one of the early legislative weapons brandished by segregationist lawmakers. It was used to club school boards into line when they wavered and moved toward compliance. Such laws either gave local boards the option of closing schools or ordered them to do so when admission of Negro pupils was ordered by the courts. The first test of that legislation came in Louisiana, when a three-judge federal district court invalidated a statute which provided "a means by which public schools under desegregation orders may be changed to 'private' schools operated in the same way, in the same buildings, with the same money, and under the same supervision as the public schools," in the words of the district court. The same statute also provided that where the public schools were "closed," the school board was "charged with responsibility for furnishing free lunches, transportation, and grants-in-aid to the children attending the 'private schools.'" The Supreme Court affirmed the district court's judgment that this statute was a mere device to continue segregation and a denial of equal protection of laws, in the case of *St. Helena Parish School Board v. Hall* [13] in 1962. There were some significant differences between Virginia and Louisiana school closing statutes.

As we have seen, following the 1955 Brown decision, the federal district court enjoined Prince Edward County's school board from "refusing on account of race or color to admit . . . any child to enter" its schools, with the proviso that the injunction should go into effect only after the board had made "necessary arrangements . . . with all deliberate speed." At that time, there were about 1700 school-age Negro children and 1400 whites in that same category. In May, 1956, the county board of supervisors decided that it would not levy a tax for the support of integrated schools.

That same year, the Virginia constitution was amended to authorize the legislature and local government bodies to appropriate funds
to assist students to go to public or nonsectarian private schools.
The legislature passed such a statute.

Meanwhile, the plaintiffs asked the district court to fix a date for
the beginning of integration in the county schools. The judges refused to do so, in an opinion filed in January, 1957, on the ground
that conditions were too unsettled. The Court of Appeals for the
Fourth Circuit reversed that ruling in November, 1957, and ordered it to set a date for desegregation. In July, 1958, the judge
heeded the Court of Appeals and set the time for compliance as the
date of the beginning of the school year for 1965, *ten years after the
decision in the second Brown case!* However, he reserved the right
to shorten or *extend* that time. The board was ordered to report on
its progress in setting up procedures toward formulation of a plan
on January 1, 1959. Another appeal followed, and on May 5, 1959,
the court of appeals directed the entry of an order requiring the
schools to be operated on a nondiscriminatory basis beginning in
September, 1959. After further legal skirmishing, an order was
finally issued on April 22, 1960, enjoining the board from any action
that regulated or affected enrollment of Negro children in the high
school on the basis of race and requiring the board to make plans to
admit Negro children to elementary schools.

Nothing came of these orders because the county supervisors refused to levy school taxes for the year 1959-60, and education of
white children was turned over to a private corporation which enrolled some 1400 white children in private schools, originally supported by private contributions. Negroes refused an offer to set up
a private corporation for the education of Negro children, and Negroes were without a school for four years from 1959 to 1963. They
clung to a steadfast course of demanding the reopening of public
schools on an integrated basis. The 1956 Virginia statute which had
provided for closing of integrated schools was held invalid by the
Virginia courts, but the legislature tried again in 1959 by providing
tuition grants for elementary and secondary pupils, repealing compulsory school laws, and approving tax credits. The board of supervisors granted tax credits to persons using private schools. No other
Virginia county closed its public schools under that law.

Negroes were back in federal court again in 1961, seeking an
injunction against payment of tuition grants and tax rebates and

demanding an order requiring the reopening of public schools. After some delay, the district judge decided in 1962 that "the public schools of Prince Edward County may not be closed to avoid the effect of the law of the land as interpreted by the Supreme Court, while the Commonwealth of Virginia permits other public schools to remain open at the expense of the taxpayers." The court of appeals reversed that decision, on the narrow technical ground that the judge should have waited for a ruling by the Virginia court of appeals on the validity of Virginia laws under the state constitution. Before the state court acted to uphold the laws, the Supreme Court granted a review in the case now known as *Griffin v. County School Board.*[14]

Justice Black spoke for the majority of the Court when the case was decided on May 25, 1964—ten years and one week after the school children of Prince Edward County had been told that segregation in public schools deprived them of equal protection of the law and nine years after Prince Edward County had been directed to proceed with deliberate speed in implementing their constitutional rights. "[W]e agree with the District Court that, under the circumstances here, closing the Prince Edward schools while public schools in all the other counties of Virginia were being maintained, denied . . . Negro students . . . the equal protection of the laws guaranteed by the Fourteenth Amendment," Justice Black said.

The justice agreed that a state has wide discretion in deciding whether laws should apply to one county or all of its counties, but, he said, "Whatever nonracial grounds might support a State's allowing a county to abandon public schools, the object must be a constitutional one, and grounds of race in opposition to desegregation do not qualify as constitutional." The troublesome problem was what remedy the Court could, or should, grant.

Justice Black, for the Court majority, took a broad view. "The injunction against paying tuition grants and giving tax credits while public schools remain closed is appropriate and necessary since those grants and tax credits have been essential parts of the county's program, successful thus far, to deprive [Prince Edward Negro children] of the same advantages of a public school education enjoyed by children in every other part of Virginia," he said. "For the same reasons the District Court may, if necessary to prevent further racial discrimination, require the Supervisors to levy taxes to raise funds adequate to reopen, operate and maintain without racial discrimination a public school system in Prince Edward County like that operated in other counties in Virginia." Justices Harlan and Clark agreed with the rest of their colleagues that the Court could enjoin payment of tuition grants and granting of tax credits but were of the opinion that it could not order the reopening of schools. The balky supervisors let the district judge know that they would not voluntarily levy taxes and appropriate school funds for desegregated schools. He ordered them to do so by the beginning of the 1964 fall term.

Desegregated schools opened their doors in September, 1964, but only a handful of whites appeared. How long disgruntled whites will, or can, cling to their private schools, nobody knows. Apparently they will have to do so without state aid and assistance.

The list of cases examined here does not include all instances of avoidance and delay undertaken by school boards or of state statutes devised to defy or undermine the Brown case. A volume could be written on the subject, but we must be content with this sampling that highlights what happened after 1954. The Court disposed of many other cases with short one- or two-sentence judgments, affirming opinions of lower courts or refusing to review— denying writs of *certiorari*, in technical legal terms—in cases where it agreed with the results arrived at by lower courts. Included were a variety of cases invalidating ingenious attempts of the Louisiana legislature to forestall desegregation of that state's schools, denying attempts to lease public schools to private groups for operation, and refusing approval to obviously dilatory desegregation plans and the use of pupil placement plans to retain school segregation.[15]

Although the Brown cases specifically limited disapproval of the separate-but-equal rule of the Plessy case to public education, the decisions were soon construed to mean that racial segregation was impermissible in all public facilities. Supreme Court decisions in *Holmes v. City of Atlanta*,[16] involving Negro use of a golf course, and *Mayor and Council of Baltimore City v. Dawson*,[17] concerning swimming pools, bore out this view. As early as 1958, it was apparent that *Plessy v. Ferguson* could no longer be relied upon to justify racial segregation in publicly owned and operated facilities. The Court did not, however, write a sweeping opinion overruling the case. It was content to rob it of vitality in a case-by-case method. As a last resort, southern states attempted in some instances to apply the deliberate-speed formula in desegregation of public facilities, but the Court rejected all such attempts. That aberrant doctrine was held to have no efficacy except in the case of public schools. In every other instance, the right to be free from segregation was held personal and present.

Whatever its shortcomings as regards the deliberate-speed formula, *Brown v. Board of Education* is a great landmark case in American constitutional law. The Court did turn the clock back—back toward the bright promise of 1868, when the Fourteenth Amendment was ratified and when the nation wrote into its fundamental law the proposition that there is no color and there is no caste here, as the first Justice John Marshall Harlan had seen so clearly and said so eloquently. The Court's long backward step in *Plessy v. Ferguson* disrupted but did not destroy that principle. When the Supreme Court restored that principle in the Brown case, it broke down a blockade of law and custom and reopened the road toward equality, a road beset with many obstacles—obstacles growing out of slavery and out of the institutionalization of racial discrimination created by the separate-but-equal rule and by other cases in which the Court restricted constitutional rights.

As for the deliberate-speed formula, it has nearly run its course. The Court's increasing dissatisfaction with and criticism of the application of the rule presages the day when it will declare its end and restore the constitutional doctrine that a right imbedded in the Constitution is always personal and present. Meanwhile the 1964 Civil Rights Act has provided additional leverage for desegregation through provisions that the federal government may withhold school funds where no adequate desegregation plan has been undertaken by a school board. That provision hastened desegregation in the fall of 1965 and will become an increasingly important device to disestablish separate schools.

The Court's secrets are its own, and we do not know why it was so hesitant about issuing a forthright opinion overruling *Plessy v. Ferguson*. Future historians will wrestle with that question and construct an answer based on letters and other documents that will explain why it left the question open and answered it on a piecemeal basis. One of the last answers came in the field of transportation, where the separate-but-equal rule was born and from which it spread to other areas. The first skirmishes in transportation began in the 1930's and involved a Chicago congressman.

One does not speak of the rope
in the house of the hanged.

OLD PROVERB

Arthur W. Mitchell was a member of the House of Representatives when he set out on a trip from Chicago to Hot Springs, Arkansas, via the Illinois Central and Rock Island Railroads on April 20, 1937. As befitted a man in his station in life, he bought a first-class Pullman ticket to his destination and all went well until the train crossed the Mississippi river from Memphis to Arkansas. At that point the Rock Island conductor ordered him to leave the air-conditioned Pullman car with its flush toilets, its hot and cold running water, and other travel comforts and move into another car. That other car was divided into three sections: one for Negro smokers, one for white smokers, and another for Negro men and women; it was an old car without air conditioning; it lacked flush toilets for men; it had no running water, hot or cold, and no soap or towels. The Congressman protested in vain against the order to move and finally did so under threat of arrest.

Arthur Mitchell was a Negro.

Mightily aggrieved at what had happened to him, the congressman filed a complaint with the Interstate Commerce Commission asking it to issue an order directing the Rock Island to change its ways of treating Negro passengers. The commission, over the dissent of five of its members, rejected his plea. Arkansas, it pointed out, required the separation of the races on railroad trains. What the Rock Island had done, the commission held, was in keeping with long-established procedures and with Supreme Court decisions saying that railroads could segregate the races by rules, where such segregation comported with local custom and laws. The short of the whole matter was that the commission saw no reason to change the rules or regulations.

Congressman Mitchell's very presence in the House of Representatives was symptomatic of the change that was taking place in his native land. He was a Democrat, the first Negro Democrat ever to sit in Congress, and he came from Chicago's poverty-ridden black belt, whose voters had deserted the party of Abraham Lincoln and cast their lot with the party of Franklin Delano Roosevelt. The party with which Mr. Mitchell was affiliated was the party that had driven Negroes from office in the South in the 1870's, disfranchised them a score of years later, and then enacted Jim Crow codes in southern states, including Arkansas. As a lawyer, Mitchell knew full well that within his own lifetime the Supreme Court had formulated the separate-but-equal rule in *Plessy v. Ferguson,* a railroad case—that strange legal fiction that had come to mean the Jim Crow car to which he had been removed was "substantially equal" to accommodations available to white persons.

The legal basis of Congressman Mitchell's complaint to the commission was a provision of the Interstate Commerce Act that made it unlawful for a common carrier "to subject any particular person . . . to any undue or unreasonable prejudice or disadvantage in any respect whatsoever." The three-judge federal court to which the congressman took his case after the Commission refused to act held it had no jurisdiction and dismissed the suit. When the case reached the Supreme Court as *Mitchell v. United States,*[1] Mr. Mitchell and his lawyers broadened their plea to assault the rule in the Plessy case, and ten southern attorneys general hastened to file briefs as friends of the court, urging it to hold fast to the separate-but-equal doctrine. Something new happened—something that was a harbinger of things to come and a herald of the change enveloping the land: the Attorney General of the United States ranged himself on the congressman's side, although the United States was a nominal defendant.

The Court sidestepped a ruling on the Plessy case, and in a 1940 decision unanimously held, through Chief Justice Hughes, that the commission was wrong and that Congressman Mitchell had indeed been subjected to undue and unreasonable disadvantage, in violation of the Interstate Commerce Act. The Chief Justice said that the case did not present a "question of segregation but one of equality of treatment," because the railroad had removed the passenger from first-class accommodations afforded white persons and forced him to ride in a "second class car." That denial of equality of accommodations "because of his race would be an invasion of a fundamental individual right which is guaranteed by the Fourteenth Amendment," Chief Justice Hughes said, "and in view of the nature of the right and our constitutional policy it cannot be maintained that the discrimination . . . was not essentially unjust. In that aspect it could not be deemed to lie outside the purview of the sweeping prohibitions of the Interstate Commerce Act."

What the Court had done was to give greater substance to the equality factor in the separate-but-equal equation. In practice it meant that the railroads must exercise great, or greater, care, to see to it that every accommodation provided for white persons was also afforded Negro passengers. The Plessy rule was still in full force and effect, but Negroes must be afforded Pullman accommodations.

Irene Morgan took a bus running from Gloucester County, Virginia, through the District of Columbia to Baltimore, her destination. Virginia law provided that white and colored persons could be segregated on buses within the state, and when Miss Morgan refused to move to the back of the bus on the driver's order, she was arrested and fined ten dollars. Under Virginia law, the Negro passenger could be required to change seats at any time in order to effectuate segregation. The state's highest court held the law constitutional and decided that it applied to all passengers, whether they were in interstate commerce or not. When the case reached the Supreme Court as *Morgan v. Virginia*,[2] Justice Reed, for the majority, held that "This appeal presents the question of validity of a statute that compels segregation of interstate passengers in vehicles moving interstate."

The ultimate question, he said in a 1946 decision, was whether or not the state statute unduly burdened interstate commerce in a situation in which Congress had not acted. The Court had held that where Congress had not acted, it could inquire into the burdens imposed and decide whether or not an undue burden had been levied. Pointing out that Miss Morgan might have been required to change seats several times in Virginia at the direction of the driver and then left free to make her own choice of seats when the bus reached the District of Columbia, Justice Reed came to the conclusion that "seating arrangements for the different races in interstate motor travel require a single, uniform rule to promote and protect national travel. Consequently, we hold the Virginia statute in controversy invalid."

The decision was apparently written in a careful vein to exclude any possibility of its application to segregation on railroads. There was some question as to whether it covered the situation where the bus lines imposed segregation by their own rules and regulations. It mustered a strange majority, with three other justices apparently in complete agreement with Justice Reed. Justice Jackson took no part in the case; Justice Rutledge agreed only with the result. Justice Black concurred with the notation that he believed the issue as to imposition of burdens on interstate commerce to be a matter for Congress alone, but that since the Court had taken an opposite view, he would accept its formula. Justice Burton dissented on the ground that the states should be left free to make their own rules as to racial segregation on motor carriers. Justice Frankfurter, who saw great merit in Justice Burton's view, concurred in the result only because of his conviction that the seventy-year-old case of *Hall v. De Cuir* was controlling.[3] (In that case a Louisiana law *forbidding* racial segregation by public carriers was held invalid as a burden on interstate commerce.) In practice, the case had little immediate result; bus lines continued to segregate. The Plessy case was not mentioned.

Elmer Henderson, an employee of the President's Committee on Fair Employment Practices, took a routine train trip from Washington, D.C., to Birmingham on May 17, 1942, to investigate discrimination in Alabama war industries. Thanks to Congressman Mitchell's case, he had no difficulty in securing Pullman accommodations on the Southern Railroad. He ran into trouble when he got ready for dinner. In what it chose to regard as compliance with the holding in the Mitchell case that all facilities furnished white passengers must be supplied to Negroes, the Southern had set aside two tables for Negro diners in the section of the dining car nearest the kitchen. The two tables were curtained off and "Reserved" cards placed on them. If all other seats were taken before a Negro appeared for a meal, however, "the curtains should be pushed back, the cards removed and white passengers served." Henderson went to the diner at 5 P.M., but white passengers were seated at the end tables. He returned at 7 P.M. and again at 7:30 P.M., but white passengers were still occupying the tables. The dining car was detached at 9 P.M. and the hungry Mr. Henderson got no dinner.

In October, 1942, Henderson filed a complaint with the Interstate Commerce Commission charging that the failure to serve him subjected him to "undue or unreasonable disadvantage," in violation of the Interstate Commerce Act, and asking the commission to issue a cease-and-desist order against the Southern. The commission refused to issue the requested order, holding that while Henderson had been put to some disadvantage in the particular incident, the railroad's rules met the fundamental requirements of the act. On an appeal, a three-judge federal court reversed the commission's order and sent the case back for further proceedings.

When the commission finally got around to rehearing the case, the Southern submitted a new set of rules that had been in effect since March 1, 1946, which set aside a four-seat table nearest the kitchen for exclusive use of Negro passengers. Curtains were replaced by a five-foot high wooden partition enclosing the four seats. The seats set aside for Negro use represented 8.33 per cent of dining car space; studies showed that Negro passengers ordinarily used from 3 to 4 per cent of such space. The new rules satisfied the commission and the federal district court but not Henderson, who took his case to the Supreme Court. There he urged in *Henderson v. United States*[4] that the new segregatory rules violated the Interstate Commerce Act, and he also attacked them as derivatives of what he said was the wrongfully decided case of *Plessy v. Ferguson*. He wanted the Court to invalidate the separate-but-equal rule.

The federal government, although also sued by Henderson, agreed with him and filed a brief on his behalf, arguing vigorously that dining car segregation violated the Interstate Commerce Act and voicing a straightforward plea for overruling the Plessy case. The U. S. Solicitor General appeared at the oral argument to repeat these arguments with eloquence and fervor.

The Supreme Court again evaded a direct ruling on the Plessy case, in a unanimous 1950 opinion written by Justice Burton. Where "a dining car is available to passengers holding tickets entitling them to use it . . . denial of dining services to any such passenger . . . subjects him to a prohibited disadvantage," he said. He ridiculed the racial signs and partitions as serving no purpose except to humiliate Negroes: "We need not multiply instances in which these rules sanction unreasonable discrimination. The curtains, partition and signs emphasize the artificiality of a difference in treatment which serve only to call attention to a racial classification of passengers holding identical tickets and using the same public dining facility." The Interstate Commerce Commission was directed to issue appropriate orders abolishing segregation in dining cars.

The Court had further weighted the equal factor in favor of Negroes in the separate-but-equal equation, but it had not invalidated the Plessy rule as such. Construed together, the Mitchell and Henderson cases had created a situation in which the more advantaged Negro middle-class person could secure first-class railroad accommodations equal, because identical, to those afforded white passengers. The Negro who had to use the day coach, whether for economic reasons or because first-class accommodations were not furnished between particular places, could still be required to ride in a Jim Crow coach. But it was becoming apparent that the Plessy case was living on borrowed time; every Supreme Court assault on it resulted in a limitation on its scope.

When Justice Brown formulated the separate-but-equal rule for the Court in *Plessy v. Ferguson,* he relied heavily, and erroneously, on state and lower federal court cases tolerating segregation in public schools as justifying state laws requiring railroad segregation. He reasoned that if separate schools were permissible under the Fourteenth Amendment, state laws ordering separate railroad accommodations were likewise tolerable. After the decision in the Plessy case, the courts in turn relied on that decision as a precedent for segregation in public schools. This merry-go-round performance came home to roost after the Court held in the 1954 School Segregation cases that "in the field of public education the doctrine of 'separate but equal' has no place." Despite the Court's language limiting its school ruling to the "field of public education," lower courts began to cast doubt on the validity of the separate-but-equal doctrine in interstate travel. Responding to an NAACP petition, the Interstate Commerce Commission held in 1955 that segregation of passengers on railroads or in terminals subjected Negroes to undue prejudice or disadvantage, in violation of the Interstate Commerce Act, and in doing so relied on the School cases. It ordered the end of all railroad segregation in interstate commerce. There was no Supreme Court challenge to that order, perhaps because the railroads had lost the battle for passenger service to the airlines and were no longer inclined to pay the cost imposed by a dual transportation system.

The commission had no jurisdiction over intrastate transportation, such as that furnished by city bus or transit lines, or local motor carriers, or railroads operating within one state. There was considerable sentiment, however, that the School cases also invalidated segregation laws and ordinances of all kinds. Not all judges agreed.

Federal Judge George Bell Timmerman of South Carolina was one of them; he held that his state's segregation statute governing local transportation was still valid. On appeal, the Court of Appeals for the Fourth Circuit reversed his ruling, saying "We do not think that the separate but equal doctrine of *Plessy v. Ferguson* can any longer be regarded as a correct statement of the law . . . recent decisions, which relate to public schools, leave no doubt that the separate but equal doctrine has been repudiated." [5] The Supreme Court summarily dismissed an appeal from the court of appeals decision in *Flemming v. S. C. Electric & Gas Co.*,[6] on April 26, 1956, by simply citing an old case holding that dismissal was proper where an appeal was frivolous. It declined the opportunity to write an opinion overruling the Plessy case, however.

The Court then bypassed another opportunity to spell out its repudiation of the Plessy case in *Gayle v. Browder*,[7] on which it acted on November 13, 1956. That case grew out of the famed Montgomery Bus Boycott and a subsequent attack on the constitutionality of Montgomery ordinances and Alabama statutes requiring racial segregation on municipal transit lines. The three-judge federal court confronted the issue directly, and Circuit Court Judge Richard Rives spoke for the two-to-one majority in an opinion taking direct issue with Justice Brown's Plessy opinion.[8]

Judge Rives drew a legal bead on the Plessy case fatuity that the protest against enforced segregation on a common carrier was a demand for "social equality." He said: "In their private affairs, in the conduct of their businesses, it is clear that the people themselves have the liberty to select their associates. . . . There is, however, a difference, a constitutional difference, between voluntary adherence to custom and the perpetuation and enforcement of that custom by law." Then he pronounced the judgment that should have been pronounced in the Plessy case in 1896: "We hold that the statutes . . . requiring segregation of the white and colored races . . . on a common carrier violate the due process and equal protection of the law clauses of the Fourteenth Amendment. . . ."

The dissenting judge argued that the Supreme Court had not directly invalidated the Plessy case rule in the area of transportation and protested that a lesser federal court was bound to follow that case until it was specifically overruled. Judge Rives answered that "the [Supreme] Court has first weakened the vitality of, and has then destroyed, the separate but equal concept." He said that "Even a statute can be repealed by implication . . . a judicial decision, which is simply evidence of the law and not the law itself, may be so impaired by later decisions as no longer to furnish any reliable evidence." When the case reached it, the Court contented itself with affirming Judge Rives by a perfunctory reference to the School cases.

The reluctant Supreme Court was proffered another opportunity to directly overrule the Plessy case on December 15, 1958, when *Evers v. Dwyer*[9] was decided. In that case a three-judge federal court dismissed Evers's suit attacking bus segregation in Memphis, Tennessee, on the ground that he had filed it simply to test constitutionality of segregation laws and that, therefore, it did not present a genuine controversy. The Court was satisfied with reversing the lower court on the ground that, even as a one-time rider of a bus, Evers had a right to test the constitutionality of a statute which imposed segregation on him. There was no hint that the Court had overruled the Plessy case. Nor did the Court seize the opportunity to set the entire matter at rest.

Meanwhile, the Freedom Riders, who swarmed through the South in their giant protest against all bus segregation, had thrown that issue into bold relief. They began their rides in May, 1961, and on September 22, 1961, the Interstate Commerce Commission found the Morgan case pregnant with new meaning and issued an order requiring every interstate bus to display a sign stating:

> Seating aboard this vehicle is without regard to race, color, creed, or national origin, by order of the Interstate Commerce Commission.

The Plessy case was on its deathbed.

In 1961, Mississippi's attorney general Joe Patterson, protesting that *Plessy v. Ferguson* was still applicable in transportation cases, put reliance on it to defend himself and his state against a suit for injunction in a federal court, *Bailey v. Patterson.*[10] The Supreme Court handed down a very short perfunctory opinion on February 26, 1962, saying "*We have settled beyond question that no State may require racial segregation of interstate or intrastate facilities. The question is no longer open; it is foreclosed as a litigable issue.*" (Emphasis added.) *Plessy v. Ferguson* had been executed in a manner reminiscent of the cat who was choked to death on buttermilk.

The student of the law will look in vain for the words in which important cases are ordinarily overruled: "*Plessy v. Ferguson is overruled.*" He will not find them. Nor will he find anywhere a Supreme Court opinion refuting the grievous errors contained in Justice Brown's opinion for the Court in that case or a repudiation of the evil that it wrought in the almost sixty years that it guided state and federal courts and inspired racial discrimination in every aspect of American life. Perhaps no justice on the Court wanted to speak of the rope in the house of the hanged, or perhaps all considered it impolitic to do so. Some future historian may unravel the question, as he threads through the decisions and gains access to unpublished material.

The failure of the Court to write an opinion directly overruling the Plessy case also foreclosed its opportunity to pay deserved tribute to the first and great John Marshall Harlan and his accurate prediction in 1896 that "the judgment this day rendered [*Plessy v. Ferguson*] will, in time prove to be quite as pernicious as the decision made by this tribunal in the *Dred Scott* case," and his inquiry, "What can more certainly arouse race hate, what more certainly create and perpetuate a feeling of distrust between these races, than state enactments, which, in fact, proceed on the ground that colored citizens are so inferior and degraded that they cannot be allowed to sit in public coaches occupied by white citizens?" The reversal of the case, no matter how circuitous, bore out his prescience that the Negro "objects and ought never to cease objecting to the proposition that citizens of the white and black races can be adjudged criminals because they sit, or claim the right to sit, in the same public coach on a public highway." He was a prophet who deserved honor, not silence, in his own Court.

No matter what is said about the manner in which it was done or the failure of the Court to act in a more forthright fashion, the fact is that racial segregation was ultimately forbidden on common carriers. The consequences were important because the Plessy case had become symbolic of racial segregation and had been interwoven into the Southern Mystique. A great legend had fallen into disrepute, and it could no longer be said that the Constitution permitted classification of American citizens on the basis of race in order to impose racial segregation on a common carrier. In time, the concept of equalitarianism implicit in the new ruling would seep into the consciousness and subconsciousness of Americans and move them closer to a realization of the American Dream of the equality of all men before the law. And on a practical day-to-day basis, men would learn to live together by living together. The Court had vindicated the wisdom of the framers of the Fourteenth Amendment by returning to their principles.

Everywhere they turned, white Southerners found the NAACP and its lawyers arrayed against them. Angered over defeat in the courts and in legislative halls, southern politicians began to vent their wrath against the association by enacting laws designed to cripple it and drain off its energies in self-defense.

*There's none so blind
as they that won't see.*

JONATHAN SWIFT, *Polite Conversations* [Dialogue iii]

White Southerners have always insisted that Negro Southerners are and always have been happy with their lot, and that there would be no racial conflict, were it not for outside agitators bent on stirring up discontent. Slaveholders clung to that belief prior to and during the Civil War. The enlistment of 200,000 Negroes in the Union cause did not shake that faith; it is still reflected in southern-oriented history textbooks filled with stories of happy, singing slaves. Carpetbaggers—northern whites who went South after the Civil War—and power-hungry northern politicians are popularly supposed to have forced the vote and the desire for public office on unwilling Negroes. Southern folklore has it that Negroes literally loved, and still love, the segregation system. Contrary evidence is scornfully rejected by white southern politicians and public figures blinded by their own beliefs.

Self-armed with this set of beliefs, white Southerners have struck back at these "outside agitators" by repressive legislation. Abolitionist literature was barred from the mails, and abolitionists were subjected to heavy penalties. Carpetbaggers and New England teachers who ventured south after the "War Between the States" were targets of laws and Klan violence. For many years, the NAACP has been the villain of the southern piece, and after it assumed almost complete command of the civil rights movement, southern legislators set out to cripple it and hamper its activities.

There was a certain apparent justification for white southern hos-

tility to the NAACP which was not diminished by the observation
that it enlisted the loyalties of many southern Negroes. Under the
leadership of the quiet and always polite but tough-minded Roy
Wilkins, NAACP pressure for civil rights was relentless after the
Brown decision, and its involvement in civil rights litigation was
much greater than we have had time to describe here. Before and
after the Brown decision, its legal arm, the NAACP Legal Defense
and Educational Fund headed by Thurgood Marshall—first as an
adjunct of the parent organization and later as an independent corporation—supplied counsel or aided local counsel in day-to-day litigation and in the great cases that reached the Supreme Court. Resistant white Southerners undertook to put the association on the
defensive after the Brown case. Litigation was inevitable.

The counter-defensive against the NAACP took three main
forms: (1) administrative action to apply old and unused laws or
hastily passed new statutes regulating the conduct of foreign, that
is, out-of-state, corporations; (2) legislation designed to hamper
the association's support of civil rights litigation and to subject its
lawyers to the threat of prosecution or disciplinary action by state
bar associations; and (3) investigations by state legislative committees modeled after the congressional Un-American Activities Committee. Concurrently, there was an upsurge of popular retaliatory
measures against members of the NAACP through economic and
social pressures and outright violence. Legislative and administrative arms of the states tried to dredge up and publicize the association's membership lists for the obvious purpose of frightening away
its supporters.

Alabama led the way when its attorney general filed a suit on
June 1, 1956, to oust the NAACP from the state, on the ground that
it had failed to register as a foreign or out-of-state corporation as
required by the state's 1940 laws. The NAACP had begun operations in Alabama in 1918 and had had a regional office in Birmingham since 1951 but had never been asked to comply with registration laws. But the attorney general suddenly filed a suit to oust the
association, alleging that it was "causing irreparable injury to the
property and civil rights of residents and citizens of the State."
Boiled down to their essentials, the activities complained of were
that the NAACP had "employed or otherwise paid money" to Autherine Lucy in her ill-starred attempt to gain admission to the University of Alabama, that it had furnished Miss Lucy with legal

counsel, that it had "engaged in organizing and financing an illegal boycott" against the Montgomery bus lines, that it had "falsely charged" state and university officials with violations of law, that it had supported breaches of the peace in order to "raise funds under a false claim that it is for the protection of alleged constitutional rights," and that it had "encouraged, aided, and abetted a course of conduct, seeking to deny to the citizens of Alabama the constitutional right to voluntarily segregate."

On the day the complaint was filed, the attorney general sought a temporary restraining order barring the association from conducting any business or *from taking any steps to qualify to do business in the State while the suit was pending.* The NAACP filed a motion to dismiss the suit on the ground that there was no substance to the state's complaint. The trial judge then issued an order requiring the association to produce voluminous papers and records, including its membership lists. It produced or offered to produce all the demanded records except the membership lists, tendered compliance with Alabama's registration statute, answered that production of membership lists would subject members to harassment, loss of employment, and reprisals, and asserted that compliance would deny members freedom of speech and assembly. The judge countered by finding the NAACP in contempt of court and by imposing a $10,000 fine for its failure to produce the membership list, with a proviso that the fine would be increased to $100,000 unless the list was produced within five days. He also provided that no further action would be taken in the case until the fine was paid. The list was not produced. Instead, the association appealed to the Alabama supreme court. The $100,000 fine became effective.

The state's highest tribunal rebuffed the association, on the ground that its lawyers had chosen the wrong legal remedy in its attack on the judgment, and let the lower court order stand. At that stage a Supreme Court review was sought and secured, and the Court decided the issues before it on June 30, 1958, in *NAACP v. Alabama.*[1] Justice Harlan spoke for a unanimous Court. He disposed of the Alabama supreme court's claim that the NAACP lawyers had chosen the wrong remedy by citing Alabama cases in which that court had approved the very procedures taken by the lawyers! The Supreme Court, he said in effect, would not tolerate deprivation of constitutional rights through evasive application of obscure procedural rules.

Alabama asserted that the NAACP as an organization could not claim protection of the constitutional rights of its members, even if it were assumed that they, as individuals, had been or would be deprived of the rights of freedom of speech or assembly. Justice Harlan observed that for all practical purposes the NAACP and its membership were identical and answered that "Effective advocacy of both public and private points of view, particularly controversial ones, is undeniably enhanced by group association. . . . It is beyond debate that freedom to engage in association for the advancement of beliefs and issues is an inseparable aspect of that liberty assured by the Due Process Clause of the Fourteenth Amendment which embraces freedom of speech." He also said that "compelled disclosure of affiliates with groups engaged in advocacy may constitute as effective a restraint on freedom of association as the forms of governmental action." The NAACP, he observed, had made "an uncontroverted showing that on past occasions revelation of the identity of its rank and file membership has exposed these members to economic reprisal, loss of employment, threats of coercion and other manifestation of public hostility."

Nor could Justice Harlan "perceive that the disclosure of the names of . . . rank and file membership [had] a substantial bearing" on the issue of whether or not the NAACP should be permitted to do business in Alabama. The state argued, correctly, that the Ku Klux Klan had been forced to divulge the names of its members under state law upheld by the Supreme Court.[2] That was true, the justice said, but that ruling was "based on the particular character of the Klan's activities, involving acts of unlawful intimidation and violence." In short, the cases were not comparable. Alabama had one last objection: even if private parties did undertake reprisals on NAACP members after learning their names, that retaliatory action would not be "state action" but individual wrongdoing, and the Fourteenth Amendment, as had been said so many times, did not proscribe individual action, no matter how wrongful. Justice Harlan had no fault to find with the proposition that the amendment does not condemn wrongful private action but, he said, "The crucial factor is the interplay of governmental and private action, for it is only after the exertion of State power represented by the production order that private action takes hold." What he had said was that the state had made no case against the NAACP but had attempted to deny its members the rights of freedom of association and assembly protected by the Constitution.

Finally, Justice Harlan said that "the civil contempt order of the Alabama court and the $100,000 fine . . . must fall." The case was sent back to the Alabama supreme court with implicit directions that the trial court consider the NAACP's defenses and decide the case on its merits. Alabama's highest court did nothing of the kind. It affirmed the contempt sentence and the $100,000 fine levied on the NAACP, and sent back word that the Supreme Court's judgment had rested on the "mistaken premise" that the NAACP had done everything ordered except furnish membership lists. Its decision amounted to the claim that the NAACP was in contempt of court on grounds other than its failure to furnish membership lists. The NAACP returned to the Supreme Court, and on June 8, 1959, the Court rendered its *second* decision in *NAACP v. Alabama.*[3]

In the second case, the Court said summarily that the premise of its prior decision had been one which the state had "plainly accepted" in the first case and that Alabama couldn't switch grounds in the midst of the lawsuit. It observed with some acerbity that the Alabama court was "evidently not acquainted with the detailed basis of [its] proceedings." The case was sent back to Alabama with the mandate that "We assume that the State Supreme Court . . . will not fail to proceed promptly with the disposition of the matters left open under our mandate for further proceedings . . . rendered in the prior case." In short, there was nothing for Alabama to do except try the case under the rules laid down in the Court's first opinion.

The Alabama supreme court went on a sit-down strike of its own when the case was returned to it. It did exactly nothing. Finally, in June, 1960—exactly one year after the *second* decision—the frustrated NAACP filed a suit in the U. S. District Court asking for an injunction to restrain the enforcement of the Alabama judgment. The district judge dismissed the case on the ground that he would not assume that Alabama executive and judicial officers would fail to protect "the constitutional rights of all citizens." The case of *NAACP v. Alabama* under the title of *NAACP v. Gallion* went back to the Supreme Court for the *third* time, and on October 23, 1961, the Court directed the federal district judge to proceed with the trial of all issues in the case, "unless with a reasonable time, no later

than January 2, 1962, the State of Alabama shall have accorded to
[the NAACP] an opportunity to be heard on its motion to dissolve
the state restraining order of June 5, 1956, and upon the merits of
the action in which the order was issued." [4] Alabama dragged its
feet to the very last, and finally on December 29, 1961—two court
days before the Supreme Court deadline—the Alabama trial court
heard the case, found that the association had continued to do business in the state "in violation of the Constitution and laws of the
state" and that its activities "are and have been a usurpation and
abuse of its corporate functions and detrimental to the State of Alabama. . . ." The decree "forever" enjoined the NAACP from doing
business in the state. The association appealed to the state supreme
court.

Alabama's highest court again refused to consider the case on its
merits. This time it said that the association briefs did not comply
with its rules on appeal! The basis for its decision was that "under a
rule of long standing and frequent application . . . where unrelated assignments of error are argued together and one is without
merit, the others will not be considered." The court found that vice
in every single one of the NAACP arguments and affirmed the
lower court's ruling ousting the association from the state.

NAACP v. Alabama went back to the Supreme Court for the
fourth time and on June 1, 1964—eight years after the issuance of
the *temporary* restraining order—Justice Harlan again spoke for a
unanimous Court and reversed the Alabama decision.[5] He was able
to demonstrate without much difficulty that the Alabama court had
misconstrued its own rules and that it had often decided cases on
their merits despite variances between its technical rules and briefs.
He repeated the language of the first case that "novelty in procedural requirements cannot be permitted to thwart review in this
Court applied for by those who, in justified reliance upon prior
decisions, seek vindication in state courts of their federal constitutional rights." In other words, Alabama couldn't deny constitutional
rights by hiding behind a maze of procedural rules.

Alabama asked that if the Court found its decision on procedural
grounds inadequate, the case be returned to it for decision on the
merits. Justice Harlan refused that request. He indicated that the
Court had lost faith in the Alabama courts. "While this might be
well enough in other circumstances," he said, "in view of what has
gone before, we reject that contention and proceed to the merits."

If Alabama wouldn't decide the case, the Supreme Court would. He found no merit in the charges revolving around NAACP conduct in the Autherine Lucy case or in its action in reference to the Montgomery boycott. Nor did he think it was legally significant, as charged, that the NAACP had attempted to "pressure" the mayor of Philadelphia, the governor of Pennsylvania, and the Penn State football team into a "boycott of the Alabama football team" when it played in the Liberty Bowl. These matters, he concluded, presented no reasons for barring the NAACP from Alabama.

"This case, in truth," said Justice Harlan, "involves not the privilege of a corporation to do business in a State, but rather the freedom of individuals to associate for the collective advocacy of ideas. 'Freedoms such as . . . [this] are protected not only against heavy-handed frontal attack, but also from being stifled by more subtle governmental interference.'" The case was sent back to the Alabama supreme court with a mandate directing it to order the trial court to vacate its prior injunction and issue an order "permitting the Association to take all necessary steps to qualify it to do business in Alabama. Should we unhappily be mistaken in our belief that the Supreme Court of Alabama will properly implement this disposition, leave is given the Association to apply to this Court for appropriate relief," he added. What he was saying was that if the Alabama supreme court didn't follow the order, the Court would draw a decree of its own on the request of the NAACP. Alabama knuckled under to the Supreme Court ultimatum, and in the fall of 1964 the NAACP reactivated its branches in the state. Civil rights agitation had not ceased in the enforced eight-year moratorium on NAACP activities and when it returned, it found a vastly expanded field for its operations.

The blind had led the blind into a legal ditch.

While Alabama was playing hide and seek with the Supreme Court, Louisiana and Arkansas tried to utilize laws and ordinances to ferret out NAACP membership lists. In 1957, Little Rock and North Little Rock, Arkansas, amended their ordinances regulating out-of-state corporations to provide that such organizations must list their members with a municipal officer. Mrs. Daisy Bates, as custodian of the Little Rock NAACP branch, refused to do so and was arrested, convicted, and fined $25. Her conviction was affirmed on appeal to the state court, but on Supreme Court review the ordinances were invalidated insofar as they required listing of members. Referring to evidence showing that NAACP members feared reprisals and that membership declined when disclosure was compelled, Justice Potter Stewart spoke for seven members of the Court on February 23, 1960, in *Bates v. Little Rock* to say that "freedom of association for the purpose of advancing ideas and airing grievances is protected by the Due Process Clause of the Fourteenth Amendment from invasion by the States." [6] He concluded that the "municipalities have failed to demonstrate a controlling justification for the deterrence of free association which compulsory disclosure of membership lists" would involve. Justices Black and Douglas concurred in the result on free-speech grounds.

Arkansas then tried to attain at least a portion of its objective by a state statute that required all school teachers to list in detail all organizations to which they belonged, a patent attempt to strike at NAACP members who were teachers. Booker T. Shelton had taught in Little Rock schools for 25 years, but when he refused to list his organizational memberships, his contract was not renewed. He filed suit in a federal court claiming that the law requiring his listing of all memberships was invalid as an attempt to deny his rights of freedom of association and speech. A three-judge federal court refused to enjoin enforcement of the law, and the case reached the Supreme Court as *Shelton v. Tucker*,[7] decided on December 12, 1960. Justice Stewart, who spoke for a five-to-four majority of the Court, agreed that a state had a legitimate and substantial interest in an inquiry into the fitness and competency of its teachers. But, he said, "That purpose cannot be pursued by means that stifle fundamental personal liberties. . . ." The sweeping statute was invalidated on the ground that many organizational memberships "could have no possible bearing upon the teacher's occupational competence or fitness." Chief Justice Warren and Justices Douglas, Black, and Brennan agreed with Justice Stewart, while Justices Frankfurter and Harlan dissented in opinions joined in by Justices Clark and Whittaker. The dissenters said that the interest of the state was broad enough to warrant the inquiry.

Louisiana's attorney general, John P. F. Gremillion, one of the most persistent state officials in the attempt to undermine enforcement of the Brown cases, filed suit in an attempt to enforce a 1958 statute aimed at the NAACP. The statute prohibited all "nontrading" organizations from doing business in Louisiana if any of the officers or directors of its out-of-state affiliate was a member of

"Communist, Communist front or subversive organizations, as cited by the House of Congress [*sic*] Un-American Activities Committee or the United States Attorney." Every organization covered by the statute was required to file an annual affidavit that "none of the officers" of the affiliate was a "member" of such organizations. A Louisiana state court upheld the law, but the case was removed to a federal court which found the statute invalid. In the same hearing the NAACP sought to enjoin enforcement of a 1924 Louisiana statute requiring annual disclosure of membership lists. The law was originally passed to hamper Ku Klux Klan activities; members of organizations whose lists had not been filed were barred from holding or attending any meeting of the group. The federal court granted the NAACP request for the injunction.

The two cases were heard together as *Louisiana ex rel. Gremillion v. NAACP*[8] in the Supreme Court, and on May 22, 1961 the Court speaking through Justice Douglas held both laws invalid as applied to the NAACP.[9] The decision rested on the principles announced in the first *NAACP v. Alabama* case and in *Shelton v. Tucker*.

The states had failed in their initial efforts to secure NAACP membership lists.

The southern crusade against NAACP lawyers took the form of strengthening and broadening statutes against solicitation of clients and stirring up of litigation. State law and professional ethics had always forbidden lawyers from feathering their own nests by seeking out clients and drumming up lawsuits for money-making purposes. There were no profits in civil rights litigation. The NAACP interest in furthering and financing such litigation lay in attaining its objective of establishing constitutional rights for all Negroes. Lawyers who furnished services in NAACP lawsuits were ordinarily members of the association, with a commitment to its purposes and with a willingness to engage in long and tedious litigation at a financial sacrifice to themselves. The practical fact was that southern segregationists had complete command of state machinery, with virtually unlimited public funds at their disposal to defend assaults on segregation laws or ordinances; they were represented by attorneys general, district attorneys, lawyers for school boards, and other publicly paid counsel. No, or very few, individual litigants could oppose the panoply of state power thus arrayed against them. They had to band together. There was the added fact that many Negroes did not even know the extent of their own constitutional rights and privileges, and they had to be informed and educated.

NAACP officials, and sometimes NAACP lawyers, appeared before branch meetings to advise members of their rights and to encourage them to exercise those rights through judicial challenges to discriminatory or segregatory laws, customs, and practices. In the ordinary case, a plaintiff or plaintiffs had to be found who were willing to spearhead the lawsuit. There is no blinking the fact that the NAACP did stir up civil rights litigation and did solicit litigants in some instances in a manner that would not have been tolerated in commercial law. As a part of its massive resistance program, Virginia hit upon the idea that if the rules against stirring up of litigation and solicitation of litigants that prevailed in commercial law could be applied to civil rights litigation, it could throttle lawsuits against segregation and discrimination. Chapters 31, 32, 33, 35, and 36 of the 1956 Acts of the Virginia Assembly sought to reach these objectives.

The assembly's announced purpose was that of maintaining "continued harmonious relations between the races . . ." in Virginia. Chapters 31 and 32 were basically registration statutes that required detailed listing of members, sources of revenue, expenditures of funds, names and addresses of officers and directors of organizations which engaged in activities for "the passage of legislation by the General Assembly in behalf of any race or color" or with "advocating of racial integration or segregation," or which raised or expended funds "for the employment of counsel or payment of costs in connection with litigation in behalf of any race or color. . . ." Chapter 35 was aimed against "the offense of stirring up litigation," commonly called barratry. Chapter 33 was directed against "runners and cappers," persons who solicit business for lawyers. The definition of a "runner and capper" was extended to include an agent for an individual or organization that retained a lawyer in connection with a lawsuit in which it had no pecuniary interest. "Running and capping" in commercial cases had long been frowned upon by the law and by the canons of ethics of the American Bar Association. Chapter 36 in essence forbade advocacy of suits against the state and the giving of any assistance, financial or otherwise, to such suits.

The campaign against Virginia laws opened with companion

suits by the NAACP and the NAACP Legal Defense and Educational Fund in the federal district court, in which they asked that the Chapters 31, 32, 33, 35, and 36 be declared unconstitutional as applied to them, on the ground they denied freedom of speech and association and equal protection of the laws. A three-judge federal district court found Chapters 31, 32, and 35 invalid for constitutional reasons but refused to rule on Chapters 33 and 36, on the ground that these chapters should first be construed by state courts before federal courts acted. The refusal to rule on the two chapters was in response to previous Supreme Court rulings and insistence that where several constructions were open, state laws should first be construed by state courts in order to minimize interference with a state's construction and application of its own statutes.[10] Thereafter, federal courts could act if the state court construction of the law infringed constitutional rights. The federal district court thought that Chapters 31, 32, and 35 were invalid on the face of their language but that the constitutionality of Chapters 33 and 36 depended on the construction put upon them by the state courts.

That case reached the Supreme Court as *Harrison v. NAACP* and was decided on June 8, 1959, with Justice Harlan holding for a six-to-three majority that all the chapters should first be construed by Virginia's courts before federal courts intervened.[11] Justices Douglas and Brennan and Chief Justice Warren dissented on the grounds that the Court should determine all the issues presented by all sections of the state law. While the appeal was pending in the Harrison case, the NAACP sued in Virginia courts to test the constitutionality of Chapters 33 and 36. Virginia courts found Chapter 36 invalid but upheld Chapter 33, the so-called "running and capping" section. Chapter 33 was a source of particular danger to the NAACP, because it subjected the organization to heavy penalties where "running and capping" was proved, and also made its attorneys liable for loss of licenses and to suspension or disbarment at the discretion of the courts. Specifically, the Virginia court held that past activities of the NAACP, the NAACP State Conferences of Branches, and the Legal Fund constituted "fomenting and soliciting legal business in which they are not parties and have no pecuniary right or liability and which they channel to the enrichment of certain lawyers employed by them. . . ." The NAACP, but not the Legal Fund, sought a review, and the Supreme Court reviewed the case and decided it as *NAACP v. Button*[12] on January 14, 1963.

Justice Brennan wrote the opinion for the majority, in which he explained, "We hold that the activities of the NAACP, its affiliates and legal staff . . . are modes of expression protected by the First and Fourteenth Amendments which Virginia may not prohibit, under its power to regulate the legal profession, as improper violations of Chapter 33 and the Canons of Professional Ethics." Justice Douglas agreed but would have gone further. Justice White agreed with the result but not with the majority reasoning. Justices Harlan, Clark, and Stewart dissented.

"In the context of NAACP objectives," Justice Brennan wrote, "litigation is not a technique of resolving private differences; it is a means of achieving the lawful objectives of equality of treatment by all governmental, federal, state and local for members of the Negro community in this country. It is thus a form of political expression." He was convinced that the "NAACP is not a conventional political party; but the litigation it assists while serving to vindicate the legal rights of the American Negro community, at the same time and perhaps more importantly, makes possible the distinctive contribution of a minority group to the ideas and beliefs of our society. For such a group, association for litigation may be the most effective form of political association."

The justice asserted that Virginia's construction of Chapter 33 would make into a criminal a person who advised another that his constitutional rights had been violated and referred him to a particular attorney. Thus, he said, the statute presented the "gravest danger of smothering all discussion looking to the eventual institution of litigation on behalf of the rights of an unpopular minority." The Court, he insisted, could not close its eyes to the fact that the "militant Negro civil rights movement has engendered resentment and opposition of the politically dominant white community of Virginia." Nor could he find any overriding state interest in the "regulation of the legal profession . . . which justifies limiting . . . First Amendment rights." Under all of the circumstances, he concluded that, as interpreted by the state court, Chapter 33 was also void because it was too vague to define the offense.

The *NAACP v. Alabama* cases were cited as precedents for the right of freedom of association and for the proposition that the NAACP "and its members are in every practical sense identical." Finally, he said, "Resort to the courts to seek vindication of constitutional rights is a different matter from the oppressive, malicious or avaricious use of the legal process for purely private advantage. Lawsuits attacking racial discrimination, at least in Virginia, are neither very profitable nor very popular. They are not an object of general competition among lawyers . . . the problem is . . . an apparent dearth of lawyers who are willing to undertake such litigation."

Justice Douglas agreed with the majority but would have broadened the decision on Fourteenth Amendment grounds. Justice White wrote that the majority opinion, while justified, seemed to imply too sweeping a rule and he would have narrowed it. Justice Harlan, who spoke for himself and Justices Clark and Stewart, wrote that the "litigation program of the NAACP . . . falls within an area of activity which a State may constitutionally regulate." He justified his opinion by drawing analogies between the conduct of NAACP lawyers and attorneys in private litigation, where the state admittedly had a right to impose regulations. Nor could he find any room in the Virginia decision "for any findings of discriminatory purpose" in the enactment or application of the laws or any vice of vagueness.

When Chapters 31, 32, and 35 were construed by Virginia courts as required in the Harrison case, the Circuit Court of the City of Richmond found most of the three chapters unconstitutional. The final result was that the NAACP defended itself and its lawyers quite effectively from a state-inspired offensive that seemed to promise disaster. Similar statutes were enacted by Arkansas, Florida, Georgia, Mississippi, South Carolina, and Tennessee, but after the Virginia experience, little effort was made to use them extensively. The Arkansas statutes were attacked by the NAACP in a federal district court that referred the issues to state courts for construction. After its decision in the Harrison case, the Supreme Court affirmed the district court opinion in *NAACP v. Bennett* [13] on June 22, 1959. Justices Douglas and Brennan and Chief Justice Warren dissented and would have directed the district court to proceed with a hearing without state court hearings.

The Florida legislature went fishing for NAACP membership lists in 1956 by setting up a committee for the purpose of investigating the association. When that committee's authority expired in 1957, a new committee was named, and it tried to subpoena the Miami chapter's entire membership list. After a refusal to produce that list, the Florida supreme court held that while the association could not be compelled to give the entire list to the committee, the custodian of branch records could be required to attend committee hearings and bring the list in his possession to answer whether specific individuals, otherwise identified as, or "suspected of being," Communists were NAACP members. The Supreme Court refused to review that ruling.[14]

In 1959, a successor committee, authorized by the Florida legislature, subpoenaed Father Theodore Gibson, an Episcopal clergyman and custodian of the Miami branch records, to appear on November 4, 1959, and bring the records with him. He was informed that the committee would be concerned with "activities of various organizations which have been or are operating in this State in the fields of race relations," with the "coercive reform of social and educational practices and mores by litigation and pressured administrative action" and "other vital phases of life in this State." The chairman stressed that the committee inquiry would be directed to Communists and communist activities, including infiltration into organizations.

Called to the stand, Father Gibson said he was custodian of the Miami membership records but that he had not brought them with him and would not produce them, but he added that he would testify from personal knowledge as to any persons whose names were brought to his attention. He based his refusal to produce the list and testify from it on the ground that to do so would interfere with the right of association guaranteed to the NAACP members by the Fourteenth Amendment. Some fourteen names said to be Communists or members of communist fronts were suggested to him, but he could not associate any of them with the NAACP. He was found in contempt of the committee for failing to produce the list at the hearing and sentenced to a six-month jail term and a fine of $1200. Florida's supreme court upheld the contempt order and the Supreme Court reviewed the case and decided it as *Gibson v. Florida*[15] on March 25, 1963.

Justice Albert Goldberg was spokesman for the five-to-four majority which reversed the Florida court over the vigorous dissent of Justices Harlan, Clark, Stewart, and White. In the final analysis, Justice Goldberg's opinion rested on the proposition that there was no adequate basis for the legislative investigation, in light of the fact that the NAACP had long pursued an anticommunist course. The committee, he said, "has laid no adequate foundation for its direct demands upon the officers and records of a wholly legitimate organization for disclosure of its membership; the Committee has neither demonstrated nor pointed out any threat to the State by virtue of the existence of the NAACP. . . ." In summary, he said, "To permit legislative inquiry on less than an adequate foundation would be to sanction unjustified and unwarranted intrusions into the very heart of the constitutional privilege to be secure in associations in legitimate organizations engaged in First and Fourteenth Amendment rights. . . ." Chief Justice Warren and Justice Brennan agreed with Justice Goldberg, and while Justices Black and Douglas supported his opinion, they also advanced additional grounds arising out of beliefs in severe limitations on all legislative inquiries.

Justice Harlan, joined by Justices Clark and Stewart, dissented on the ground that the legislative investigation was entirely proper, since the information sought was that of activity *by* Communists in NAACP branches. They could see no difference "in the degree of governmental investigatory interest as between Communist infiltration *of* organizations and Communist activity *by* organizations." (Emphasis original.) Justice White in his dissent said that he had thought "that the freedom of association which is and should be entitled to constitutional protection would be promoted, not hindered, by disclosures which permit members of an organization to know with whom they are associating. . . ."

The victory was a narrow but very significant one for the NAACP. A contrary decision almost certainly would have resulted in similar legislative inquiries in southern states immersed in their program of massive resistance to school desegregation. What the states were seeking was a device that would give them access to NAACP membership lists. Those lists had no value in and of themselves; the only purpose of disclosure was their publication, with inevitable and wholesale reprisal against NAACP members by private persons. A legislative finding, no matter how flimsy, that there had been Communist infiltration into the NAACP would certainly have popularized retaliatory action.

Supreme Court decisions fending off attacks on the NAACP followed the Court's trend of extending federal supremacy in the protection of civil rights and of asserting federal power as contemplated by the framers of the Fourteenth Amendment where the states were laggard in enforcing equality before the law. The

Court's actions inspired complaints that it had intruded into areas long held to have been reserved to the states. But such complaints were beside the point; at issue was the question of what the Constitution commanded. In the first *NAACP v. Alabama* case, for example, it overruled the Alabama supreme court's interpretation of state statutes and decisions, and decided for itself that NAACP lawyers had chosen the correct procedural method of attacking a contempt-of-court ruling on appeal to state courts. Its conduct in doing so flew straight in the face of what it had done 60 years earlier in the Alabama voting case of *Giles v. Teasley*,[16] where it had eagerly embraced an Alabama supreme court interpretation of procedural rules obviously designed to forestall federal intervention in protection of franchise rights under the Fifteenth Amendment.

In the third *NAACP v. Alabama* case, the Court went to the length of ordering a federal district court to decide issues of law and fact in a case pending in the Alabama supreme court, unless that court acted within a specified time—an order that amounted to intervening directly into the state's judicial affairs. In the fourth *NAACP v. Alabama case, the* Court brushed aside an Alabama supreme court's interpretation of its own rules as to form and content of briefs on appeal and held those briefs adequate. Having done that, it proceeded to decide the very issues it had once ordered Alabama to decide and told the state court in no uncertain terms that, unless Alabama's supreme court judges wrote the proper directive to the trial court, it would also perform that task.

Federal supervision could hardly go further; federal supremacy in the protection of civil rights could not have been more aptly asserted. The precise purpose of the Fourteenth Amendment was to assure that supremacy where the states failed or refused to protect the rights of their citizens. That failure was apparent.

The Court's intervention in Alabama's affairs rested on its determination that its conduct was necessary to preserve constitutional rights and defend them against state procedural stultification, and it found precedents of a sort to bolster its actions. But beyond that facile dependence on precedent lay the fact that the Court had harked back to a realization that protection of the rights of Negroes was the *all-pervading purpose* and command of the Civil War Amendments, a realization that carried with it an acknowledgment that almost one hundred years of deference to state control and regulation of civil rights had failed to reach the end envisaged by the amendments.[17] Justice Bradley's witless dictum in the 80-year-old *Civil Rights Cases* that the time had come when the Negro's rights could be "vindicated by resort to the laws of the State for redress" was as bankrupt of reality in 1964 as it was when uttered in 1883.

What Alabama demonstrated in hostility to the rights of its Negro citizens, Virginia, Florida, Arkansas, and Louisiana confirmed with their persistent efforts to cripple the NAACP and expose its members to private reprisals and violence. These purposes were not ends in themselves but efforts to subvert and undermine Supreme Court civil rights decisions, particularly the rulings in the School Cases. State control and supervision of civil rights had yielded not protection for Negro citizens but a shameless harvest of racial discrimination. And here again, the Supreme Court could find no remedy except a return to that federal protection and control of civil rights interwoven in the fabric of the Civil War Amendments.

What the Court learned for itself as to the necessity for restoration of federal supremacy in the area of civil rights, it taught the nation. As its decisions laid bare the cauldron of racial discrimination that bubbled beneath the surface of southern life, the Court's decisions, more than any other single factor, prepared the way for change to enlarged federal action. The first changes were mild enough: the federal Civil Rights Acts of 1957 and 1960.

Every social reform is pregnant with the promise, or threat, of further reform; every social change arms its beneficiaries with the possibilities of exacting more change.[18] Segregationists had a phrase for these truths: "Give the nigger an inch," they said, "and he'll want a mile." Suddenly and almost without warning, Negro students turned to new tactics in 1960 in an attempt to walk that next mile toward equality. The Supreme Court was soon wrestling with a new set of constitutional problems in the sit-in cases.

> *They sat down that they might
> grow tall—tall like men, tall
> like free men.*

ANONYMOUS

On February 1, 1960, four freshmen students of North Carolina Agricultural and Technical College at Greensboro walked into the Woolworth five-and-ten-cent store, seated themselves at the white lunch counter, and asked for coffee. The manager said he couldn't serve Negroes because of local customs. They just sat and waited. At the obvious prompting of the manager, some Negro employees of the store came out and told the boys they were doing a bad thing. They did not reply. Other Negro students shopping in the store looked at them, some in wonder, some in amazement, but all in silence. Franklin McClain, Joseph McNeil, David Richmond, and Ezell Blair didn't even know that the date they chose was the ninety-fifth anniversary of Freedom Day as proclaimed by Abraham Lincoln for February 1, 1865. Their actions were the result of "bull sessions" in which they engaged after nightly studies with endless complaints to each other about North Carolina's segregation laws and customs. The previous night, Sunday, McNeil announced that he was going to start a boycott of Woolworth's the next day and said that the others would be "chicken" if they didn't join him. No college freshman can afford to be chicken; the other three had to go along.

Five years later, they had slipped into obscurity, their very names forgotten. But they had lit the fuse that would precipitate a great constitutional debate. Before that crisis had been resolved, the Supreme Court of the United States had solemnly considered a score of cases involving breach of the peace, trespass, freedom of speech and assemblage, and the meaning of the Fourteenth Amendment, for the right the students had asserted lay close to the hearts of all Negroes. Moreover, the duty of an innkeeper to serve all who applied for food was rooted deeply in the common law, so deeply that among the first equalitarian statutes enacted after the Civil War were laws forbidding discrimination in places of public accommodation. Even Mississippi once had and enforced such a law.[1]

Laws forbidding discrimination in places of public accommodation have a symbolism of their own. Those who can be denied services in places of *public* accommodation for other than purely personal reasons are pariahs and outcasts among men—they are in truth nonpeople. Negroes knew without further asking that a state that lacked such a law was a state in which their rights were neglected and they were subject to discrimination in all other aspects of their lives. Americans knew without much reflection—they simply felt it in their bones—that the 1883 Supreme Court's invalidation of the Civil Rights Act of 1875 marked the beginning of the end of the Negro's quest for full equality under the Civil War Amendments. The end man in Haverly's minstrel show at the Atlanta Opera House interrupted the performance to announce the decision to the audience and, while Negroes sat in stunned silence, the dress-circle and orchestra seat holders stood and gave three rousing cheers. Eighty years later, the most bitterly fought section of the new federal Civil Rights Act of 1964 was that forbidding discrimination in places of public accommodation.

Long before the upsurge of sit-ins, Negroes had been casting about for ways and means of gaining access to places of public accommodation. Discrimination had been considerably weakened in the North and West through revival of older laws as well as passage of new legislation. Such discrimination was particularly galling in Washington, as the capital of the nation, and was wiped out by a judicial windfall. In its self-rule days, the District of Columbia prohibited discrimination of service by restaurants and similar places to "well-behaved and respectable persons" by an 1872 enactment. Violators were subject to criminal prosecution. The law was codified in the 1894 statutes but was dropped from the 1901 code, with no notation or record as to repeal, apparently because it had fallen into disuse. District of Columbia law enforcement authorities were prodded into resurrecting it after the Truman Committee's civil rights report of 1948. In 1953, the Supreme Court held through Chief Justice Vinson in *John R. Thompson v. District of Columbia*[2] that the law was in full force and effect and had not been superseded by congressional legislation of 1878. President Eisenhower seized the occasion to urge the end of all discrimination in places of public accommodation, and almost total discrimination and segregation in Washington hotels, restaurants, and like places vanished overnight.

Discrimination in bus terminal restaurants was struck a heavy blow in 1960, when the Supreme Court, speaking through Justice Black, upset a Virginia conviction of Bruce Boynton, a Howard law student, for his refusal to leave the "white" counter in a Richmond station. The Court held, over the dissents of Justices Whittaker and Clark, that as an interstate passenger, he was subjected to "undue or unreasonable" treatment under the Interstate Commerce Act when refused service at a restaurant located in a terminal which was an integral aspect of passenger service. The case, *Boynton v. Virginia*,[3] rested on the principles announced in the Mitchell and Henderson cases and, while important in the instance of bus travelers, had no application to privately owned restaurants or places of public accommodation. Justices Whittaker and Clark could find no evidence that the bus companies had any control or interest in the restaurant.

These were important but piecemeal victories that left discrimination intact in southern cities and towns. Students wanted more.

After February 1, 1960, sit-ins spread like a wild prairie brushfire over the South. Restless Negro students swept their sometimes disapproving elders along with them as they barged into restaurants for sit-ins, into the ocean for wade-ins, and into churches for pray-ins. White students joined them. Sit-ins flowered into street demonstrations and into parades and finally into Freedom Rides. Stunned and panicky southern states struck back with hasty and ill-considered arrests under old breach-of-the-peace statutes, trespass laws, or makeshift ordinances regulating parades. The prime legal difficulty facing the states was that the laws they tried to apply had been enacted to meet other law enforcement needs long before sit-ins were conceived and were ill adapted to exigencies of the new situation. Adoption of the nonviolent technique by the sit-inners and demonstrators robbed breach-of-peace laws of much of their vitality and applicability, while the sharp edge of trespass laws was blunted by the fact that the sit-inners chose variety stores to which they were welcome in all departments except the restaurant or café —they were not trespassers in the stores.

The first sit-in case to reach the Supreme Court came from Louisiana as *Garner v. Louisiana*[4] and was decided on December 11, 1961. Sixteen students were arrested in Baton Rouge for disturbing the peace after they had refused to leave lunch counters when asked to do so by proprietors. Three cases were combined: one involving a drug store, another the Kress department store, and the third a lunch counter in a bus terminal. The stores involved welcomed Negro patronage and did not discriminate except at their lunch counters, while the bus company maintained separate counters for the races. There was no evidence that the students had done anything except sit peaceably at the counters when asked to move. The trial court decided that the students at the drug store had done an "act . . . in a manner calculated to, and [one that] actually did, unreasonably disturb or alarm the public"; that the Kress sit-inners' conduct was "an act, on their part, as would unreasonably disturb or alarm the public," and that the bus sit-in students were guilty of conduct which "foreseeably could alarm and disturb the public." The state penal code defined as a misdemeanor fighting, use of loud or boisterous language, appearing in an intoxicated condition, engaging in loud and tumultuous conduct by three or more persons, holding an unlawful assembly, interruption of a lawful assembly of people, or the "Commission of any other act in such a manner as to unreasonably disturb or alarm the public." The judge found all defendants guilty and sentenced them to 30-day jail terms and fines of $100. He was upheld by the state supreme court.

The Supreme Court was unanimous in reversing all convictions, but there were four opinions: one by Chief Justice Warren, joined by Justices Black, Whittaker, Clark, Brennan, and Stewart; and others by Justice Frankfurter, Justice Douglas, and Justice Harlan. Although all agreed on reversal in this case, the varying points of view bared important differences that would emerge as fundamental before and after sit-in litigation was settled.

Quite simply, Chief Justice Warren, speaking for the majority, held that there was *no* evidence upon which to base a conviction and that, as a consequence, the defendants had been denied due process of law as prescribed by the Fourteenth Amendment.

That resolution of the case drew its support from a prior case involving Sam Thompson, a Louisville ne'er-do-well who was fined ten dollars in a magistrate's court for loitering and disorderly conduct. The only evidence against him was that he was found in a public restaurant, patting his foot to the rhythm of jukebox music, when officers made a routine check of the place. He had 60 prior arrests, and the officers decided to "run him in" on a loitering charge. Officers said that when he protested, "we placed a disorderly on him." At the trial, it appeared that he had a place to live, did odd jobs for a living, and that he had bought a can of beer in the restaurant the afternoon of his arrest. The proprietor of the restaurant had no fault to find with his conduct. The Supreme Court, speaking through Justice Black, reversed his conviction in *Thompson v. Louisville*[5] in 1960, and in the process announced the very important principle that "it is a violation of due process to convict and punish a man without evidence of his guilt." [6]

What Chief Justice Warren said in the Garner case was that sit-inners could not be found guilty of disturbing the peace when they did nothing except sit peaceably at a lunch counter. There was *no* evidence. He rejected the argument that their mere presence might provoke their opponents to violence. It was, he said, no "breach of the peace for [them] to sit peacefully in a place where custom decreed they should not sit. Such activity, in the circumstances of these cases, is not evidence of any crime and cannot be so considered either by the police or the courts." The sit-inners had won an important victory.

Justice Frankfurter said in his concurrence that there was no "evidence of disturbance or alarm in the behavior of café employees or customers or even passers-by." The inference was that if such disturbance had been proved, there might have been a basis for conviction. But, he said, "Conviction under this Louisiana statute cannot be sustained by reliance upon likely consequences in the generality of cases. Since particular persons are being sent to jail for conduct allegedly having a particular effect on particular occasion under particular circumstances, it becomes necessary to appraise that conduct and its effect by the particularity of evidence adduced." His subtleties would have narrowed the sit-inners' victory.

Justice Douglas was dissatisfied with that disposition of the case by his colleague. He was convinced that the mere presence of Negro sit-inners might lead to serious breaches of the peace in a state such as Louisiana, and he said he would have difficulty in reversing the cases under Chief Justice Warren's assessment of the issues. But, he thought, "the constitutional questions must be reached and they make reversal necessary." A state, he reminded his colleagues, acts through legislation, through executive action, through judicial action, and by enforcement of local customs. He reviewed history to show that Louisiana had a long custom of racial segregation and that in 1960 its legislature had proclaimed it "is the intention of the citizens of this sovereign state that such policy be continued." He deemed it "plain that the proprietors in the instant cases were segregating . . . pursuant to Louisiana's customs."

Drawing upon the first Justice Harlan's dissent in *Plessy v. Ferguson*, Justice Douglas said that "It is my view that a State may not constitutionally enforce a policy of segregation in restaurant facilities." A restaurant was a *public* place, and it was required to secure a license to do business in the state, he pointed out. And, he protested, "those who license enterprises for public use should not have under our Constitution the power to license it for the use of only one race." He found forbidden state action in support of racial discrimination in the cases before the Court and closed with the first Justice Harlan's stirring words that ". . . in view of the Constitution, in the eye of the law, there is in this country no superior, dominant, ruling class of citizens. There is no caste here. Our Constitution is color-blind. . . ."

The second Justice Harlan was not persuaded by Justice Douglas's quotation from his illustrious grandfather. His views were more restricted. He thought the generalized breach-of-the-peace statutes did not fit the situation in the sit-in cases before the Court and that the statute under which they were prosecuted suffered from vagueness in application. He would have set aside the convictions on that ground. In a long and discursive opinion, he also arrived at the conclusion that the drug store and Kress sit-inners were exercising a right of freedom of speech with the implied consent of the owners and that the evidence was not conclusive as to whether such consent was given in the bus counter case. Therefore, he agreed that the convictions should be reversed, but he ended with a strong intimation that Louisiana might enact an enforceable law to proscribe the conduct of sit-inners under similar circumstances. It was plain that he did not share Justice Douglas's viewpoint that the Fourteenth Amendment prohibited discrimination by restaurant keepers.

The next of such cases to reach the Court did not settle the fundamental issue. Leverett Taylor and six companions went to the Shreveport bus terminal as an aftermath of the Freedom Rides. Taylor and three of them went to the white waiting room, while the other three sat outside in an automobile. All were arrested and convicted of disturbing the peace, after they refused to move on at the command of the chief of police. The statute under which they were convicted defined a breach of peace as the conduct of any person who went "with others . . . in or upon . . . any . . . public place or building . . . and who fails to disperse or move on" when ordered by proper authorities. The record showed that Taylor and his companions were "quiet, orderly and polite" and that, although others in the waiting room grew quite excited, there was no violence. Their convictions by Louisiana courts were upset by the Supreme Court in *Taylor v. Louisiana*,[7] decided June 4, 1962, in a summary and unsigned opinion, on the ground that the "only evidence was that [they] were violating a custom that segregated people in waiting rooms according to their race, a practice not allowed in interstate transportation facilities." Again, there was *no* evidence of wrongdoing. Justice Harlan disagreed with that disposition of the case; he thought it should have been set down for argument and exploration of the question. Justice Frankfurter took no part in the proceedings because of illness.

The second cluster of sit-in cases decided by the Court involved state trespass statutes in five actions and a breach-of-the-peace law in a sixth. The five cases involving trespass arose out of restaurant sit-ins, and the other from use of a public playground. All were announced on two court days, May 20 and 21, 1963, with Chief Justice Warren speaking for the majority and upsetting convictions in all cases, one each from South Carolina, Louisiana, North Carolina, and Georgia, and two from Alabama. Justice Douglas wrote a special concurring opinion in the Louisiana case that had significance for all restaurant cases; Justice Harlan dissented in four cases, concurred in some aspects of the South Carolina case, and joined in a unanimous opinion in the Georgia case.

In the bellwether case, *Peterson v. City of Greenville*,[8] that South Carolina city had an ordinance prohibiting Negroes and white persons from dining together. A South Carolina statute aimed at sit-in demonstrations defined trespass as failure or refusal to leave a place of business after a request to do so. The evidence showed plainly that the ten students involved had violated that statute. There was no room to argue that there was *no* evidence to support a conviction. The Chief Justice rested the reversal on the ground that a state cannot compel racial discrimination by law or ordinance. He said that the "conviction had the effect, which the State cannot deny, of enforcing the ordinance passed by the city . . . an agency of the State. When a state passes a law compelling persons to discriminate against other persons because of race, and the State's criminal processes are employed in a way which enforces the discrimination mandated by law . . . [there is] a palpable violation of the Fourteenth Amendment. . . ." The sit-inners had taken a new forward stride; they could not be prosecuted for a sit-in demonstration in protest of state-imposed segregation.

Louisiana had no law, and New Orleans no ordinance, requiring segregation in public eating places. In 1960, the state enacted what it called a public mischief statute, obviously intended to fit the sit-in situation, which provided that any person who took temporary possession of a part of a business and failed to leave the store after a request to do so was guilty of a misdemeanor. Four college students, three Negroes and one white, went to a white lunch counter and announced they would sit there until served. They were arrested, convicted, and fined under the 1960 law, although they were orderly and polite. Prior to their sit-in, the superintendent of police and mayor of New Orleans had issued statements praising the "good race relations of the city" and announcing that "such demonstrations [must] cease and that henceforth they [will] be prohibited by the police department." The Court reviewed the convictions in *Lombard v. Louisiana*[9] and found that "the evidence all tended to indicate that the store officials' actions were coerced by the city." That being so, the Chief Justice said, the convictions could not stand, because "A State or a city may act as authoritatively through its executive as through its legislative body. . . . Consequently, the city must be treated as if it had an ordinance. . . . The official command here was to direct continuance of segregated service in restaurants, and to prohibit any conduct directed toward its discontinuance. . . ." The sit-inners had scored another triumph: in the absence of a discriminatory ordinance, public authorities could not lend assistance to segregation in restaurants.

In the case of *Avent v. North Carolina*,[10] the Supreme Court told that state's highest court to reconsider the conviction of John Thomas Avent and five other Negro and two white students who sat in at a Durham luncheonette. Durham had a segregative ordinance, but the students were arrested by a city police officer and convicted for violation of a state trespass statute. Birmingham, Alabama, ordinances required segregation in places serving food. James Gober and ten other Negro students were convicted of violating a state trespass statute for sitting in at a department store lunch counter, only to have the Supreme Court reverse the convictions in *Gober v. Alabama*[11] for the reasons explained in the Peterson case. Two Negro ministers, the Reverend Fred Shuttlesworth and C. Billups, had been convicted of inciting a misdemeanor by aiding and abetting the conduct of Gober and his companions, but they were freed in *Shuttlesworth v. Alabama*[12] on Chief Justice Warren's holding that "there can be no conviction for aiding and abetting someone to do an innocent act"—Gober was innocent and those who counseled him to sit in were likewise innocent.

Justice Douglas concurred in a written opinion in the Lombard case to bolster the views he had expressed in the earlier Louisiana cases. He cited an old English case of 1701, in which a court had held that an innkeeper must serve all applicants because he has "made Profession of a Trade which is for the Public Good. . . ." The law of innkeepers had followed that precedent, he said, and it seemed to him that an American restaurant keeper cannot discriminate on racial grounds where state action is found. He cited the race restriction cases to show that judicial action is state action and argued that where a state court imposed a penalty against a person seeking service in a public restaurant, there was sufficient state action to invoke the equal-protection and due-process clauses of the Fourteenth Amendment. Restaurant keepers are state licensees, he also pointed out, adding that "There is no constitutional way, as I see it, in which a State can license and supervise a business serving the public and endow it with the authority to manage that business on the basis of *apartheid* which is foreign to our Constitution."

Justice Harlan wrote a blanket opinion, partially in dissent and partially in concurrence, of all the cases. His chief concern, he said, was with the state action issue. He was especially alert to the need for preserving the limitations of the Fourteenth Amendment as forbidding only discriminatory action by the states and *not* private individuals. "Freedom of the individual to choose his associates or his neighbors, to use and dispose of his property as he sees fit, to be irrational, arbitrary, capricious, even unjust in his personal relations are things all entitled to a large measure of protection from governmental interference," he wrote. "This liberty would be overridden, in the name of equality, if the strictures of the Amendment were applied to governmental and private action without distinction . . . there are areas of private rights upon which the federal power should not lay a heavy hand and which should properly be left to the more precise instruments of local authority." His was the timeworn argument in favor of state regulation, control, and supervision of civil rights.

He seemed to be unaware of the fact that the framers of the Fourteenth Amendment had made a deliberate choice that the "federal power should lay . . . a heavy hand" on state control and regulation of civil rights and that the well-being of Negro citizens should not be "left to the more precise instruments of local authority," out of the historically justified fear that "local authority" would maintain and perpetuate racial discrimination. The very problems before the Court were the problems the Fourteenth Amendment was designed to solve by asserting the supremacy of federal power.

Justice Harlan did not doubt that state-compelled discrimination against Negroes offended the guarantees of the amendment, but he insisted that the private restaurant keepers might have chosen to segregate customers even without the compulsion of law. He would have left it to trial courts to determine whether the segregation was the result of law or the free choice of the proprietor, and if it was the free choice of the proprietor, he could see no compelling state action. In his view, proprietors were free to discriminate if they chose. Therefore, he would have reversed the North Carolina, Louisiana, and the two Alabama cases and remanded them to the states for a determination of whether or not the proprietors discriminated in response to laws or ordinances or of their own volition. As for the Greenville, South Carolina, case, he pointed to the proprietor's testimony that the city ordinance required segregation. "That," he said, "suffices to establish state action and leads me to join the judgment of the Court."

In the case of *Wright v. Georgia*,[13] six young Negroes were convicted of disturbing the peace because they played basketball in a "white public park" in Savannah on January 23, 1961. No disturbance of any kind resulted, but they were arrested by a city police officer and convicted. A unanimous Court agreed with Chief Justice Warren that disturbance-of-the-peace charges could not be based on a refusal to obey an unconstitutional order of the police to leave the park or upon the vague fear that the exercise of constitutional rights by a Negro might lead to disorder.

At the same term, the Court summarily reversed without opinions five sit-in cases from Virginia and ordered that state's courts to reconsider them in the light of what it had said in the Peterson and Avent cases.[14]

Accompanying sit-in cases were mass marches of Negro students on state capitols or city halls, leading to mass convictions for breach of the peace. In *Edwards v. South Carolina*,[15] decided February 25, 1963, that state's supreme court upheld the convictions for breaches of the peace against 187 Negro students who marched on the state capitol in Columbia. The students' avowed purpose was to "submit a protest to the citizens of South Carolina, along with the Legislative Bodies of South Carolina, with our feelings and our dissatisfaction with the present condition of discriminatory actions against Negroes. . . ." There was no evidence of violence on the part of students or onlookers. Over the dissent of Justice Clark, the Supreme Court reversed the convictions, on the ground that rights of freedom of speech and petition, as guaranteed by the Constitution, had been infringed. Justice Stewart said for the Court that the "Fourteenth Amendment does not permit a State to make criminal the peaceful expression of unpopular views." In another case, 349 Negro students marched on the main business section of Orangeburg, South Carolina, and were also convicted of a breach of the peace, only to have their convictions reversed in a summary and unsigned opinion in *Fields v. South Carolina*,[16] March 18, 1963, on the authority of the Edwards case. Negro students could not only sit in to gain their objectives; they could conduct mass marches to advertise those grievances.

The historian will be struck with the fact that in every case in which it granted review—as it did in most cases—the Supreme Court upset convictions upheld by state courts of last resort in the great sit-in controversy. Time and again, the Court put its own construction on the facts and came to conclusions opposed to those of the state courts. Federal supremacy was asserted with a vengeance, and no ingenious interpretation of state laws governing breach of the peace, unlawful assembly, or trespass was availing against what seemed the obvious determination of the Supreme Court to protect sit-in defendants against the wrath of the states. These decisions had significance beyond protection of individual rights: they left the students and their sympathizers free to pursue their massive assault on discrimination in places of public accommodation, to keep the controversy open, and to marshal public sentiment for congressional action.

A last wave of sit-in cases reached the Court before Congress finally enacted the Civil Rights Act of 1964, two from South Carolina, one from Florida, and two from Maryland. And again the students emerged as victors and upset state court convictions. The decisions were all announced on June 22, 1964.

In *Barr v. City of Columbia*,[17] convictions of five Negro sit-in defendants on charges of breach of the peace were overturned on the ground that there was no evidence that their peaceful conduct created any breach. In *Robinson v. Florida,* the Court held that state regulations requiring separate toilet and lavatory facilities for Negro and white customers embodied "state policy putting burdens to discourage the serving of the two races together" and consequently constituted state action to coerce segregation. Justice Black wrote both opinions.[18] He disagreed with the Court majority on the issue of the validity of trespass convictions.

In *Bell v. Maryland*,[19] Justice Brennan spoke for a six-to-three Court majority which held that sit-in convictions should be reversed because Maryland later enacted a public accommodations statute forbidding racial discrimination. Thus, a Negro's request for service that had been held to constitute trespass before passage of the law was thereafter permitted. Justice Brennan said it was unlikely that a "legislature which passes a public accommodations law making it unlawful to deny service on account of race [desired] that persons should still be prosecuted and punished for the 'crime' of seeking service from a place of public accommodation which denies it on account of race." [20] The case was sent back to the Maryland courts for a consideration of that issue, over the dissents of Justices Black, Harlan, and White.

In *Griffin v. Maryland*,[21] two groups of individuals were convicted of trespass in connection with a demonstration against a privately owned amusement park. They were arrested and jailed by a deputy sheriff who was also a guard employed by the park. Chief Justice Warren and a six-to-three majority held that his participation as a state officer, a deputy sheriff, constituted state action in aid of discrimination as forbidden by the Fourteenth Amendment.[22] Again, Justices Black, Harlan, and White disagreed.

In *Bouie v. South Carolina*, Justice Brennan was spokesman for a six-to-three majority that held that two Negroes were not guilty of violation of a state trespass statute, because they had entered the store with the permission of the management and were arrested only when they sought lunch counter service.[23] The South Carolina law was held to have no application to persons who refused to leave a store after a lawful entry, with Justices Black, Harlan, and White in the minority. Four other trespass cases were summarily disposed of by remanding them to state courts for consideration in light of what had been said in the five cases, and another was summarily reversed outright on the basis of the Bouie case.[24]

Again, Negroes had emerged winning in the Supreme Court after state convictions. The Court had clung to its policy of rebuffing the state courts and had insisted on putting its own construction on the facts. But the practical unanimity of the earlier cases was shattered, as has been indicated. There were strong and insistent dissents from Justices Black, Harlan, and White in the *trespass* convictions in all the cases. Even more important, the cases opened up a great constitutional controversy, with Chief Justice Warren and Justices Douglas and Goldberg ranged on one end, Justices Harlan, Black, and White on the opposite pole, and Justices Stewart, Clark, and Brennan occupying middle ground and taking no part in the debate. That debate involved the fundamental meaning and thrust of the Fourteenth Amendment and was opened by a special concurring opinion by Justice Douglas in *Bell v. Maryland*. Nothing like it in the area of civil rights had been heard, or written in the Court, since the first Justice Harlan had disputed his colleagues in the *Civil Rights Cases* and in *Plessy v. Ferguson*.

"I reach the merits of this controversy," Justice Douglas said in opening the debate. "The time is ripe for decision and [those] who have been convicted of asking for service . . . are entitled to an answer to their complaint here and now." He cited the long time-lag between the date the case had reached the Court and the date of decision. "The whole Nation," he wrote, "has to face the issue; Congress is conscientiously considering it; some municipalities have had to make it their first order of business; law enforcement officials are deeply implicated, north as well as south; the question is at the root of demonstrations, unrest, riots, and violence in various areas. . . . Yet we stand mute, avoiding decision of the issue by an obvious pretense."

It seemed to him that the Negro customer and the restaurant owner "each claims protection by the Constitution and tenders the Fourteenth Amendment as justification for his action. Yet we leave resolution of the conflict to others, when, if our voices were heard, the issues for the Congress and for the public would become clear and precise. The Court was created to sit in troubled times as well as in peaceful days." For him the answer was clear: The Civil War Amendments had "one pervading purpose . . . we mean the freedom of the slave race, the security and firm establishment of that freedom, and the protection of the newly-made free man and citizen from . . . oppression of those who had formerly exercised unlimited domination over him." Those words, he pointed out, had been written by the Court in 1873 in the *Slaughter House Cases*. He said that "prior to the Amendments Negroes were segregated and disallowed the use of public accommodations unless the owners chose to serve them. To affirm these judgments [of conviction in the sit-in cases] would remit those Negroes to their old status and allow the States to keep them there by force of police and their judiciary."

Justice Douglas then reviewed history. Civil rights created by the Civil War Amendments, he insisted, "owe their existence to the Federal Government, its national character, its Constitution, or its laws." And, he said boldly, "the right to be served in places of public accommodation is an incident of national citizenship." He returned to what he had said in the Lombard case about the historical duty of the innkeeper to serve all travelers and to the license requirements of the states. "Segregation of Negroes in the restaurants and lunch counters . . . is a relic of slavery," he believed. States act, he argued, by their executive, their legislative, and their judicial arms, and he drew on *Shelley v. Kraemer,* the race restriction case, to assert that where state law was used to protect or conserve segregation or discrimination, there was state action condemned by the equal-protection clause of the Fourteeth Amendment. "When the state police, the state prosecutor and the state courts unite to convict Negroes for renouncing that relic of slavery, the state violates the Fourteenth Amendment." In a lengthy appendix, he showed that the restaurant business was largely in the hands of corporations that had no "personal" prejudices or predilections and were not entitled to claim protection for their "rights" to "choose" business associates or friends. The corporate claim to segregate or discriminate was only a consideration for profits, he urged. And he found no merit in the claim that constitutional guarantees armed the corporation with the privilege of closing its doors to those citizens protected by the Civil War Amendments. He cited the dissent of the first Justice Harlan in the *Civil Rights Cases* of 1883 as undergirding his argument and his views.

Justice Goldberg, with whom the Chief Justice joined in another concurring opinion, agreed with much, perhaps most, of what Justice Douglas said. He was sure of one thing: "the Constitution guarantees to all Americans the right to be treated as equal members of the community with respect of public accommodations." He centered his first fire on the dissenting argument that "the Constitution permits American citizens to be denied access to places of public accommodation solely because of their race or color." That view, he wrote, "does not do justice to a constitution which is color-blind. . . . The denial of the constitutional right of Negroes to access to places of public accommodation would perpetuate a caste system in the United States."

After a lengthy review of the debates on the Fourteenth Amendment at the time of its proposal, Justice Goldberg came to the conclusion that the framers intended to protect the common-law right of all persons to service in places of public accommodation. That was a "civil right," he argued, and not a "social right." He took another look at the phrase *equal protection of the laws* and called attention to the fact that Justice Bradley who had written the *Civil Rights Cases* majority opinion had written Justice Woods that "denying includes inaction as well as the omission to pass laws for protection." Therefore, he reasoned, Maryland's "inaction" in failing to pass laws for the protection of Negroes who sought the use of public accommodations gave the Court a constitutional warrant to strike down the use of penal laws to abet racial discrimination. "The constitutional right of all Americans to be treated as equal members of the community with respect to public accommodations is a civil right granted by the people in the Constitution—a right which is 'too important in our free society to be stripped of all protection,'" he concluded.

Obviously, Justices Douglas and Goldberg and Chief Justice Warren were as irked at the failure of Justices Clark, Stewart, and Brennan for their refusal to come to grips with the constitutional issue as they were with Justices Black, Harlan, and White for their rejection of the proposition that the Fourteenth Amendment, *per se*, doomed discrimination in places of public accommodation. But neither Justice Clark, nor Stewart or Brennan, made any rejoinder —they were content to leave the matter to Congress. Justice Black, however, spoke for the trio to which he belonged. It was a strange combination—Justice Black, a great and sincere southern libertarian who had spoken out so many times and with such a clear voice against all racial discrimination; Justice Harlan, grandson of the great dissenter in the *Civil Rights Cases* from whose dissent Justice Douglas had borrowed so many ideas and phrases, and Justice White, northern-born, northern-educated lawyer, who had given his heart to legal niceties that seemed to preclude his understanding of the *Realpolitik* of the closed, segregated society of the South.

Justice Black made it plain that his rejection of the view that the Fourteenth Amendment could not be applied as Justice Douglas or Justice Goldberg demanded did not mean that he rejected the idea that Congress could not legislate to reach those ends. It was the essence of his position that Congress had not legislated. There was, he said, nothing in the Fourteenth Amendment that forbids a "state to prosecute for crimes committed against a person or his property however prejudiced or narrow the victim's views may be. . . . It would betray our whole plan for a tranquil and orderly society to say that a citizen, because of his personal prejudices, habits, attitudes, or beliefs, is cast outside the law's protection and cannot call for the aid of officers sworn to uphold the law and perserve the peace."

He turned to the congressional debates on the Civil War Amendments and could find little to uphold Justice Douglas's view that the framers intended to ban discrimination in places of public accommodation by force of the Fourteenth Amendment itself. He pointed out that Senator Charles Sumner, perhaps the greatest of the abolitionist lawmakers, was the author of the 1875 Civil Rights Act to prohibit such discrimination and did not entertain the view that the Fourteenth Amendment prohibited discrimination by an innkeeper. "The Court," he said, "has done much in carrying out its solemn duty to protect people from unlawful discrimination. . . . But the Fourteenth Amendment itself does not compel either a black man or a white man running his own private business to trade with anyone against his will. We do not believe that section I of the Fourteenth Amendment was written or designed to interfere with a storekeeper's right to choose his customers, his social or his business associates, so long as he does not run counter to valid state or federal regulations." Until the state or federal legislature acted, he was saying, discrimination by the restaurant keeper was permissible.

Turning to the argument that pickets and sit-inners were only exercising their right to freedom of speech, Justice Black said that the "right to freedom of speech is a right to express views—not a right to force other people to supply a platform or a pulpit. It is argued that this supposed right to invade other people's property would not mean that a man's home, his private club, or his church could be forcibly entered—only his store or place of business which he has himself 'opened to the public.' But the whole quarrel . . . was that instead of being open to all, the restaurant refused to serve Negroes."

Justice Black found nothing in the Shelley case that supported his opponents' views, for, he said, that case rested on the proposition that there was a willing buyer and a willing seller whose transaction had been interfered with by the state for racial reasons. In the case before the Court, he pointed out, there was no state statute, rule, or regulation of any kind imposing or requiring or encouraging discrimination. The licensing argument, on which Justice Douglas had placed such reliance, had no cogency for Justice Black. "Businesses owned by private persons do not become agencies of a State because they are licensed; to hold that they do would be completely to negate our private ownership concepts and practices," he said.

"At times," Justice Black concluded, "the rule of law seems too slow to some for the settlement of their grievance. But it is the plan our Nation has chosen to preserve both 'Liberty' and equality for all. On that plan we have put our trust and staked our future. This constitutional rule of law has served us well. Maryland's trespass law does not depart from it. Nor shall we."

There the argument rested. It was inconclusive. Neither side had come to grips with the fact that the 1964 debate arose out of the monumental error of the Supreme Court when it invalidated the 1875 Civil Rights Act, by which Congress had sought to implement the equalitarianism that suffused the Civil War Amendments.

The debate took place in June, 1964. A month later, the filibuster blockade broke and Congress enacted another civil rights act prohibiting discrimination in places of public accommodation. The Court had a second chance to decide how far Congress could go in opening the doors of such places and removing the brand placed on Negro citizens. The answer was certain and sure. It came six months later from a unanimous Court.

Yesterday is a wind gone down,
A sun set in the west.

CARL SANDBURG

Bird Cee had to wait eight years, from 1875 to 1883, to get a Supreme Court answer to his complaint that Murray Stanley had violated the Civil Rights Act of 1875 in refusing to serve him because he was a person of color. When the answer came, it was adverse: the Court said that Mr. Stanley was well within his rights in refusing to serve Negroes at his Kansas restaurant despite what the act said. It took Lester Maddox less than eight months to get a Supreme Court answer to his insistence that he, too, was within his rights in refusing to serve persons of color despite the Civil Rights Act of 1964. He also got an adverse answer: the Court said that Mr. Maddox was a law violator for closing his doors against Negroes at his Georgia restaurant. There was precious little difference between the Civil Rights Act of 1875 and the Civil Rights Act of 1964, insofar as each prohibited racial discrimination in places of public accommodation. Not a word, not a syllable, not a phrase of the Fourteenth Amendment had been changed from 1875 to 1964. The commerce clause of the Constitution remained unchanged. Yet the Court had held the 1875 Act unconstitutional and the 1964 Act constitutional.

There were two quick test cases of the 1964 Civil Rights Act: *Heart of Atlanta Motel v. United States* and *Katzenbach v. McClung,*[1] argued at the same time and decided on the same day, December 14, 1964. In each case, the decision was unanimously in favor of constitutionality, with Justice Clark writing the Court's opinion and with Justices Douglas, Goldberg, and Black each writing special concurring opinions.

The 1964 Act rested on two constitutional grounds: (1) that Congress could prohibit racial discrimination in business establishments, under its power to regulate the conduct of business enterprises engaged in interstate commerce or where their business affected interstate commerce under the commerce clause, that section of the Constitution which gives Congress jurisdiction to "regulate Commerce with foreign Nations, and among the several states . . ." and to "make all Laws which shall be necessary and proper for carrying" that section into effect, and (2) that Congress had such power under Section 5 of the Fourteenth Amendment, which provides that "The Congress shall have power to enforce, by appropriate legislation, the provisions of this article," because one of the provisions of the amendment requires equal protection of the laws.

The act also declared that segregation or discrimination was supported by state action when carried on under color of any law, statute, ordinance, regulation, or any custom or usage required or enforced by officials of the state or any of its subdivisions. It declared that all persons "shall be entitled to be free, at any establishment or place, from driscrimination or segregation of any kind on the ground of race, color, religion, or national origin, if such discrimination or segregation is or purports to be required by any law, statute, or ordinance, regulation, rule or order of a state or any agency or political subdivision thereof."

In sum, Congress had asserted its authority to prohibit segregation or discrimination in places of public accommodation under (1) the commerce clause, (2) under Section 5 of the Fourteenth Amendment, or (3) under that interpretation of the Fourteenth Amendment which limited such power to prohibition of "state action" in aid of segregation or discrimination. It left nothing to chance.

The broad. almost unlimited, power of Congress to decide for itself what activities affect interstate commerce is part of an old constitutional story. Chief Justice John Marshall speaking for the Court interpreted the commerce clause in a famous case in 1824 and gave it broad content and sweeping meaning. It meant, he said, "that these words comrephend every species of commercial intercourse. . . . No sort of trade can be carried on . . . to which this power does not extend." [2] He found that "This power, like all others vested in Congress, is complete in itself, may be exercised to its utmost extent, and acknowledges no limitations, other than those prescribed in the Constitution." Under that sweeping language, Congress has long been able to have power to regulate business establishments using articles moving in interstate commerce, the conduct of persons dealing with such articles, and interstate travelers. Justice Clark had no difficulty in dredging up a spate of cases under the commerce clause supporting what Congress had done in the 1964 Civil Rights Act.

The Heart of Atlanta case involved a large Georgia motel that advertised in national magazines for patronage, entertained national conventions, and three-fourths of whose patronage came from out-of-state guests. Much of the food it served moved in interstate commerce. The Katzenbach case involved a Birmingham, Alabama, family-owned restaurant that "purchased locally $150,000 worth of food, $69,783 of which was meat that it bought from a local supplier who had procured it from outside the State . . . a substantial portion of the food served in the restaurant had moved in interstate commerce." The Atlanta motel sued the United States to prevent enforcement of the Civil Rights Act; Nicholas deB. Katzenbach, as U. S. Attorney General, sued Ollie McClung, as proprietor of the Birmingham barbecue place, to restrain him from discriminating against Negro applicants for food and service.

The results were predictable. The Supreme Court found the 1964 Act valid, insofar as it rested on the commerce clause for congressional authority to enact public accommodation statutes. Ultimately, injunctions were issued restraining both places from racial discrimination. In our increasingly closely knit society with constant growth of interstate commerce, it is plain that virtually all places of public accommodation are subject to terms of the act, except those small enterprises specifically exempted by congressional fiat.

The determination that Congress had power to prohibit racial discrimination in places of public accommodation in 1964 under the commerce clause raised the question of whether or not it had that same power in 1875. Also raised was the issue of whether it had such power under the Fourteenth Amendment. There was a certain embarrassment for the Court in articulating answers to those questions. If the interstate commerce clause did in fact vest

Congress with authority to enact the 1875 Act, as it was said to give it the power to enact the 1964 Act, did it not follow that the *Civil Rights Cases* of 1883 were wrongly decided and that Negroes had suffered a deprivation of their constitutional rights for the 81 years between the 1883 Supreme Court decision invalidating the 1875 Act and the Court's 1964 decision validating the 1964 Act? The same question arose if Congress had power under Section 5 of the Fourteenth Amendment to pass the 1964 Act. If so, why did it not have power under that same section to enact the 1875 Act? Justice Clark found answers of a sort to both questions.

He observed that "certain kinds of businesses may not in 1875 have been sufficiently involved in interstate commerce to warrant bringing them within the ambit of the commerce power." Congress, he said, had carefully considered the question in 1964 and had noted that civil rights legislation "could be readily achieved by congressional action based on the commerce power of the Constitution." He noted for the Court that "Our populace had not reached its present mobility, nor were facilities, goods and services circulating as readily [in 1875] as they are today." Therefore, he said, "Our study of the legislative record, made in the light of prior cases has brought us to the conclusion that Congress possessed ample power [to enact the 1964 Act], and we have . . . not considered the other grounds relied upon." That was fair enough, as far as it went, but it did not supply an answer to the question of why the 1883 Court did not sustain the 1875 Act on the commerce clause, just as the 1964 Court was doing. Justice Clark's answer was an admission that "there is language in the Civil Rights Cases [of 1883] which indicates that the Court did not fully consider whether the 1875 Act could be sustained as an exercise of the commerce power."

That admission was tempered, as it had to be, by the fact that Justice Bradley who wrote the eight-to-one majority opinion in 1883 had given at least some attention to the commerce power. Justice Bradley said as much in the course of his own opinion when he wrote that his remarks as to lack of congressional authority to enact civil rights laws "do not apply to those cases in which Congress is clothed with direct and plenary power of legislation over the whole subject, accompanied with an express or implied denial of such power to the States, as in the regulation of commerce with foreign nations, [and] among the several states. . . . In these cases Congress has power to pass laws for regulating the subjects mentioned in every detail, and the conduct and transactions of individuals with respect thereof." Justice Clark suggested that Justice Bradley's failure to pursue the inquiry he had opened up in 1883 might have been due to the fact that "Since the commerce power was not relied upon by the Government [in 1883] and was without support in the record, it is understandable that the Court narrowed its inquiry and excluded the Commerce Clause as a possible source of power." That being so, he said, it was clear that the *Civil Rights Cases* of 1883 had no value as a precedent for the argument that the 1964 Act, resting on the commerce clause, was unconstitutional.

Justice Clark was certainly correct in his contention that the 1883 decision had no value as a precedent in an inquiry into the constitutional validity of the 1964 Act under the commerce clause, but that did not shed light on whether the 1883 Court was right or wrong in failing to uphold the 1875 Act on the commerce-clause ground. The Court has always insisted that its power to invalidate congressional legislation is a "very delicate" one, to be exercised only if there was no *possible* ground to justify what Congress had done.[3] It is no answer to say that it is "understandable that the Court narrowed its inquiry" in 1883 merely because the commerce clause was not thrust into the foreground of the argument. There is a strong presumption that congressional acts are valid, and the 1883 Court had the constitutional duty to inquire closely into that subject matter in detail and, if at all possible, to uphold the 1875 Act on the authority of the commerce clause. The conclusion is almost inescapable that, if the 1883 Court had considered the reach and scope of the commerce clause in respect of the 1875 Act and in light of the precedents initiated by Chief Justice Marshall, it would have been impelled to find the 1875 Act within the scope of congressional authority. That it did not do so is understandable in light of its well-intentioned but mistaken zeal to curb the federal power and restore control and regulation of civil rights to the states.

Justice Clark carefully bypassed the question of whether or not the 1964 Act was justified under the congressional authority to enact civil rights legislation under Section 5 of the Fourteenth Amendment, which gives Congress the express right to enforce the amendment by "appropriate legislation." He said that the 1964 Court had not considered that ground but added quickly that "This is not to say that . . . it . . . was not adequate, a question upon which we do not pass, but merely that since the commerce power is sufficient for our decision here, we have considered it [the commerce power] alone." This careful abstention relieved the Court of having to overrule or uphold the *Civil Rights Cases* of 1883, and in the event of overruling, to have to tacitly concede that there had been 81 years of wrongful deprivation of civil rights in places of public accommodation.

Justice Douglas, who had argued in the later sit-in cases, particularly in *Bell v. Maryland,* that the Fourteenth Amendment, *per se,* gave the Court authority to prohibit discrimination in places of public accommodation, readily agreed that Congress had authority to enact the 1964 Civil Rights Act under either the commerce clause or the Fourteenth Amendment. But, he said, "our decision should be based on the Fourteenth Amendment, thereby putting an end to obstructionist strategies and allowing every person—whatever his race, creed, or color—to patronize all places of public accommodation whether he travels interstate or intrastate." Justice Goldberg agreed in his concurring opinion that the 1964 "Act is a just law and, in my view, Congress had the authority both under Section 5 of the Fourteenth Amendment and the Commerce Clause to enact the Civil Rights Act of 1964."

Justice Black, who had strongly disagreed in the Bell case with Justices Douglas and Goldberg and Chief Justice Warren in their contention that the Fourteenth Amendment sanctioned judicial action to prohibit discrimination in places of public accommodation, wrote in his concurring opinion that the "Civil Rights Act of 1964 as applied here is wholly valid under the Commerce Clause and the Necessary and Proper Clause [and] there is no need to consider whether [it] is also constitutionally supportable under Section 5 of the Fourteenth Amendment which grants Congress 'power to enforce by appropriate legislation, the provisions of this article.'"

Congress had finally achieved in the Civil Rights Act of 1964 what it had sought to do 89 years earlier in the Civil Rights Act of 1875: it had enacted and won Supreme Court approval of federal legislation prohibiting segregation or discrimination in places of public accommodation. Moreover, it had repudiated the Supreme-Court-contrived fiction that state control and regulation of civil rights offered assurance or hope to Negroes that their rights would be respected or enforced. It had re-established federal supremacy, on which the framers of the Fourteenth Amendment had rested their case for the amendment and for the equalitarian legislation that had been so ruthlessly decimated by haggling Supreme Court decisions. In its proper turn, the Court had bowed to the congressional will and had approved in 1964 what it had disapproved in 1883. In all honesty, it must be added that the Court had led the way in churning up the public opinion that eventuated in the passage of the 1964 Act by its great equalitarian decisions of the preceding quarter of a century.

On the same day that it announced its decisions in the Heart of Atlanta and Katzenbach cases, the Court tidied up some of the last of the demonstration and sit-in cases. It overturned Louisiana breach-of-the-peace, obstructing-public-passage, and obstructing-justice convictions of the Reverend B. Elton Cox, a Baton Rouge minister who led a 1961 demonstration against segregation in that city. In his case, *Cox v. Louisiana*,[4] Justice Goldberg spoke for the majority in holding that the breach-of-peace conviction violated free speech rights. There were no dissents. He held the obstructing-public-passage convictions invalid, because "the practice in Baton Rouge of allowing unfettered discretion in local officials in the regulation of the use of streets for peaceful parades and meetings is an unwarranted abridgement of . . . freedom of speech and assembly. . . ." Justices White and Harlan dissented, while Justices Black and Clark concurred on the ground that other groups had been permitted to do the acts for which Reverend Mr. Cox was convicted.

The obstructing-justice conviction was based on a statute prohibiting picketing near a court house or residence or other building used by judges, juries, witnesses, or court officers. All justices agreed that the law was valid, but Justice Goldberg and the majority held that the Reverend Mr. Cox had been permitted by the sheriff to hold the demonstration near the court house in question. Justices Black, Clark, Harlan, and Stewart dissented, on the ground that no permission by the sheriff could vary the terms of the law.

In *Hamm v. Rock Hill*,[5] the Court, speaking through Justice Clark, found a formula to overturn sit-in convictions that drew vigorous dissents from Justices Harlan, White, Black, and Stewart. The Court held that because passage of the 1964 Civil Rights Act gave Negroes the right to be seated and served in the very restaurant in which they had sought service that led to their convictions, the convictions should be reversed. As Justice Clark phrased it: "Now that Congress has exercised its constitutional power in enacting the Civil Rights Act of 1964 and declared the public policy of our country is to prohibit discrimination in public accommodations . . . there is no public interest to be served in the further prosecution" of the sit-inners.[6] Justices Douglas and Goldberg concurred, on the ground they had asserted in *Bell v. Maryland* that the Fourteenth Amendment itself prohibited enforcement of the laws in question.[7] Dissenting Justices Harlan, Black, and White could find no congressional intent to terminate prosecutions for prior offenses and insisted that the rule of law was best served by respecting the statutes in force at the time the offenses were committed. Justice Stewart said the issue should be sent back to state courts for decision. The same results and the same dissents occurred in *Lupper v. Arkansas*[8] and *Blow v. North Carolina*,[9] where the facts were virtually the same as in the Hamm case.

Disposal of the Cox case and the Hamm case (and those decided on its authority) followed the Court's pattern of refusing its approval of sit-in convictions in those instances in which it granted review. Grounds of refusal for overturning state convictions had shifted from time to time and from case to case, but the results did not vary. Federal supremacy based on the Court's own determination of law and fact ran like a red thread through these cases.

A century before the 1964 Civil Rights Act was decided by the Court, the Civil War was drawing to a close. Emancipation had been proclaimed in 1863, and two years later, on December 18, 1865, the Thirteenth Amendment was added to the Constitution. The Fourteenth Amendment was ratified on July 28, 1868, and the Fifteenth on March 30, 1870. Congress enacted the first civil rights legislation in 1866 and completed that task with the Civil Rights Act of 1875. There was some concern but little fear about what the Supreme Court would do in respect of the amendments or the great sweep of equalitarian legislation. At that point, the Court was in eclipse and in some disrepute because of the Dred Scott case and what was popularly regarded as its obstructionist tactics during the war years. Congressional power was ascendant. Congress had carried the day against the stubborn President Andrew Johnson and had bolstered its authority to chart its own way in civil rights with the War Amendments providing that "Congress shall have power to enforce" each of them "by appropriate legislation." There were few, very few, Americans who would have hazarded a prediction in 1875 that in 1965, a hundred years after the end of the Civil War, the Supreme Court of the United States would have had a controlling or indeed an important voice in the civil rights issues.

On the other hand, few, very few, Americans would have hazarded a prediction in 1930, the two-thirds mark of a century after the close of the Civil War, that by 1965 the Supreme Court would have:

1. Upheld a federal civil rights act that in effect overruled the *Civil Rights Cases* of 1883;

2. Toppled the separate-but-equal rule of *Plessy v. Ferguson* and overruled that case;

3. Prohibited all state-imposed segregation in all public schools;

4. Forbidden segregation in all public carriers, whether in interstate or intrastate commerce and whether imposed by law or ordinance or by rules or regulations of carriers;

5. Interdicted judicial enforcement of racially restrictive covenants and closed the doors of federal and state courts against litigants seeking to collect damages for sales in violation of such agreements;

6. Overthrown the white primary system, even in the situation where such primaries were established by political parties without any state statutory sanction and even where all state law regulating primaries had been repealed;

7. Construed the due-process-of-law clause of the Fourteenth Amendment to mean that the Court could and would look behind and through state court construction of state law and determine for itself whether or not a Negro defendant had had a fair trial where mob violence or threat of mob violence permeated the trial atmosphere, or where adequate counsel was not provided or given time to prepare for trial, or where defendants' confessions were used in evidence.

8. Protected Negro civil rights organizations, particularly the NAACP, from having to disclose membership lists in response to law, ordinances, or to inquiries by state legislative committees, upon the claim that such disclosure might subject NAACP members to reprisals by *private* persons.

9. Construed the equal-protection-of-the-law clause of the Fourteenth Amendment to mean that Negro sit-inners in places of public accommodation could not be successfully prosecuted under state breach-of-the-peace or trespass statutes in cases where racial segregation was compelled by state law or city ordinance or imposed by

executive order of municipal authorities or, in the attenuated case, where state law required separate toilet and sanitary facilities for Negro and white customers.

10. Forbidden labor unions and employers from entering into discriminatory agreements against Negro nonunion members of the same craft where federal law had clothed the union with bargaining rights, or against Negro members of another union where bargaining rights flowed from federal laws.

These decisions were not announced in that order nor in any neat, categorical fashion. They were imbedded in a long list of cases in which the Court dealt with perplexing day-to-day problems that arose out of litigation that came before it. In almost every instance the Court had precedents in its own decisions that would have justified other, and often contrary, conclusions. The very fact that it neglected and distinguished old cases is proof enough of a determination to find new solutions and of its recognition that it had strayed from the course prescribed by the Civil War Amendments.

✠ 29 ✠ *Bright Before Us*

We have tomorrow
Bright before us.

LANGSTON HUGHES, "Youth"

What Americans like to call the Negro problem took on new dimensions after World War I. Negro urbanization was growing, and Negroes had become political factors to be reckoned with in the larger northern and western cities. Negro soldiers, from both the South and North, came home from European experiences with new concepts about their place in the social order and their claim for constitutional rights and privileges. Negro organizations grew rapidly, including the NAACP, the National Urban League, and kindred groups. A bombastic West Indian named Marcus Garvey fanned the fires of incipient black nationalism and enlisted almost a million Negroes in a Back to Africa movement before his scheme collapsed.

The attitudes of many white Americans also underwent profound changes on racial issues during the same period. Social scientists pricked the bubble of white supremacy. Organized labor dropped many racially exclusionary practices, as it was confronted with the necessity of adapting its tactics to the presence of Negroes in the northern work force. Politicians bid for votes of Negroes out of simple self-interest. Communist and fascist revolutions stirred worldwide unrest and roused debate on equality and on racial issues. A new generation of law students began to question and reexamine Supreme Court precedents in every field, including decisions on racial issues. The collapse of the American economy in 1929 exacerbated trends in every one of these fields and in many more. Restless Negroes, egged on by sympathetic whites, began a systematic presentation of many more cases to the Court after the early 1930's. The Court simply had more cases involving Negroes on its docket and, of course, it dealt with them within the context of the times.

It is not at all surprising that the Court broke with old precedents. As we have noted, it was under heavy attack, which culminated in Franklin Roosevelt's famous "court-packing" plan of 1937, in which he proposed to raise the number of justices from nine to fifteen. Although that attack was beaten back, it had its effects, and as new justices came to the Court, they brought new ideas and new attitudes toward all constitutional problems, including racial issues. From today's vantage point, the Court's profound change, even reversal, of stands on racial issues does not appear as unlikely as it would have loomed to the person invited to make a prediction in 1930. At that time, the Court's record was a discouraging one in the area of civil rights. A capsule review will put the matter in perspective.

The Court laid waste to the privileges-and-immunities clause of the Fourteenth Amendment, upon which the framers of that Amendment had put so much dependence, in the 1873 *Slaughter House Cases,* which did not involve Negroes. In 1875, it applied the *Slaughter House Cases* rule in a civil rights case and returned to the Dred Scott concept that, as far as Negroes were concerned, there were still two categories of citizenship, national and state. In that case, *United States v. Cruikshank,*[1] it said that protection of "civil rights was originally assumed by the states; and it still remains there." Hard on the heels of the Cruikshank case, the Court decided *United States v. Harris*[2] in 1883, in which it held that the equal-protection-of-the-law clause of the Fourteenth Amendment meant only that the states could lay no affirmative racial disabilities on Negroes and that Congress had no authority to protect the freedmen from state inaction and inability or unwillingness to conserve their rights. In *United States v. Reese,*[3] also decided in 1875, it narrowed the impact of the Fifteenth Amendment by holding that the amendment did not confer the franchise on Negroes but only prohibited racial discrimination in voting. In that same decision it overthrew a congressional statute designed to protect Negroes against wholesale violation of the voting privilege.

The Court stunned the nation with its 1883 ruling in the *Civil*

Rights Cases, holding flatly that Congress had no authority to enact public accommodations statutes, and announcing the sweeping rule that Congress could not proscribe individual invasion of civil rights unless such invasion was supported by "state authority in the shape of laws, customs, or judicial or executive proceedings." The case made it clear beyond all doubt that control and supervision of civil rights was vested in the states and that failure of the states to protect the Negro's civil rights left him with no federal remedy.

In 1896, the Court devised the separate-but-equal rule of *Plessy v. Ferguson,* leaving the states free to classify Negroes on the basis of race and deny them access to state institutions and public facilities where separate institutions and facilities were provided for them. In the area of the franchise, the Court put its stamp of approval on Mississippi's constitution, which openly swept "the circle of expedients" to curb the Negro's voting privilege. At the turn of the century, it blandly refused to intervene in the cases where legislators and constitution makers boasted that they were out to keep Negroes from polling places. There was small wonder that Frederick Douglass, the great Negro abolitionist and leader, cried out that "The citizenship granted in the Fourteenth Amendment is practically a mockery, and the right to vote . . . is literally stamped out in the face of government."

These ground rules for the exercise of civil rights were not explicit in the War Amendments. They were interpolated by the Supreme Court through its interpretations of those amendments—interpretations that in many instances ran directly counter to those placed on that same language by the great lawyers who wrote the amendments and by the congressmen who enacted legislation to give them meaning and purpose. Nor were these interpretations crystal clear to all the judges who sat on the Court. The *Slaughter House Cases,* which emasculated the privileges-and-immunities clause, drew the impassioned protest of four out of nine justices. The first Justice Harlan, as we have seen, thundered lone dissents in the *Civil Rights Cases* and in *Plessy v. Ferguson,* and time has vindicated his judgments. Other justices joined him from time to time in lesser cases. Today's Supreme Court construction of what the War Amendments mean in terms of civil rights is far closer to Justice Harlan's views than to those voiced by the majorities that overwhelmed him.

The third of a century after the Civil War until the early 1900's was given over to the fundamental and restrictive interpretations put on the War Amendments by the Supreme Court, and to the invalidation of equalitarian legislation enacted by Congress. It was the period during which state regulation and control of civil rights was restored and in which the Court reduced the Negro to almost complete dependence on its fiat for the exercise of his rights. When all was said and done, the Negro had no rights but those which the Court was willing to grant him. The Court was his guardian, the Negro its unwilling ward. He was not a *free man;* he was a *freedman* cadging for judicial favors.

The second third of a century, from the early 1900's to the early 1930's, was the time of the application of the constitutional interpretations of the preceding years. These were the years of Supreme Court validation of the racist doctrine of the unbelievable Berea College case, which loosed a flood of other state legislation forbidding voluntary interracial association. Within that period, the Court validated the white primary and gave tacit approval to judicial enforcement of racially restrictive covenants. It put the great seal of federal approval on racial segregation in public schools and assented to rigid segregation in interstate travel. It left the states free to impose segregation in every nook and cranny of American life, even to separate telephone booths. There was almost no phase of American life in which it could not be argued with a show of great reason that the Supreme Court would tolerate whatever racial segregation the states chose to levy. But man does not live by the letter of the law alone; he also dwells in its spiritual temple.

The spirit of Supreme Court decisions during the second period was such that racial segregation and discrimination were stimulated to take root and flower everywhere. The states of the old Confederacy far outran their formal statutes and barred the Negro from the polling places by custom and violence, while a three-time Democratic presidential candidate and ultimate Secretary of State openly condoned disfranchisement. A horde of federal and state office seekers sought and won public office by promising to eliminate the last handful of Negro voters. Congressmen and senators praised lynch law and promised more of it in the legislative halls of the nation. Southerners lived their lives without seeing a Negro serve on a grand or a trial jury; Negroes were segregated in courtrooms. President Wilson issued an executive order imposing racial segregation in federal services. The Supreme Court did not give formal approval to these practices—it was not asked to do so, but its decisions had made them possible; the temper of the times gave them birth and nurtured them.

There were bright spots from the very beginning. The Supreme Court always insisted that discriminatory state action exercised through legislative, judicial, or executive branches of government offended the equal-protection clause, although its approval of the separate-but-equal rule put severe limitations on that doctrine. It voided convictions where Negroes were openly excluded from juries that indicted or tried Negro defendants, although, unfortunately, its decisions permitted the untrammeled growth of the white jury system except in the cases where Negroes were on trial. It turned its face resolutely against state legislation enacted to protect peonage. The Court blotted out the excrescences of the grandfather clauses in state voting legislation and overturned state laws directly establishing a white primary system. It saved the nation from the disgrace of the legally constituted ghetto by invalidating racial zoning legislation. It called an abrupt halt to mob-dominated trials in the Arkansas riot cases. Even where it was remiss in protecting the rights of Negroes, it proclaimed adherence to the great equalitarian principles of the Constitution, a not inconsiderable contribution when similar sentiments were muted in the executive and legislative halls of the federal government.

We must not blink at the fact, however, that the Supreme Court strayed far from the equalitarian commands of the amended Constitution during the first two-thirds of a century after the war. And we must face up to the further fact that the Court's establishment and constant expansion of judicial supremacy made a tremendous impact on popular beliefs, attitudes, and actions, for Americans are idolatrous in their attitude toward their Constitution; they look to it for moral as well as legal guidance. The Constitution was what the Court said it was, and when the Court said it brooked racial segregation, that dogma took on an aura of wisdom and morality. After all, as children learned from their textbooks, as men read in their newspapers, and as the great and learned proclaimed on every public platform, the Constitution was a near perfect document. As such it demanded allegiance and respect. The common man had but to heed it and obey it as the Supreme Court interpreted it, in order to reach the zenith of good citizenship; he heeded it as it was interpreted to mean that it sanctioned the color-caste system.

The Court's own assessment of what it was required to do under the rule of law to which it was genuinely committed was a compound of many factors. The William Graham Sumner dictum, that law ways could not change folkways, permeated sociological thought, and Justice Brown looked to that principle for guidance in the Plessy case, when he said that "legislation is powerless to eradicate racial instincts." Justice Oliver Wendell Holmes's concept that the life of the law was not logic but the experience of the community concerned played its great part because of his weighty influence on his liberal colleagues. He voiced that attitude in the first Giles voting cases from Alabama, with the flat statement that "equity cannot . . . enforce political rights" and that if "the great mass of white population intends to keep the blacks from voting . . . a name on a piece of paper will not defeat them." It followed that the Court could do nothing to stay encroachment on the franchise and that Negroes must turn to the state legislatures to change the consensus of what was expedient for the community.

Justice Holmes and such other great liberal luminaries of the Court as Justices Brandeis and Cardozo were also consistently critical of the use of the Fourteenth Amendment to invalidate wages-and-hours and child-labor legislation and other state social reforms, and consistently urged that the amendment did not prevent the states from a wide area of experimentation in social legislation. That same attitude carried over into their beliefs as to the authority of the states where civil rights was concerned. Thus, Justice Holmes said in his decision for the Court in the first white primary case that "States may do a good deal of classifying that it is difficult to believe rational but there are limits, and it is too clear for extended argument that color cannot be made the basis for a statutory classification affecting the right" to vote.[4] The statement illustrates the judicial error. The truth was that the all-pervading purpose, the express command, of the Fourteenth Amendment was that as far as civil rights were concerned, there was no margin for state classification and experiment as there was in other cases. Justice Frankfurter phrased the issue correctly in another case: "The majestic generalities of the Fourteenth Amendment are thus reduced to a concrete statutory command when cases involve race or color which is wanting in every other case. . . ."[5]

The subscription of some justices to the Sumner dictum that law could not change folkways, that of others to expedient doctrine of

Justice Holmes, and that of still others to the erroneous belief that the Fourteenth Amendment left the states free to experiment in the amendment's application to civil rights misled the Court into relaxing federal supremacy and leaving the states in even greater control and regulation of civil rights. And as Robert J. Harris observes, "It is melancholy to record that the southern states, instead of using their newly restored powers over race relations to bring about a gradual improvement of the legal, political and economic status of Negroes, used them in a discriminatory and oppressive manner, with a view of keeping the colored race in a low, servile and cringing status. . . ." 6

We have arbitrarily selected the first Scottsboro case in 1932 as the time of the beginning of the return of the Court to the Constitution and the original intent of the Civil War Amendments. As we have seen, the Court marched steadily forward under that banner, with an occasional tactical retreat here and there. Between 1932 and 1965, the last third of a century after the close of the Civil War, it had reached the imposing list of constitutional decisions that has been recited. These decisions wrought a judicial revolution in race relations and swept aside restrictive decision after restrictive decision, some by open renunciation but most by ignoring precedent or through subtle and ingenious distinctions. And, again, as the letter of the law was changed in Court decisions, the spirit of the law was varied. Lower federal courts and state courts accommodated their decisions to the predictable trend of Supreme Court change. Exclusion of Negroes from grand and trial juries was subjected to closer judicial scrutiny; confessions of defendants were examined more carefully for evidence of coercion; the right to counsel at all stages of criminal trials was extended; the due-process clause of the Fourteenth Amendment was extended to new areas; old Reconstruction statutes giving the right to removal of cases to federal courts where state court bias was alleged were resuscitated and put to use; and legal subtleties difficult to catalogue, but nonetheless very important, were resolved in favor of civil rights claims.

As new questions arose, particularly in the application of what were supposed to be dead-letter Reconstruction statutes, the Court itself found them still vital, as it did in the Screws case. In *Monroe v. Pape*, decided on February 20, 1961, it held that an 1871 statute permitted a damage suit against police officers for unreasonable searches, seizures, and detention, over Justice Frankfurter's protest that the Court was undermining the Cruikshank and similar cases.[7] In other cases the Supreme Court refused to review very important cases where results favorable to Negroes were reached, as it did in *Simkins v. Cone Memorial Hospital*.[8] There the Court of Appeals for the Fourth Circuit held that a hospital accepting federal funds under the federal Hill-Burton Act, which expressly permitted separate but equal facilities, could not bar Negro doctors from its staff, and that insofar as the Hill-Burton Act approved such a rule, it was unconstitutional. Of course, the Court has repeatedly said that denial of review does not mean approval of a decision, but it is hard to believe that the Court would have rejected review of a case freighted with such great consequences for southern hospitals, if the issue had been in doubt. In relatively minor matters, such as addressing a Negro witness by given name and in segregation in a traffic court, the Court intervened on behalf of Negroes. In *McLaughlin v. Florida*, decided on December 7, 1964, it invalidated a Florida statute imposing penalties on members of different races for cohabiting together, overruling an old Alabama case of the same import.

In legal contemplation, the Court's invalidation of the separate-but-equal rule simply amounted to prohibiting the states from classifying persons within their jurisdiction on the basis of race. The states were told to stop racial classification of applicants for admission to *state* graduate or professional schools, or to *state* parks, or playgrounds or swimming pools, or libraries, or to *state* facilities of any kind. A state which cannot classify by race cannot segregate or discriminate by race. It must serve all persons or it can serve none of them. The injunction against racial classification was also applied to *state* political subdivisions, to *state* agencies, and to *state* agents of every kind: to the school board when a pupil knocked at the schoolhouse door; to the bailiff when a person attended a trial at the courthouse; to the greenskeeper when a person wanted to play a round of golf on a city-owned course; to the manager when a person sought to rent an apartment in a publicly owned housing project; or to the doorkeeper when a person asked to see an exhibit at a county museum; to the administrator when a doctor applied for a place on a hospital staff. The list is endless. A person is a person is a person. A state which cannot classify by race no longer has any basis upon which it can order a railroad, or a bus line, or a hotel, or a restaurant, or a taxi driver, or an airport, or a pool hall, to segregate customers by race. Of course, the state or the political subdivision could still prescribe rules for the conduct of a facility open to the public, but those rules had to be rules for customers *as customers*—an inevitable consequence since the state could no longer classify those customers and put them into separate categories as "white" customers or "Negro" customers.

Put another, and more poetic way, the Court in the process of destroying the separate-but-equal rule ordered the states, their cities, their subdivisions, and their agents of all kinds to become color-blind. Texas was told to become color-blind when Heman Sweatt or any other applicant sought admission to its law school, and Oklahoma was ordered to remain color-blind when George McLaurin or any other student entered a classroom or a cafeteria at the University of Oklahoma. Jury commissioners were directed to become color-blind when they sought grand or trial jurors, and the election judges were told they must become color-blind when a qualified voter sought to cast a ballot at a primary election. The list is as extensive as the roll call of state functionaries.

That was not quite the end of the matter. The Court went further and extended and strengthened former decisions proscribing state aid or assistance or sanction to private discriminatory conduct. It found "state action" where state involvement was minute or attenuated, as in the case where a restaurant was a lessee from the state. It said that the private individual could not classify applicants for his goods or services on the basis of race, on pain of forfeiture of the state aid or assistance theretofore extended to him. He, too, must become color-blind. In the sit-in cases, the Court extended that doctrine to mean that the keeper of the place of public accommodation could not call upon law enforcement authorities to enforce breach-of-the-peace or trespass statutes where cities or states had segregation laws or where the mayor or chief of police proclaimed an intention of enforcing customary segregation and, in the extreme case, where the state did no more than require separate toilet or sanitary facilities when a restaurant served members of both races.

Civil rights legislation affecting places of public accommodation goes a long step beyond proscription of racial classification by states or political subdivisions and of enforcing color-blindness on them or by those who receive state aid or sanction or assistance. Public accommodation statutes operate directly on the individual

and order him to stop classifying applicants for his goods or services on the basis of race. They order him to become color-blind
also. The circle is then complete. The state is enjoined from classifying persons within its jurisdiction on the basis of race; the purveyor
of goods or services is enjoined from classifying applicants for those
goods and services on the basis of race. The state is color-blind; the
keeper of the place of public accommodation is color-blind. Every
person then stands as the equal of every other person, as he seeks to
enjoy the goods and services available in the society in which he
lives. That is what Congress sought to achieve in the Civil Rights
Act of 1875; that is what it did achieve in the Civil Rights Act of
1964. It failed in 1875, only because the Supreme Court aborted its
will; it succeeded in 1964, because the Supreme Court approved its
attempt.

The achievement of the color-blind state—using the term *state* in
its broadest sense to mean all federal, state, and local political subdivisions—was the great purpose of the Civil War Amendments.
That color-blindness was meant to be all-encompassing.

First came the Thirteenth Amendment, destroying slavery and
making free men of all who lived under the American flag. And free
men, the philosophers said and everybody knew, were endowed
with certain unalienable rights. Among them were life, liberty, and
the pursuit of happiness. Congress had power, the amendment
said, to enforce "this article" and, of course, to insure the rights that
arose under that article. Congress wrote the Civil Rights Act of
1866 as the appropriate legislation it was commissioned to write. It
searched the Dred Scott decision to find an answer to every thrust
Chief Justice Taney had made to prove his contention that under
the original Constitution the Negro had no rights which a white
man was bound to respect. It answered them all. Now all men were
free men, their rights spelled out in plain language saying that the
newly freed men should have the *same* rights in every state and
territory as those enjoyed by their one-time masters.

Then the doubts came. Common-sense constitutional lawyers
said that such vast changes should be written into the fundamental
law. Cautious others feared that some future Congress might undo
the Civil Rights Act of 1866. Congress acted. It proposed and secured the ratification of the Fourteenth Amendment. The provisions of the Civil Rights Act of 1866 were written into that amendment in constitutional shorthand. Every free man was a citizen—a

citizen of the United States *and* of the state wherein he resided. No state, it was written, could make or enforce any law which should abridge the privileges and immunities of citizens—those priceless privileges and immunities that were the inheritance of a free man, his by the mere right of birth. And what were they, these privileges and immunities, these pearls of such great price? Why, they were so all-pervasive, so deeply rooted in constitutional soil that no man needed to list them, no man dared list them, lest by mistake or inadvertence he neglect one and make it seem that it did not exist when all men felt them in their bones. And now no free man could be denied due process of law—the Fifth Amendment laid that restraint upon the federal government, and the Fourteenth Amendment enjoined that burden on the states. Every Free Man would have equal protection of the laws, which could only mean that the *same* law would be applied in the *same* manner to every man.

Congress, it was written again, could enforce that article by appropriate legislation. Congress responded. It wrote great sheafs of laws wiping out all racial distinctions, invoking penalties against those who transgressed its will that all men, all free men, should walk equal before the law. And then the doubts came again.

Free men, the doubters said, could not be secure unless they could vote, unless they could protect themselves at the ballot box. Congress acted again. It proposed and secured the ratification of the Fifteenth Amendment striking all color shackles on the right to cast a ballot. The *right* of *citizens* to vote could not be abridged by the United States or any state because of race or color. Voting was a *right* now, not a privilege, lodged in every citizen. Wherever and whenever a polling place was opened to any citizen, it was opened to every citizen.

And, it was underscored, Congress should have power to enforce the Fifteenth Amendment by appropriate legislation.

Congress expressed its final will in the Civil Rights Act of 1875, where it distilled its judgment of what was appropriate legislation under the Thirteenth Amendment, and the Fourteenth Amendment, and the Fifteenth Amendment. The color-blind state, again using that term in its broadest sense, was reality now. Its powers were summed up in three constitutional amendments and ingrained in congressional statutes protecting the free man in every phase of his life against any possible assault on his prerogatives as a free man.

The evidence is clear and abundant, and abundantly clear, that the framers of the Civil War Amendments intended to place civil rights under the protection and control of the federal government. Congress, they said—Congress, not the states and not state legislators, was vested with power to enforce those articles by appropriate legislation. It is true, as was said then and is said now, that these amendments aggrandized the powers of the federal government at the expense of the states and disturbed the delicate balance of federalism and states' rights. But the safety and security of the slave system in the face of expanding federal power was what the Civil War was about, and it is idle to talk as if, and act as if, the victors did not accomplish their purpose. They did accomplish their purposes, and they wrote these accomplished purposes into the fundamental law of the land.

In the first two-thirds of a century after the Civil War, the Supreme Court diffused the federal congressional power in many respects, and denied it altogether in others, by narrow interpretations of the Civil War Amendments and by its construction of congressional enactments, through what the first Justice Harlan called "ingenious verbal criticism." The results, as we have seen, were the debasement and denial of the rights of the Negro as a free man. It was when the Court faced up to what it had done in those respects that it began its return to the Constitution in the last third of a century after the war. And, of course, that return was marked by a new aggrandizement of federal power and a new disturbance of the delicate balance of federalism and states' rights. The manner in which federal supremacy has been asserted time and again in the great civil rights decisions found necessary to protect the Negro's rights in the past 35 years has been pinpointed here in discussion of particular cases.

As the Supreme Court broke with old precedents and either overruled them directly or indirectly to find a path back toward the goal of the color-blind state envisioned by the framers of the Civil War Amendments, it acted as a catalytic agent to loose other great equalitarian forces. It refurbished the concept of the Constitution as the fountainhead of equality when it appealed to that document for justification of the decisions it rendered. More and more often U. S. Attorneys General, who had been worse than laggard in enforcement of old civil rights statutes, appeared as a friend of the court—often at the invitation of the justices—to throw the weight of the executive branch of government behind racial reforms. The Court's constant reiteration of the sentiment that its civil rights decisions were required responses to constitutional guarantees stimulated and helped create a climate of public opinion that demanded extension and intensification of the very reforms it had initiated.

Northern and western states strengthened their public accommodations statutes and added fair employment, fair education, and fair housing laws that quickly won the Court's approbation. In their proper turn, northern and western politicians won elections to the House and the Senate on the basis of their approval of equalitarian Court decisions. Democrats and Republicans alike found it profitable and expedient to include commendation of the Court's civil rights decisions in quadrennial platforms. There were other forces at work also, both on the national and international fronts, to spur racial reforms. One of the Court's greatest contributions was that it gave voice and leadership to those sentiments.

There is something of an anomaly in the spectacle of the judicial branch of government as the leader of social reform in a democratic society. The traditional role of the judiciary has been that of declaring and interpreting the law as enacted by the legislative branch and as enforced by the executive arm of government. The Supreme Court has come in for its share of criticism on that very ground, but such criticism neglects the tremendous impact of the doctrine of judicial supremacy on our institutions. As the final repository of state power, our Supreme Court plays a primary role in American government. Those who now complain most bitterly of the Supreme Court's present role had no similar criticism when the Court took similar leadership in weakening and emasculating the Civil War Amendments. They praised the Court for doing then what they damn it for doing now.

The sum of the whole matter is that the Supreme Court has been bold, aggressive, and creative in resuscitating civil rights and in restoring them to the place assigned to them in the constitutional firmament by the Civil War Amendments. It has had to break old shackles and depart from old precedents of its own making. It has rarely hesitated. Where it could have taken refuge in those old precedents, it has resisted the temptation to do so and has remained undaunted by shock waves of criticism and abuse. It has been tried and found worthy of the past moments of its own greatness. In its great decisions in the white primary cases, the confession cases, the race-restrictive covenant cases, the school cases, the sit-in cases, the new civil rights cases, and a host of other cases of slightly less but similar import, the Supreme Court has moved at an ever accelerating pace toward making the Negro more and more a *free man* and less and less a *freedman*. And as the Negro becomes a free man, he becomes less and less the Court's ward and more and more his own master.

Since Franklin D. Roosevelt in his third term issued his famed executive order establishing a fair employment practices committee, every President has issued executive orders striking at discrimination embedded in the constitutional crevices where it could not be reached by judicial decrees, and where Congress would not act. Executive orders ended segregation in the armed forces, discrimination in government contracts, and in some aspects of housing. Every one of those orders owes something to the Supreme Court example, and every one was grounded on the sure knowledge that each would win Supreme Court sanction in the event of judicial test. Judicial action and executive action helped spur the demand for legislative action. Congress had to act, but it acted timorously in the Civil Rights Act of 1957, more boldly in the Civil Rights Act of 1960, and aggressively in the Civil Rights Act of 1964. In 1965, we cannot know or predict the full effect of this legislative push toward full equality. What we do know is that the end is not in sight. President Lyndon B. Johnson demanded more, much more, in a message delivered to the joint session of Congress on March 15, 1965, in language not heard in the halls of Congress since Reconstruction. Bitter, old Thaddeus Stevens and the erudite Charles Sumner must have stirred comfortably in their graves. For the first time since the early years after the Civil War, all branches of the federal government—executive, legislative and judicial—are united in a determination to obliterate the color line in American society.

The Supreme Court of the United States does not deserve all credit for the nation's new march toward the color-blind society, but what it has done in the last third of a century since the close of the Civil War has helped mightily. Certainly it broke the log jam of law and precedent without which little or nothing could have been done. It would take blindness of another sort and of great dimensions to conceal the fact that much remains to be done. But there is hope now where there was once despair; there is faith now where there was once doubt and cynicism.

There is Tomorrow Bright Before Us!

Notes

CHAPTER 1

1 *Civil Rights Cases*, 109 U.S. 3.
2 *Marbury v. Madison*, 1 Cranch 137.
3 For attacks on Supreme Court, see Charles Warren, *The Supreme Court in United States History* (Boston: Little, Brown & Co., 1924), Vol. III, pp. 91, 143–156, 167–176.
4 For attacks on Supreme Court in Congress during this period, see 40th Congress, 2d Session, *Congressional Globe*, pp. 478 ff., 1859, 1889 ff.
5 *Brown v. Board of Education*, 347 U.S. 483 (1954).
6 *Dred Scott v. Sandford*, 19 Howard 393.
7 As examples, see *United States v. Cruikshank*, 92 U.S. 542; *United States v. Reese*, 92 U.S. 214.
8 *Civil Rights Cases, op. cit.*
9 *Plessy v. Ferguson*, 163 U.S. 537.
10 See Warren, *op. cit.*

CHAPTER 2

1 George Livermore, *Negroes as Citizens, as Slaves and as Soldiers* (Boston: John Wilson & Sons, 1862), p. 23.
2 *Ibid.*, p. 15.
3 *Ibid.*, p. 23.
4 *Ibid.*, p. 24.
5 *University and Others v. Cambreling*, Yerger's Tenn. Reports, p. 79 (1834).

6 Livermore, *op. cit.*, p. 94.
7 *Ibid.*, p. 64.
8 *Ibid.*, p. 65.
9 *Marbury v. Madison*, 1 Cranch 137.

CHAPTER 3

1 *Scott v. Negro London*, 7 U.S. 324.
2 *Scott v. Negro Ben*, 10 U.S. 3.
3 *Negress Sally v. Ball*, 14 U.S. 1.
4 *Williamson v. Daniel*, 25 U.S. 567.
5 *McCutcheon v. Marshall*, 33 U.S. 218.
6 *The Antelope*, 23 U.S. 66.
7 *The Plattsburg*, 23 U.S. 133.
8 *United States v. Gooding*, 25 U.S. 460.
9 Marion Mills Miller (ed.), *Great Debates in American History* (New York: Current Literature Publishing Co., 1913), Vol. IV, Chapter 2, p. 42 ff.
10 *Ibid.*, p. 42 ff.
11 *Ibid.*, p. 42 ff.
12 *McCulloch v. Maryland*, 4 Wheaton 316.
13 *Bank of United States v. Deveaux*, 5 Cranch 61.
14 *Gibbons v. Ogden*, 9 Wheaton 1.
15 Louis B. Boudin, *Government by Judiciary* (New York: William Godwin, Inc., 1932), Vol. I, p. 310.
16 Quoted in Charles Warren, *The Supreme Court in United States History* (Boston: Little, Brown & Co., 1924), Vol. II, p. 86.
17 Taney kept two slaves because they were too old to shift for themselves. For an excellent short biography of Taney and assessment of his judicial philosophy, see Robert J. Harris, "Chief Justice Taney, Prophet of Reform and Reaction," 10 *Vanderbilt Law Rev.*, No. 2, p. 227 (Feb. 1952).

CHAPTER 4

1 See Robert J. Harris, "Chief Justice Taney: Prophet of Reform and Reaction," 10 *Vanderbilt Law Rev.*, No. 2, p. 227 (Feb. 1952).
2 *The Amistad*, 40 U.S. 518.
3 *Groves v. Slaughter*, 40 U.S. 448.
4 *Gibbons v. Ogden*, 9 Wheaton 1.
5 *Prigg v. Commonwealth*, 16 Peters 539.
6 *Abelman v. Booth*, 62 U.S. 506.
7 *The Passenger Cases*, 48 U.S. 283.

Notes [437]

8 Quoted in Louis B. Boudin, *Government by Judiciary* (New York: William Godwin, Inc., 1932), Vol. I.

9 Marion Mills Miller (ed.), *Great Debates in American History* (New York: Current Literature Publishing Co., 1913), Vol. IV, p. 133 ff.

10 *Ibid.*

11 *Ibid.*

12 James K. Polk, *Message to Congress*, 2d Session, December, 1848.

13 *Scott, Man of Color, v. Emerson*, 15 Mo. 576.

14 Mills, *op. cit.*, Vol. IV, p. 133 ff.

15 *Ibid.*

16 *Ibid.*

17 *Ibid.*

18 *Ibid.*

19 Carl Sandburg: *Abraham Lincoln, The Prairie Years* (New York: Blue Ribbon Books, 1925), p. 314 ff.

20 Mills, *op. cit.*, Vol. IV, p. 133 ff.

21 *Ibid.*

22 *Scott v. Emerson Ibid.*, Note 13.

23 *Scott v. Sandford*, 19 Howard 393. For histories of this complex and curious case, see Thomas Hart Benton, *Historical Examination* . . . (New York: D. Appleton & Co., 1858); Elbert Ewing, *Legal & Historical Status of the Dred Scott Decision* (Washington: Cobden Printing Co., 1909); Vincent Hopkins, *Dred Scott's Case* (New York: Fordham University Press, 1951).

CHAPTER 5

1 *Dred Scott v. Sanford*, 19 Howard 393.

2 *Dred Scott v. Sandford*. A clerk had misspelled his name.

3 Justice Nelson's opinion appears as a concurring opinion in the case.

4 Carl Sandburg, *Abraham Lincoln, The Prairie Years* (New York: Blue Ribbon Books, 1925), pp. 314 ff.

5 *The Life and Writings of Benjamin Robbins Curtis* (Boston: Little, Brown and Company, 1879), Vol. I, pp. 168–180.

6 Charles Warren, *The Supreme Court in United States History* (Boston: Little, Brown & Co., 1924), p. 822.

7 Gustavus Myers, *History of The Supreme Court* (Chicago: Charles Kerr, 1925), pp. 469–476.

8 *Ibid.*, p. 470.

9 Library of Congress, *Buchanan Mss.*, Letter of Catron to Buchanan, Feb. 19, 1857.

10 *Ibid.*, Letter of Grier to Buchanan, Feb. 23, 1857.

11 Warren, *op. cit.*, Vol. I, p. 304 ff.

12 *Ibid.*

13 *Ibid.*

14 *Ibid.*
15 *Ibid.*
16 *Ibid.*

CHAPTER 6

1   Howard Devon Hamilton, *The Legislative and Judicial History of the Thirteenth Amendment,* pp. 27–48. (IX National Bar Journal, March, 1951).
2   *Ibid.*
3   Charles Warren, *The Supreme Court in United States History* (Boston: Little, Brown & Co., 1924), pp. 91 ff.
4   *Ex parte Merryman,* Taney's Decisions 246 (the decision was made on circuit), Fed. Cases 9487.
5   *The Prize Cases,* 2 Black 635.
6   *Ex parte Vallandigham,* 1 Wallace 243.
7   *Greenback Cases* (*Roosevelt v. Meyer,* 1 Wallace 512; *Trebilcock v. Wilson,* 12 Wallace 687).
8   Hamilton, *op. cit.,* pp. 27-48.
9   *Ibid.*
10 *Blyew v. United States,* 13 Wallace 581.
11 *Ex parte Garland,* 4 Wallace 333.
12 Quoted in Louis B. Boudin, *Government by Judiciary* (New York: William Godwin, Inc., 1932), Vol. II, p. 75.
13 *Ibid.*
14 *Mississippi v. Johnson,* 4 Wallace 475.
15 *Georgia v. Stanton,* 6 Wallace 50.
16 *Mississippi v. Stanton,* 6 Wallace 50.
17 Warren, *op. cit.,* Vol. III, pp. 91, 143–156, 167–176.
18 *Ex parte McCardle,* 6 Wallace 318.
19 Benjamin B. Kendrick, *The Journal of the Joint Committee of Fifteen on Reconstruction* (New York: Columbia University Press, 1914), p. 46.
20 Quoted by Alfred H. Kelley, unpublished ms. used in briefs in *Brown v. Board of Education,* 347 U.S. 483. Kelley's research was the cornerstone upon which the NAACP rested its case as to the meaning and scope of the Fourteenth Amendment.
21 39th Congress, 1st Session, *Congressional Globe,* pp. 2540–2543.
22 Kelley, *op. cit.*
23 Robert J. Harris, *The Quest for Equality* (Baton Rouge: Louisiana State University Press, 1960), p. 39.
24 2 Congressional Record 948.
25 Kelley, *op. cit.*
26 39th Congress, 1st Session, *Congressional Globe,* pp. 2458–2459.
27 39th Congress, 1st Session, *Congressional Globe,* pp. 2540–2542.
28 42nd Congress, 1st Session, *Congressional Globe,* p. 1000.

29 42nd Congress, 1st Session, *Congressional Globe*, p. 697.
30 2 Congressional Record 3554.
31 Harris, *op. cit.*, Chapter 2.
   This book is the best short treatment of the meaning of the Fourteenth Amendment, particularly the equal-protection clause. Chapter 2 should be consulted by any person interested in a short and accurate review of the motives of the framers of the amendment.
   There are many excellent articles on the antislavery background of the amendment. Jacobus Ten Brock, *The Anti-Slavery Origins of the Fourteenth Amendment* (Berkeley: University of California Press, 1951); Howard Jay Graham, "Our Declaratory Fourteenth Amendment, 7 *Stanford Law Rev.* 1.
   For the student interested in a complete history, Horace Flack, *The Adoption of the Fourteenth Amendment* (Baltimore: The Johns Hopkins Press, 1908), and Kendrick, *Journal of the Joint Committee,* are indispensable.
32 Boudin, *op. cit.*, Vol. II, p. 75.

CHAPTER 7

1 *Slaughter House Cases,* 16 Wallace 36.
2 The appearance of senators as advocates in the Supreme Court was a matter of course in early history. Daniel Webster and Henry Clay appeared for example in *Groves v. Slaughter,* 15 Peters 518.
3 Alfred H. Kelley, unpublished ms. used in briefs in *Brown v. Board of Education,* 347 U.S. 483.
4 Everett V. Abbot, *Justice and the Modern Law* (New York: Houghton Mifflin Company, 1913), pp. 75–76.
5 Charles Fairman, "Samuel F. Miller, Justice," 10 *Vanderbilt Law Rev.* No. 2, p. 193.
6 William L. Royall, 4 *Southern Law Rev.* 563 (1879).
7 *Corfield v. Coryell,* 6 Fed. Cases 3230 (1823).
8 *United States v. Cruikshank,* 92 U.S. 542.
9 Strangely enough, the Court constantly assumed that rights inhering in and enjoyed by white persons had also always been enjoyed and exercised by Negroes under the original Constitution. This was obviously not true of slaves, and the Dred Scott case denied that free Negroes enjoyed such rights under the federal Constitution. When the Court says a right existed prior to the Constitution, all it could mean is that such a right existed for *white* persons.
10 *United States v. Reese,* 92 U.S. 214.
11 *United States v. Harris,* 106 U.S. 629.
12 Charles Francis Adams, in introduction to Marion Mills Miller (ed.), *Great Debates in American History* (New York: Current Literature Publishing Co., 1913), Vol. IV.

13 Philip S. Foner, *Frederick Douglass: Selections from His Writings* (New York: International Publishers, 1945), pp. 81–82.

14 Howard Jay Graham, "An Innocent Abroad, The Constitutional Corporate Person," 2 *UCLA Law Rev.* No. 2, Feb. 1955, presents a quick and incisive look at the growth of the Supreme Court doctrine regarding corporations and the Fourteenth Amendment. See authorities cited therein.

15 Robert J. Harris, *The Quest for Equality* (Baton Rouge: Louisiana State University Press, 1960), p. 59.

16 See 40th Congress, 2nd Session, *Congressional Globe*, pp. 478 ff, 1859, 1889 ff.

17 In time, as will appear, Harlan did voice his opinion on the Harris holding. See *Baldwin v. Franks*, 120 U.S. 678, where the same question was in issue; Harlan dissent.

CHAPTER 8

1 The federal Constitution guarantees trial by jury. Most, if not all, state constitutions grant jury trials in all serious offenses.

2 As a practical matter, most offenses by slaves were summarily punished by the master or by white persons. The right to a trial was little honored. See Frederick Douglass, *The Life and Times of Frederick Douglass* (Hartford: Park Publishing Co., 1882), p. 129 ff.

3 Section 5508 was originally a section of the 1875 Civil Rights Act.

4 *Strauder v. West Virginia*, 100 U.S. 303.

5 *Ibid.*

6 *Virginia v. Rives*, 100 U.S. 313.

7 *Ex parte Virginia*, 100 U.S. 339.

8 *Neal v. Delaware*, 103 U.S. 370.

9 *Bush v. Kentucky*, 107 U.S. 110.

10 State procedures were devised to forestall service of Negroes on juries, and conformity with them was made exceedingly difficult. See *Norris v. Alabama*, 294 U.S. 587.

11 The Court gradually abandoned the full import of this rule. See Chapter 19, Post.

   The Court has moved toward but never quite implemented such a rule. Note Goldberg, dissenting, in *Swain v. Alabama*, 380 U.S. 202.

12 *Andrews v. Swartz*, 156 U.S. 272.

13 *Williams v. Mississippi*, 170 U.S. 213.

14 For the Court's progressive later attitude, see Chapter 19, Post.

15 For contemporaneous example, note failure of white trial jury to convict Alabama Klansman for killing of white civil rights worker in 1965. The proof of guilt was overwhelming. The defense was a ringing appeal to racial prejudice, in which the deceased was branded a "white nigger."

16 Walter White, *Rope and Faggot* (New York: Alfred A. Knopf, Inc., 1929), p. 252 ff.
17 See *Screws v. United States*, 325 U.S. 91.

CHAPTER 9

1 Sumner as a lawyer argued what was probably the first school segregation case in the nation twenty years before ratification of the Fourteenth Amendment. *Roberts v. City of Boston*, 5 Cushing Reports 198.
2 *Civil Rights Cases*, 109 U.S. 3.
3 See Concurring Opinion, Justice Goldberg, *Bell v. Maryland*, 378 U.S. 226, Footnotes 29, 30, 31.
4 Justice Harlan had reference to the fact that some 200,000 Negroes served in the Union Army. Lincoln said that without their aid the Union cause might have been lost. Revisionist historians never refer to the fact that Negroes were not *given* their freedom. They fought for it. See James McPherson, *The Negro's Civil War* (New York: Pantheon Books, 1965).
5 Southerners were not content with a Supreme Court decision that Congress could not interdict discrimination by places of public accommodation. They were soon demanding, and securing, rulings that the states could forbid Negro usage of places of public accommodation. See *Plessy v. Ferguson*, 163 U.S. 537; *Berea College v. United States*, 211 U.S. 45.
6 *Shelley v. Kraemer* made that tabulation in 334 U.S. 1.

CHAPTER 10

1 *United States v. Cruikshank*, 92 U.S. 542.
2 *Strauder v. West Virginia*, 100 U.S. 303.
3 *United States v. Reese*, 92 U.S. 214, Hunt, dissenting.
4 *Ibid.*
5 *Ibid.*
6 James Weldon Johnson, *Negro American, What Now?* (New York: The Viking Press, 1935), pp. 39–57.
7 See *Prigg v. Commonwealth*, 16 Peters 539.
8 See Chapter 7, p. 109.
9 *United States v. Harris*, 106 U.S. 629.
10 *Baldwin v. Franks*, 120 U.S. 678.
11 *Ex parte Yarborough*, 110 U.S. 651.
12 *James v. Bowman*, 190 U.S. 127.
13 Congressional intent is plain from the fact that it legislated in that vein within two years after the enactment of the Fifteenth Amendment. Under

that amendment it was the judge of what was "appropriate" legislation. The Court should not have substituted its judgment for the congressional will.

14 *James v. Bowman*, 190 U.S. 127.

15 This was a familiar statement in state disfranchising conventions. See William A. Sinclair, *The Aftermath of Slavery* (Boston: Small, Maynard & Co., 1903).

16 William Jennings Bryan, Cooper Union, New York, 1908. Bryan was a Northerner and his statement is indicative of the manner in which many Northerners had succumbed to the South.

17 See Justice Black for Court in *United States v. Mississippi*, 380 U.S. 128.

18 *Williams v. Mississippi*, 170 U.S. 213.

19 *Giles v. Harris*, 189 U.S. 475.

20 *Giles v. Teasely*, 193 U.S. 146.

21 *Jones v. Montague*, 194 U.S. 147; *Selden v. Montague*, 194 U.S. 147.

22 See *Mills v. Green*, 159 U.S. 651.

23 See C. Vann Woodward, *The Strange Career of Jim Crow* (New York: Oxford University Press, 1957).

24 The probabilities are that the railroad was a party to the test case and was well informed that Mr. Plessy was on the train to test the Louisiana law. See John A. Garraty, *Quarrels That Have Shaped the Constitution* (New York: Harper & Row, 1964), p. 145 ff.

CHAPTER 11

1 *Plessy v. Ferguson*, 163 U.S. 537.

2 *Hall v. De Cuir*, 95 U.S. 485.

3 In fact, such legislation had come from Congress. The 1875 Civil Rights Act did forbid discrimination by public carriers.

4 *L., N.O. & T. Rwy. v. Mississippi*, 133 U.S. 587.

5 *Gayles v. Browder*, 352 U.S. 903.

6 Senator Glenn Taylor, vice-presidential candidate on the Henry Wallace ticket in 1948, was arrested, convicted, and fined for entering the "Negro entrance" of a Negro church to attend a political meeting!

7 *Johnson v. Virginia*, 373 U.S. 61.

8 Formal Jim Crow laws never kept pace with informal segregation practices. See C. Vann Woodward, *The Strange Career of Jim Crow* (New York: Oxford University Press, 1957).

9 Robert J. Harris, *The Quest for Equality* (Baton Rouge: Louisiana State University Press, 1960), p. 108.

10 The debate as to the Court's correctness in the assumption of the right to judicial review is almost endless. We are not concerned with the merits of that debate. But see Justice Robert Jackson, *The Supreme Court in the American System of Government* (Cambridge, Mass.: Harvard University Press, 1955).

11 Woodrow Wilson issued such an executive order.

12 After 1875, Congress enacted no more civil rights legislation, as such, until 1957.

13 The Attorneys General justified their inactivity by pointing out the major difficulties in securing indictments or convictions.

14 Significantly, as we shall see, the dissents in all of those cases except the *Slaughter House Cases* have been incorporated to lesser or greater degrees in prevailing Supreme Court opinions since 1935.

CHAPTER 12

1 Booker T. Washington, *Up From Slavery, An Autobiography* (New York: Doubleday, Page & Co., 1902), p. 206 ff.

2 See Charles Francis Adams, Introduction to Marion Mills Miller (ed.), *Great Debates in American History* (New York: Current Literature Publishing Co., 1913), Vol. IV.

3 Carey McWilliams, *Brothers Under the Skin* (Boston: Little, Brown & Co., 1946).

4 *Plessy v. Ferguson*, 163 U.S. 537.

5 Justice Frankfurter described Justice Harlan as such in a comment on the privileges-and-immunities clause.

6 Thomas Dixon, Jr. His pro-Klan, anti-Negro novel, *The Leopards Spots*, was converted into "Birth of A Nation" by Hollywood and did much to spur the growth of the Ku Klux Klan.

7 The favorite excuse for a lynching was that the victim had "attacked a white woman." See Walter White, *Rope and Faggot*. The excuse was a mere rationalization, as White shows.

8 *Hodges v. United States*, 203 U.S. 1.

9 *Clyatt v. United States*, 197 U.S. 207.

10 *Strauder v. West Virginia*, 100 U.S. 3, 303.

11 *Clyatt v. United States*, 197 U.S. 207.

12 Apparently, the pair had signed a Georgia labor contract and had failed to fulfill it, which constituted a crime under Georgia law. However, as the Supreme Court later held, arrests and detention under such contracts constituted peonage. Hence, the government charge of "return" to peonage.

13 Justice Brewer was incorrect in finding reversible error under the circumstances in light of Note 12.

14 The convict "leasing" system was in full flower in the South during the period. See William H. Skaggs, *The Southern Oligarchy* (New York: Devin-Adair Co., 1924).

15 *Bailey v. Alabama*, 211 U.S. 452 (1908).

16 *Bailey v. Alabama*, 219 U.S. 219 (1911).

17 See August Meier, *Negro Thought in America, 1880–1915* (Ann Arbor: University of Michigan Press, 1963).

18   *United States v. Reynolds,* 235 U.S. 133.
     United States v. Broughton, 235 U.S. 133.
19   See Chapter 21, Post.
20   *Berea College v. Kentucky,* 211 U.S. 45.

CHAPTER 13

1   Oklahoma, Georgia, and other states enacted similar laws. The climate of public opinion stimulated by almost universal segregation often dictated segregatory practices where there was no formal statutory requirement. See C. Vann Woodward, *The Strange Career of Jim Crow* (New York: Oxford University Press, 1957).
2   Negro students returned to Berea after the School Segregation Cases in 1954—*Brown v. Board of Education,* 347 U.S. 483; 349 U.S. 294.
3   Quoted from William A. Sinclair, *The Aftermath of Slavery* (Boston: Small, Maynard & Co., 1903), pp. 187–196.
4   Winfield H. Collins, *The Truth About Lynching and the Negro in the South* (New York: Neale Press, 1918), Chapter 4. Collins was an all-out apologist for lynching.
5   Albert Bushnell Hart, *The Southern South* (New York: Appleton-Century-Crofts, Inc., 1910), Chapter 10.
6   *Ibid.*
7   Collins, *op. cit.,* p. 58.
8   *Jackson* (Mississippi) *Daily News,* June 20, 1919.
9   Quoted in Sinclair, *op. cit.,* p. 196.
10 William Benjamin Smith, *The Color Line, A Brief in Behalf of the Unborn* (New York: McClure, Phillips & Co., 1905). See also A. H. Shannon, *Racial Integrity* (Nashville: Methodist Publishing Co., 1907); author unlisted, *Appeal to Pharaoh* (Fords, Howard & Hulbert, 1889). These and many similar books preached an unceasing doctrine of racial superiority and antipathy.
11 Hart, *op. cit.,* Chapters 22, 23.
12 *Roberts v. City of Boston,* 5 Cushing 198. The case was decided before the Civil War and, of course, was no precedent after ratification of the Fourteenth Amendment with its requirement of equal protection and due process.
13 *Cummings v. Board of Education,* 175 U.S. 528.
14 The Courts had fallen back on the doctrine of "substantial equality" to cover up the obvious fact that facilities were in fact unequal. See *McCabe v. Atchison, etc. Railways,* 235 U.S. 151.
15 *Gong Lum v. Rice,* 275 U.S. 78.

CHAPTER 14

1   See Douglass dissenting in *United States v. Classic*, 313 U.S. 299.
2   *Williams v. Mississippi*, 170 U.S. 213.
3   It later became Section 19 of the Penal Code and was such at the time of the grandfather clause cases.
4   *Guinn v. United States*, 238 U.S. 347. The companion Maryland case is *Myers v. Anderson*, 238 U.S. 368.
5   *United States v. Mosely*, 238 U.S. 383.
6   Woodrow Wilson promised "justice" to Negroes during his 1912 campaign. See *Crisis Magazine*, New York, 1912, months of June to January for Du Bois views.
7   *Newberry v. United States*, 256 U.S. 232.
8   *Nixon v. Herndon*, 273 U.S. 536.
9   Max Lerner, *The Mind and Faith of Justice Holmes* (Boston: Little, Brown & Co., 1943), p. 329.
10   *Nixon v. Condon*, 286 U.S. 73.
11   *Grovey v. Townsend*, 295 U.S. 45.
12   *Bank of United States v. Deveaux*, 5 Cranch 61.
13   Chief Justice Stone in *Smith v. Allwright*, 321 U.S. 649.

CHAPTER 15

1   U.S. Census Reports, 1920.
2   *Moore v. Dempsey*, 261 U.S. 86.
3   *Frank v. Mangum*, 237 U.S. 309.
4   Jury case reversals 1892–1923: *Carter v. Texas*, 177 U.S. 442; *Rogers v. Alabama*, 192 U.S. 226. Jury case reversals 1923–1953: *Norris v. Alabama*, 294 U.S. 587 (1935); *Hollins v. Oklahoma*, 295 U.S. 394 (1935); *Hale v. Kentucky*, 303 U.S. 613 (1938); *Pierre v. Louisiana*, 306 U.S. 354 (1939); *Smith v. Texas*, 311 U.S. 128 (1940); *Hill v. Texas*, 316 U.S. 400 (1942); *Patton v. Mississippi*, 332 U.S. 463 (1947); *Brunsen v. North Carolina* (five cases), 333 U.S. 851 (1948); *Cassell v. Texas*, 339 U.S. 282 (1950); *Shepherd v. Florida*, 341 U.S. 50 (1951); *Avery v. Georgia*, 345 U.S. 559 (1953). Other reversals since 1953: *Reece v. Georgia*, 350 U.S. 85 (1955); *Eubanks v. Louisiana*, 356 U.S. 584 (1958); *Anderson v. Alabama*, 366 U.S. 208 (1961). See also *U.S. ex rel. Goldsby v. Harpole*, 263 Fed. 2d 71; Cert. Denied Supreme Court 361 U.S. 838 (1959); *Hernandez v. Texas*, 347 U.S. 475 (1954), person Mexican descent.
5   *Martin v. Texas*, 200 U.S. 316 (1906).
6   *Gibson v. Mississippi*, 162 U.S. 565 (1896).
7   *Franklin v. South Carolina*, 218 U.S. 161.

8 Herbert Seligman, *The Negro Faces America* (New York: Harper & Row, 1920), Chapter 8.
9 *Chiles v. Chesapeake Rwy. Co.*, 218 U.S. 71.
10 *Butts v. Merchants and Mining Transportation Co.*, 230 U.S. 126.
11 *McCabe v. Atchison, etc. Rwy. Co.*, 235 U.S. 151.
12 *So. Covington & Cincinnati Rwy. Co. v. Kentucky*, 252 U.S. 408.

CHAPTER 16

1 *In re Lee Sing*, 43 Fed. 259.
2 *Pace v. Alabama*, 106 U.S. 583.
3 *Buchanan v. Warley*, 165 Ky. 559.
4 *Buchanan v. Warley*, 245 U.S. 60.
5 *City of Richmond v. Deans*, 281 U.S. 704; *Harmon v. Tyler*, 273 U.S. 668.
6 *Monk v. Birmingham*, 185 Fed. 2d 859 (Cert. Denied by Supreme Court, 341 U.S. 940).
7 *Jimmerson v. Bessener*, Civ. No. 10054, Northern District of Alabama. Comments on cities which ignored Supreme Court ruling.
8 *Gandolfo v. Hartman*, 49 Fed. 181.
9 *Queensborough Land Co. v. Cazeaux*, 136 La. 724; *Los Angeles Investment Co. v. Gary*, 181 Cal. 680.
10 *Koehler v. Rowland*, 275 Mo. 573.
11 *Parmalee v. Morris*, 218 Mich. 625.
12 *Corrigan v. Buckley*, 299 Fed. 899; *Corrigan v. Buckley*, 271 U.S. 323.
13 Charles Abrams, *Forbidden Neighbors* (New York: Harper & Row); Robert C. Weaver, *The Negro Ghetto* (New York: Harcourt, Brace & World, Inc., 1948).
14 *Bank of United States v. Deveaux*, 5 Cranch 1.

CHAPTER 17

1 Some of them: William H. Hastie, judge, U. S. Court of Appeals; Thurgood Marshall, judge, U. S. Court of Appeals; Robert C. Weaver, administrator, U. S. Housing & Home Finance Agency; Ralph Bunche, assistant secretary, United Nations, Nobel Prize winner; James Nabrit, president, Howard University; Raymond Pace Alexander, judge, court of common pleas, Philadelphia; Earl B. Dickerson, president, Supreme Liberty Life Insurance Co., Chicago; W. Robert Ming, former professor Constitutional Law, University of Chicago; Spottswood Robinson, U. S. District Judge; Carl Johnson, Kansas City municipal judge (deceased); Loren Miller, Los Angeles municipal judge; Franklin Williams, Ambassador to United Nations Cultural Agencies; Edward Dudley, New York Supreme Court judge;

Constance Baker Motley, president, Borough of Manhattan, New York; Oliver Hill, Richmond city councilman, Federal Housing Agency official; Theodore Spaulding, county judge, Philadelphia.

CHAPTER 18

A NOTE ON APPEALS

The Supreme Court is not required to review all cases in which review is asked. The ordinary way in which a case gets before the Court is through a grant of *certiorari*—that is, a writ of review—which is granted by a vote of four members of the Court, upon application of the losing party in either state or lower federal courts. If the Court grants *certiorari*, it may then (a) order the lower court record sent to it, (b) set the case down for argument, (c) hear the argument and decide the case. Where the point on appeal is well settled, the Court may (a) grant *certiorari*, (b) summarily affirm the decision, or (c) summarily reverse the decision without hearing or argument. Most applications for *certiorari* are denied, in which case the law reports simply say "*cert. den.*" The Court insists that a denial of *certiorari* does not mean Supreme Court approval or disapproval of the decision in the case. It may only mean that certain procedural rules were not complied with. Be that as it may, when lawyers note that the Court consistently denies *certiorari* on a particular state of facts, they come to the conclusion that the Court has adopted a particular point of view. Only when the Court is reconstituted by deaths or resignations will the lawyers try again.

Where a state law is attacked as unconstitutional, that issue, under modern practice, is submitted to a three-judge federal court. The loser *appeals* to the Supreme Court. The Court then (a) affirms the decision, (b) reverses it, or (c) notes "probable jurisdiction." In the latter event, it sets the case down for argument, hears the argument, and one of the justices writes an opinion.

Laymen should be warned—as lawyers will know—that this is a short-hand and oversimplified description of the appeals practice in the Supreme Court, but it may help them to understand some of the terms that are used.

1   *Powell v. Alabama*, 287 U.S. 45.
2   *Norris v. Alabama*, 294 U.S. 587; *Patterson v. Alabama*, 294 U.S. 600.
3   *Powell v. Alabama*, 287 U.S. 45.
4   *Norris v. Alabama*, 294 U.S. 587.
5   *Gibson v. Mississippi*, 162 U.S. 565; *Brownfield v. South Carolina*, 189 U.S. 426.

CHAPTER 19

1 *Brown v. Mississippi*, 297 U.S. 278.
2 *State v. Brown*, 173 Miss. 563.
3 *Hurtado v. California*, 110 U.S. 516; *Maxwell v. Dow*, 176 U.S. 581; *Twining v. New Jersey*, 211 U.S. 78. Significantly, the Supreme Court is veering ever closer to the views expounded by the first Justice Harlan in the areas of the law considered in these cases. He clung steadfastly to the belief that the Fourteenth Amendment made the Bill of Rights binding on the states.
4 *Chambers v. Florida*, 309 U.S. 227.
5 *White v. Texas*, 309 U.S. 530; *Canty v. Alabama*, 309 U.S. 629; *Lomax v. Texas*, 313 U.S. 544; *Haley v. Ohio*, 332 U.S. 596; *Watts v. Indiana*, 338 U.S. 49; *Harris v. So. Carolina*, 338 U.S. 68; *Fikes v. Alabama*, 352 U.S. 191; *Payne v. Arkansas*, 356 U.S. 560; *Blackburn v. Alabama*, 361 U.S. 199; *Rogers v. Richmond*, 365 U.S. 534. These cases all involve Negroes. There are a few other cases involving white persons and Mexicans.
6 *Watts v. Indiana*, 338 U.S. 49.
7 *Fikes v. Alabama*, 352 U.S. 191.
8 *Blackburn v. Alabama*, 361 U.S. 199.
9 *Mapp v. Ohio*, 367 U.S. 643.
10 *Escobedo v. Illinois*, 378 U.S. 478.
11 *Gideon v. Wainwright*, 372, U.S. 335.
12 *Douglas v. California*, 372 U.S. 353.
13 *Johnson v. Virginia*, 373 U.S. 61.
14 *Hamilton v. Alabama*, 376 U.S. 650.
15 *Screws v. United States*, 325 U.S. 91.
16 *Hamilton v. Alabama*, 376 U.S. 650.
17 See U. S. Commission on Civil Rights Report, 1961: *Justice.*
18 See "A Note on Appeal," in Notes, Chapter 18.
19 See U. S. Commission on Civil Rights Report, 1961: *Voting.*
20 *Pierre v. Louisiana*, 306 U.S. 354.
21 *Eubanks v. Louisiana*, 356 U.S. 584.
22 *Avery v. Georgia*, 345 U.S. 559.
23 *Akins v. Texas*, 325 U.S. 398.
24 *Cassell v. Texas*, 339 U.S. 282.
25 *Brown v. Allen*, 334 U.S. 469.
26 *U.S. ex rel. Goldsby v. Harpole*, 263 Fed. 2d 71.
27 *Ibid., Cert.* Denied by Supreme Court, 361 U.S. 839.
28 See *Hill v. Texas*, 316 U.S. 400.
29 See *Walker v. Collins*, 335 Fed. 2d 417; (Cert. Denied by Supreme Court, November 10, 1964).
30 *Swain v. Alabama*, 380 U.S. 202 (March 8, 1965).

CHAPTER 20

1 *Smith v. Allwright*, 321 U.S. 649.
2 *Rice v. Elmore*, 333 U.S. 875 (Cert. Denied).
3 *Brown v. Baskin*, 78 Fed. Supp. 933, Affirmed 174 Fed. 2d 391.
4 *Terry v. Adams*, 345 U.S. 461.
5 *Lane v. Wilson*, 307 U.S. 268.
6 *Breedlove v. Suttles*, 302 U.S. 277.
7 For progressive discriminatory steps taken by Mississippi as an example, see Brief *Amicus Curia* filed by American Civil Liberties Union in *United States v. Mississippi*, 380 U.S. 145.
8 This practice prevailed in a number of black belt counties, notably in Lowndes County, Alabama. See U. S. Commission on Civil Rights Report, 1961: *Voting*.
9 Robert J. Harris, *The Quest for Equality* (Baton Rogue: Louisiana State University Press, 1960), p. 108.
10 *Davis v. Schnell*, 336 U.S. 933.
11 *Gomillion v. Lightfoot*, 364 U.S. 339.
12 *United States v. Reese*, 92 U.S. 214.
13 *United States v. Raines*, 362 U.S. 17.
14 *United States v. Thomas*, 362 U.S. 58.
15 *United States v. Alabama*, 362 U.S. 602.
16 *Hannah v. Larche*, 363 U.S. 420.
17 *Anderson v. Martin*, 375 U.S. 399.
18 *Louisiana v. United States*, 380 U.S. 145; *United States v. Mississippi*, 380 U.S. 128.

CHAPTER 21

1 *Taylor v. Georgia*, 315 U.S. 25.
2 *United States v. Gaskin*, 320 U.S. 527.
3 *Pollock v. Williams*, 322 U.S. 4.
4 *New Negro Alliance v. Sanitary Grocers*, 303 U.S. 552.
5 *Hughes v. Superior Court*, 339 U.S. 460.
6 *Steele v. L.&N. R.R. Co.*, 323 U.S. 192.
7 *Turnstall v. Brotherhood*, 323 U.S. 210.
8 *Graham v. Brotherhood*, 338 U.S. 232.
9 *Brotherhood of Railway Trainmen v. Howard*, 343 U.S. 768.
10 *Conley v. Gibson*, 355 U.S. 41.
11 *Syres v. Oil Workers Union*, 350 U.S. 892.
12 *Mail Handlers Union v. Corsi*, 326 U.S. 88.
13 *Colorado Anti-Discrimination Commission v. Continental Airlines*, 372 U.S. 714.

CHAPTER 22

1   For history of judicial action in reference to racial covenants, see Mc-
    Govney, "Racial Residential Segregation," 33 *Cal. Law Rev.* 5; Miller,
    *Race Restrictions on Ownership or Occupancy of Land, 7 Lawyers Guild
    Rev.* 99.
2   See McGovney and Miller, *op. cit.*
3   *Corrigan v. Buckley,* 271 U.S. 323.
4   For history of organized assault on enforcement of covenants, see Clement
    E. Vose, *Caucasians Only* (Berkeley: University of California Press,
    1959).
5   *Ibid.*
6   *Shelley v. Kraemer,* 334 U.S. 1.
7   *McGhee v. Sipes,* 334 U.S. 1.
8   *Hurd v. Hodge,* 334 U.S. 24.
9   *Barrows v. Jackson,* 346 U.S. 249.
10 *Barrows v. Jackson,* 112 Cal. App. 2d 534.
11 *Banks v. Housing Authority,* 120 Cal. App. 2d 1 (Cert. Denied by U.S.
    Supreme Court, 347 U.S. 974).
12 See U.S. Civil Rights Commission Report, 1961: *Housing.*
13 See John H. Denton (ed.), *Race and Property* (Berkeley: Diablo Press,
    1964).
14 *Burton v. Wilmington Parking Authority,* 365 U.S. 715.
15 Between 1926 and 1948, the Court refused to review (denied *certiorari*
    in) at least four cases that attacked judicial enforcement as "state action"
    —the issue decided in *Shelley v. Kraemer,* 334 U.S. 1, and *Hurd v.
    Hodge,* 334 U.S. 24. See U. S. Civil Rights Commission, 1961 Report:
    Housing.

CHAPTER 23

1   *Pearson v. Murray,* 169 Md. 478.
2   *Missouri ex rel. Gaines v. Canada,* 305 U.S. 337.
3   *Sipuel v. Board of Regents,* 332 U.S. 631.
4   *Fisher v. Hurst,* 333 U.S. 147.
5   *Ibid.*
6   *McLaurin v. Oklahoma State Regents,* 339 U.S. 637.
7   *Sweatt v. Painter,* 339 U.S. 629.
8   Kentucky, Arkansas, West Virginia, among others, opened their graduate
    professional schools. See 21 *Journal Negro Education* 3 (1952).
9   *Ludley v. Bd. of Supervisors, La. State Univ.,* 252 Fed. 2d 372.
10 *Ibid.,* Cert. Denied by Supreme Court, 358 U.S. 819.
11 In the widely known James Meredith case, a Mississippi federal district

court agreed with Mississippi contentions that he had been denied admission to the University on nonracial grounds. See *Meredith v. Fair*, 202 Fed. Supp. 224; Reversed 305 Fed. 2d 343.

12   *Florida ex rel. Hawkins v. Board of Control*, 350 U.S. 413.
13   The Court honored the rule that a civil right was "personal and present" in all but the cases involving grade-school segregation.
14   *Brown v. Board of Education of Topeka*, 347 U.S. 483 (1954).
15   *Bolling v. Sharpe*, 347 U.S. 497 (1954).
16   *Harry Briggs, Jr., v. R. W. Elliott*, 347 U.S. 497 (1954).
17   The Courts never devised a way for the Negro complainant to enjoy equality while unequal facilities were being "equalized," nor did the Supreme Court find any such device for use pending admission of Negro children to schools under the "deliberate speed" formula of *Brown v. Board of Education*, 349 U.S. 294 (1955).
18   *Brown v. Board of Education*, 347 U.S. 483 (1954).
19   *Davis v. County School Board of Prince Edward County*, 347 U.S. 483.
20   *Gebhart v. Bolton*, 33 Del. Chan. 144, decided under *Brown v. Board of Education*, 347 U.S. 483.
21   *Bolling v. Sharpe*, 347 U.S. 497 (1954).

CHAPTER 24

1   *U. S. Bank v. Deveaux*, 7 Cranch 1.
2   Thus, each case was returned to the Court from which it had come for application of "deliberate speed" rule.
3   For over-all view of school cases, see Albert Blaustein and Charles Clyde Ferguson, *Desegregation* (New Brunswick, N.J.: Rutgers University Press, 1957).
4   *Aaron v. Cooper*, 243 Fed. 2d 361 (1956), affirming *Aaron v. Cooper*, 143 Fed. Supp. 855.
5   *U.S. v. Faubus*, No. 3113 Eastern District Arkansas, 2 *Race Relations Law Reporter* 958; 254 Fed. 2d 797.
6   *Cooper v. Aaron*, 358 U.S. 1.
7   *Shuttlesworth v. Alabama*, 358 U.S. 101.
8   *Goss v. Board of Education*, 373 U.S. 683.
9   *Watson v. City of Memphis*, 373 U.S. 526.
10   *Calhoun v. Latimer*, 377 U.S. 263.
11   *Griffin v. County School Board*, 377 U.S. 218.
12   *Allen v. County School Board* was decided with Brown case, 347 U.S. 483.
13   *St. Helena Parish School Board v. Hall*, 368 U.S. 515.
14   *Griffin v. County School Board*, 377 U.S. 218.
15   These transparent efforts to evade desegregation were usually dressed up as "desegregation plans" and were the inevitable result of the Court's deliberate speed formula. See Jack Greenberg, *Race Relations and American Law* (New York: Columbia University Press, 1959), Chapter 7.

16   *Holmes v. City of Atlanta,* 350 U.S. 879.
17   *Mayor, etc. v. Dawson,* 350 U.S. 877.

CHAPTER 25

1   *Mitchell v. United States,* 313 U.S. 80.
2   *Morgan v. Virginia,* 328 U.S. 373.
3   *Hall v. De Cuir,* 95 U.S. 485.
4   *Henderson v. United States,* 339 U.S. 816.
5   *Flemming v. S.C. Electric & Gas Co.,* 224 Fed. 2d 752.
6   *Flemming v. S.C. Electric & Gas Co.,* 351 U.S. 901.
7   *Gayle v. Browder,* 352 U.S. 903.
8   *Browder v. Gayle,* 142 Fed. Supp. 707.
9   *Evers v. Dwyer,* 358 U.S. 202.
10 *Bailey v. Patterson,* 369 U.S. 31.

CHAPTER 26

1   *NAACP v. Alabama,* 357 U.S. 449 (1958).
2   *Bryant v. Zimmerman,* 278 U.S. 63.
3   *NAACP v. Alabama,* 360 U.S. 240 (1959).
4   *NAACP v. Gallion,* 368 U.S. 16 (1961).
5   *NAACP v. Alabama,* 377 U.S. 288 (1964).
6   *Bates v. Little Rock,* 361 U.S. 516.
7   *Shelton v. Tucker,* 364 U.S. 479.
8   *Louisiana ex rel. Gremillion v. NAACP,* 366 U.S. 293.
9   Justice Douglas noted that it would have been impossible for any local
    chapter of a national organization to comply with the law.
10 The rule is one of convenience and may be bypassed—as it sometimes is
    —when the Court wants an early opportunity to test the validity of a
    state statute.
11 *Harrison v. NAACP,* 360 U.S. 167.
12 *NAACP v. Button,* 371 U.S. 415.
13 *NAACP v. Bennett,* 360 U.S. 471.
14 *Gibson v. Florida,* 108 Southern 2d 729; Cert. Denied by U. S. Supreme
    Court, 360 U.S. 919.
15 *Gibson v. Florida,* 372 U.S. 539.
16 See *Giles v. Harris,* 189 U.S. 475, and *Giles v. Teasley,* 193 U.S. 146.
17 The Court, of course, made no such announcement. Understanding of its
    course must be governed from what it *did,* from the spirit and direction
    of its decisions.
18 Marshall left the NAACP Legal Defense & Educational Fund to accept an

appointment from President Kennedy to the U. S. Court of Appeals. He later became Solicitor General of the United States, appointed by President Lyndon Johnson. He was succeeded by the equally capable and determined Jack Greenberg. Robert Carter became special counsel for the NAACP, proper, which defended itself in cases aimed at it and also undertook some other defensive and offensive cases. As the states soon learned, there was no diminution in quality of its work or zeal under Carter.

CHAPTER 27

1 See Justice Goldberg concurring and dissenting in *Bell v. Maryland,* and citing *Donnell v. State,* 48 Miss. 661, upholding Mississippi's civil rights statute.

2 *John R. Thompson v. District of Columbia,* 346 U.S. 100.

3 *Boynton v. Virginia,* 364 U.S. 454.

4 *Garner v. Louisiana,* 368 U.S. 157.

5 *Thompson v. Louisville,* 362 U.S. 199.

6 The decision marked an important extension of the reach of the due-process-of-law clause of the Fourteenth Amendment. The Supreme Court again had substituted its judgment for that of a state court.

7 *Taylor v. Louisiana,* 370 U.S. 154.

8 *Peterson v. City of Greenville,* 373 U.S. 244.

9 *Lombard v. Louisiana,* 373 U.S. 267.

10 *Avent v. Louisiana,* 373 U.S. 375.

11 *Gober v. Alabama,* 373 U.S. 374.

12 *Shuttlesworth v. Alabama,* 373 U.S. 262.

13 *Wright v. Georgia,* 373 U.S. 284.

14 *Daniels v. Virginia; Randolph v. Virginia; Henry v. Virginia; Thompson v. Virginia; Wood v. Virginia,* were all reversed in June, 1963, after summary grants of *certiorari,* because the facts were parallel to those in the Petersen and Avent cases, 373 U.S. 954.

15 *Edwards v. South Carolina,* 372 U.S. 229.

16 *Fields v. South Carolina,* 372 U.S. 522.

17 *Barr v. City of Columbia,* 378 U.S. 146, 1734.

18 *Robinson v. Florida,* 378 U.S. 153. Justice Black wrote the prevailing opinion in reference to the breach-of-peace charges but dissented on the trespass aspects of both cases.

19 *Bell v. Maryland,* 378 U.S. 226. (Maryland held that its laws did not call for dismissal of the case, but the U. S. Supreme Court in effect dismissed it after passage of the federal Civil Rights Act.)

20 The dissenters said that such considerations were matters for the state courts and were not properly considered by the Supreme Court. Maryland refused to free the defendants, holding them liable to punishment.

21 *Griffin v. Maryland,* 378 U.S. 130.

22 The majority saw the deputy as acting for and in the name of the state. The minority viewed him as an employee of the private owner.
23 *Bouie v. Columbia,* 378 U.S. 347.
24 *Drews v. Maryland,* 878 U.S. 547.
    Williams v. North Carolina, 378 U.S. 548.
    Green v. Virginia, 378 U.S. 550.
    Fox v. North Carolina, 378 U.S. 587.
    Mitchell v. Charleston, 378 U.S. 551.

CHAPTER 28

1 *Heart of Atlanta Motel v. United States,* 379 U.S. 241; *Katzenbach v. McClung,* 379 U.S. 294.
2 *Gibbons v. Ogden,* 9 Wheaton 1.
3 The Constitution gives the Court no plenary power to invalidate congressional legislation. That power exists only if a congressional enactment violates a constitutional provision or exceeds the power under which Congress acts. As Justice Harlan pointed out in his dissent, the Court had just said that "Every possible presumption is in favor of the validity of a statute and this continues until the contrary is shown beyond a rational doubt (*Sinking Fund Cases,* 99 U.S. 718)." He also pointed out that one of the cases before the Court involved *interstate* travel and that, as to that case, the Statute was undoubtedly valid, even supposing Congress had mistakenly depended on the Thirteenth and Fourteenth Amendments rather than on the Commerce Clause. The majority's cavalier course in invalidating the 1875 Civil Rights Act in face of these facts underscores its determination to reach that end at whatever cost.
4 *Cox v. Louisiana,* 379 U.S. 536 and 379 U.S. 559.
5 *Hamm v. Rock Hill,* 379 U.S. 306.
6 Again the dissenters held the matter was one for the states, not the federal courts.
7 Chief Justice Warren who had joined the dissenters in *Bell v. Maryland* did not join them in their special concurrence.
8 *Lupper v. Arkansas,* 379 U.S. 306.
9 *Blow v. North Carolina,* 379 U.S. 684.

CHAPTER 29

1 *United States v. Cruikshank,* 92 U.S. 542.
2 *United States v. Harris,* 106 U.S. 629.
3 *United States v. Reese,* 92 U.S. 214.

4 *Nixon v. Herndon,* 273 U.S. 536.
5 *Corsi v. Mail Handlers Union,* Justice Frankfurter concurring, 326 U.S. 88.
6 Robert J. Harris, *The Quest for Equality* (Baton Rogue: Louisiana State University Press, 1960), p. 95.
7 Justice Frankfurter, great scholar that he was, never looked behind the standardized prosouthern historical version of Reconstruction and therefore was prone to make statements and pronounce judgments on the basis of "historical facts" which were not facts. For balanced view of Reconstruction, see John Hope Franklin, *Reconstruction* (Chicago: University of Chicago Press, 1961). See also Henrietta Buckmaster, *Freedom Bound* (New York: The Macmillan Company, 1965), and *The Strange Career of Jim Crow* (New York: Oxford University Press, 1957).
8 *Simkins v. Moses Cone Hospital,* 323 Fed. 2d 959 (*Cert.* Denied by Supreme Court, March 3, 1964).

Table of Cases